Epicentre to Aftermath

Epicentre to Aftermath makes both empirical and conceptual contributions to the growing body of disaster studies literature by providing an analysis of a disaster aftermath that is steeped in the political and cultural complexities of its social and historical context. Drawing together scholars from a range of disciplines, this book highlights the political, historical, cultural, artistic, emotional, temporal, embodied and material dynamics at play in the earthquake aftermath. Crucially, it shows that the experience and meaning of a disaster are not given or inevitable, but are the outcome of situated human agency. The book suggests a whole new epistemology of disaster consequences and their meanings, and dramatically expands the field of knowledge relevant to understanding disasters and their outcomes.

Michael Hutt is a scholar of Nepali literature and Emeritus Professor of Nepali and Himalayan Studies at SOAS, University of London. He has authored and edited fourteen books and over fifty articles and book chapters on Nepali and Himalayan topics. He co-edited, with Pratyoush Onta, *Political Change and Public Culture in Post-1990 Nepal*, which was published by the Press in 2017.

Mark Liechty is Professor of Anthropology and History at the University of Illinois at Chicago. He is a cultural anthropologist by training and has been a student of Nepali and South Asian culture and history for more than three decades. He is the author of influential books on modern Nepal and a founding co-editor of the journal *Studies in Nepali History and Society*.

Stefanie Lotter is Senior Teaching and Research Fellow in the Department of Anthropology and Sociology at SOAS, University of London. She is currently exploring the dynamics of heritage decision making in post-conflict, post-earthquake Nepal.

EPICENTRE TO AFTERMATH

REBUILDING AND REMEMBERING IN THE WAKE OF NEPAL'S EARTHQUAKES

Edited by

Michael Hutt

Mark Liechty

Stefanie Lotter

CAMBRIDGE
UNIVERSITY PRESS

CAMBRIDGE
UNIVERSITY PRESS

University Printing House, Cambridge CB2 8BS, United Kingdom

One Liberty Plaza, 20th Floor, New York, NY 10006, USA

477 Williamstown Road, Port Melbourne, vic 3207, Australia

314 to 321, 3rd Floor, Plot No.3, Splendor Forum, Jasola District Centre, New Delhi 110025, India

79 Anson Road, #06–04/06, Singapore 079906

Cambridge University Press is part of the University of Cambridge.

It furthers the University's mission by disseminating knowledge in the pursuit
of education, learning and research at the highest international levels of excellence.

www.cambridge.org
Information on this title: www.cambridge.org/9781108834056

© Cambridge University Press 2021

First published 2021

Printed in India by Avantika Printers Pvt. Ltd.

A catalogue record for this publication is available from the British Library

Library of Congress Cataloging-in-Publication Data

Names: Hutt, Michael (Michael J.), editor. | Liechty, Mark, 1960- editor. |
    Lotter, Stefanie, editor.
Title: Epicentre to aftermath : rebuilding and remembering in the wake of
    Nepal's earthquakes / edited by Michael Hutt, Mark Liechty, Stefanie Lotter.
Description: Cambridge, United Kingdom ; New York, NY : Cambridge
    University Press, 2021. | Includes bibliographical references and index.
Identifiers: LCCN 2021005349 (print) | LCCN 2021005350 (ebook) | ISBN
    9781108834056 (hardback) | ISBN 9781108991636 (ebook)
Subjects: LCSH: Earthquake relief--Nepal. | Nepal Earthquake, 2015 (April
    25) | Earthquakes--Social aspects--Nepal. | Nepal--Social
    conditions--21st century. | Nepal--Politics and government--21st century.
Classification: LCC HV600 2015.N35 E65 2021 (print) | LCC HV600 2015.N35
    (ebook) | DDC 954.96--dc23
LC record available at https://lccn.loc.gov/2021005349
LC ebook record available at https://lccn.loc.gov/2021005350

ISBN 978-1-108-83405-6 Hardback

CONTENTS

FIGURES

ABBREVIATIONS

ADA	Architects Design Associates
ADWAN	Association for Dalit Women's Advancement of Nepal
AJWS	American Jewish World Service
CBO	community-based organization
CCA	climate change adaptation
CDO	Chief District Office
CEO	Chief Executive Officer
CGI	corrugated galvanized iron
CPN-UML	Communist Party of Nepal-Unified Marxist–Leninist
CRK	Campaign to Rebuild Kasthamandap
CSO	civil society organization
CTEVT	Council for Technical Education and Vocational Training
DDC	District Development Committee
DoA	Department of Archaeology
DPNN	Disaster Preparedness Network Nepal
DUDBC	Department of Urban Development and Building Construction
ENPHO	Environment and Public Health Organization
EPF	Employees Provident Fund
ESA	European Space Agency
GDP	gross domestic product
HRRI	Himalayan Risk Research Institute
HRRP	Housing Recovery and Reconstruction Platform

ICDO	integrated community development organization
ICOMOS	International Council on Monuments and Sites
INGO	international non-governmental organization
IOM	International Organization for Migration
IOR	India Office Records
JICA	Japan International Cooperation Agency
KII	key informant interview
KMC	Kathmandu Metropolitan City
KRC	Kasthamandap Reconstruction Committee
KVPT	Kathmandu Valley Preservation Trust
LPG	liquefied petroleum gas
LWF	Lutheran World Federation
MOHA	Ministry of Home Affairs
NOAA	National Oceanic and Atmospheric Administration
NEPAN	Nepal Participatory Action Network
NFP	National Forestry Plan
NGO	non-governmental organization
NIP	National Integrity Policy
NMKP	Nepal Majdoor Kisan Party
NPC	National Planning Commission
NPR	Nepali rupee
NRA	National Reconstruction Authority
NSET	National Society for Earthquake Technology–Nepal
NWPO	Nepal Workers and Peasant Organisation
PA	participation agreement
PDNA	Post-disaster Needs Assessment
PDRF	Post-disaster Recovery Framework
PwDs	persons with disability
RC	reinforced concrete
RPP	Rastriya Prajatantra Party
RSDC	Rural Self-reliance Development Centre

SAARC	South Asian Association for Regional Cooperation
SDC	Swiss Agency for Development and Cooperation
SOAS	School of Oriental and African Studies
SSB	Social Science Baha
UBC	University of British Columbia
UCPN-M	Unified Communist Party of Nepal-Maoist
UNESCO	United Nations Educational, Scientific and Cultural Organization
UNOPS	United Nations Office for Project Services
USGS	United States Geological Survey
UTKHPL	Upper Tamakoshi Hydropower Limited
VDC	Village Development Committee
WASH	water, sanitation, and hygiene
WCF	Ward Citizen Forum
WFP	World Food Programme
WHR	Women for Human Rights Nepal

PART I

Contextualizing Disaster

Reconstituting Pasts and Futures

Contextual Agency in a Disaster Aftermath

Mark Liechty and *Michael Hutt*

> [The earthquake] came
> just as threats sometimes come,
> it went
> just as assurances vanish....
> —Peshal Acharya, 'Aagaman' (Arrival), tr. Michael Hutt

Drawing together a range of scholars—from ethnographers to geographers, historians to literary critics, political scientists to art historians—this volume lays out a host of perspectives on Nepal's 2015 earthquakes that highlight the political, historical, cultural, artistic, emotional, temporal, embodied, and material dynamics at play.[1] By approaching the 2015 disaster

---

[1] This volume grew out of contributions to an academic conference entitled 'From Epicentre to Aftermath: Political, Social and Cultural Impacts of Earthquakes in South Asia' held at the School of Oriental and African Studies (SOAS), University of London on 11–12 January 2019. The conference was hosted by SOAS South Asia Institute and the research project 'After the Earth's Violent Sway: The Tangible and Intangible Legacies of a Natural Disaster' funded by the UK's Global Challenges Research Fund through the Arts and Humanities Research Council, grant number AH/P003648/1. In seismological terms, the earthquake that struck on 25 April 2015 with its epicentre near Barpak in Gorkha district and the many smaller quakes and tremors that followed, with their epicentres at different locations, were all part of a single seismic event—just one earthquake. However, this book is concerned with the impact this earthquake had on those affected by it, who experienced it as a long series of linked but separate events. Therefore, in what follows 'the earthquake' should be taken to refer to the Gorkha earthquake of 25 April 2015 specifically, and 'the earthquakes' to the whole sequence of quakes, tremors and aftershocks that continued for months thereafter.

and its aftermath from multiple analytical and methodological perspectives, the book not only dramatically expands the field of knowledge relevant to this particular disaster, but also suggests a new way of approaching and understanding disasters more generally. Many studies of disaster aftermaths follow relatively narrow pragmatic approaches which view disasters as mainly technical or material challenges to be assessed and addressed by experts in relief and reconstruction. This volume pursues a more holistic approach—one that recovers the disaster aftermath as a lived human experience in which it is the disaster-affected people themselves, individually and collectively, who work to build new lives, sometimes with and sometimes against the efforts of the outsiders who come to assist them.

Epicentre to Aftermath captures the richly complex currents that were stirred up in the 2015 earthquakes' aftermath. These include outpourings of grief, rage, and commemoration in poetry and song, artistic representation, documentation, and memorialization. With greater temporal distance from the event, pledged commitments turn into complex discourses about long-term visions and aspirations for society. They include debates over state intervention, bureaucracy, and corruption; questions of risk and the material and symbolic standards of reconstruction; and struggles over what constitutes and who owns the discourse over 'heritage', leading to questions about *which pasts* to rebuild and *which futures* to claim. In the disaster's aftermath, it is not just homes and other infrastructure that must be reconstructed. Even more challengingly, people must rebuild their lives and livelihoods, their senses of self, their families, their communities, their pasts and futures: in short, they must reconstruct the edifices of meaning that were profoundly affected by the disaster.

Thus, the chapters of this volume document how people *work* to rebuild lives, meaning, memory, and social relations. Yet what is rebuilt is hardly ever a return to the past. Rebuilding is about actively crafting a future within the constraints and possibilities that unfold in the disaster's wake. Disaster aftermaths do not *happen to* people: they are collective constructions that emerge as all kinds of individuals, groups, and institutions simultaneously engage in the same (often desperate and conflicting) rebuilding projects. The experience and meaning of a disaster are never given or inevitable, but are, rather, the outcome of situated human agency. Contributors show how—from the realms of politics to art to commemoration to rebuilding—people actively work to create the event as it unfolds through various temporal frames and degrees of relational embeddedness. This volume provides insights into how disaster-affected people in Nepal actively shaped the lived event that spread from the disaster's historic epicentre to its aftermath.

To begin with, we present a brief survey of modern Nepali history leading up to the 2015 earthquakes that provides important insights into the complex historical and political processes that were underway on the eve of the disaster, and which unfolded in surprising ways in its immediate aftermath. Readers familiar with this context may wish to skip to the following section, which lays out the book's conceptual agendas.

Setting the scene

Nepal, a medium-sized, mostly mountainous country with an ethnically diverse population of approximately 30 million, is located between the rapidly growing economic powers of India and China, which compete for influence within it. Nepal assumed what are more or less its present territorial dimensions 200 years ago and, for most of its history, was constituted as a Hindu monarchy.

Although it is probably the oldest surviving state in the region, political modernity came late to Nepal, even in comparison with other South Asian countries. A century of autocratic rule by the Rana family ended in 1951, soon after the departure of British colonial power from the Indian subcontinent. After this, the palace, the new political parties, and the feudal landlords of the displaced old order jostled for power. The Nepali Congress Party appeared to have brought an end to the ongoing contestation when it won a majority in the general elections of 1959, but King Mahendra dismissed the Congress government less than two years later and established a new political system, the Panchayat Vyavastha. Political parties and organizations advancing sectional interests and agendas were banned under this regime, and 'development' (driven mainly by international aid) became the all-encompassing theme of government programmes. Nepal benefited from its strategic location during the Cold War and received massive quantities of aid. Literacy and public consciousness of the wider world grew in leaps and bounds as a consequence, but the Panchayat regime set out to homogenize Nepal's national identity around the three pillars of the monarchy, the Nepali language, and Hinduism, while political and cultural dissent was harshly suppressed.

By the late 1980s, the Panchayat system had lost much of its legitimacy, especially when a major disagreement with India over the terms of trade and transit between the two countries led to shortages of essential commodities in the capital, Kathmandu. In 1990, a popular movement—the first *jan andolan*—forced King Birendra to dismantle the Panchayat system and give way to the re-establishment of multi-party democracy. A new constitution was promulgated and the Nepali Congress Party won the first general election. The opposition was dominated by parties espousing various forms of communist ideology, along with other more conservative elements who were disgruntled by the constitutional change.

The early 1990s saw a major upsurge in the claiming of civil, economic, and political rights by marginalized sections of the population—notably the Adibasi Janajatis ('indigenous nationalities'), the Madhesis of the southern plains districts, and the Dalits of the lowest rungs of the Hindu caste hierarchy. This period also saw transformations in 'development' practices in the form of increased foreign aid, experts, and non-governmental-organization (NGO) involvement, along with new discourses of participatory development and local governance: these themes come into play in many of the chapters in this volume. But the new democratic dispensation failed to deliver on its promises, leading to war between the Nepal Communist Party (Maoist) and the Nepali state. The conflict began in the mid-western hills in 1995–96 and had spread to almost every district of Nepal by 2003. Over 16,000 lives were lost during a 10-year period, and Nepal saw severe abuses of human rights. In 2001, the family of King Birendra was massacred in Narayanhiti Palace, and this event was followed by the king's brother, Gyanendra, ascending the throne. Within five years, the new king had succeeded in alienating both the mainstream parties and civil society so much that they made common cause with the Maoists against him.

The war ended in a ceasefire in 2006 after the Maoist insurgents and the parliamentary parties aligned themselves against the monarchy, giving rise to a second *jan andolan*. In 2007 an Interim Constitution was promulgated and a new national anthem was adopted, and in 2008 a Constituent Assembly was elected to draft a new constitution for a secular, democratic, federal, republican state of Nepal. The new constitution, it was promised, would ensure greater inclusivity and representation in a country where people other than men from among the upper castes (Bahuns and Chetris) of the hill regions and the upper strata of the Newar society of the Kathmandu

Valley had been largely excluded from avenues of advancement and power. The Maoists, who had now renounced armed struggle, confounded expectations by becoming the largest party in the Constituent Assembly. At its first meeting, in May 2008, the Assembly voted to abolish the Shah monarchy.

Although the Constituent Assembly elected in 2008 was probably the most representative legislative body ever established in South Asia, its proceedings and decisions quickly came to be dominated once again by political-party leaders who failed to agree on a range of key issues, including the form of government and the structure of the new federal state: an agreement to establish the latter had been one of the key planks of the 2006 peace agreement. Adibasi Janajati activists insisted this should be determined by the geographical distribution of minority ethnic groups, and Madhesi activists demanded the creation of Tarai-only provinces. Having failed to deliver a constitution despite extensions to its original two-year term of office, the Constituent Assembly came to the end of its life in May 2012. After an 18-month interregnum, a new Constituent Assembly was elected in November 2013. No party achieved an overall majority in these elections, but the Nepali Congress emerged as the single largest party while the Maoists' share of the vote fell dramatically, leaving them in third place. A new government based on a coalition of the Nepali Congress Party and the Communist Party of Nepal (Unified Marxist–Leninist) (CPN-UML) was formed in February 2014, with Sushil Koirala of the Nepali Congress Party as Prime Minister.

Nepal was still engaged in its protracted process of ostensible political transition to a federal, secular, democratic republic when, on 25 April 2015, its central districts were struck by a magnitude 7.8 earthquake. A second quake, of magnitude 7.3, struck the Dolakha district on 12 May, and over 400 aftershocks with magnitudes over 4.0 occurred during the next three months, maintaining a high level of public fear. The hill districts to the north, west, and east of the capital, Kathmandu, bore the very worst of the impact. The earthquakes (primarily the first, which had its epicentre in the Gorkha district) killed some 9,000 people and displaced 2.8 million. They destroyed or severely damaged over 800,000 homes, nearly 7,500 educational institutions, 1,200 health centres, and 750 temples, shrines, and other heritage sites. Damage to the region's cultural heritage had serious negative implications for Nepal's tourism industry, which accounts for some 9 per cent of its gross domestic product (GDP). If the earthquake of Saturday, 25

April, had taken place on any other day of the week, when children were at school, the death toll would have been much higher.

The political developments that took place in Nepal in the immediate aftermath of these earthquakes were tumultuous. Indian relief arrived almost immediately, followed shortly by Chinese rescue and relief teams, amid a domestic response in which the Nepal Army and spontaneously organized volunteer teams were the key players. The leaders of the main political parties came together to finalize the new constitution that had been promised for over seven years through a 'fast-track' process, resulting in approval by the Constituent Assembly less than five months after the first earthquake (Hutt 2020). Although it was warmly welcomed in the hills of Nepal, the new constitution provoked a rebellion in the southern lowlands, the Madhes, because of its perceived failure to deliver long-standing promises of greater autonomy and more proportional representation to the people of that region. After Madhesi demonstrators were killed in police firings, Madhesi political organizations blocked supply routes to Kathmandu in support of their demands. Their position was supported by the Indian government, which the government in Kathmandu accused of mounting an effective economic blockade. By November 2015, Nepal was suffering severe shortages of many basic commodities, most crucially of fuel, and it took several more months to re-normalize the bilateral relationship.

Although the Nepal government produced a Post-disaster Needs Assessment (PDNA) very quickly after the April earthquake, on the basis of which the international community pledged a total of USD 4.4 billion for relief and reconstruction (see Shakya, this volume), Nepal's National Reconstruction Authority (NRA) did not begin to function properly until 2016, by which time hundreds of thousands of earthquake survivors had spent the first of several Himalayan winters in temporary shelters. Four years after its establishment in December 2015, the NRA's government-subsidized 'owner-driven' reconstruction programme was still ongoing, with 62 per cent of the 825,439 private households that were deemed eligible for the housing grant of NPR 300,000 (approximately USD 2,700) completely reconstructed, and work on 24 per cent of them ongoing (NRA 2019: 2).[2]

---

[2]   Throughout this volume, conversions of NPR to USD in discussions of reconstruction finance in the aftermath of the 2015 earthquakes will employ the exchange rate NPR 110 = USD 1, which was current in mid-2015.

On the morning of 25 April 2015, Nepal was still groping its way towards agreement on a new post-conflict political conception of itself. The largest slice of its GDP consisted of remittances from overseas labourers in the Gulf and Malaysia. Although the average level of prosperity was improving, the economic gulf between the elite of the capital valley and the rural poor of the hills and plains was wide, and widening. International donors, aid agencies, and international non-governmental organizations (INGOs) were active in almost every sphere, but a significant portion of the population was still excluded structurally from avenues of socioeconomic advancement on grounds of caste, ethnicity, gender, and region. This was the context in which the first earthquake struck.

Aftermath, context, and intervention

Major disasters in low-income countries, like the earthquakes that struck Nepal in 2015, frequently unleash torrents of international aid. However, the effectiveness of these donor-driven relief efforts is often poor (Schuller 2012). Why is it that bilateral and I/NGO-driven relief and reconstruction programmes—however well-intentioned—frequently founder and fail in the chaotic context of a disaster's aftermath? Why do disaster aftermaths so often stymie the best laid plans of international experts who sweep into disaster zones bearing not only tents and blankets, but also elaborate predetermined reconstruction protocols and 'best practices'? As documented in this volume, why now—just five years after the earthquakes of 2015—is Nepal's landscape already strewn with disaster relief and reconstruction programmes whose success is so often partial and contested? (see Baniya; Gurung and Baniya, this volume).[3]

The answer, we contend, lies in how willing actors are to engage with the complex realities of context. As Button and Schuller (2016:1) state in their introduction to a recent edited volume on contextualizing disasters:

---

[3] We would point to the construction of new 'integrated settlements' at Majhigaon (Baniya, this volume) and Laprak (Hutt and Shreesh 2019; Lal 2019) as perhaps the most egregious example of initiatives that have ignored the contextual lives of those they seek to benefit.

... disasters are grounded in a larger social, political, historical, and spatial context that very often reflects the historical processes that surround the economic and political processes of both the nation-state and the global economy.

As its title suggests, this book stakes out the territory *from epicentre to aftermath* to make the case that close attention to the cultural, historical, societal, and political aspects of a disaster is essential—not merely to understand, document, and produce a better ethnographic account of its consequences, but also in order to have any meaningful chance of effectively intervening in, and alleviating, its impacts. Without an appreciation of the powerful cultural and sociopolitical currents that churn unpredictably through a disaster's aftermath context, and of the local historical consciousness of disasters (see Whelpton, this volume), even the most well-intentioned relief and reconstruction interventions are likely to end up twisted and incapacitated.

Why does the aftermath context matter? To begin with, such a focus reminds us that what makes disasters *really disastrous* is not the initial triggering event itself—in this case, the earthquake of 25 April 2015—but the minutes, hours, days, weeks, months, and years following this event in which, for those most affected, all hell breaks loose in spasms of terror, pain, grief, loss, mourning, and recuperation. To varying degrees, affected people must grapple with the existential crisis that Hoffman (2002: 129) neatly refers to as 'the monster' of 'ontological liminality' and 'anti-diachronicity'. The taken-for-granted, foundational patterns of cause and effect, routine, and even power (in a word, culture) are suddenly undermined, rendered fluid like the seemingly solid ground liquidated by an earthquake's shockwaves. As Simpson remarks, 'almost all the ordinary actions of our social lives require that the ground should remain motionless under our feet, our settlements and our philosophical systems' (2013: 202). Thus, for many, life becomes a struggle to reconstitute a viable existence.

This points to another critical significance of understanding disaster aftermaths: rebuilding social life or lives is never about some kind of 'return to the normal', the *status quo ante*. There is no going back, and never was. Rebuilding is about actively crafting a future, not a passive return to the past. With the old normal in ruins, people must work to construct a new normal that acknowledges what was lost and, potentially, what was gained. Efforts to aid disaster-affected people have to fit into larger projects of constituting a future, not of reconstituting the past.

Crucially, such a focus on disaster aftermaths helps to foreground the agency of the disaster-affected. Albala-Bertrand characterizes this as the 'endogenous response' and argues that it is too often overlooked in writings on disaster response:

> Exogenous as distinct from endogenous response is more easily observable and, therefore, more amenable to study. Not surprisingly, most writings on disaster response overlook or disregard the endogenous response. For some authors, the ongoing social system often appears as a nuisance to the visible response represented in prominent national and international organizations. This lopsidedness feeds the technologically biased approach to disaster response, at the expense of political and socio-economic structure and dynamics. (1993: 23)

Similarly, Roberto Barrios documents the ways in which disaster recovery experts construct their assumptions about the natures of affected communities, and uphold these assumptions 'as matters of fact, applicable and relevant anywhere regardless of cultural context', so that 'the knowledge of experts is readily applicable across space and time, anywhere, anytime' (2016: 135, 149; see Shneiderman et al., Dhungana, this volume). The relief discourse may portray survivors as passive victims—and people may indeed be in serious need of assistance, both immediate and long term. But even the most seriously incapacitated people will almost immediately begin actively shaping new lives, even if the contours of those new lives only emerge gradually within the constraining conditions and possibilities of the aftermath itself. In myriad ways, people learn to cope with and adapt to the threats and challenges thrown down in front of them, displaying behaviours which are often referred to as 'resilience', as if it was some instinctive trait and not a powerfully agentive response born of historical circumstances of neglect or even oppression by the state (see Oven et al., this volume). As Ben Campbell writes of Tamang villagers in the Rasuwa district of Nepal in the immediate aftermath,

> As things came tumbling down, people lurched into a limbo land of space and time, confronting the extremes of human predicaments

and finding the resourcefulness to remake a rough-and-ready home base. In doing so they took stock of where and how they now stood on the earth, while waiting for the lights to come back on. They made new kinds of judgements about where they now stand and who they can rely on. (2018: 122)

Disaster assistance must acknowledge its place within a range of competing exigencies that disaster-affected people must resolve, many of which may be more highly prioritized than the goals of the aid providers. To quote Barrios once more, 'recovery experts must be able to recognize the variable, historically configured, and locality-contingent ways people meaningfully engage their environment' (2016: 149). That this agency is not always acknowledged or valued by those who come from outside to help the affected means that valuable social capital generated in the immediate aftermath is often quickly dissipated:

> ... many of the benefits and potentials that emerge in the oft-witnessed post-impact solidarity and other forms of social capital that occur after a disaster might not be lost if a culturally knowledgeable mediator were available to work with communities and agencies. Unfortunately, in-depth sociocultural data are *rarely asked for and more rarely appreciated.* (Oliver-Smith and Hoffman 2001: 15, emphasis added)

A focus on affected people's agency in a disaster's aftermath will help us to recognize that aftermaths are *created* by the collective agency of many individuals, families, communities, and institutions (including states), each working to claim space and meaning in a world that is radically changed. Disaster aftermaths do not *just happen*, either as the *outcome* of preconditions or as a *return to* preconditions. Rather, at every level, society works to reconstitute not just houses and infrastructure but, even more importantly, social networks, livelihoods, memory, and the epistemological means with which to carry on: in short, new lives.[4] People work to create the

---

[4]   The impact of the 2015 earthquakes on mental health in Nepal is an aspect of the aftermath that is not explored in depth in this volume, though the chapter by Lord and Bradley touches upon it. For more detailed analyses, see articles by Chase et al. (2018) and Seale-Feldman (2020).

event's meaning, its narrative, its material outcomes, its past and future, its memory and message. They work to turn an act of nature into an object of culture, to transform the incomprehensible into the manageable, the surreal into what they must accept as the new reality. The contingent and chaotic conditions of the aftermath form the context in which collective agency will determine the disaster's outcomes. Aftermaths are collective creations. People do not so much 'work in' disaster aftermaths as they *work on* and shape the very elements that will, collectively, constitute the disaster as an event and an outcome: every contributor to this volume recognizes this fact, and presents examples. As lived events, disasters are not brief moments of violent destruction; they are *the aftermath*, the experiences of individual and collective sensation, labour, and memory, gradually diminishing like ripples radiating out through time from a historical epicentre.

Of course, these acts of aftermath creation are inevitably conflicting and contingent. What gets rebuilt, and how and why, is never predetermined. Rather, it is always *worked out*, and often bitterly contested, in the aftermath context, as a wide range of people, groups, and institutions struggle to rebuild in sometimes conflicting ways (see Lotter, Ninglekhu, this volume). These struggles occur within uneven fields of power, and the outcomes of competing projects to shape the event and its meaning are never foregone conclusions (Dhungana, this volume). Disaster aftermaths institute a kind of generative process, marked by contingency across shifting temporalities rather than law-like outcomes. The contributors to this book consider how agents create the aftermath at every level, from the state's immediate efforts to claim the disaster for 'the nation' and therefore use it as a political tool; to Nepali artists who mobilized to help fellow citizens to salvage meaning and memory from the rubble; to hill villagers, devastated by loss, who must choose what to remember and what to forget; to householders navigating the financial, political, and aesthetic hurdles between them and the building of homes in which they feel able to reconstitute their lives (see Shneiderman et al., Baniya, this volume).

This focus on the aftermath also reminds us that pre-disaster conditions cannot in any straightforward way be the template for post-disaster reconstruction. Preconditions neither predict what will happen in the disaster's aftermath (preconditions are both plural and contradictory), nor are they ever actually reproduced. As this volume documents, even when people consciously set out to literally 'reconstruct' the past, as in heritage restoration projects, the pasts which they reconstruct ultimately have much more to do with the present than with what stood before. People may try to 'rebuild the past' but inevitably they end up imposing the present onto the past by rewriting history to suit the political demands of the present (Lotter, this volume). And the same goes for rebuilding anything else, from individual to institutional lives. Efforts to go back, to return, will inevitably reflect the conditions and demands of the new normal, not the old.

Implicit in our call for attention to the aftermath context is the argument that for post-disaster interventions to have any hope of succeeding, they must take fully into account the complex, dynamic, combative, and contingent conditions within which affected people must work to constitute new social worlds. Earthquakes destroy and damage lives, not just houses and roads. Rebuilding houses and roads is important, and will benefit from outside assistance. But to view this material rebuilding merely as a technical challenge to be addressed by preordained, one-size-fits-all technocratic fixes applied by state and I/NGO entities is to ignore the vastly larger and more powerful societal rebuilding projects within which relief and reconstruction efforts must try to operate. To attempt to ignore, or work outside of, the powerful and, ultimately, determining holistic aftermath context is to risk being scuttled by those very forces. Disaster aftermaths are like a mill, powered by collective agency, within which those affected by the disaster will grind out their future. Relief and reconstruction efforts that ignore this larger, more powerful, context are likely to be ground up in the process. Writing about the impact of the 25 April 2015 earthquake upon the Tamang communities of Rasuwa district, Ben Campbell states that it 'reverberated through time and space and amplified associations between poverty, place, nature and power' (2018: 111). Those who work to assist disaster-affected people must recognize that the new houses they are trying to build are only one part of a massive sociocultural rebuilding process that draws in everyone, from individuals to families to communities to the state. It is a complex, disorderly, and contingent process that we can probably never fully grasp. But to pretend that this larger context does not exist is to doom interventions to failure.

Disaster studies, area studies

This point may be restated in terms of competing claims to authoritative knowledge about disasters and how best to intervene. This volume argues that disaster relief and reconstruction efforts will succeed only to the extent that they bring together people with generic disaster assistance experience *and* people with deep knowledge of the relevant local historical, social, and cultural context. In short, effective post-disaster interventions can only emerge at a committed intersection between disaster studies and area studies.[5] Yet this joining of forces seems almost unthinkable to many, and perhaps especially to those who are most deeply entrenched within the existing division of academic labour. Indeed, an anonymous reviewer of an earlier draft of this introductory chapter remarked that this volume's primary contribution would be to 'area studies' and 'cultural heritage studies', and that its contribution to the field of 'disaster studies' would be of less significance. It is precisely this kind of self-defeating binary compartmentalization that this volume seeks to challenge.

Any catastrophe, whether it proceeds from a natural event or is human-made, is likely to attract the attention of these two academic communities— disaster studies, area studies—each claiming to possess authoritative knowledge. To date, the tensions, and even contradictions, between these two forms of knowledge production have often been tangible. Much of the literature categorized as 'disaster studies' and published in the journals of this field is authored by researchers who have little prior experience of or grounding in the political, cultural, and linguistic contexts of the disaster-affected society or societies about which they write.[6] Emic perspectives are

---

5   The field of disaster studies that has emerged since the 1960s is largely anchored in the social sciences and supports several high-ranking international journals. 'Area studies' refers to the in-depth, long-term, language-based study of regions and societies (see Dominguez 2009; Hutt 2019a).

6   There is also an important and influential body of work which approaches and analyses disasters, either singly or collectively, through a quasi-disciplinary comparative and theoretical framework. Some of this framework derives from research that attempts to formulate generalizing statements on the basis of case studies. Brancati (2007), for instance, conducts a statistical analysis of the effects of earthquakes on intrastate conflicts in 185 countries between 1975 and 2002, and Drury and Olson (1998) undertake a statistical analysis of the political impacts of disasters that occurred in various countries between 1966 and 1980. Meanwhile, Mark Pelling and Kathleen Dill discuss the potential for a disaster to provide either a 'critical juncture' (a contestation of established political, economic, and cultural power) or an 'accelerated status quo' (a successful concentration of that power—'a concentration or speeding up of pre-disaster trajectories which remain under the

also often conspicuously absent. As a result, the literature often focuses on problems concerning infrastructure and physical reconstruction from the point of view of I/NGO- and/or state-based relief practitioners (Lindell 2011). By contrast, area specialists, whether locals or foreigners, typically bring extensive research experience in the region conducted from a range of physical science, social science, and humanities perspectives. But to the extent that major disasters are rare in any given region, area-studies scholars rarely devote sustained attention to disaster consequences, and when they do, their studies are framed in ways that make them seem unapproachable and/or irrelevant to disaster-studies experts.[7]

As Nepal area-research specialists with a range of disciplinary backgrounds, the contributors to this volume are not disaster-studies experts. However, all of them engage with literature from that field in order to illustrate both the problems that can arise from the continuing separation of these perspectives (such as failed relief assistance initiatives) and the potential for new forms of meaningful intervention that might arise if and when the contradictions between them are shown to be false. At the level of policy, effective disaster relief has to emerge from initiatives that embody a folding-together of the *breadth* of disaster studies and the *depth* of area studies. Let us make it clear that we are not fantasizing about some supremely enlightened confederation of experts. What we *are* arguing is that post-disaster interventions that ignore the powerful, all-encompassing sociocultural processes and contexts in which disaster-affected people struggle to build their futures will almost certainly be ineffective. Sophisticated understandings of the powerful, complex, holistic aftermath context must inform the choice of the forms and methods of disaster relief and reconstruction that will be used. To be effective, disaster relief has to amplify the agency of the disaster-affected, not that of the disaster experts.

---

control of powerful elites …') and ask whether it is possible for us to identify 'tipping points, critical historical moments or broader influences on systems (internal and external) that determine the direction and significance of change' (2010: 22).

[7] There are, of course, examples of studies of disasters authored by scholars who were, or have since become, members of both of these communities, such as Bankoff's (2003) work on the Philippines, Clancey's (2006) historical work on Japan, and Simpson's study (2013) of the political aftermath of the 2001 Gujarat earthquake in India, to cite just a few.

The only way to achieve this is through the integration of disaster- and area-studies perspectives.

Epicentre to aftermath

By approaching the 2015 Nepal earthquakes from a wide range of analytical and methodological perspectives, this volume aims to contribute to disaster studies literature and practice by dramatically expanding the field of knowledge relevant to understanding disasters, their meanings, and their outcomes. Its 33 authors and co-authors (14 of them Nepali nationals) are all people who have been conducting research in Nepal for many years (in several cases many decades), each compelled by different backgrounds and circumstances to try to understand and explain this particular disaster aftermath. The (non-Nepali) editors are acutely aware of the dangers of imposing their own meanings on Nepal's earthquake aftermath experiences, especially in light of the fact that the project that gave birth to this volume was designed by researchers based in London, albeit in close consultation with Nepali counterparts, and funded by a United Kingdom (UK) research council. As S. Tamang (2019) points out, there is 'a certain deployment of the politics of knowledge' which leaves little room to question the expert, and 'cements a distinction between "academic" and "non-academic" knowledge and Western "experts" and others'. But we believe that the contributors to this volume have followed Mallika Shakya's (2015) request to 'consider the overlap between categories of insider and outsider while digging through localized experiences of the event and its aftermath'.

Part I of the volume, 'Contextualizing Disaster', consists of two introductory chapters, of which this is the first. Shakya (2015) records that 'Nepalis tried to make sense of the calamity by connecting their own experiences with those of their kin during a similar earthquake in 1934'. However, survivors of the 1934 earthquake were hard to find 81 years later, and published accounts were rare. In Chapter 2, John Whelpton situates the 2015 earthquakes in the context of the local history of disasters, with particular reference to the two major earthquakes that struck Nepal during the 20th century. By identifying recurring themes that run across these events, the chapter both provides historical context for the most recent earthquakes, and makes the case for the value of historical perspectives.

Part II, 'Rebuilding Lives and Livelihoods', complicates the notion of disaster recovery by looking closely at how it actually plays out on the ground. Where within the spectrum of victimhood and opportunity should we locate the pre-existing conflicts, hierarchies, aspirations, vulnerabilities, and needs of a specific disaster context? How does the arrival of new agents influence individual and group decision-making? How do humanitarian agencies replicate globally designed recovery models while also reacting to local circumstances via open source maps? How do government officials assess damage or establish ownership when life's circumstances are more complicated than formal categories allow? And where does individual and communal agency lie, amid disaster mapping, building-approval processes, and the arrival of construction materials?

In Chapter 3, Sara Shneiderman et al. draw upon research conducted at three sites in the districts of Bhaktapur, Dhading, and Sindhupalchok to explore the lived experience of reconstruction at household level, paying particular attention to the roles played by 'experts' (engineers, lawyers, and NGO staff) and the impact of high labour costs. The chapter demonstrates that a nexus of law, construction, and finance not only produces, or fails to produce, material outcomes, but transforms knowledge and the material conditions for people's livelihoods, and alters the value of skills and contextualized knowledge. Variables such as the availability of and demand for labour at different locations and pressures to sell or divide land mean that the reconstruction process can easily tilt social relations in unforeseen directions.

Chapter 4 continues this theme as Shyam Kunwar, Elsie Lewison, and Katharine Rankin focus their attention on the socially transformative effects of two major post-earthquake labour upheavals in Dolakha district of central Nepal. The earthquakes forced the massive displacement of labour at the site of a major infrastructure development project, and the arrival of hordes of international experts and volunteers engaged in humanitarian and reconstruction assistance had contradictory implications for local labour markets.

In Chapter 5, Jeevan Baniya describes the conceptualization and construction of a new 'integrated settlement' for a small marginal community in Sindhupalchok and explores how it has been changed by its interactions with new institutions, actors, and ideas. He asks who has benefited and who has lost from delays in the reconstruction process, and assesses the extent to which reconstruction activities have been owned and driven by the community concerned.

In Chapter 6, drawing upon fieldwork conducted in Gorkha, Sindhupalchok, and southern Lalitpur districts, Amrita Gurung and Jeevan Baniya turn a similarly critical eye on the role played by INGOs and NGOs in the earthquake aftermath, particularly in the context of partnerships forged with local community-based organizations (CBOs). They find that the I/NGOs' strategies are shaped by a range of different policy frameworks, priorities, and pre-existing networks, and that partnerships between I/NGOs and local organizations rarely translate into substantial changes at the local level.

Of course, it is at the 'local' level that a disaster is most immediately experienced, and that the new risks it introduces to the environment are first assessed. In Chapter 7, the status of local systems of knowledge of landslide hazards and their relationship to science and technical expertise is explored by Katie Oven et al. in the context of disaster risk governance in Nepal.

Part III, 'Rebuilding Structures', looks at the intersection of the social and built environments—of houses, heritage, and infrastructure—and examines the positionalities and relationships of stakeholders who participate in the political, administrative, and advocatory processes of reconstruction. The negotiation of frameworks for future cities, whether this is via civil society, INGOs, NGOs, central or local authorities, provides a platform from which a shared future of community can be envisaged. How do bureaucracy, aid, and activism structure the process of physical reconstruction in order to fulfil the development objective of 'building back better'? How, for example, are the strength and safety of traditional and modern structures perceived when the failure of certain categories of structure to withstand an earthquake is clearly visible and apparent? How does a pride in traditional architecture in private and public buildings promote a strengthened identity?

In Chapter 8, Nimesh Dhungana raises related questions about participation and ownership in his case study of the earthquake aftermath in the small Newar town of Sankhu. He describes how the Government of Nepal instrumentalized the spaces of participatory governance in order to legitimize its decision to implement 'owner-led reconstruction' while also pursuing its agenda of governance reforms in Nepal's aid sector, and argues that post-disaster participatory politics may shape longer-term state–society relations.

In Chapter 9, Shobhit Shakya finds increasing evidence that the experience of the 2015 earthquakes has led to significant changes in the Nepali state's perspective on international aid, over which it seeks to assert greater control. Citing the case of Bhaktapur, where the municipal administration rejected an offer of financial aid from a major German donor, he argues that this changed attitude towards aid has reached the local government level too.

In Chapter 10, Sabin Ninglekhu et al. investigate the politics of rebuilding in the traditional Newar settlement of Bungamati in the Kathmandu Valley, exploring how a community's claim to the right to rebuild according to its own desires conflicts with governmental programmes which seek to encode norms of 'heritage' into the rebuilding bylaws, thus making rebuilding more expensive. The chapter also connects to and addresses the core argument developed in Chapter 3, about the relationship between land, knowledge, and immaterial values being transformed through the reconstruction process.

In Chapter 11, Stefanie Lotter focuses on two examples (the Hanuman Dhoka Palace Complex (a historic monument) and Kasthamandap (a living monument) to describe the complex claims to ownership and authority and the re-negotiation of power relations that emerged as plans were being laid for the reconstruction of monuments in the medieval heart of Kathmandu. This chapter claims that a paradigm shift took place as the reconstruction approach changed from an 'authoritative government-led approach' to a 'community-led participatory approach'.

Part IV, 'Building Memory', understands the commemoration of a disaster as an active process of expression and articulation. Nepal's 2015 earthquakes have been reflected through the visual and performing arts in virtual spaces, planned memory centres, and existing museum galleries. There is a need to communicate shared experience and remember not only those who lost their lives but also those who survived, but this changes with the emotional and temporal distance from the event. These chapters capture instances of memorialization connected by either the form of artistic expression or the location of collective trauma. They analyse how commemorative spaces, both virtual and physical, are curated in collaborations between artists and communities, and how the medium as well as the facilitation by anthropologists, architects, curators, and editors influences the content.

In Chapter 12, Katharina Weiler analyses curatorial decision-making at the Patan Museum as it prepared its display of Newar architecture in the aftermath of the 2015 earthquakes. She discusses the values and identities projected onto these cultural goods by both local and international agents, and asks how the earthquakes were addressed in this exhibition of Nepali cultural heritage. The chapter's focus on authenticity provides a context for reflections upon the validity or otherwise of universal concepts applied in the preservation of heritage.

In Chapter 13, Christiane Brosius focuses on an individual artist's photographic, diary-like engagement with the urban landscape surrounding his home in Kathmandu in the weeks after the earthquake and the development of this work into an installation made up of oral histories and individual portraits in Bhaktapur, and on an innovative community-art project instituted by a Kathmandu-based artist collective in one of the worst affected neighbourhoods in the Kathmandu Valley. She asks how artists should respond to a catastrophe without simply aestheticizing tragedy, and how the artist-as-activist ensures a space for critical reflection or intervention in a dramatically changing reality.

In Chapter 14, drawing on their ongoing community-engaged visual ethnographic work, Austin Lord and Jennifer Bradley ask how photographs and photographic practices articulate with and help to shape different kinds of 'memory work' in the wake of a disaster. They describe the ways in which survivors of the co-seismic Langtang avalanche have used images and visual materials to reorganize the temporalities of memory, aftermath, recovery, and rejuvenation and create new forms of subjectivity, exposure, and agency.

Finally, in Chapter 15, Michael Hutt subjects a corpus of nearly 300 Nepali-language poems that were published in the *bhukampa visheshank* (earthquake special issues) of Nepali literary journals within three months of the April earthquake to a detailed thematic analysis, asking how this literature might help us to distinguish the endogenous response from the 'exogenous' response that, according to Albala-Bertrand (1993) and others, dominates writing about disasters. The chapter raises important questions about representation, which resonate throughout this volume and the issues and concerns it has raised: how should those who have not suffered the worst impacts of a disaster represent or give voice to those who have?

In closing, we would like to draw readers' attention to the SWAY archive within the Digital Library of SOAS University of London at https://digital.soas.ac.uk/SWAY. When completed, this archive will provide free and open access to some 3,000 documents in both English and Nepali, most of them generated locally, from the first three years of the aftermath of Nepal's 2015 earthquakes. It is our hope that the archive will be used by researchers, both now and in years to come, who wish to better understand the cultural, social, and political impacts of these earthquakes, and draw lessons from them for future occurrences of this kind.

2

Earthquakes in Nepali History[*]

John Whelpton

Introduction

The major earthquakes of 25 April and 12 May 2015 were the most recent in the long chain of such events to which the Himalayan region, at the junction of the South Asian and Eurasian tectonic plates, has been subject. For the inhabitants of the region, earthquakes are a significant part of historical memory, whether in the form of oral tradition or, as with the *vamsavalis* (chronicles) of the Kathmandu Valley, of written record. This chapter is intended to put the events of 2015 into historical context, looking in particular at the Nepal–Bihar earthquake of 1934 and the 1988 Nepal earthquake. The search for a historical perspective, whether formalized or not, follows naturally from human beings' need to see themselves as part of a community existing over time. Specifically, in keeping with the theme of this volume, I will discuss the impact of these earthquakes on social, political, and cultural change.

Living with earthquakes in the pre-modern period

A list of major earthquakes in Nepal since 1100 is given as Appendix 2A. The first for which any details are recorded occurred on 7 June 1255, during

---

[*] This chapter is based upon research conducted as a part of the project 'After the Earth's Violent Sway: The Tangible and Intangible Legacies of a Natural Disaster' funded by the UK's Global Challenges Research Fund through the Arts and Humanities Research Council, grant number AH/P003648/1. The main archival sources are the India Office Records (IOR), now housed in the British Library in London, in particular the IOR/L/PS/12 series, which covers British India's external relations from c. 1931 onwards, and, for more recent events, the *Nepal Press Digest* and *Nepal Press Report* published by the Regmi Research Institute in Kathmandu.

the reign of King Abhayamalla:

> The earthquake toppled very many houses and temples. It claimed the lives of one-third of the whole population, and the king himself died eight days later as a result. People left their houses and lived outside for a period of a fortnight to a month after the earthquake, while aftershocks were felt for the succeeding four months. (Pant 2002: 30)

The most destructive earthquake known from the historical record, rather than merely from geological evidence, was probably that of June 1505, which devastated much of Tibet, western Nepal, and Uttarakhand (D. Jackson 2002), and which may have killed one-third of the population of what is now Nepal (Himalayan Risk Research Institute n.d.). Such events must have had effects on political processes and on mentalities, but their detailed stories are not recoverable. We might, however, expect to find some indication of adaptation to risk in the choice of construction sites and methods, as is certainly the case in the traditional building practices of other civilizations, for example the pyramids of ancient Egypt (Morsy and Halim 2015)[1] and the Forbidden City in Beijing.[2]

Bharat Sharma (2072 v.s.) argued shortly after the April 2015 earthquake that earlier generations of Nepalis, who understood their relationship with the geological environment better, had built low-rise houses on high ground with courtyards and open space around them, using thick mortar and small windows and doors. Rather more tentatively, Mukunda Raj Aryal has suggested that some of the damage in 2015 was due to the neglect—or the forgetting—of traditional methods in the reconstruction effort between 1934 and 1938, and possibly also due to faulty methods introduced in restoration and preservation work from the 1950s onwards with the help of foreign consultants.[3] The question of the earthquake resilience of traditional

---

[1] See also '10 Interesting Facts about the Pyramids of Giza', https://www.onthegotours.com/blog/2015/08/10-interesting-facts-about-the-pyramids-of-giza/ (accessed 24 May 2019).

[2] Channel Four, 'Secrets of China's Forbidden City' (TV documentary), 2017, https://www.channel4.com/programmes/secrets-of-chinas-forbidden-city (accessed 28 May 2019).

[3] Mukunda Raj Aryal, interview, Kathmandu, 8 September 2017.

Nepali architecture and the impact of modern methods is fiercely debated between local people and outside experts.[4]

Whilst some traditional techniques do seem to have evolved in response to earthquake hazard, they clearly did not offer complete protection, and the major form of adaptation must be seen in the resilience with which the communities coped with disaster and with rebuilding. Resilience in the reconstruction phase is perhaps also demonstrated by the use of brick rather than stone for temple construction from the end of the Licchavi period down to the reign of Pratap Malla (1641–74).[5]

The 1833 earthquake

The first Nepali earthquake for which we have any detailed knowledge of the contemporaneous political situation (both domestic and international) is that of 26 August 1833. The most detailed account is that provided by Archibald Campbell, the British Residency doctor in Kathmandu: this records two milder shocks earlier in the evening followed by the main tremor just before 11 p.m.:

> … at 10.48 a third and most violent [shock] commenced: at first it was a gentle motion of the earth, accompanied by a slight rumbling noise; soon however it increased to a fearful degree, the earth heaved as a ship at sea, the trees waved from their roots, and houses moved to and fro far from the perpendicular. Horses and other cattle, terrified, broke from their stalls, and it was difficult to walk without staggering as a landsman does on ship-board. This shock lasted for about three minutes in its fullest force. (A. Campbell 1833: 564)

Campbell states that the earthquake's effects were the most severe to the east of Kathmandu, and records 401 dead, 172 injured, and 4,040 houses destroyed across the whole country—figures compiled without access to official Nepali records, and probably an underestimate for areas outside

---

[4]   See, for example, D'Ayala and Bajracharya (2003), UNESCO (2019), and Lotter (2019).

[5]   Mukunda Raj Aryal, interview, Kathmandu, 8 September 2017.

the Kathmandu Valley.[6] Aftershocks continued for some time, and their psychological effect on the inhabitants of Kathmandu was described by the Resident, Brian Hodgson, writing two days after the main quake:

> Whilst I write the Earth is trembling under my feet and the unhappy population of the crowded Capital are responding with an audible wail of woe and fear to every mutter of the Earthquake.[7]

The death the previous year of the Queen Regent, Lalita Tripura Sundari, had weakened the position of her political ally, the *mukhtiyar* (minister) Bhimsen Thapa, who had dominated the political scene since 1806. In January 1834, the Senior Queen Samrajyalakshmi approached the British Residency, hoping that it would back her against Bhimsen. Those pressing for the young King Rajendra to take direct control of the administration himself helped to convince Hodgson that Nepal would pose less of a threat to British interests if Bhimsen, whose power base was the army, could be disposed of. The process that led to Bhimsen's removal from office in 1837 was well underway before the earthquake of 26 August 1833, but the quake might conceivably have quickened developments.[8] The collapse of the two *dharahara* minarets that Bhimsen had erected adjacent to his palace very recently (see Hutt 2019b) may have encouraged rivals to believe that the minister's time was coming to a close.[9]

The 1934 earthquake

By the time of the 1934 Bihar–Nepal earthquake, Nepal was in a fundamentally different relationship with British India. The Rana family, who had since the mid-19th century ruled the country as Maharajas, reducing the king (Maharajadhiraj) to a mere religious symbol, were now

---

[6]   The figures given in a Nepali *vamsavali* (chronicle) composed shortly after the event are slightly lower (Wright 1966 [1877]: 183).

[7]   Hodgson to Macnaghten, 28 August 1833, IOR/R/5/47.

[8]   For a succinct overview of political developments in the 1830s, see Rose (1970) and for fuller details Pradhan (2001, 2012) and Whelpton (1991).

[9]   Pradhan (2012: 145) suggests that the earthquake was regarded as a 'portent predicting dire consequences for the state'.

military allies of the British and providers on a massive scale of recruits
for the British Indian Army's Gurkha regiments. A much larger quantity
of information is available on this earthquake, albeit mostly from official
sources.[10]

The earthquake struck at 2.15 p.m. on 15 January 1934. Lt. Col. G. H.
Smith, the British Legation surgeon, delivered first aid in Kathmandu on
the 15th and 16th and reported that almost every house had been damaged,
with around one in five completely collapsed, but stressed that there was no
panic and that people were moving patiently into open areas.[11] Like Brahma
Shumshere Rana, whose account of this earthquake was written from the
Nepal government's perspective, Smith emphasizes the swift and effective
action taken by the authorities:

> For two nights following the earthquake there was considerable
> looting by large organised bands. Owing to profiteering, food stuffs
> in the Bazaar soared to famine prices. Both these evils were promptly
> and successfully dealt with by the Nepal Government.... In two days
> the looting had ceased and prices had dropped to normal.[12]

Smith similarly notes the rapid restoration of basic infrastructure: piped
water supply was available again on the 17th, and electric street lighting
restored on the 19th, the latter greatly helping public morale. Although not
mentioned by Smith, the resilience of the Kathmandu Valley's population
was also helped by the traditional *guthi* (temple trust) organizations of the
indigenous Newar population, as highlighted in an article published just
after the 2015 quake by the cultural historian Satyamohan Joshi, who had
himself also experienced the 1934 disaster (Joshi 2072 v.s.). The account by
the British Minister[13] Clendon Daukes of his return journey to Kathmandu
at the end of February similarly includes an appreciation of self-help efforts

---

[10] The best-known account is by Brahma Shumshere J. B. Rana (2013), a senior Rana
who was in charge of hospital administration in 1934.

[11] G. H. Smith, report of 24 January 1934 to Secretary, FPD (IOR/L/PS/3056).

[12] Smith, undated report, forwarded to Secretary, FPD (19 April 1934, IOR/L/
PS/12/3036-3A).

[13] The title of the British representative in Nepal was successively 'Resident' (from
1816 to 1920), 'Envoy' (to 1934), 'Minister' (to 1947), and finally 'Ambassador'.

at the village level and an upbeat assessment of prospects for reconstruction across the country:

> Great as is the calamity, Nepal possesses a priceless asset in her sense of national unity which combined with the great energy of her people will in all probability enable her to recover in a surprisingly short space of time.[14]

Daukes' optimism has to be tempered by the opinion of his successor, Frederick Bailey, who wrote that the houses of the poor had been rebuilt hurriedly and were of very low quality.[15] A fair conclusion might still be that, given the limited number of functions the Rana regime normally attempted to perform, the government of Juddha Shamsher Rana handled the immediate crisis reasonably well.

The issue of external assistance

Juddha Shamsher stressed the virtues of self-reliance at the grassroots level in his appeals to his countrymen and is still seen as someone who preferred self-reliance at national level (L. M. S. Karki 2015; M. Sharma 2072 v.s.). This image needs to be tempered in two ways. First, in line with Nepal's policy even before she became closely allied to British India,[16] he was prepared to ask for assistance where specific technical expertise was clearly necessary. Second, his reluctance to accept either money or material assistance from British India was not rooted in opposition to assistance *per se*: he was primarily opposed to anything which might strengthen the widespread impression that, despite the 1923 treaty between Nepal and Great Britain,

---

[14] Daukes to Metcalfe, 3 March 1934, IOR/L/PS/12/3036. In his covering note to Smith's report cited earlier (Daukes to Secretary, FPD, 19 April 1934, IOR/L/PS/12/3036-3A), Daukes estimates a recovery period of three to five years. However, the reconstruction seems to have been completed by 1938.

[15] F. M. Bailey, Legation Report for 1935 and 1936, forwarded to A. Eden, 15 January 1937, IOR/L/PS/12/306 -3A.

[16] In 1816, shortly after the end of the war between Nepal and British India, Bhimsen Thapa, who had headed the administration since before the conflict, asked the British to provide vaccination against smallpox (Heydon 2019).

Nepal was in reality a part of India. He was probably also worried that assistance might involve 'an invasion of Nepal by an army of British Relief Officers and Doctors'.[17]

On the technical side, Juddha Shamsher asked for and received the services of 'engineering advisors', who were lent by the Government of India,[18] but they do not seem to have arrived before mid-March, and they left on 26 April.[19] Their exact duties are uncertain but most likely involved repairing public utilities and possibly assisting with the demolition of dangerous structures: although the coverage of the earthquake aftermath in the government's mouthpiece newspaper, the *Gorkhapatra*, was highly positive, it did note in its issue of 26 Jyestha (c. 8 June) that fatalities were still occurring during the demolition process. The government was also ready to bring in new materials from foreign sources to help with relief and reconstruction. Joshi's (2072 v.s.) eyewitness account notes the appearance for the first time in Kathmandu of parboiled rice, corrugated steel, and cement, from Burma, Belgium, and Britain, respectively.

Juddha Shamsher also allowed J. B. Auden of the Geological Survey of India to visit Nepal to report on the causes of the earthquake and make recommendations for the future. As well as visiting the Kathmandu Valley, Auden was given unprecedented permission to travel to Dhankuta and Udaypur, where the damage was believed to be particularly severe. Some of his findings were incorporated in the accounts of the Bihar–Nepal earthquake published by the Geological Survey of India (Dunn, Auden, and Ghosh 1934; Dunn et al. 1939) and a summary was also published in Nepali in the *Gorkhapatra* (12 Shravan, c. 11 July) under his by-line. (This was subsequently incorporated in Brahma Shumshere's book.) Auden's conclusions, which included recommendations on building design and locations for future industrial development, may not have had much practical effect, but the fact that he was allowed in at all and that his advice was publicised enhanced the

---

[17] This was a guess hazarded by a British official reporting Juddha's polite refusal of an offer of food and other supplies (Gorakhpur Collector to Secretary to UP Government, 30 January 1934, F & P External 39-X 1934 [National Archives of India]).

[18] Government of India Home Department, reply telegram to Secretary of State for India, 14 February 1934, IOR/L/PS/12/3036.

[19] Daukes to Metcalfe, 12 March 1934 and Daukes to W. K. Fraser-Tytler, 29 April 1934, IOR/L/PS/12/3036.

image Juddha Shamsher desired for himself as an enlightened ruler, and was hailed as such in the same issue of the newspaper.

Juddha Shamsher was out hunting in far-western Nepal at the time of the earthquake, and his request for engineers seems to have been made shortly after his return to the Valley on 4 February. Whilst still *en route*, he declined an offer from the government of the United Provinces (in British India) to provide food and medicine or other necessary supplies.[20] He framed his decision as taken 'not because of pride but because of profound sympathy in their own distress' and because of the need, at a time when both countries were suffering, to 'be as self-supporting as possible'.[21] This sentiment might have been genuine: the Nepal government was able to make enough rice available in the Kathmandu Valley by using supplies amassed for a possible conflict with Tibet and by bringing additional supplies up from the Tarai, whilst Juddha Shamsher himself collected thatch and bamboo *en route* (Prasad 1975: 82). Nonetheless, the wish to be seen as wholly independent politically was the most important factor. This was seen very clearly in the unwillingness to share in the Viceroy's Relief Fund, which, as Juddha Shamsher's son Bahadur emphasized personally to government officials in Delhi, might strengthen the mistaken notion that Nepal was part of India.[22] The Ranas were particularly sensitive on this point, because it was obvious by the 1930s that India was well on the way to achieving internal self-rule, if not complete independence, and that many in the Indian Congress did not see Nepal itself as truly independent.[23] Bahadur also told officials in Delhi that his country would accept 'any spontaneous subscriptions made by the public in England or India earmarked for Nepal'. However, the Government of India did not want to set up a separate conduit for donations to Nepal:

> We are strongly opposed to making any offer of financial assistance to be given by opening a separate fund since they might feel it incumbent on them to accept, and, apart from possible diversion

---

[20] Private telegram from Viceroy to Secretary of State for India, 5 February 1934, IOR/L/PS/12/3036.

[21] Juddha to Daukes 11 February 1934, IOR/L/PS/12/3036.

[22] Government of India Home Department telegram to Secretary of State for India, 14 February 1934, IOR/L/PS/12/3036.

[23] As emphasized by Bahadur's remarks to Daukes' successor in 1936 (Bailey's note of 1 October 1936, Bailey Collection, Mss Eur F157 (IOR)).

of subscriptions from Bihar, we consider that it would be most undesirable to have two funds in competition with each other.[24]

The 1934 relief loans

Juddha Shamsher established a loan fund of 50 lakh (5 million) Nepali rupees (NPR) for house rebuilding,[25] originally on the understanding that if loans were not repaid within four years his government would take ownership of the rebuilt house. In 1938, however, he announced that repayment of the housing loans would be waived entirely, and that those who had already repaid them would have their money returned (Figure 2.1).

This decision has usually been portrayed as one that was taken by Juddha Shamsher alone. However, at least one oral tradition has him giving in to public pressure,[26] and one of his daughters claimed that he had intended all along to make grants but disguised them initially as loans so that people would not apply for excessive amounts.[27] It has also been plausibly suggested that decisions on earthquake relief were sometimes the result of political manoeuvring within the Rana family (Mishra and Aryal 2015); indeed, this is precisely what Geoffrey Betham, the British Minister in Nepal from 1938 to 1944, believed had happened. In the Legation Report for 1938, he claimed that Juddha originally wanted to enforce repayment but had given way to pressure for leniency from Mohan, Baber, and Kaiser, the sons of his predecessor Chandra Shamsher, who had inherited Chandra's wealth and influence.[28]

---

[24] Government of India Home Department, telegram to Secretary of State for India, 14 February 1934, IOR/L/PS/12/3036.

[25] This equates to c. USD 27 million at January 2021 prices.

[26] According to senior Nepali scholar Mukunda Raj Aryal (interview, Kathmandu, 8 September 2017) when invited to inaugurate the re-constructed Mahabouddha temple in Patan, Juddha spontaneously announced at the ceremony that the loan to the *guthi* (temple trust) involved would not have to be repaid. This led to further requests from *guthis* responsible for other temples, and later from individuals, and Juddha eventually complied.

[27] Janak Rajya Laxmi Devi Shah, eldest daughter of Juddha's youngest Maharani, interviewed in 1999 by Stefanie Lotter.

[28] Betham, Annual Report for 1938, submitted to Foreign Office, 12 January 1939, IOR/L/PS/12/306-3A.

Figure 2.1 The 1934 earthquake memorial at Bhugol Park, just off New Road (Juddha Sadak) in Kathmandu. It is inscribed with the text of the speech delivered by Juddha Shamsher Rana in 1938 in which he announced that the repayment of housing reconstruction loans would be waived.

Source: Photograph by Michael Hutt.

In accepting this account, Betham may have been unduly swayed by the Chandra family itself, and also by an initial British view of Juddha Shamsher as a weak character, easily manipulated by priests, his son Bahadur, and his nephews.[29] Nevertheless, Betham's version is the only account available from someone who was reasonably well informed but not an interested party.

Political consequences of the 1934 earthquake

An immediate consequence of the 1934 earthquake was the removal of the 'C-class Ranas' (the illegitimate sons of previous Maharajas) from the line of succession to the Maharajaship, and their banishment to the provinces. Their inclusion on the Roll of Succession, and in particular the position of

---

[29] See, for example, Clendon Daukes to Sir John Simon, 15 January 1935, IOR/L/ PS/12/3051.

Rudra Shamsher as Commander-in-Chief, had disadvantaged Chandra's sons, but Juddha Shamsher justified the timing of his move, made on 18 March, in terms of it sparing those who were to be expelled from the Valley the wasted expense of reconstructing their palaces. The move had been under discussion for some time and the decision to act was revealed by Juddha to his 'A-class' relatives two days before he reached the Kathmandu Valley. The 'C-class' Ranas were aware of what was likely to happen but had decided that there was nothing to be done (S. Rana 2017: 99–100; P. Rana 2062 v.s.: 263).

British diplomats knew that political dissidence had been slowly growing for some time before the 1934 earthquake and that it was not entirely confined to the Kathmandu Valley and the Nepali diaspora in India.[30] Writing in 1940, Betham saw rising political consciousness as the natural result of education and travel, and he stressed in particular recent improvements in communications with India.[31] Although the effects of the earthquake were marginal to these long-term factors, the Rana regime's opponents, based in India, included allegations of mismanagement of financial relief in their propaganda. D. R. Regmi (1950: 209–10) alleges that the Ranas themselves were favoured in the distribution of the relief, with individual members of the clan receiving NPR 20,000–30,000 against a normal limit of NPR 500,[32] and that 25 of the NPR 30 lakh (3 million) distributed were found after the cancellation of debts to have gone to members of the ruling family. Purushottam Rana, grandson of Commander-in-Chief Rudra Shamsher, alleges (2062 v.s.: 256–57) that Juddha Shamsher's agents were expected to minimize the amount given out, and claims that the loans that were written off were only 20 per cent of the total, because repayment of the rest was already underway. He even suggests that some people had already been imprisoned for defaulting. These claims contradict Juddha's own assertion that those who had already returned their loans would have them refunded (Prasad 1975: 95), and are probably partisan exaggerations. If abuses on this scale were really happening, it is unlikely that rumours would not have reached the British Legation, whose sources of information included Indian and Nepali staff who mingled freely with the general population.

---

[30] Daukes to Sir John Simon (Foreign Secretary, London), 15 January 1935, IOR/L/PS/12/3051.

[31] Betham to Halifax, 27 July 1940, IOR/L/PS/12/3012.

[32] The actual limit appears to have been NPR 1,500 (Sever 1993: 318).

There is, however, evidence of some internal discontent: Hem Prasad Timilsina, a survivor of both the 1934 and 2015 earthquakes, told an interviewer that the government had not done much for them on either occasion (*The Times of India* 2015). Additionally, even though most Nepalis probably did not expect their government to provide assistance for the rebuilding of private homes in 1934, some of the educated minority may have felt that this should have been given as loans right from the start, particularly if they shared the erroneous belief that the relief money had been provided by Japan (Gong 2014). Gautam (2046 v.s.: 53–54) argues also that the earthquake experience encouraged radicalism, which was channelled at first into social and religious organizations but contributed also to the emergence of the Praja Parishad, the most important dissident group formed within Nepal during the Rana period, rather than among Nepalis based in India.[33]

Betham came to believe that the spread of disaffection to at least part of the army was the result of Juddha's misstep over relief payments. His annual report for 1940 claims that the army was discontented because, in contrast with the treatment of loans to civilians, they had been required to return the four months' advance of pay they had received in 1934. He was also told that the outbreak of the Second World War in 1939 was welcomed by Juddha Shamsher because he was able to include the most disaffected regiments in the brigade that was sent to India for garrison duty, replacing British Indian Army units that were now needed at the battle front.[34]

Again, it is possible that Betham was unduly influenced by the Chandra family or its supporters after his initial inclination to downplay the significance of the army's complaints.[35] However, a mutiny in January 1941 by a Nepali battalion stationed at Kohat, in what is now Pakistan's

---

[33] Gong (2014), apparently relying on the autobiography of a Praja Parishad leader, Ramhari Sharma Nepal (2006), and Gautam (2046 v.s.) both claim that the loans were made from Japanese funds. Since the uneducated generally believed that the earthquake had been caused by divine anger at Lord Clydesdale's flight over Everest the previous year (Daukes, report on Nepal in 1929–34, forwarded to London 15 January 1935, IOR/L/PS/12/3051), the rulers may have also been blamed for authorizing the flight.

[34] Betham, Annual Report for 1940, forwarded to Foreign Office 22 January 1941, IOR/L/PS/12/306, pp. 1–2.

[35] Betham to Lord Halifax, 2 May 1940, IOR/L/PS/12/3012.

Khyber Pakhtunkhwa province, suggests that the discontent continued. The following month Betham wrote of the 'very grave mistake' which Juddha had made by not giving the soldiers the requested refund.[36]

There are conflicting reports of the Kohat incident, but the immediate spark was the men's anger when an expected supplementary payment was given in kind as extra rations—probably milk, to counteract a vitamin deficiency (P. Rana 2062 v.s.: 294). Some of the rank and file rioted and their own officers were either unable or unwilling to control them. However, a British officer managed to secure the armoury, leaving the rioters armed with only their *kukris*. Bahadur Shamsher, the Maharaja's son, who was in overall command of the Nepali regiments in India, was brought from Delhi and the battalion was paraded (with fully armed British and Indian troops nearby) and obeyed his order to ground their *kukris*. Twenty-two men were sent back to Nepal: the supposed chief instigator was hanged, another was given life imprisonment, and shorter sentences were imposed on the others. Betham linked the incident both to pre-existing resentment and to the poor quality of the Nepali officers, many of whom, he said, were 'illegitimate' ('C-class') Ranas.[37] Purushottam Rana, himself a member of the 'C-class', refers also to a belief that a Nepali officer was embezzling funds earmarked for the soldiers, and claims that the Nepali officers who were attacked were the ones who had sided with the British in insisting that the supplement could not be paid in cash.

In addition to Betham and Purushottam's versions of events, a detailed account of the episode is provided by Uprety (1984: 200–07), drawing primarily on Nepal Foreign Office Archives, including British correspondence not preserved in London. Uprety makes no mention of the earthquake issue and focuses only on the grievance that arose over rations, though he also refers to a problem of cultural adjustment for the Nepalese army contingent as a whole. His sources blame the unit's officers, without singling out the Ranas among them. Memories within the Nepal Army are more or less in line with Uprety, with rations and poor discipline seen as key but also a hint that discomfort in a Muslim environment might have been an additional factor.[38]

---

[36] Betham to Foreign Secretary, Government of India, 7 February 1941, IOR/L/PS/12/3012.

[37] Legation Annual Report for 1941, IOR/L/PS/12/306 -3A.

[38] J. P. Cross, Personal Communication, 30 June 2018.

Whatever concrete grievances lay behind it, discontent in the army appeared to be widespread. The author of a Government of India Intelligence Department Report compiled around the same time expressed surprise at how many Thakuri and Chettri officers from the Kathmandu Valley in the Nepal contingent expressed anti-regime feelings to him. English-speaking officers were particularly resentful of the restrictions imposed on them by the Rajguru, whom they termed the 'Guru Maharaj' or 'Pope of Nepal' and believed to be partly controlling Juddha.[39] Whilst such growing resentment had deep causes, Juddha's lack of flexibility in 1938 may have exacerbated it.

The 1988 earthquake

During the 50 years that followed the formal end of the post-1934 reconstruction period, there were a number of lesser earthquakes affecting areas far from the Kathmandu Valley (see Appendix 2A). However, apart from the panic in 1941 when an astrological prediction of a similar conjunction of planets to that of January 1934 prompted the closure of government offices and led a number of Ranas to camp out in their grounds, little attention was given to the issue of earthquake safety. This changed dramatically with the earthquake of 21 August 1988 which, at 6.6 on the Richter scale, was the largest to hit Nepal since 1934 and led to a strong focus amongst professionals and the media on the danger of future, bigger disasters (Whelpton 2019).

The 1988 disaster caused up to 1,091 deaths, with 6,553 injured, 21,973 houses destroyed, and 42,198 damaged (P. Nepal 2016: 107) There was also extensive damage to public buildings, including the destruction of a large number of schools.[40] The epicentre was in Udaypur district,[41] and the physical

---

[39] Undated Intelligence Report (probably January or February 1941), IOR/L/PS/12/3012.

[40] Kandel, Pandey, and Dixit (2004) claim that 6,000 schools were damaged, but Marichman Singh gives a total of 1,202 (*Gorkhapatra* 24 September, *Nepal Press Digest* 32: 39), and a January 1989 World Bank report gives a total of 1,122.

[41] Although most authorities name Udaypur as the epicentre, Chinese measurements placed it just to the west of Dhankuta. Fujiwara et al. (1989: 84) argue that this is more consistent with the observed pattern of damage.

destruction was the most severe in the eastern hills (Figure 2.2), although the highest number of deaths was in the town of Dharan at the foot of the Chure range.[42] The earthquake was felt across the country, including in the Kathmandu Valley, where Bhaktapur, due to the thickness of the alluvium beneath it, as usual suffered the worst damage (N. Thapa 2045 v.s.). Overall, around 460,000 persons were estimated to have been rendered homeless and the total damage was around NPR 4.1 billion, equivalent to approximately NPR 39 billion at current prices (World Bank 1989).[43]

After the collapse of the Rana regime in 1951 and a brief experiment with parliamentary democracy, political power was now again in the hands of the king, who presided over the Panchayat system of non-party, 'guided democracy'. Although the most important decisions were made in the royal palace, day-to-day administration was in the hands of politicians working within this system, known as *panchas*. The relief operation in 1988 was under the overall direction of a Natural Disaster Relief Committee, headed by the Minister of State for Home Affairs, Niranjan Thapa. To coordinate between this body and relief committees in individual districts, Natural Disaster Relief Coordination Committees were set up separately for the eastern and central regions, the former based at Biratnagar airport (N. Thapa 2045 v.s). Donations were to be channelled through a Central Earthquake Relief and Rehabilitation Fund chaired by the Prime Minister, Marichman Singh Shrestha. The Panchayat Policy and Evaluation Committee also appointed a team of senior *panchas*, including former Prime Ministers, to encourage popular participation in relief measures (N. Thapa 2045 v.s.: 52).

In addition to the immediate rescue operation, which, as in 2015, involved neighbours, local social services, and volunteers, as well as the security forces, the government announced grants of NPR 2,000 to each bereaved family and NPR 1,000 to those whose homes had collapsed or been rendered uninhabitable. To help meet the need for immediate shelter and food, plastic sheeting was made available for distribution, and affected families were promised an allocation of 40 kilograms of rice. As of

---

[42] Niranjan Thapa reproduces the official, district-wise casualty figures in an appendix to his book (N. Thapa 2045 v.s.: 121, 122). The total number of houses damaged but still habitable in the central region was 13,959 (including 133 in Bara district). No comparable figure is provided for the eastern region.

[43] At the current (January 2021) exchange rate, NPR 39 billion would amount to approximately USD 330 million.

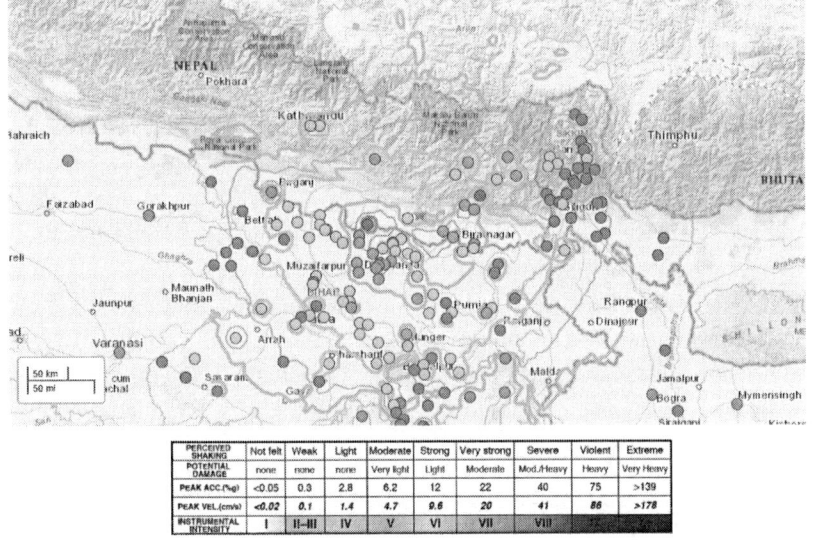

PERCEIVED SHAKING	Not felt	Weak	Light	Moderate	Strong	Very strong	Severe	Violent	Extreme
POTENTIAL DAMAGE	none	none	none	Very light	Light	Moderate	Mod./Heavy	Heavy	Very Heavy
PEAK ACC.(%g)	<0.05	0.3	2.8	6.2	12	22	40	75	>139
PEAK VEL.(cm/s)	<0.02	0.1	1.4	4.7	9.6	20	41	86	>178
INSTRUMENTAL INTENSITY	I	II–III	IV	V	VI	VII	VIII		

Figure 2.2 Map: intensity of the 21 August 1988 earthquake.

Source: https://earthquake.usgs.gov/earthquakes/eventpage/usp0003k6t/shakemap/intensity (accessed 8 December 2018).

Note: Map shows general locations and does not represent authentic international boundaries.

mid-March 1989, official figures showed expenditure on the relief operation of NPR 154.4 million (approximately 1.46 billion at 2018 prices),[44] of which around 30 per cent had been provided by foreign sources and 27 per cent by local organizations and individuals. The total reached NPR 204 million (1.9 billion at current prices) if estimates for the value of help in kind or resources mobilized by local organizations are included (N. Thapa 2045 v.s.: 137–39).

Without an independent evaluation, it is difficult to assess the effectiveness of the 1988 operation. Whilst the best description of the actual damage is probably that given by a Japanese team (Fujiwara et al. 1989), the fullest account available of the relief effort is Niranjan Thapa's self-published

---

[44] Calculating on the basis of the inflation statistics at https://knoema.com/atlas/Nepal/Inflation-rate (accessed 18 December 2018), the 1988 figures have to be multiplied by 9.444 to give 2018 equivalents.

5 *Bhadauko Bhukampa* (The 5 Bhadra Earthquake). This, like Brahma Shumshere Rana's book on the 1934 earthquake, which Thapa took as his model, is an account written by a man who himself played a leading role in the events he describes. Unsurprisingly, Thapa paints a highly positive picture. He pays tribute to the first responders, but then goes on to claim that the affected population were greatly impressed by the government's efforts. As was customary in the Panchayat era, Thapa is particularly appreciative of the role played by the royal family, and is at his most gushing when describing an inspection visit by Queen Aishwarya:

> In Her Majesty's actual presence, it seemed that in this country there are no children without parents, no orphans, that all Nepalis are safe in the sacred, pure and broad shade of the monarchy. (N. Thapa 2045 v.s.: 82; translation mine)

Thapa omits any mention of the criticism voiced in the press of the speed with which relief was delivered and of corruption and favouritism in the process. This included a report of the Udaypur Chief District Officer (CDO) admitting that the relief operation did not get properly underway until 8 September, even in one part of the district headquarters.[45] Thapa does, however, mention the difficulties of obtaining information from and getting relief to the remoter areas, and the lack of helicopters and other aircraft. His recommendation that rapid-response teams and supplies should be in place before future disasters struck betrays an awareness that the response in 1988 left something to be desired.

The existence of private newspapers, which, while subject to intermittent official harassment, were not controlled by the authorities, meant that opposition voices were heard—particularly those of the leaders of the still officially banned political parties. Although the multi-party side had lost a referendum on the future of Nepal's national political structure in 1980, the general atmosphere was more open than in the preceding decades, and the post-referendum introduction of direct elections to the Rastriya Panchayat (National Assembly) meant that the space for opposition activities was now somewhat wider.[46] All of this was a complete contrast with 1934, when the

---

[45] *Matribhumi*, 13 September 2018 (*Nepal Press Digest* 32: 38).

[46] For a discussion of politics in this period, see Hoftun, Raeper, and Whelpton (1997: 96–114).

only newspaper was the official *Gorkhapatra*, and even the reports that appeared in the Indian press generally reflected the Rana regime's line.[47]

The leaders of the Nepali Congress and of the different Communist factions complained of general inefficiency and a lack of urgency, and accused the government of wasting resources on transporting senior *pancha*s around the country on inspection visits.[48] This complaint presumably referred in particular to the veteran politicians selected for this role by the Panchayat Policy and Evaluation Committee, a body whose general regulatory powers were in any case resented both by party activists and the more liberal-minded of the Panchayat system's own workers.

There was also indignation over the government's insistence that it would assume total control of the relief operation. Prime Minister Marichman Singh made it clear on 5 September that all relief contributions would have to be channelled through official District Relief Committees 'so as to maintain law and order and avoid duplication and partiality'.[49] A number of Nepali Congress Party workers and activists of other parties who were involved in the unauthorized soliciting of donations or transportation of supplies were arrested. The political parties were even banned from turning up as a group to donate blood, even if not marching under their party flags. Participation had to be purely on an individual basis or as a member of a government-approved organization.[50] Whilst decrying all this obstruction, the Nepali Congress Party eventually gave up attempts to act on its own and deposited NPR 900,000 in the government's Central Relief Fund.[51]

---

[47] Dilli Raman Regmi, a Nepali dissident based in India at the time, claimed during the Second World War that the Ranas bribed the Indian press to provide favourable coverage. He also criticized the Indian nationalists for their reluctance to criticize 'native states' so as to concentrate solely on the anti-British struggle and pointed out that the Reuters correspondent in Kathmandu, the superintendent at the British Legation, would be reluctant to criticize the pro-British Ranas. 'An Appeal to Congressmen', Ext Affairs 626-C.A./44 (Secret), ff. 214–20, (National Archives of India).

[48] *Rastra Pukar*, 25 August 1988 (*Nepal Press Report*, 26 August 1988, p. 136).

[49] *Rising Nepal*, 6 September 1988 (*Nepal Press Digest* 32: 37).

[50] Information from C. K. Lal, who was involved as an engineer in post-earthquake reconstruction, Kathmandu, 30 August 2018.

[51] Statement by Krishna Prasad Bhattarai, *Matribhumi*, 20 September 1988 (*Nepal Press Digest* 32: 39).

The government was also accused of obstructing foreign organizations and individuals, including the British Gurkha camp at Dharan and Mother Teresa of Calcutta, who arrived in Kathmandu with relief supplies on 25 August. Allegedly, no helicopter was made available for her to travel to Dharan and she was not allowed to visit Bhaktapur as the situation was not 'normal' there, so she left Nepal four days later.[52] Marichman Singh later denied in the Rastriya Panchayat that obstacles had been put in her way,[53] and the government did accept the assistance of a British Brigade of Gurkhas medical team sent from Hong Kong (N. Thapa 2045 v.s.: 100), but it remains possible that sensitivity over Christian missionaries and over the role of the British in Dharan had made the government wary[54]

There was also criticism of the government's appeal for assistance from abroad, which was voiced most trenchantly by former-minister-turned-prominent-dissident Rishikesh Shaha:

Even before full details about the extent of loss of life and property caused by the earthquake are available, [ministers] have appealed for international assistance. This clearly reveals that the Marich Man Singh regime lacks a spirit of self-reliance and is totally helpless.... As many as 7000 people had died in the 1934 earthquake, and foreigners had offered relief aid, but the then rulers of our country had refused to accept it. But today, we are dependent on foreign assistance not only for economic development but even for the relief of disaster victims. Is not this shameful for us?[55]

This criticism was made at a time of increasing concern over the role played by foreign aid in Nepal's development, reflecting not only unease

---

[52] *Nepali*, 29 August 1988 (*Nepal Press Digest* 32: 36); *Matribhumi*, 13 September 1988 (*Nepal Press Digest* 32: 38).
[53] *Rising Nepal*, 24 September 1988 (*Nepal Press Digest* 32:39).
[54] The shortage of helicopters and the tense situation in Bhaktapur following the murder of an ex-Member of the Rastriya Panchayat, Karna Hyaju, on 25 August might explain the government's reluctance to facilitate Mother Teresa's visit. However, the recent (February 1988) conviction of a group of Catholic priests and nuns for proselytizing may have also made it particularly wary of a high-profile Catholic visitor.
[55] *Rastra Pukar*, 25 August 1988 (*Nepal Press Report*, 26 August 1988, p. 138).

over a perceived undermining of self-reliance but also a belief that aid was being captured by a corrupt elite, rather than benefitting the bulk of the population (see, for example, Panday 1983). Unfavourable comparisons with Juddha Shamsher Rana's policy of self-reliance in 1934 would be made again strongly after the 2015 earthquake, especially in monarchist circles.

The charge that the distribution of relief was being distorted by corruption and favouritism was the most damaging for the government. In addition to broad accusations from opposition figures, the official media reported the arrest of the vice chairman of a village *panchayat* in Udaypur district, together with a government employee, for misappropriating relief materials and issuing receipts for NPR 1,000 (the amount each homeless family was entitled to) after distributing only 700 or 800.[56] Marichman Singh insisted that irregularities like this were only isolated cases, but corruption certainly was a problem, as was also the case in affected areas across the border in India.[57]

Accusations of malpractice had lethal consequences in Bhaktapur on 25 August 1988, when the former Member of the Rastriya Panchayat for the area, Karna Bahadur Hyaju, was accused of improper distribution of relief supplies and lynched in the street by an angry mob. Although the Panchayat system remained officially partyless, Hyaju had originally been elected with the support of a Leftist group, the Nepal Workers and Peasants Organisation (NWPO), which had long been the dominant force in Bhaktapur politics. Once in the legislature, Hyaju succumbed to the blandishments of the Panchayat establishment and lost the 1986 election to a candidate who was still loyal to the NWPO. He was therefore considered a traitor by many in Bhaktapur. Even though many Leftists claimed that he had actually been killed in a 'false flag' operation by 'Mandales', hoodlums who acted as enforcers for the Panchayat hardliners, he was most probably the victim of an attack by rank-and-file local communists which got out of hand.[58] In any case, the government seized its chance to arrest the head of the NWPO, Narayan Bijuchke (who had actually been at his home throughout the day of the lynching), and other leading members of his group, including the National Panchayat member for Bhaktapur and the city's mayor. They were convicted by a special court and remained in prison until the victory of the 1990 People's Movement and the

---

[56] *Rising Nepal*, 14–15 September 1988 (*Nepal Press Digest* 32: 38).

[57] For Marichman Singh's statement, see *Rising Nepal*, 24 September 1988 (*Nepal Press Digest* 32:39) and for the earthquake in India, see Ahmed (1988).

[58] Krishna Hachhethu, personal communication, May 2020.

dismantling of the Panchayat system. The Bhaktapur Panchayat itself was dissolved and replaced by a government-appointed committee.

The main lines of the reconstruction programme were announced in September 1988 and included an elaborate scheme for the rebuilding of Dharan town. Families who had lost their homes were to be given loans of NPR 5,000 at 1 per cent interest, with the possibility of a second tranche of 5,000 at 10 per cent, and 15 per cent on any amount beyond that. No repayment of the basic loan would be required for two years.[59] There was also to be free technical advice on the reconstruction of village houses, with a grant of NPR 600 to any family that opted to install a toilet and smokeless stove, features which would be compulsory in district headquarters and urban areas. The reconstruction of destroyed infrastructure was to be completed rapidly and a Reconstruction and Rehabilitation Committee was to be set up under the Ministry of Housing and Physical Planning. Financing was to be shared between the centre and local governments, with off-setting cuts in other parts of the budget (N. Thapa 2045 v.s.: 106–11). Additional financial support was secured from the World Bank, which agreed in April 1989 to provide a credit line of USD 41.5 million for a programme which rolled together an urban development scheme (already under discussion before the earthquake) and help with reconstruction (*Gorkhapatra*, 5 May 1989, reproduced in N. Thapa 2045 v.s.: 142; World Bank 1989).

The progress of the reconstruction programme at the centre of political power in the Kathmandu Valley does not appear to have been a major issue, but houses in the eastern hills do appear to have been reconstructed to a different standard, as compared to the pre-earthquake situation. The World Bank's 1997 final report on the project indicates that while the take-up of grants for the installation of improved stoves and toilets had been disappointing, and the town development component was ineffective, the home reconstruction loans scheme had generally been a success. In 1992, the Nepali Congress government decided to waive repayment of the basic NPR 5,000 loan for those who had not borrowed more than NPR 10,000 in total (World Bank 1997b: 18–19), a move which the Panchayat regime, shortly before its collapse in 1990, appears to have approved in principle.[60] The World Bank was not opposed to grants as such, but argued that allowing

---

[59] As inflation at this time was running at close to 10 per cent, any rate of interest below this was negative in real terms.

[60] Madhab Mathema, personal communication, 31 May 2019.

only partial relief had resulted in those who had been excluded withholding repayments, in the hope that the scheme would be extended to them. As a consequence of this, the commercial banks running the scheme had many bad loans on their books.

The 1988 earthquake, like the much bigger quake of 2015, occurred shortly before a major political transformation and a crisis in relations with India. The collapse of the Panchayat system in 1990 in the face of popular protests came after India restricted the movement of goods across the border because of a dispute over trade and transit issues (Whelpton 2005: 113). The promulgation of Nepal's new constitution in autumn 2015 led to India again introducing restrictions, this time in support of the blocking of border crossing points by Madhesi activists who were protesting the constitution's failure to meet some of their demands. However, there is no obvious link between the 1988 earthquake and the radical political changes that followed two years later. It is possible that discontent over the handling of the relief operation strengthened public discontent with the Panchayat system, even though this was primarily the result of other factors, but it is difficult to quantify this in the absence of the systematic surveying of public opinion that only got underway after 1990. Private sector newspapers are of limited use in filling this gap because they were few in number and often tied to the line of particular political parties. Whatever the actual state of public opinion, these papers painted a picture of a discontented population, just as Niranjan Thapa painted one of loyal and grateful subjects.

Conclusion

Assessments of the political significance of earthquakes have to steer between opposing pitfalls: regarding disasters as purely interruptions to the broad course of political and social development, or seeing them as critical determinants. The 1976 Tangshan disaster in China, which killed between 242,000 and 750,000 people in Northeast China, can be cited as an example. On the one hand, it is sometimes completely ignored as a factor in the changes that occurred after Mao's death later that year. On the other, Palmer (2012) and Robinson (2016) present it as a central factor in the ending of the cultural revolution and the triumph of Deng's 'capitalist road'. More plausible is the more modest claim that the disaster, while not decisive, did enable Premier Hua Guofeng to display leadership skills and weakened his political opponents, the Gang of Four, who appeared callous when they demanded that the earthquakes should not be allowed to distract attention from the campaign against Deng Xiaoping.

Looking at the events of 1833, 1934, 1988, and 2015 in Nepal, we can see how an earthquake certainly accelerated events in the most recent case, helping to produce a constitution which many regarded as more conservative than it otherwise might have been (see Hutt 2020). In the earlier cases, the picture is less clear, but forces for political change may have been strengthened and so the pace of developments increased, even if we cannot claim that the direction of change was fundamentally altered.

Appendix 2A   Major historic earthquakes

Date	Place	Deaths	Magnitude[i]	Source
c. 1100	Eastern Nepal	?	8.8	Lave et al. 2005[ii]
1223	Kathmandu Valley	?	?	Pant 2002
7 June 1255	Kathmandu Valley	2,200	7.8	Pant 2002, Sapkota et al. 2013
1260	Sagarmatha	100	7.1	DPNN[iii]
1344	Mechi	100	7.9	DPNN
August 1408[iv]	nr. Nepal–Tibet Border, Bagmati Zone	2,500	8.2	DPNN
7(?8) June 1505	Near Saldang, Karnali zone	6,000	8.2–8.8	HRRI and D. Jackson (2002)[v]
May/June 1681	Northern Kosi zone	4,500	8.0	DPNN[vi]
July 1767	Northern Bagmati zone	4,000	7.9	DPNN
4 June 1808	Kathmandu Valley	?	?	Pant 2002
26 August 1833	Kathmandu/Bihar	405[vii]	$8.0 \, M_s$[viii]	NOAA[ix]
7 July 1869	Kathmandu	?	$6.5 \, M_s$	NOAA[x]
28 August 1916	Nepal/Tibet	?	$7.7 \, M_s$	NOAA[xi]
15 January 1934	Nepal/India/Tibet	8,519	$8.0 \, M_w$	NOAA[xii]

Date	Place	Deaths	Magnitude[i]	Source
27 June 1966	Nepal/India border	*80*	6.3 M$_s$[xiii]	NOAA[xiv]
29 July 1980	Nepal/Pithoragarh	200[xv]	6.5 M$_s$	NOAA[xvi]
20 August 1988	Kathmandu/Bihar	1,091	6.6 Ms[xvii]	NOAA[xviii]
1993	Mid-west Nepal	1	5.1M$_b$	P. Nepal (2016)
2001	Far-western Nepal	2	?	P. Nepal (2016)
2003	Syangja	2	?	P. Nepal (2016)
18 September 2011	Sikkim, India	11[xix]	5.1–6.9 M$_s$	P. Nepal (2016); NOAA[xx]
25 April 2015	Gorkha district, Nepal	8,922	7.8 M$_w$	NOAA[xxi]
12 May 2015	Dolakha district, Nepal	213	7.3M$_w$	NOAA[xxii]

Source: Adapted from the list at https://en.wikipedia.org/wiki/List_of_earthquakes_in_
Nepal (accessed 11 November 2020). Differing magnitudes for the same earthquake may be
derived even by modern instruments at different stations and so estimates for earlier quakes
are extremely speculative. The NOAA entries sometimes provide only date and magnitude
and the sources for fatalities are then unclear. Where these appear to include deaths outside
Nepal, the figures are italicized.

Notes: i   The abbreviations Mw, Ms, and Mb represent moment magnitude, surface-wave
magnitude, and body-wave magnitude scales, which are variations on the original
Richter scale. The figure given in reports of recent earthquakes is normally the Mw.

   ii There is no written record of the earthquake and its occurrence has been deduced
from examination of the geological record.

   iii Disaster Preparedness Network Nepal, 'Historical Earthquakes in Nepal' (now
removed from website).

   iv The precise date is uncertain (Petech 1984: 160).

   v   Risk Research Institute (https://hri.org.np/lo_mustang_earthquake_1505/;
accessed 1 May 2020) and D. Jackson (2002). The latter gives the date of 7 or 8
June from Tibetan sources and notes that Indian sources appear to conflate it
with a subsequent quake on 6 July.

   vi Brahma Shumshere Rana puts the earthquake on the day of *jestha sukla sapthami*,
five months after the appearance of a comet and 'a strange sound from the sky' on
paush krishna asthami (B. Rana 2013: 106). Assuming the solar and lunar months
were roughly in step at this time, the first date might have been 12 December,
as there was a full moon on 5 December 1680. The comet was presumably the
Great Comet (that is, Kirch's or Newton's Comet) observed in Europe between
November 1680 and March 1681. If the lunar and solar month of Jestha roughly
coincided, the quake could have been around 23 May or 22 June, a week after a
new moon.

   vii Figure provided by Cambell (1833), probably an underestimate.

   viii Szeliga et al. (2010) estimate the magnitude at 7.3 (+/- 0.1).

   ix National Oceanic and Atmospheric Administration, https://www.ngdc.noaa.
gov/nndc/struts/results?eq_0=1758&t=101650&s=13&d=22,26,13,12&nd=display
(accessed 24 December 2018).

x National Oceanic and Atmospheric Administration, https://www.ngdc.noaa.gov/nndc/struts/results?eq_0=2153&t=101650&s=13&d=22,26,13,12&nd=display (accessed 24 December 2018).

xi National Oceanic and Atmospheric Administration, https://www.ngdc.noaa.gov/nndc/struts/results?eq_0=3060&t=101650&s=13&d=22,26,13,12&nd=display (accessed 24 December 2018).

xii National Oceanic and Atmospheric Administration, https://www.ngdc.noaa.gov/nndc/struts/results?eq_0=3528&t=101650&s=13&d=22,26,13,12&nd=display (accessed 24 December 2018).

xiii Agrawal (1969), citing the US Geological Survey, gives 6.1 as the magnitude of the first tremor.

xiv National Oceanic and Atmospheric Administration, https://www.ngdc.noaa.gov/nndc/struts/results?eq_0=4369&t=101650&s=13&d=22,26,13,12&nd=display (accessed 24 December 2018).

xv The Earthquake Engineering Research Institute (EERI) (2016) gives 125 total fatalities, which might be meant for Nepal alone. Fujiwara et al. (1989) give 178 (mainly in Darchula and Bajhang districts) but acknowledge that the data are incomplete.

xvi National Oceanic and Atmospheric Administration, https://www.ngdc.noaa.gov/nndc/struts/results?eq_0=4888&t=101650&s=13&d=22,26,13,12&nd=display (accessed 24 December 2018).

xvii The EERI (cited in Petal at al. 2017: 15) gives 6.9.

xviii National Oceanic and Atmospheric Administration, https://www.ngdc.noaa.gov/nndc/struts/results?eq_0=5167&t=101650&s=13&d=22,26,13,12&nd=display (accessed 24 December 2018).

xix My own notes. Chan and Lee (2016) suggest 6–8. The EERI (in Petal 2017: 15) gives 3 fatalities—this figure is just for Kathmandu, where 3 people were killed by the collapse of the British Embassy perimeter wall.

xx The NOAA gives the lower magnitude and lists no deaths.

xxi National Oceanic and Atmospheric Administration, https://www.ngdc.noaa.gov/nndc/struts/results?eq_0=10134&t=101650&s=13&d=22,26,13,12&nd=display (accessed 1 May 2020).

xxii National Oceanic and Atmospheric Administration, https://www.ngdc.noaa.gov/nndc/struts/results?eq_0=10141&t=101650&s=13&d=22,26,13,12&nd=display (accessed 1 May 2020).

PART II

Rebuilding Lives and Livelihoods

3

Expertise, Labour, and Mobility in Nepal's Post-conflict, Post-disaster Reconstruction

Law, Construction, and Finance as Domains of Social Transformation*

Sara Shneiderman, Dan Hirslund, Jeevan Baniya, Philippe Le Billon, Bina Limbu, Bishnu Pandey, Katharine Rankin, Nabin Rawal, Prakash Chandra Subedi, Manoj Suji, Deepak Thapa, and *Cameron Warner*

Introduction

How have people affected by Nepal's 2015 earthquakes experienced the reconstruction process on the ground? This chapter draws on ethnographic

* This research was funded by the Social Sciences and Humanities Research Council of Canada through Partnership Development Grant number 890-2016-0011, with additional support from the Peter Wall Institute for Advanced Studies, the Faculty of Arts, the School of Public Policy and Global Affairs, and the Department of Anthropology at the University of British Columbia (UBC) in Vancouver, Canada; Aarhus University and Copenhagen University in Denmark; and Social Science Baha in Kathmandu, Nepal. We thank all partnership members for their contributions at three workshops in Vancouver (2017), Kathmandu (2018), and Denmark (2019); members of the SWAY project for insights offered at our joint workshop in Kathmandu (2018); and participants in the 'Epicentre to Aftermath' conference at the School of Oriental and African Studies (SOAS) (2019). We thank the staff and students at our institutions who supported this project, the editors of this volume for their feedback and patience, and above all, the community members in Bhaktapur, Dhading, and Sindhupalchok who shared their experiences.

data collected during Nepal's post-earthquake reconstruction to inform theoretical questions about relationships between expertise, labour, and mobility in shaping post-disaster outcomes, including broader societal transformations. Based on a collaborative research project conducted between 2017 and 2020 in three of Nepal's earthquake-affected districts (Bhaktapur, Dhading, and Sindhupalchok), we point to legal, material, and financial processes that constitute lived experiences of reconstruction at the household level.

Since its inception in 2017, our project has explored the domains of law, construction, and finance to ask: How successful has Nepal's 'owner-driven' reconstruction model for households been at ensuring positive outcomes, on material, sociocultural, and subjective levels? How have domestic (that is, Nepali national) professionals, such as engineers, lawyers, and non-governmental organization (NGO) staff, served as mediators between earthquake-affected community members and institutional actors implementing reconstruction at the scale of local governance? How have relations of power and their material outcomes been negotiated? How have worldviews and practices been reshaped along the way? And how have fluctuating labour markets and conditions of high mobility shaped these interactions?

Such questions are important both for evaluating the often contradictory outcomes of reconstruction's multiple interventions and for examining the wider sociopolitical context of disaster and relief projects, such as Nepal's post-conflict process of state restructuring that devolved power to local governments in 2017. In this context, we suggest that political and material transformations—at local, regional, and national levels—must be understood as intersecting with each other, rather than as separate trajectories.

As detailed in the introduction to this volume (Liechty and Hutt), Nepal's earthquakes struck at a period of protracted political impasse which politicized and delayed the establishment of a central state agency to coordinate relief efforts by nearly seven months. The National Reconstruction Authority (NRA) only unveiled its first 'four-phase plan' in January 2016, and it took another three months for the first housing grants to be released, not least because an entire infrastructure of relief coordination needed to be erected (*The Kathmandu Post* 2015b, 2016c).

The NRA opted for an 'owner-driven' model of reconstruction, under which beneficiaries would themselves be responsible for rebuilding their houses under the supervision of external 'experts', with the grant divided into three instalments, or 'tranches' (*kista*), dependent on these experts' assessment of progress.[1] However, bureaucratic processes to assess needs, verify claims, and disburse funds have complicated access. Seventeen months after the 25 April earthquake, less than 7 per cent of the damaged houses had been rebuilt, and at the time of writing in April 2020, a full five years after the seismic events, only 550,532 households had actually received the full three tranches—66.5 per cent of the total (*The Himalayan Times* 2017b).

In this chapter, we consider the factors that have led to this situation of protracted and partial reconstruction. As highlighted in this volume's introduction (Liechty and Hutt), a realistic understanding of the politics of disaster aftermaths requires a complex consideration of the overlapping and interweaving forms of agency exercised by differentially positioned actors. From the start, our research project was set up as a collaborative effort that sought to complicate a monolithic narrative of reconstruction as being driven by particular actors and having singular outcomes. The methodological approach we adopted therefore foregrounded the local, highlighting in particular the tensions resulting from the intense mobility of people as both experts and labourers, as well as homeowners. Building on these localized histories of complexity and the deep empirical nature of the research, the chapter provides a ground-up view of the reconstruction process from the perspective of the various actors with whom our research team has engaged, including householders, engineers, local political leaders, government officials, and NGO workers. The first part of the chapter introduces the thematic and methodological framework, and the second part presents our main findings. We argue that the reconstruction process has produced not only new physical structures in the form of houses, but also new structures of knowledge, work, and political engagement, which coexist in articulation with new forms of state consolidation and governmentality.

---

[1] The initial grant for a 'fully damaged' house was set to NPR 200,000 (c. USD 1,800), with the first 50,000 to be given unconditionally to all eligible households. The two remaining tranches were subject to approval. The grant amount was extended to NPR 300,000 (c. USD 2,700) the next year, following the return of the Unified Communist Party of Nepal (Maoist) to power in August 2016.

Law, construction, and finance

The formal reconstruction process in Nepal has been a highly centralized and state-led effort. Before setting up the NRA, the government sought to control and coordinate relief through its centralized Prime Minister's Relief Fund. Despite the NRA's rocky start, it became a hegemonic institution which employed thousands of engineers to oversee the reconstruction process across the affected districts. From the early days of the reconstruction programme, it was clear that the process of rebuilding would be entangled with already existing processes of political and administrative restructuring, as well as economic and infrastructural development. Focusing on law, construction, and finance enabled us to define concrete domains of inquiry within the broad field of reconstruction, and link these to ongoing trajectories of social transformation. To frame the findings presented in the second half of this chapter, we provide here an overview of how we conceptualized these domains. We acknowledge at the outset that they are in practice deeply interconnected, yet we find it useful to distinguish between them for analytical purposes.

Within our research framework, *law* encompasses all of the issues related to government policies and provisions, access to housing grants, legal documentation, and political influence in the reconstruction process. We seek to understand how earthquake-affected people understood and interacted with the laws and policies of reconstruction, particularly in relation to the citizenship and landownership documents that were required for anyone to become enrolled as a beneficiary. Further, we consider how experiences of these regulatory dimensions of reconstruction intersected with the post-conflict constitutional process to yield subjective understandings of lawfare (Comaroff 2001) as the means to survival. Building upon existing scholarship on Nepal's constitutional process (Malagodi 2013) and citizenship challenges (Rai and Shneiderman 2019), as well as broader scholarship on the biopolitical dimensions of disaster responses (Marchezini 2015), we ask: how do populations who may not have access to full documentation navigate their relationship with the state through the reconstruction process? Key actors include earthquake-affected citizens, civil servants, political party representatives, and donors who seek to govern reconstruction through regulatory regimes.

With over 800,000 homes to be rebuilt, in addition to religious, community, and government facilities, everything in Nepal's earthquake-affected districts is, in a sense, under the *construction* domain. This domain of inquiry connects post-earthquake reconstruction with the country's existing emphasis on infrastructural development, which predated the earthquake and is especially visible in the areas of road-building (B. Campbell 2010; Murton 2013; Rankin et al. 2017), hydropower (Lord 2016; Butler and Rest 2017), urban expansion (Nelson 2017), and new linkages with China (Murton 2017; Paudel and Le Billon 2018). Articulating with recent general social scientific interest in infrastructure (Appel, Anand, and Gupta 2015; Harvey, Jenson, and Morita 2017; Larkin 2013), it also entails attention to cultural heritage, materials, and social relations (Schild 2012), as well as engineering approaches to earthquake-resilient building (Pandey et al. 2016). A focus on construction considers how reconstruction must be understood as a cultural as well as technical process for earthquake-affected homeowners, artisans, wage labourers, engineers, and contractors, all of whom combine community-based knowledge and building practices in ways that produce new forms of governmentality, materiality, and subjectivity.

NRA policies have been particularly capital-intensive in their model for private housing reconstruction, making the domain of *finance* central to our inquiry. Rural financialization was already well underway in Nepal at the time of the earthquakes (Rankin 2001), with much recent research focusing on hydropower development as a site for the cultivation of financial subjectivities (Lord 2016; Murton, Lord, and Beasley 2016). The earthquakes caused a loss of almost one third of Nepal's national gross domestic product (GDP), yet new flows of financial resources ensued at every scale of intervention, and have led towards deeper rural financialization. Resonating with scholarly interest in financialization processes (for example, Mawdsley 2018), we also look at the monetization of social relations. Affected families were required to set up bank accounts, in many cases for the first time, and to develop new forms of financial expertise (Paudel, Rankin, and Le Billon 2020; Le Billon et al. 2020). Moreover, due in large part to high mobility and shifting labour markets—nearly one third of Nepal's working male population is believed to be outside the country (World Bank 2011)—current family structures and residence patterns differ from past expectations in ways that remain poorly understood. Under these conditions, we ask: What are the multiply-scaled sources of reconstruction finance? What political rationalities and geopolitical dynamics govern these financial flows? What modes of financial subjectivity and patterns of resource distribution emerge? Key actors include aid recipients, bankers, corporate investors, cooperative fund managers, donors, and consultants.

Expertise, labour, and mobility

Across each domain, we focus on the three themes of *expertise, labour,* and *mobility*. In Nepal, as elsewhere, seismic and political transformations are entangled with trajectories of mobility shaped by local and transnational labour markets. Families who once built their own homes are now required to draw upon the professionalized expertise of engineers if they wish to qualify as beneficiaries. They are also lacking domestic labour power due to high levels of rural out-migration for wage labour—a pattern that accelerated through the conflict period and was well-established by the time of the earthquakes.

In January 2016, the NRA deployed 2,700 newly educated domestic civil engineers to affected districts to assess damage claims and oversee reconstruction according to a newly introduced building code. These largely inexperienced domestic technicians were tasked with executing new house designs in districts characterized by mountainous terrain, limited connectivity to state institutions, and hierarchical patterns of social exclusion. These multidirectional flows of people—and the forms of expertise that come and go with them—require us to pay attention to the relationships between *expertise, labour,* and *mobility* as vectors of social transformation shaping the twin projects of state restructuring and post-earthquake reconstruction in Nepal.

Within the flux of these encounters, we foreground the roles and potential of domestic expertise and local governance in disaster response, building upon emerging work that moves beyond exclusively Euro-American conceptualizations of humanitarianism to consider how regional and domestic expertise intersects on the ground with both local desires and the cosmopolitan knowledge circulated by multilateral organizations (Watanabe 2015). While we recognize the unmistakable imprint of 'disaster capitalism' (Klein 2007; Simpson 2013; Matthew and Upreti 2018) in Nepal, we find value in the supplementary notion of 'disaster nationalism' (Choi 2015), which we would nuance further to focus on 'disaster state-ism' and 'disaster financialization' (Paudel, Rankin, and Le Billon 2020; Le Billon et al. 2020). Centralization of funds, homogenization of design, and deployment of newly educated engineers together point towards re-territorialization and consolidation of state power through reconstruction, precisely at the moment that the state had grudgingly committed to its own devolution through federal state restructuring.

While the obviously visible 'experts' are domestic professionals such as engineers, lawyers, and bank managers, we view local knowledge resources in earthquake-affected areas as equally relevant forms of expertise for the reconstruction process: for instance, how to negotiate with the state to gain recognition and resources (*law*), how to build houses with local materials according to indigenous design principles (*construction*), and how to manage labour and agrarian production to secure viable livelihoods in a rapidly transforming economy (*finance*). Each of these localized bodies of knowledge has been affected in practice by shifts in labour markets that yield increasing patterns of mobility, moving some forms of expertise out and others in (Hirslund 2019; Kunwar, Lewison, and Rankin, this volume). Further, such patterns are framed by long-standing trajectories of 'NGO-ization' and development broadly conceived (Heaton-Shrestha and Adhikari 2011; Panday 2011).

Methods and fieldsites

We situate our inquiry within a critical transdisciplinary framework that is also in self-reflexive conversation with scholars and practitioners from the relevant disciplines and professions themselves. Our partnership includes colleagues with backgrounds in anthropology, art history, community and regional planning, development studies, economics, educational studies, engineering, geography, law, political science, policy studies, and religious studies.[2] At a start-up workshop in 2017, we collectively developed the terms of reference for three full-time research associates (Bina Limbu, Prakash Chandra Subedi, and Manoj Suji), who would be based at Social Science Baha (SSB) in Kathmandu. Under the supervision of two senior researchers, Jeevan Baniya of SSB and Nabin Rawal of the Tribhuvan University Department of Anthropology, the research team conducted ethnographic

---

[2]　See https://elmnr.arts.ubc.ca/partners/collaborators/ for the full list of participants.

Nepal and Bagmati Province

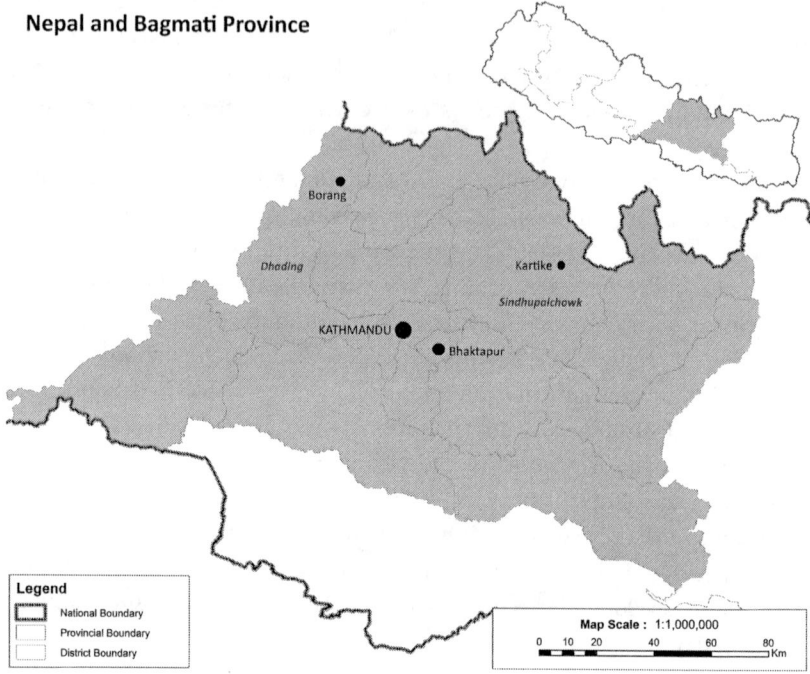

Figure 3.1 Research sites for our project in Nepal's Bagmati province.

Source: Cartography by Naxa for Social Science Baha.

Note: Map shows general locations and does not represent authentic international boundaries.

fieldwork at three sites in Bhaktapur, Dhading, and Sindhupalchok districts (Figure 3.1). Throughout the process, diverse members of the partnership team provided input on research design and contributed to analysis.

The three study districts of Bhaktapur, Dhading, and Sindhupalchok together demonstrated important variations, including in terms of demography, geography, economy, rural–urban dynamics, and proximity to state presence, which influenced the reconstruction process in each site differently. Bhaktapur Municipality offers a view into the challenges of urban housing reconstruction as well as the reconstruction of major heritage sites. The village of Borang, located in the northern part of Dhading district, was chosen, first, to serve as a rural counterpart to Bhaktapur in terms of housing reconstruction and, second, because it is a site of the technical assistance programme, Baliyo Ghar,[3] implemented by NSET, the National Society for Earthquake Technology-Nepal,[4] the premier Nepali non-governmental agency working on issues of seismic preparedness and, since the 2015 earthquakes, reconstruction. In Sindhupalchok, the research site was Kartike Bazaar and the adjoining villages of Manje and Golche. This part of Sindhupalchok is predominantly rural in nature but with road access, and was chosen in order to understand the dynamics in a setting where the Baliyo Ghar programme is not being implemented.

Research was conducted in two phases in all three field sites, supplemented with a third phase of work primarily conducted with national-level stakeholders such as the NRA, NSET, and the central Department of Archaeology (DoA). In the first phase, from 12 March to 15 May 2018, the team primarily conducted interviews with individuals at the household level. In the second phase, from 25 September 2018 to 13 January 2019, the focus was on key local institutions and individuals, as well as government agencies and other relevant organizations. This chapter draws primarily on findings from the first phase, using information collected through interviews conducted with householders in all three sites, as well as with some key informants such as community leaders, elected representatives, and NRA engineers. The research team conducted formal and informal[5] interviews with 153 individuals across three districts and observed interactions in and around the district headquarters, mainly in banks, around public infrastructure (police stations, road construction projects, local schools, hydropower projects, and so on), and cultural heritage sites under reconstruction. Interviews were conducted in Nepali, and translated into English for circulation among international team members.

---

[3] Baliyo Ghar (Strong Home) is a five-year (October 2015–September 2020) programme implemented in the four districts of Kathmandu, Dolakha, Dhading, and Nuwakot with the support of USAID. More details can be found at http://www.nset.org.np/nset2012/index.php/programs/programdetail/programid-93 (accessed 10 November 2020).

[4] More information on NSET can be found at www.nset.org.np.

[5] 'Formal interview' refers to interviews that were pre-scheduled and 'informal interview' refers to conversations that occurred spontaneously without pre-planning.

Law[6]

Documentation

In order to understand how law operated in practice, we paid close attention to the various items of paperwork and documentation that materialized relationships between actors such as politicians, engineers, and households. The first step in receiving a housing reconstruction grant was to sign a Participation Agreement (PA), and be issued with the Housing Reconstruction Grant Agreement Card, which is also referred to as the 'PA card'. At the time the householders signed the PA, the federal restructuring of Nepal had not yet taken place.[7] Hence, most interviewees in all the sites had signed their PAs at VDC (village development committee) or municipal ward offices.[8] People also referred to the PA card as the 'Red Card', the 'Beneficiary Card', and the 'Earthquake Victim Card'.

The PA card was issued in the name of the head of the household who was required to submit his or her citizenship and landownership certificates. While government representatives often assumed that the household head would be male, it was in fact possible for women to claim this position if they had the requisite landownership documentation and/ or if they had been nominated as a proxy by their absent husband. Other legal documents such as a marriage certificate or certificate of relationship were also required if the household head wished to nominate another family member as the beneficiary in his or her stead. Most of our interviewees said that they did possess citizenship papers and other required documents prior

---

[6]   For a more extensive presentation of the data-set utilized in the subsequent sections, see Limbu et al. (2019).

[7]   Prior to the division of the country into federal units in 2017 under the Constitution of Nepal 2015, the subnational bodies consisted of 75 district development committees (DDCs), 217 municipalities, and 3,117 village development committees (VDCs). The new Constitution divided the newly formed Federal Democratic Republic of Nepal into three tiers of government: federal, provincial, and municipal. The previous VDCs and municipalities were entirely restructured into 753 local units, consisting of six metropolises, 11 sub-metropolises, 276 municipalities, and 460 rural municipalities.

[8]   Every municipality in Nepal is divided into a number of smaller administrative units known as wards.

to the earthquake; what many of them did not have was a landownership certificate.

Therefore, landownership documentation was a major hurdle in all three sites, although to varying degrees. The grant distribution guidelines mandated that each beneficiary should submit the land title of the plot on which they intended to reconstruct their house (NRA 2015b). However, it was often the case that the land title had not been formally transferred for two or three generations. To accomplish this, the land had to be divided among brothers and then to their grown-up children. However, this was not an easy feat if the family could not reach an agreement on property division.

Problems related to landownership were most acute in Bhaktapur since the lots were very small, often less than 1 *aana* (31.80 square metres).[9] Bhaktapur is a very dense urban environment, mainly comprising multi-storey houses which often share one or two walls with adjacent homes. These were jointly owned by brothers and/or other male members of the family such as paternal uncles, although the title to the land could be in the name of their parents or grandparents. We often found instances of multiple families living in the same house but functioning as different households, a distinction that is made in Nepal on the basis of families having separate kitchens. However, the NRA's initial beneficiary selection guidelines[10] recognized only landownership as the necessary prerequisite to receive a grant and did not consider the situation of multiple households living in the same building.[11] In the case of joint ownership, all the families had to

---

[9]   According to Bhaktapur Municipality's 'Physical Infrastructure and Construction Guidelines Related Bylaws 2060 [v.s.]', for the construction of a new house, the minimum ground coverage for land areas of up to 2 *aana* 2 *paisa* (855.62 square feet) is 90 per cent and for bigger areas, it is 80 per cent. Plots smaller than 855.62 square feet cannot get building permits to build a new house. However, in the case of earthquake-damaged houses in the core heritage areas, they can be reconstructed on the same plot as before with 100 per cent coverage, regardless of land size.

[10] National Reconstruction Authority, http://nra.gov.np/np/resources/details/ebUVx ZtX4uarwnIddiIrr4Ia7SwaObKpVmXg2wpApCs (accessed 10 November 2020).

[11] But in coordination with the Chief District Officer, Bhaktapur Municipality also carried out damage assessments and considered multiple families living in the same house as separate earthquake-affected households. Since the multiple ownership issue was prevalent in traditional settlements like Bhaktapur, the NRA eventually revised its policies and allowed all affected households to be eligible for the reconstruction grant. See 'Revisions to the Grant Disbursement Procedures for Private Houses

agree on someone amongst themselves receiving the grant. When relatives could not come to an agreement on this matter and on other reconstruction issues—which was often the case in Bhaktapur—it tended to result in family disputes.

Even when multiple owners could reach a common understanding about who should receive the grant, they sometimes could not decide whether to rebuild their house or not. The main reason for this was that house lots in Bhaktapur's core heritage areas are often too small to build anything big enough to accommodate growing families. Hence, some of the multiple owners no longer wanted to live together. There were many who chose to shift to another location where those with sufficient resources built new houses for themselves. But, even after they had moved, they were not willing to let go of their share of the small yet valuable ancestral property. Meanwhile, those who stayed back were left in a dilemma as to whether or not to rebuild a house on land that was owned jointly with others, since, should they decide to rebuild, there was a danger that the other co-landowners might have a right over their house as well. As one of the interviewees said, 'Now, every brother owns a right over the house. The house is also very small. How do we divide it?'[12]

One solution to this problem could be that one of the co-owners would buy the others' share of the land. But the price of land in the core heritage area was very high, ranging from NPR 1,500,000 (c. USD 13,600) to NPR 3,000,000 (c. USD 27,200) per *aana*. Due to this, one informant from Bhaktapur said he was not able to buy land from his four brothers. Another informant had ventured to buy his brother's share of the land, but to his consternation, his brother had refused and insisted on dividing the property instead:

> In 300 square feet of land, if I give half a portion to him, then can you imagine what my situation would be? On 300 square feet of land, how many houses can you make after all? How much can you do in it? How many pillars can be accommodated in it? That's why I haven't done anything in that place right now.[13]

Destroyed by the Earthquake (Second Amendment), 2075 (As per the decision of the Council of Minister dated 04/02/2019)'.

[12] Interview no. 24, Bhaktapur, 16 March 2018.
[13] Interview no. 18, Bhaktapur, 15 March 2018.

Figure 3.2 A private house under construction in Dattatreya Square, Bhaktapur.
Source: Photograph by Manoj Suji.

Several interviewees claimed that there had been a rise in the number of family disputes due to such complications in landownership, which hindered the reconstruction process. Many house lots before the earthquake were already too small to feasibly be subdivided. The very small house lots meant that disputes arose between neighbours during reconstruction over land encroachments of just a few inches.

People from Bhaktapur faced another set of problems while they were constructing their houses. They had to hire registered architects or engineers to come up with a design, reportedly at a cost of NPR 10,000–30,000 (c. USD 90–275). They then had to get the designs approved by the municipality and, following the completion of each storey, they had to secure verification from the municipal authorities that there was no deviation from the approved design. But, inside the core heritage areas, house designs had to follow not only the general government guidelines on earthquake resilience, but also match the requirements of a traditional appearance (Figure 3.2).[14]

---

[14] Hereafter, we shall refer to the municipal guidelines pertaining to house construction in core heritage areas as 'heritage codes'.

Landownership in Dhading and Sindhupalchok was less complicated but homeowners did grapple with issues nonetheless. As in Bhaktapur, Borang residents had occupied their homesteads for many generations but without formally transferring the property from previous ones. In Kartike Bazaar and adjoining areas (including Golche and Manje), some people possessed land titles, but not everyone did. After the earthquakes, the need arose to transfer people's land titles to the new generation in order to access housing grants. Hence, people from Borang had to go to the land revenue office at the district headquarters of Dhading Besi, which took a whole day of travel, while people from the Kartike Bazaar area had to go to Chautara, four or five hours away by bus. People from all sites talked about delays in services in the land revenue offices due to the rush of people and the lack of capacity in the offices to process the sudden increase in the number of service-seekers.

The NRA's grant disbursement guidelines (NRA 2015b) also permitted beneficiaries to rebuild their house on land that was in the name of another family member, as long as the landowner provided written consent to the beneficiary. In cases where beneficiaries who owned the land were unable to make the journey to sign the PA in person, they were allowed to nominate someone else, who might or might not be a family member. This flexibility came in handy for many households in all sites, but particularly in Borang, where people owned land in some abundance and did not mind giving close family members and relatives a small plot on which to build their houses. Many of our research participants had accessed grants and built new houses on land that was registered in the name of their parents, grandparents, and even siblings.

Housing reconstruction grants

Householders received reconstruction grants from the government in stages, tied to the progress of construction and the relevant documentation of that fact. After the landownership documents were prepared and PA cards received, people were eligible to receive three tranches, of NPR 50,000, 150,000, and 100,000 (c. USD 450, 1,350, and 900) respectively, through banks designated by the central Nepal Rastra Bank. In order to receive the grant, people had to build 'earthquake-resistant houses' according to the technical designs prescribed by the NRA and the Department of Urban

Development and Building Construction (DUDBC).[15] In all three sites, most people were able to access the first tranche. But, to get the second tranche, people had to have laid their house foundations, completed construction to the plinth level, and received approval from an NRA field engineer. At the time of our fieldwork in April 2018, people from the Sindhupalchok site had made the most progress compared to the other locales and had already received the second tranche. This was due in part to better access to materials and other sources of finance (as well as fewer reconstruction design constraints and land conflicts, compared with Bhaktapur).[16] In contrast, only three people from the Dhading site—Borang—had received the second tranche at that time.[17]

People had to travel from Borang to the authorized banks in Dhading Besi, the Dhading district headquarters, and those from Kartike in Sindhupalchok district had to go to Jalbire, a small town about half an hour's drive away. Travel in both these places is difficult, especially in the monsoon when the roads tend to get blocked by landslides. Moreover, people in both districts complained about the delayed process of grant distribution. A ward chairperson in Kartike said that the bank tended to delay the distribution of tranches for more than 14 days after the funds had been transferred by the District Coordination Committee.

Many people suspected that the bank deliberately withheld the money, and the ward chairperson referred to earlier also suspected that the bank delay was a ruse to earn some kind of interest on the grant money. Although several bank officers denied this at the time, it was confirmed by a bank officer in Dhading Besi in an interview in February 2020. He stated that banks had some discretion when choosing which villages they would serve—and that they all sought to select the most remote villages, because people from those locations would take the longest time to reach the bank to

[15] In October 2015, the DUDBC first published *Design Catalogue, Volume 1*, which included only 17 house designs based on the National Building Code. However, the need for more variation in house designs led to the publication of *Design Catalogue, Volume 2* about one and half years later in March 2017. Volume 2 consisted of 17 more designs, with use of alternative materials and technologies that were not covered by the National Building Code.

[16] KII (Key Informant Interview) no. 29, Sindhupalchok, 14 May 2018.

[17] KII no. 12, Dhading, 7 April 2018.

process their grant. The banks intentionally sought to extend the process as long as possible in order to benefit from the interest in the meantime.

By contrast, in Bhaktapur the banks were easily accessible; yet only a few people had received the second tranche. This was due to several factors, such as disputes over land encroachments, the municipality's heritage codes, and, most importantly, multiple landownership rights over small plots of land which had led to intractable family disputes.

In all sites, people noted that the reconstruction grant was insufficient to meet the actual cost of rebuilding their houses. From the perspective of the NRA and donors, the grant was never intended as full compensation but rather as a partial subsidy. As stated in the NRA's Grant Distribution Procedures document, if the cost of the house construction exceeded NPR 200,000 (c. USD 1,800) (later this was increased to NPR 300,000 [c. USD 2,700]), homeowners would have to bear the rest of the cost (NRA 2015b: 4). There was a significant gap between the intention of this and its interpretation by recipients. The shortfall was the most severe in Bhaktapur, because all homeowners were building reinforced concrete (RC) houses. As illustrated in the quote below, numerous interviewees complained about the grant being too small:

> I had saved about 12 lakhs [1.2 million] in advance and had to take about 10 lakhs [1 million] as a loan at 12 per cent interest from Siddhilaxmi Cooperative. So, this 3 lakhs [300,000] was simply nothing in terms of reconstruction contribution since it is just enough to pass the house blueprint [design].[18]

In Sindhupalchok, many people were also unhappy with the stipulation that a toilet had to be constructed in order to receive the third tranche. That was because many households already had access to a usable toilet (usually an outhouse) of their own or of their neighbours.

In each site, there was a small number of people whose names had been left out of the beneficiary list. People from Bhaktapur seemed less concerned about these omissions because the grant money did not make much of a difference to their reconstruction plans. The grant was much more significant for people in Dhading and Sindhupalchok because it comprised a substantial part of their reconstruction cost. Hence, people who did not

---

[18] Interview no. 24, Bhaktapur, 16 March 2018.

figure in the beneficiary list constantly pestered their local representatives about amending the list to include them, but often remained unsuccessful.

The NRA's Post-disaster Recovery Framework 2016–2020 (PDRF) stipulates that grievance redressal mechanisms must be established to 'address the grievances, suggestions, and complaints of the communities in the reconstruction process'. At the ground level, although people had a number of complaints, they did not know how and where to air their grievances. People largely thought that the only form of grievance redressal for victims left out of the grant beneficiary list was to apply for a re-survey. But they had other grievances too, primarily revolving around the delay in reconstruction due to lack of landownership papers, conflicts over property, houses not matching the designs prescribed by the NRA, and delays in grant distribution by the banks. Another source of grievance was the intense time pressure to finish reconstruction and access the subsequent tranches within government deadlines.[19] However, people did not feel that such complaints would be heard—let alone addressed—even if they voiced them to the concerned authorities unless they did it as part of a group.

Technical expertise and political capital

In addition to the distribution of three tranches of reconstruction grants, the central government attempted to exhibit its control over the reconstruction process through state-certified engineers who were deputized to oversee best practices, while locally elected politicians often advocated on behalf of constituents. Engineers from the NRA were accorded a great deal of importance in the reconstruction process due to the power they had in terms of certifying houses for the second and third tranches. While on the one hand they could be seen as embodying state power, on the other, many people did not fully understand the source of their authority. The majority of the interviewees said that they had never even heard of the NRA, the apex

---

[19] The NRA's deadline for beneficiaries to receive all tranches of the reconstruction grant was mid-July 2018. The first tranche was to be disbursed by 13 January 2018, the second by 13 April 2018, and the third by 15 July 2018. Since all of these deadlines were missed by a large number of beneficiaries, the NRA extended the deadlines time and again. During our first fieldwork, however, people were under pressure to meet the deadlines mentioned above.

government body facilitating reconstruction. Some said that they had heard about the NRA on the radio and television but, even in a city like Bhaktapur, people seemed unaware of what the NRA actually did.

Most research participants said they had had frequent interactions with *sarkarko engineer* (government engineers). Upon probing further, it became clear that people were not sure whether these 'government engineers' were actually from the NRA, I/NGOs, or some other organization. In Dhading, for example, people confused NSET staff working in the area with the NRA engineers. An NSET official said that, due to Borang's remote location, the government engineers came only occasionally and only for short periods of time.[20] Engineers had the difficult task of convincing people—most of whom had already rebuilt or repaired their houses to live in—to build according to the government's requirements, and then conducting inspections to see whether the new houses qualified for subsequent tranches. Disqualification could easily offend people and lead to hostility towards the engineers who felt vulnerable, being far away from the reach of the state. As an NSET official said: 'Government agencies don't come here often. They feel scared to come here.'[21]

There was fear on all sides, however. People rushed to meet the NRA engineers when they did come, fearing that they might leave without endorsing the forms that would enable them to receive the next tranche. Since NSET's Baliyo Ghar programme was being implemented in the area, the NRA field engineers also relied on the recommendations of NSET officials while certifying houses.

In Sindhupalchok, the research team met two NRA field engineers in Kartike who said they were familiar with all the households in the area, as they had been working there for around two years. They even claimed to know in detail how each house was being built and which ones were likely to qualify for further tranches. However, we also found that the NRA engineers depended heavily on local social and political leaders to gain the community's cooperation. As one of the engineers from Sindhupalchok said: 'In every place, there's a "hero" person [*sic*]. We need to gain the support of that hero to be able to work in that area. In this place, the ward chairperson is that hero.'[22]

[20] KII no. 12, Dhading, 7 April 2018.
[21] KII no. 12, Dhading, 7 April 2018.
[22] KII no. 28, Sindhupalchok, 13 May 2018.

These dynamics highlight how local political structures intersected with reconstruction outcomes. People in all sites had a fairly good understanding about the changes in the local and federal structure of the country that had begun in 2017 with elections to federal, provincial, and local governments. The transition to federalism, which happened concurrently with the institution of elected governments at the local level after a gap of almost two decades, changed how local governments functioned. While people's access to information through elected officials increased, the more important factor vis-à-vis the reconstruction process was political affiliation. People often sought out local leaders to obtain information and advice, and to share their problems with regard to reconstruction, as these were interactions that could be facilitated by party membership or connections.

The Rastriya Prajatantra Party (RPP) had won the local elections in Borang. During our stay there, we witnessed a prominent village leader negotiating with NSET officials on behalf of the villagers. Most leaders lived in Kathmandu or Dhading Besi, but they came to the village from time to time to monitor the reconstruction process. In Kartike, the Communist Party of Nepal-Unified Marxist–Leninist (CPN-UML) and the Unified Communist Party of Nepal-Maoist (UCPN-M) had been the dominant parties. The latter had the greater influence before the earthquake, and both did well in the local elections.[23] Political influence was evident in the reconstruction process, especially during the relief phase and the distribution of the PA cards. The reconstruction policy stipulates that one PA card should be distributed to each beneficiary household. However, the ward chairperson claimed that Maoist leaders had distributed cards to multiple members of the same households, favouring those affiliated with their party and in their personal networks. Field engineers also verified this statement, but added that each card holder would have to build a house if they wished to access subsequent tranches. Meanwhile, in Bhaktapur, the left-leaning Nepal Majdoor Kisan Party (NMKP) (Nepal Workers' and Peasants' Party) is synonymous with the municipality because it has led the local government since 1990.

The reconstruction of Bhaktapur's cultural heritage is managed by the municipality and the DoA,[24] but many participants noted a lack of

---

[23] The CPN-UML and the CPN-M formally unified to become the Nepal Communist Party (NCP) in May 2018.

[24] The DoA is part of the central government under the Ministry of Culture, Tourism and Civil Aviation, and is primarily responsible for archaeological research and

Figure 3.3 Tawa Sattal being reconstructed by a contractor in Bhaktapur.
Source: Photograph by Sara Shneiderman.

coordination between them (Suji et al. 2020). Of the two, people expressed more faith in the municipality. Municipality-led reconstruction was mainly carried out through users' groups consisting of local residents which were perceived to be relatively transparent in terms of budget expenditure. Meanwhile, the DoA-led reconstruction was undertaken through contracts (Figure 3.3),[25] which was where people believed corruption came into play.

A former employee of Dattatreya Museum who had closely observed the work of the DoA said:

> If they [the central government] sent one lakh [NPR 100,000; c. USD 900], then at the ground level, not even 30,000 [NPR] is utilized for work.... Funds are leaked from the director to office head, from office

---

cultural heritage protection. More information on the DoA can be found at http://www.doa.gov.np/.

[25] The DoA would be bound by the Public Procurement Act of 2007, which requires that any public construction work in excess of NPR 6 million must be awarded through a tendering process.

head to engineers, and from engineers to contractors. By that time, how much of it can be left?[26]

He also said that political parties fought with one another to get hold of the reconstruction funds. In the same vein, another interviewee claimed that other political parties tend to hinder projects under the municipality by freezing the budget from the central level in order to dent the NMKP's popularity.[27] Therefore, the kind of jockeying for political position often observed in Nepali politics played out in the reconstruction process through the assertion of central government power via technical expertise and the competition of local political actors via the discourse of corruption and misappropriation of reconstruction funds.

Construction

House designs and materials: before and after

In Dhading, most new houses in Borang were constructed with the assistance of NSET's Baliyo Ghar programme. The majority of these were one-room structures made of dry stone walls[28] with wooden bands and posts and corrugated galvanized iron (CGI) roofs, while some people used RC bands[29] in the walls instead of wood (Figure 3.4). However, the story behind these houses had little to do with people's needs. The government-approved designs for reconstruction were made available only a year after the earthquake. By that time people in Borang had already repaired their old houses. Later, rumours spread that if beneficiaries did not build a new house as prescribed by the NRA and implemented by NSET, they would have to return the first tranche of funding and their documents could be confiscated or their children would not receive birth certificates and citizenship cards.

---

[26] Interview no. 18, Bhaktapur, 15 March 2018.

[27] Interview no. 23, Bhaktapur, 16 March 2018.

[28] Dry stone walls do not use any mortar.

[29] Reinforced concrete (RC) bands, made of concrete and iron rods, are constructed to strengthen the walls of the house and are generally considered to be stronger and more durable than wooden bands.

Figure 3.4 A newly constructed one-room house in Borang, Dhading district, built with the government's housing reconstruction grant.

Source: Photograph by Prakash Chandra Subedi.

Prior to the earthquake, most houses in Bhaktapur were brick-masonry structures three to five storeys high, made from red bricks, mud mortar, wood, and clay roofing tiles called *jhingati*. People said that such houses dated from the time of their grandfathers or even earlier. In the case of Dhading and Sindhupalchok, however, houses were usually stone-masonry structures of two or three storeys using mud mortar, wood, and roofing slates. People said that the earthquake had severely damaged the stone-masonry houses in the rural sites and brick-masonry houses in the urban sites, while RC buildings were left standing. People were therefore under the impression that RC houses were stronger and safer than masonry structures.

In Sindhupalchok, post-earthquake reconstruction had introduced many variations in house design. There were stone- and brick-masonry houses, houses made of concrete hollow blocks, iron truss, or only of CGI sheets, and also RC frame structures.[30] There were also many 'hybrid

---

[30] In our study, as in many parts of Nepal, we found that people as well as the NRA manuals used 'RC structures' synonymously for buildings with frame structures made of RC columns and beams. However, stone- and brick-masonry structures may also use RC bands but they are still referred to as masonry-structures.

Figure 3.5 New construction in Kartike Bazaar, Sindhupalchok district. A frame structure stands next to a load-bearing house that has used rocks on the ground floor and bricks on the first.
Source: Photograph by Manoj Suji.

houses',[31] which, from an engineering perspective, had an inconsistent combination of a ground floor made of stones and upper storeys made of bricks or hollow concrete blocks. NRA engineers told us that such hybrid houses would not qualify for subsequent tranches but were hopeful that some correction measures could be applied for these houses to be approved in the future (Figures 3.5 and 3.6).[32]

Bhaktapur residents had to adhere to the traditional Newar-style architectural designs mandated by the municipality's 'heritage codes' for buildings in the core heritage areas, and also abide by the NRA's reconstruction guidelines (Suji et al. 2020). People were more irked by these local laws that required houses to maintain a traditional appearance. They had to use wood for their doors and windows and layer the front part of the

---

[31] 'Hybrid houses' refer to those structures that are made of a mixture of different materials, for example, one wall is made of stones while others are made of bricks.

[32] KII no. 28, Sindhupalchok, 13 May 2018.

Figure 3.6 Two-storeyed multi-roomed stone-masonry house built under the reconstruction programme in the Manje area, Sindhupalchok district. This house was built after the house design manuals were revised.

Source: Photograph by Manoj Suji.

house with veneer bricks (*dachi appa*). People complained about having to make a traditional sloping roof with *jhingati* tiles and use wood, instead of cheaper materials such as aluminium or steel. Many interviewees felt that the heritage codes were impractical and caused additional difficulties, both economically and practically. As one interviewee said: 'If we make a sloping roof, we will not have a place to put the water tank.... Now, our daily life is not possible if we don't have the water tank on the roof to supply water to toilets, bathrooms, and the kitchen.'[33]

In Dhading, the foremost cause of dissatisfaction was the size of the one-room house promoted by NSET, which was simply too small to be livable. As one respondent said: 'If you place two beds inside, where will you make

---

[33]   Interview no. 31, Bhaktapur, 19 March 2018.

the kitchen? Where to sleep? Where to keep other things?'[34] Similarly, people in Sindhupalchok were also concerned about not having enough space although most of their houses were bigger than those in Dhading. As a result, some had begun using their new toilets, which had been built in order to be eligible for the third tranche, as storage spaces for grain, firewood, agricultural tools, and other household equipment.

On the positive side, people at all sites believed that their new houses, built according to the government's prescription, were stronger than those that had existed previously. People had the highest faith in the RC 'pillar houses', which they deemed to be 'earthquake-resistant'. At the same time, they were concerned about the quality of the construction materials, and especially the bricks. In the case of stone houses being built in Borang and the periphery of Kartike Bazaar, people were unsure about the durability of the green wood that was being used.[35]

The costs of construction

The one commonality in all the sites was a unanimous sense that the price of construction materials had increased after the earthquake. In Dhading, people made use of the wood freely available in the forests, although they had to pay the labour costs for cutting and carrying this wood to their villages. Due to this, the cost of one piece of wood could range from NPR 1,200 (c. USD 11) to 1,500 (c. USD 14).[36] The nearest market centre where they could purchase cement, iron rods, and CGI sheets was the roadhead of Dundure. People said that the cost of cement had increased after the earthquake, from NPR 1,000 to 1,300 or more per 50 kilogram bag. From Dundure, all of the construction material had to be transported on mules which added further to the price and also made the use of heavy materials like cement unaffordable. All households used CGI sheets to roof their houses. The cost varied according to size, thickness, and colour. The CGI sheets were not

---

[34] Interview no. 128, Dhading, 5 December 2018.

[35] Wood from *gobre salla*, or the Himalayan white pine, a moderately hard coniferous tree, was most commonly used.

[36] Wood pieces could vary in size but were usually about 3–4 inches wide and 10–12 feet long.

Figure 3.7 Porters carrying CGI roofing sheets to Borang, Dhading district. *Source*: Photograph by Manoj Suji.

transported on mule back but carried by porters who charged NPR 3,000–3,500 (c. USD 27–31) per bundle from Dundure to Borang (Figure 3.7).

By contrast, in Sindhupalchok, construction material was bought from different locations according to need and financial capacity: Kartike Bazaar, Jalbire, Banepa, and Bhaktapur. Prices were lower further away from Kartike Bazaar. For instance, cement was around NPR 900 (c. USD 8) per bag in Banepa, while the cheapest in Kartike was NPR 1,050 (c. USD 9). However, once the cost of transportation was added to the cost of cement brought from Banepa, the price became quite similar to that in Kartike. Bricks were not available in the Kartike area, and these usually came from Bhaktapur, where the price was NPR 12–15 (c. USD 0.11–0.14) per piece. However, by the time it reached Kartike, the cost had shot up to NPR 18–20 (c. USD 0.16–0.18). Likewise, the price of CGI sheets also increased. Hiring a mini-truck to carry material from Jalbire to Kartike cost around NPR 4,000 (c. USD 36). The cost of sand varied from NPR 8,000 to 12,000 (c. USD 73–109) per load and the transportation cost was about NPR 2,300 (c. USD 23).

Bhaktapur had easier access to construction materials compared to the other sites due to its proximity to Kathmandu and to numerous brick kilns in the immediate area. Nevertheless, here too the perception was that the price of all construction materials had increased due to post-earthquake reconstruction. The price of cement had gone up from NPR 900 to 1,500

(c. USD 8 to 14) per bag, and of iron rods from NPR 66 to 92 (c. USD 0.6 to 0.8) per kilogram, and prices were continuing to increase.

Bhaktapur Municipality also had a provision for a 25 per cent subsidy on the wood used to make traditional decorative windows and doors within the core heritage sites. However, people said that these subsidies were very difficult to access because the house had to follow strict guidelines. It was also reported that people who had close relations with officials at the municipality and elected representatives received the subsidies even though they did not follow the code completely.

The differential pricing in goods in Nepal is tied into the political economy of connectivity and transportation between regions, and is based on a long history of spatial inequality in the country (Riaz and Basu 2010). Yet the 2015 closure of Nepal's border with India, as described in the introduction to this volume (Liechty and Hutt), created serious obstacles to accessing materials for RC construction, thus pushing up prices further. Moreover, the owner-driven model of reconstruction shifted the responsibility for acquiring goods onto house-owners. This had the unfortunate consequence of effectively punishing remotely located areas such as Dhading and deepening existing inequalities.

Labour

Various workers, both skilled and unskilled,[37] were employed in the reconstruction process, including masons, carpenters, stone crushers, *surei* (craftsmen who chisel stones into required shapes), and manual labourers, with varying degrees of skill, experience, and training. Before the earthquakes, residents were skilled in traditional construction techniques but knew little about building earthquake-resistant houses, because the designs for these only became widely available after the earthquake.

In our fieldwork sites, there was a preference for masons who had received training to build earthquake-resistant houses[38] but, due to the mass scale of reconstruction, there was a severe shortage of such labour.

---

[37] Here we shall categorize workers with training and/or experience in building earthquake-resistant houses as 'skilled' and those with little or no experience as 'unskilled'.

[38] Here we refer to the mason-training and on-the-job training provided by the NRA, NSET, and various other organizations.

Ongoing labour migration, both external and internal, added to the labour shortage problem, especially in Dhading and Sindhupalchok. In Dhading, one homeowner told us that he was compelled to hide the masons' tools so that they would have to come back and finish the foundation of his house. Skilled masons would often work one or two days on one building, and then move to another, because everyone was in a rush to meet the deadline of mid-April 2018 to receive the second tranche.

Labourers from non-earthquake affected districts such as Kanchanpur, Salyan, Dang, Rukum, and Rolpa migrated in great numbers to the earthquake-affected areas. Some Kartike interlocutors claimed that migrant labourers comprised a higher proportion of the labour force, and were more skilled in building houses with cement and concrete, than local labourers. This is maybe linked to histories of migration from southern provinces to Kathmandu's construction industry in the previous decades, where RC construction skills were honed among this group of labourers (Suji et al. 2020). But this also affected wage levels. Wages had increased in all sites and varied according to the demand for and availability of workers.[39] Workers also demanded three or four hearty meals a day (consisting of rice, meat, cold drinks, and even alcohol). Some homeowners complained that the food expenses exceeded the labour wages, but they had no choice but to comply with such demands.

There was an increasing trend of implementing house reconstruction on *thekka* (contract). The contract system was more expensive than hiring workers on daily wages, but freed house-owners from the trouble of finding labourers themselves. However, contractors took on multiple contracts at the same time, leading to delays in the reconstruction of all the houses. People were also suspicious of the quality of construction as contractors hastened to complete the work. As shown by Mallika Shakya (2018) and Dan Hirslund (2019), *thekka*-based work arrangements are widespread in both formal and informal sectors but reduce the transparency of work arrangements due to the many layers of informal agreements involved. For villagers unaccustomed to this arrangement, this way of organizing work added to the insecurity of managing the reconstruction process.

---

[39] The daily wage of a labourer in Dhading was around NPR 1,000 (c. USD 9); in Sindhupalchok, NPR 1,200–1,300 (c. USD 11–12); and in Bhaktapur, NPR 1,000–1,500 (c. USD 9–14). By comparison, wages for construction labourers in Kathmandu in the same period were around NPR 800 (c. USD 7), except for the most specialized.

In Dhading and Sindhupalchok, some people were engaged in systems of reciprocal labour exchange (*parma*) for both agriculture and non-agricultural purposes that were historically common in many areas of Nepal (Messerschmidt 1981). In Dhading, the preference was for labour exchange to take place with households with skilled male members present, while in Sindhupalchok, *parma* was not favoured because local masons and labourers preferred to work for wages. Likewise, in the urban site of Bhaktapur, *parma* was quite uncommon.

Mason training and gender dynamics

To compensate for the shortage of skilled masons, various organizations conducted mason training in all of the sites. The NRA did not have sufficient in-house capacity for all construction-related activities and partnered with NSET and other NGOs for training activities. At the time of our fieldwork in Dhading, an NSET official said that, under the Baliyo Ghar programme, seven-day mason training had been provided to 155 people with prior experience, and 50 days of on-the-job training to 48 people without any such experience in Sertung VDC, which included Borang. An NSET-trained mason estimated that some 15–20 people had received such training in Borang alone. In Sindhupalchok, multiple mason training sessions were held when the government building codes were introduced.

Bhaktapur's urban context differentiated it from the rural sites in this regard. There had been greater prior knowledge there about the Kathmandu Valley being an earthquake-prone area even before the 2015 earthquakes. Hence, Bhaktapur Municipality had provided mason training to 200–300 people at the local Khwopa Engineering College run by the municipality. After the earthquake, a team of engineers from the same college had organized similar training sessions.[40]

---

[40] Interview no. 5, Bhaktapur, 12 March 2018. The national institution for facilitating training for builders is the Council for Technical Education and Vocational Training (CTEVT). However, this did not have a very pronounced role in the reconstruction process, probably due to its general focus on testing, curricula-development, and diploma-courses. Construction work in Nepal, as in South Asia in general, is characterized by a lack of standardized education structures (see

Figure 3.8 Women masons in Borang, Dhading district, enrolled in training to build earthquake-resistant houses.

Source: Photograph by Manoj Suji.

These training sessions also seemed to offer a space for women in what was otherwise a highly male-dominated profession. Following mason training, there was some increase in women's involvement in masonry work in Dhading and Sindhupalchok, but not in Bhaktapur. Women's participation in this kind of work was a recent trend, especially in Dhading. At the time of our fieldwork, there were five women masons who had been trained by NSET in Borang, three of whose husbands were working as migrant labourers away from Nepal. These three women masons said that their families had supported their decision to take the training and they were also happy to work as masons (Figure 3.8).[41]

In Sindhupalchok, there was an overwhelmingly high participation of women in the training sessions, but few continued with masonry work afterwards, mainly due to a lack of interest in masonry work, the burden of household chores, and a lack of community trust in women masons. A

Hirslund 2019), and there has therefore been little coordinated national effort at formalizing the sector.

[41]   Interview no. 75, Dhading, 10 April 2018.

trained woman mason said that, out of the 30 trainees in her batch, around 25 were women but only one woman was still working as a mason.[42]

The construction sector was thus characterized by dynamics that differed from region to region and had contrasting outcomes. Whereas the very possibility of acquiring a government-funded modern-built house for many villagers was a promising asset and offered a rare public investment in rural Nepal, it also came bundled with many complications. These included the problem of procuring labourers and materials, ever higher prices the further away from Kathmandu the villages were located, and the decentralized and informal nature of managing construction. At the same time, patterns of migration both in and out of the areas we researched, and the higher participation of women in the training programmes, suggest that there might be some longer-term effects of the reconstruction process on local house construction practices that are still in the making.

Finance

Reconstruction is generally a capital-intensive process, with finance constituting a major concern for earthquake-affected households. Variations in socioeconomic and geographical contexts along with differences in house design have a direct bearing on the amount of money needed. The government reconstruction grant of NPR 300,000 (c. USD 2,700) could only cover a small proportion of actual costs. People made up for this shortfall by drawing on their own savings or borrowing from banks, micro-finance companies, and cooperatives, or taking loans from neighbours, friends, moneylenders, and informal women's savings groups. Remittances from members of the family working elsewhere further supplemented resources, while people also sold assets such as land, jewellery, and livestock. As a result of these transactions, and particularly interactions with the banking sector, there is now a heightened sense of 'financial expertise' among those involved.

The cost of rebuilding a house varied widely between sites. The one-room house design found in Dhading was the cheapest, at NPR 150,000–400,000 (c. USD 1,360–3,600), the cost varying according to the availability

---

[42] Interview no. 96, Sindhupalchok, 10 May 2018.

of labour and materials used. People from Dhading said they had repaired
or rebuilt their damaged stone houses at costs ranging from NPR 250,000
to 900,000 (c. USD 2,270 to 8,100). In contrast, in Sindhupalchok, with the
highest variations in house design, the costs also varied the most, from NPR
400,000 to 3,000,000 (c. USD 3,600 to 27,000). In Bhaktapur, as discussed
earlier, the heritage codes required for houses inside the core heritage area
increased reconstruction costs. As well as following the municipality's
heritage codes, the design of houses inside the world heritage area had to
be approved by the DoA. Most people in Bhaktapur were building three- to
five-storeyed RC houses that cost anywhere between NPR 2,000,000 (c. USD
18,000) and 5,000,000 (c. USD 45,000).

Loans: from informal to formal

Informal sources of finance played a crucial role. This was especially the
case in rural areas, where there were no banks, micro-finance companies, or
cooperatives. In Dhading and Sindhupalchok, people borrowed from their
neighbours, relatives, friends, and moneylenders at different interest rates,
ranging from 24 per cent to 36 per cent per annum. However, loans from
kith and kin had minimal interest rates or were even interest-free. People
often took loans from multiple individuals at different interest rates because
getting one big loan from a single source was generally difficult.

People had access to formal financial institutions only in Bhaktapur
and Sindhupalchok. In Bhaktapur, homeowners preferred taking loans
from cooperatives rather than from banks. The interest rates varied among
cooperatives (from 8 to 18 per cent per annum) depending on the locality,
personal relations of the borrower with officials in the cooperatives, and the
nature of their membership in the cooperatives. For instance, a woman who
had taken loans from three cooperatives said that the cooperative of which
she had been a member for a long time provided a loan at a low interest rate
and did not require land as collateral either.[43]

Taking loans from cooperatives was quite common in Bhaktapur because
even the sale of land did not generate sufficient money to build a new house (see
following section). People took loans ranging from NPR 300,000 (c. USD 2,700)

---

[43]   Interview no. 83, Sindhupalchok, 3 May 2018.

to 2,000,000 (c. USD 18,200) from cooperatives which provided loans at 10 per cent interest to earthquake-affected households.[44] But some informants also said that taking loans from cooperatives was a complicated process. For instance, one woman said that a cooperative was reluctant to provide a housing loan to her because her lot was small and she had to put forward both the land and the newly built house as collateral in order to get a NPR 1,000,000 (c. USD 9,100) loan.[45]

According to the NRA's subsidised loan guidelines (NRA 2015d), earthquake-affected households inside and outside the Kathmandu Valley would be provided up to NPR 2,500,000 (c. USD 22,700) and up to NPR 1,500,000 (c. USD 13,600) respectively as loans at the subsidized interest rate of 2 per cent from authorized banks. The guidelines also contained a provision for interest-free loans up to NPR 300,000 (c. USD 2,700) to members of micro-finance institutions with *samuhik jamani* (social collateral).[46] However, few people had been able to benefit from this provision.

In Dhading, people were not even aware of the government loan programme. Only a few people from Borang living in Kathmandu and Dhading Besi had heard about it but they were unaware of how to access it. Some said they were not interested in taking subsidized loans, as in the words of a woman who had returned from Kathmandu to build her house: 'The government is not providing that money for free; one day, we have to repay it. How can we repay that much money? If we have the capacity to pay back that much loan, why take the loan?'[47]

People in Sindhupalchok and Bhaktapur, on the other hand, were more informed about subsidized loans through community leaders, villagers, news over the radio and TV, social media, and NRA engineers. Some people in Sindhupalchok said they had consulted elected ward chairpersons and community leaders, as well as officials in the banks in Jalbire, about accessing subsidized loans. The chairperson of Ward no. 4 of Jugal Rural Municipality affirmed that he had been asked by earthquake-affected individuals for recommendation letters for the subsidized loan. But he said

---

[44]   Interview no. 21, Bhaktapur, 15 March 2018.
[45]   Interview no. 15, Bhaktapur, 14 March 2018.
[46]   In the collective collateral loan process, a group of relatives, neighbours, or friends guarantee that the loan beneficiary will repay the loan. If the borrower is not able to repay, the collective agrees to pay on his/her behalf.
[47]   Interview no. 72, Dhading, 10 April 2018.

it was a mistaken perception that they would be automatically eligible for the loan if they got a recommendation from the chairperson.

In Bhaktapur, people said that they had not benefited from the provision for subsidized loans and the municipality's heritage codes were one of the barriers to this. Most respondents said they were reluctant to follow the codes since they did not align with their everyday needs, and many had already built houses that violated them (Figure 3.9). This not only prevented them from getting subsidized loans but also from getting additional housing grants, thus putting them at odds with the infrastructures of finance.

Only a few people in Sindhupalchok, and even fewer in Bhaktapur, had taken loans from banks. This was because many people assumed that bank interest rates would be high and feared that their property would be auctioned off if they could not pay back the loan on time. People preferred to access loans from local cooperatives since the process was easier and

Figure 3.9 After the earthquake, traditional houses were replaced by concrete frame houses in Kartike Bazaar, Sindhupalchok district.

Source: Photograph by Manoj Suji.

quicker than with the banks. These semi-formal loan institutions have a long history in Nepal (Haxby 2019) and smoothed people's access to loans in some cases. But they also drew them into complicated arrangements with multiple creditors that carried other forms of social risk.

Selling property

In all three areas, people had also sold property, either to rebuild their houses or to erect temporary shelters. Such instances of monetization were highest in Dhading and Sindhupalchok. For instance, five interviewees in Sindhupalchok had sold cattle and gold jewellery to build temporary shelters. In Dhading too, some people had sold their cattle to build their houses or to pay back the loans they had taken for house reconstruction.

Unlike in Dhading and Sindhupalchok, where livestock is often more immediately valuable than real estate, selling agricultural land was common in Bhaktapur. But not everyone had that option, as one of our interviewees explained:

> We were told that if we did not start building a house the government would not provide subsequent tranches [of the grant]. But the first tranche was insufficient and those who had additional land sold it off to start laying the foundation to become eligible for the second tranche. Those who don't have land to sell, what can they do after laying the foundation?[48]

Most of our informants from Bhaktapur said that they had sold or were planning to sell their agricultural land to build their houses even though that was not something they would have preferred because they were still farming the land. During an informal conversation, an old man aptly summed up their dilemma with a saying in Newari: *Bhu chalan, chhen dhalan* (To build a house, we need to lose our land).

Most people reported selling their land at a cheap price of NPR 300,000–400,000 (c. USD 2,700–3,600) per *aana*, either to a *dalaal* (broker) or to their neighbours and friends. Brokers, who have become notorious in

---

48   Interview no. 31, Bhaktapur, 19 March 2018.

Kathmandu's land markets (Nelson 2018), pooled the individual land parcels together and converted them into residential plots, which could then be sold at a much higher price of around NPR 1,000,000–1,500,000 (c. USD 9,000–13,500) per *aana*. Consequently, in Bhaktapur, land transactions had increased. Given how lucrative it had become, one of the brokers said that even masons and other locals had begun working as *bichauliya* (middlemen), either coordinating with other brokers and sellers or acting as brokers themselves. Taking advantage of people's desperation, *bichauliya* encouraged them to sell land at cheap rates.[49]

Nepal's remittance economy also had a direct influence on the reconstruction process.[50] In Dhading and Sindhupalchok, remittances played a key role in financing reconstruction. Many men and women in these two districts had gone to work in Malaysia, the Gulf, Japan, and South Korea prior to the earthquake. In Borang, people had received and used remittances to rebuild or repair their houses prior to the introduction of the formal reconstruction programme. However, there was no significant role of remittances in Bhaktapur where it was more common for family members to go abroad for further studies than for income-generating employment.

This last distinction points to the different class dynamics among Bhaktapur city residents, as compared to the two rural sites (Figure 3.10). Whereas Bhaktapur also comprises large groups of farmers, artisans, and migrant labourers, the inner city is mostly populated by middle-class professionals and shop owners. Here, high land prices intersect with real estate markets, and finance becomes a strategy for not merely rebuilding homes but also a future investment in the profitability of property. Overall, 'disaster financialization' (Le Billon et al. 2020) has made possible an increased penetration of capital in earthquake-affected Nepal. But this has not happened without resistance from financial institutions themselves, nor without contradictory results, as alternative sources of finance, suspicion, and regulatory policies have limited its impact.

---

[49] Interview no. 31, Bhaktapur, 19 March 2018.

[50] Foreign-exchange earnings have over the past decades grown to comprise around one-third of the GDP, putting Nepal as the 5th highest recipient of remittances worldwide as a percentage of GDP, though earning almost three times as much in absolute terms as Kyrgyzstan, which was number 1 on the list for 2017. See https://www.forbes.com/sites/niallmccarthy/2018/04/26/the-countries-most-reliant-on-remittances-infographic/#17041b7e7277 (accessed 10 November 2020).

Figure 3.10 Ongoing reconstruction of the Vatsala Durga temple in Bhaktapur Durbar Square.

Source: Photograph by Sara Shneiderman.

Conclusion

Reconstruction is never just a process of designing adequate policies and building codes and putting them into action. Cataclysmic events such as earthquakes penetrate deep into the social fabric of communities and unsettle patterns of livelihood provision, local structures of cooperation, and kin solidarities. Collective responses work on and through such innumerable localized histories to reconfigure dynamics of power and agency. We have illustrated this multiplicity of effects through the comparison of three spatially distinct sites that have experienced the reconstruction process in distinctive ways, with all having been significantly transformed. An in-depth ethnographic focus on private housing reconstruction, such as we have offered here, highlights how these transformations work at the scale of individual subjectivities and kinship relations, in articulation with local, regional, and national political processes of state consolidation at a moment of political restructuring.

We might view the reconstruction process as Nepal's largest ever mass mobilization, with nearly one million householders working closely with legions of state officials, NGO workers, technical experts, and representatives of private finance institutions. Their mutual negotiation of the terms necessary to work towards the policies of post-disaster reconstruction reflects the country's long-standing history of intensive mobilization towards other political goals, such as democracy, federalism, and secularism.

At the same time, it reveals the way in which material and immaterial processes interweave to create contradictory outcomes. Bringing what we have called the 'domains' of law, construction, and finance into the same field of vision has provided a concrete framework for tracing the threads of earthquake response into areas that are normally not considered primary targets of intervention but which constitute essential *means* of reconstruction policies. How to intervene in the mass construction of more than 800,000 buildings in a country with deep geographic divisions and histories of political upheaval without significant overhauls of the infrastructures of governance, labour, and economy? The question of how centralized administrative and regulatory changes, novel work practices, and new forms of monetary transaction are absorbed and moulded by the long histories of law, construction, and finance in different localities thus becomes crucial for evaluating the actual impact of Nepal's massive state-led reconstruction programme.

In this sense, the term 'owner-driven' may indeed be appropriate to describe how the reconstruction process has unfolded in Nepal: it indicates a form of circumscribed agency but falls short of recognizing full 'ownership', in either material or affective terms. Individual householders have worked hard to access resources offered by the state as they rebuild their own residences and livelihoods, but in doing so they have been enrolled in new systems to regulate their legal, material, and financial realities. These systems offer opportunities for citizens to exercise agency through newly available forms of technical and political expertise, but they also constrain it by foreclosing the individual choice and local specificity that previously characterized house-building processes and structures of labour.

4

Labour and the Humanitarian Present

Thinking through the 2015 Nepal Earthquakes

Shyam Kunwar, Elsie Lewison, and *Katharine Rankin*

Labour offers an important arena for studying the creation of aftermaths in the wake of disaster (see Liechty and Hutt, this volume). In this chapter, we track the collective agencies that shaped post-disaster labour upheavals and transformed socioeconomic relations in Dolakha district of central Nepal, one of the regions hardest hit by the 2015 earthquakes. The upheavals included a rapid, large-scale displacement of labourers at the site of a major infrastructure project, alongside massive increases in demand for labour to carry out reconstruction work—dynamics that, in turn, contributed to a significant and widely reported increase in wage rates. These seemingly 'natural' fluxes in supply and demand were also shaped by politics and agency, as various intermediary actors with interests at stake intervened to shape both pre- and post-disaster labour markets. The chapter highlights struggles among intermediaries for control over wages, efforts to exploit differences between sectors and among labourers, and the different implications for those trying to rebuild homes and livelihoods in the wake of the disaster.

Much of the critical analysis of humanitarian relief and reconstruction following the earthquakes has centred on the failure of the Nepali state to respond effectively. Amnesty International (2017) underscores the role of state-led reconstruction works in exacerbating processes of marginalization. Yogesh Raj and Bhaskar Gautam (2015) specify the deliberate negligence of an 'amnesiac state' that 'remembers to forget' existing data and information that could support the distribution of aid—lest it face the demands of accountability (see also S. Tamang 2015). Similarly, there have been ample accounts of donor complicity in the chaos and inequities surrounding both relief and reconstruction (for example, Bhattarai, Acharya, and Land 2018). Others have analysed the post-earthquake dynamics in Nepal through the lens of disaster capitalism, emphasizing how disasters can offer new opportunities for capital accumulation while extending processes of commercialization and financialization deeper into agrarian subsistence economies (D. Paudel 2017; Paudel and Le Billon 2018; Matthew and Upreti 2018; Le Billon et al. 2020; Paudel, Rankin, and Le Billon 2020). Recent scholarship has also explored everyday relations of expertise from the perspective of residents as well as the cadres of professionals and relief workers dispatched to affected areas (Limbu et al. 2019; see also chapters by Shneiderman et al.; Baniya; Gurung and Baniya; Oven et al.; Dhungana; Shakya; Ninglekhu, Daly, and Hollenbach; Lotter, this volume). Together this work speaks to broader themes in 'critical humanitarianism studies' (Pallister-Wilkins 2018), which has highlighted the relations of power at work in the 'liberal morality' (Reid-Henry 2013, 2014) and bureaucratization of humanitarianism (Barnett 2011), as well as the violence of its instrumentalization (Weizman 2012).

In this chapter, we build on and contribute to insights from critical humanitarianism studies and critiques of disaster capitalism through a focus on construction labour (see also Shneiderman et al., this volume). This focus reveals key points of intersection between the rationalities of bureaucratic humanitarian governance and the political economy of reconstruction. As we demonstrate in the following sections, labour markets are deeply instituted and spatially variegated (Hirslund 2019). They are shaped by the internal bureaucratic logics and inertia of state and donor apparatuses, and by firms and individual labourers competing to exploit new vulnerabilities and opportunities in emerging post-disaster geographies.

The evidence in the chapter draws on research for a seven-year, multi-sited research project titled 'Infrastructures of Democracy', which employs comparative, ethnographic methods to investigate infrastructure development as a site of state building across three agrarian districts in Nepal.[1] The project

---

[1] 'Infrastructures of Democracy: State Building as Everyday Practice in Nepal's Agrarian Districts' is funded by the Canadian Social Sciences and Humanities Research Council (SSHRC Grant no 435-2014-1883), infrastructuresofdemocracy. geog.utoronto.ca.

builds on exploratory research on the meaning and practices of 'democracy' in rural areas of Nepal following the decade-long Maoist insurgency. This initial research identified roads as a key terrain of contestation and negotiation in relation to both the *material* infrastructure underpinning state reconstruction and the *social* and *political* infrastructures that govern everyday life (Rankin et al. 2018). The latter encompass a myriad of labour arrangements, ranging from contracting networks, to self-help users' groups, to various arrangements for procuring workers for construction projects.

In this chapter, we first provide a snapshot of the terrain of construction labour prior to the earthquake. Here we focus particularly on the construction site of the Upper Tamakoshi Hydroelectric Project, one of the Nepal government's National Pride Projects located near the northern border of Dolakha.[2] We then turn to the overlapping processes of labour displacement and rising demand for labour in the wake of the earthquakes. To understand how these processes have played out in Dolakha, we focus on the roles of key intermediaries working to govern and benefit from post-earthquake labour upheavals, including trade unions, government regulators, donors, and labour contractors. In the following section, we consider the differential implications for vulnerable populations in Dolakha. On the one hand, opportunity was created for both local and migrant labour—including among socially and economically marginalized populations—who now had access to reconstruction work at increased wage rates. On the other hand, the rising cost and scarcity of labour for mundane house reconstruction impeded efforts to recover livelihoods and exacerbated equity issues for poor and vulnerable households trying to rebuild their homes and communities. Together, the sections of this chapter demonstrate how post-disaster labour markets became a key arena in which the aftermath of the earthquakes was '*created* by the collective agency of many individuals, families, communities, and institutions (including states)' (Liechty and Hutt, this volume). In the concluding section, we build on this

---

[2] National Pride Projects are identified by the National Planning Commission (NPC), which is the apex advisory body of the Government of Nepal that is responsible for formulating a national vision, development policy, periodic plans, and sectoral policies for national development. Pride Projects are identified on the basis of their perceived priority for national development and, once designated, they receive significant resources every fiscal year until they are completed (NPC 2013).

analysis to argue that labour markets also represent an important arena for rethinking the politics of humanitarianism and disaster preparedness.

Pre-earthquake construction labour markets

The emergence of a labour hub

One year after the 2015 earthquakes, on 2 April 2016, we paid a visit to the town of Lamabagar, the site of the Upper Tamakoshi Hydropower Dam, as part of our research on roads (Figure 4.1). We travelled by hired jeep from the district centre, Charikot, to the village of Chhetchhet, where landslides had swept away the Singati–Lamabagar access road nearly a kilometre short of its destination (Figures 4.2 and 4.3). From there, we walked along a narrow footpath shared with *dzos* (a hybrid between the yak and the domestic cow) and mules, which had been (re-)enlisted for transportation in the absence of the motorable road. We passed electricity poles cracked

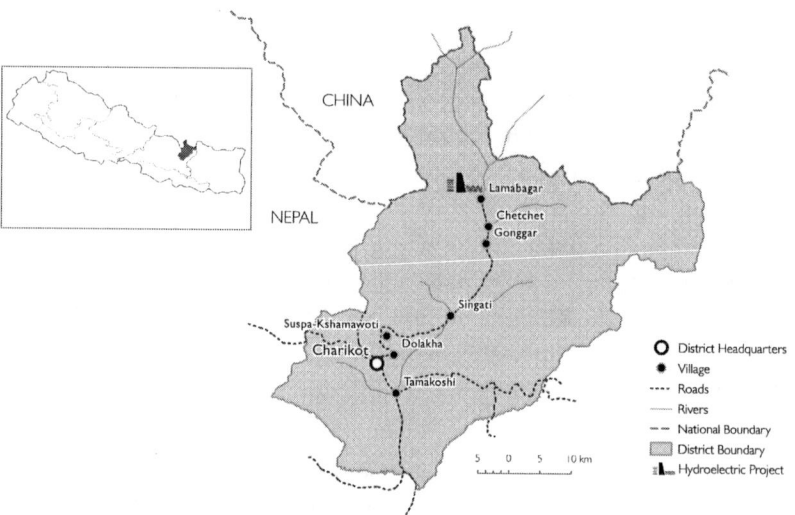

Figure 4.1 Dolakha map

Source: Elsie Lewison.

Note: Map shows general locations and does not represent authentic international boundaries.

Figures 4.2 and 4.3 View of landslide that swept away the access road just short of Lamabagar (*left*); labourer working on constructing a wall to repair the access road (*right*).
Source: Photographs by Katharine Rankin and Bicram Rijal.

in half and dangling off the edge of the trail, over the precipice forming the edge of a steep canyon about 1,000 feet above the Tamakoshi River. We passed the entrance of the tunnel for dam works, inside which warning signs of the hazards within were still intact, but the grated entrance gate was damaged and ajar. As we headed north towards the Tamakoshi's headwaters, the narrow valley began to widen and the river came level with the road. On arrival in Lamabagar,[3] all was silent except for the sounds of the wind and the river's flow. The massive concrete dam dominated the horizon of the wide river valley, surrounded by vacant labour camps and all manner of abandoned construction equipment; the dam was engulfed in silence too. The Tamakoshi River flowed slowly across the flats. We saw two or three villagers moving about in the distant foreground of the dam, and two or three army personnel guarding the Tamakoshi office building; their silhouettes were dwarfed by the vast construction site beyond.

That evening we stayed in a small hotel in Lamabagar, downriver from the dam, in an area populated by a dozen shops and hotels built since the initiation of dam construction and the arrival of the road. The owner, Tenzin, a young Sherpa man, had returned to Lamabagar after having

---

[3] *Bagar* literally translates as 'river shore', with an implication of sandiness but also suitability for settlement in an otherwise inhospitably mountainous terrain, and 'Lama' references the religious significance of the region for Tibetan Buddhists.

worked for several years in Korea.[4] He had been drawn back home by the economic opportunities opened up by the hydro project, and especially the influx of labourers. Before the earthquake, he said, as we chatted by the warmth of the hotel's wood-burning stove, Lamabagar had become 'crowded'—about 1,000 workers were needed for the day and the night shift each, as construction work ran for 24 hours a day. Lamabagar had become like a foreign country, all lit up at night; another resident who stopped by for a drink similarly remarked on the crowds of construction labourers, project officials, engineers, technicians, and visitors.

The construction company, Sino Hydro, had employed hundreds of Chinese labourers for civil engineering works. Texmaco Railway and Engineering Limited, an Indian contractor for hydro-mechanical works, brought Indian engineers and site workers to the dam site and surrounding tunnels. The construction companies had employed residents from the area as unskilled labourers in order to maintain good relations with the local population. Local residents were hired to oversee quality control, checking safety equipment used by skilled labourers, or as security guards who could be relied on to know who was an outsider and who was a local. Those with some skills were given petty contracts, such as the construction of a hostel in the labour camp. Others, like Tenzin, opened businesses which catered to the new residents of Lamabagar.

The labour camp at this site, now deteriorating behind a rusty barbed-wire fence, formerly housed over 500 workers in hostels who were served by a large 'mess' pavilion (Figures 4.4 and 4.5). As conditions grew increasingly cramped, local hotels began to offer competitive prices and better entertainment facilities. Drinking and loud socializing were prohibited inside the camps, as the 24-hour construction cycle required that half the labour force was able to rest at any given time. By contrast, the hotels offered a warm hearth, ample drink, and entertaining company. They began to draw labourers (all men) in larger numbers and to prove lucrative to local proprietors like Tenzin. People called them *chhapre* hotels—meaning that they were built as inexpensive, temporary structures that could easily be moved near the labour camp or construction site to maximize convenience for labour. Other clientele included tourists drawn by the access road and participants in education tours focused on the dam.

---

[4]   In this chapter, we follow social science convention and have changed proper names to pseudonyms to protect the privacy of interlocutors.

Figures 4.4 and 4.5 Views of the labour camp at the Upper Tamakoshi Hydropower Dam site from above, looking south (*left*), and from the side, looking north (*right*).
Source: Photographs by Shyam Kunwar and Katharine Rankin.

The economic centrality of Lamabagar in turn gave locals some unusual bargaining power vis-à-vis one of the most powerful private sectors in Dolakha—the controversial transportation 'syndicates'. Two bus companies ply the roads in the district and compete with one another through nefarious and sometimes violent practices. In violation of regulations, they also protect their mutual turf against any other private enterprise seeking to offer transportation services in the district. The vandalism, pirating, and violence surrounding transportation syndicates in Dolakha are legendary. The arrival of the competing Rolwaling Yatayat and Araniko Yatayat bus associations in Lamabagar signalled the significance of this geographically peripheral location for the economic development of the district. A bus driver in Singati (a commercial centre about 30 kilometres downriver from Lamabagar along the Tamakoshi River), who previously worked on the Singati–Lamabagar access road, recalled the 'thousands' of workers who travelled by bus to and from Lamabagar to work in dam and road construction.[5] Demand for regular service on the route was so strong that, when the bus associations tried to reduce the number of buses, locals threatened to initiate an alternative jeep service and block access for buses. Unwilling to lose territorial control, the bus companies conceded to demands to resume a twice daily service to the district centre.

In fact, labour became so well-articulated as a political force in Lamabagar that it undertook a strike in March 2015 to demand a right to shares from

---

5   Personal communication, 5 August 2017.

the publicly listed Upper Tamakoshi Hydropower Limited (UTKHPL). The project had allocated shares to the staff of investors including the Employees Provident Fund (EPF), Nepal Telecom, Citizen Investment Trust, Rastriya Beema Sansthan (National Insurance Agency), the staff of the National Electricity Authority, and the staff of UTKHPL itself. Shares were also to be made available to the residents of Dolakha—another means for building the consent of local populations. Financing development through private share offerings was a relatively new model in Nepal, one that had received widespread support amongst Dolakha residents, based on the hope that buying shares would allow them to 'make a living even while sleeping' (*suti-suti khaane*). Given these new developments, construction labour unions demanded that their members be given the right to purchase shares on the basis of their affiliation with the project.

Ultimately, despite their numerical strength, the labourers' claims were undermined by political tensions among the unions. Organized labour in Nepal is represented by multiple unions, each affiliated with a specific political party. In this instance, four unions were involved in the negotiations and their divergent agendas led to bitter disputes over negotiations to end the strike. When the Communist Party of Nepal-Unified Marxist–Leninist (CPN-UML)–affiliated union came to an agreement with the project management to end the strike, Nepali Congress and Maoist affiliated unions refused to follow their lead. Eventually, the political clout of national ministers, the district party leadership (with the CPN-UML holding a relatively dominant position at the time), and local Dolakha citizens eager to realize the benefits of their shares brought all of the unions to the bargaining table. Management, meanwhile, insisted that the project's articles of incorporation had made no provision for allotting shares to workers. Under pressure to bring the dispute to a rapid resolution, the unions jointly agreed to resume work after 18 days of failed negotiations. For our purposes, although the strike failed in terms of securing shares for workers, it nevertheless reflected an impressive consolidation of labour as a political force in Lamabagar over the course of just a few years and highlighted the significant influence of labour unions and political party institutions in mediating labour relations.[6]

---

[6]   For more detailed coverage of the strikes see *Kantipur Dainik* (2071a v.s.; 2071b v.s.); Dilbahadur KC's (2071a v.s., 2071b v.s.) coverage in *Karobaar Dainik*; and Rajendra Manandhar's (2071 v.s.) and Lokmani Rai's (2071 v.s.) coverage in *Kantipur Dainik*.

Aid for infrastructure and contracting networks

Elsewhere in Dolakha, we find significantly different modalities of construction labour prior to the earthquake. Road building in the district has long attracted a variety of interested parties with differing agendas. In the second half of the 20th century, road building in Dolakha was led by foreign aid projects, particularly by the Swiss Agency for Development and Cooperation (SDC), which provided funding for development activities across the entire district. The SDC's Lamosangu–Jiri Road Project, which ran from 1974 to 1985, was one of the first road projects in Nepal to employ a 'green roads' approach (Schaffner 1987). Relying on locally sourced, manual labour (and thus avoiding the use of heavy equipment), the green roads model was intended to optimize local economic benefits by creating employment opportunities while also reducing environmental pressures and ensuring greater sustainability (Bajracharya et al. 1995). In the 1990s, the Germans, in partnership with the World Food Programme and the Norwegians, similarly sought to link poverty alleviation and infrastructure development goals in a large-scale public works road project that compensated local labour with food supplies—a strategy intended to target the households that were most in need.

In more recent years, however, both state- and donor-funded infrastructure projects have relied increasingly on the networks of private contractors that have consolidated as influential forces in the infrastructure sector. As had become common practice across Nepal, infrastructure works in Dolakha were often carried out through systems of subcontracting to 'petty contractors' who were responsible for mobilizing and managing labourers. Contractors in Nepal are categorized as A, B, C, and D classes, with the latter two commonly working as subcontractors. Thus, for example, when the construction of the Singati–Lamabagar access road for the Upper Tamakoshi Hydroelectric Project went out to tender, it was awarded to four 'Class A' Nepali contractors who were each allocated a section of the road. In practice, however, these large firms subcontracted the work to local petty contractors from the C and D classes.[7]

---

[7] The first section of the road, a six-kilometre section from Singati to Bhorle, which was awarded to an A class contractor in 2005–06, was later cancelled and given to the Nepal Army for completion after the contractor failed to complete the section within four years (Gurung 2010).

Subcontracting for low-tech construction tasks, such as building gabion walls (walls constructed with large blocks made of a wirework container filled with rock or a similar material), typically did not require a formal bidding process, but rather operated through the word-of-mouth networks of lower-level contractors. In some cases, petty contractors were local and recruited from in-district populations. For example, the petty contractors working on the Singati–Lamabagar road reported that one of the most consistent sources of local labour for this project was the northern regions of Dolakha, where agricultural production tends to be insufficient to meet household needs. Historically, as Sara Shneiderman (2015a, 2015b) has documented, household members from these areas, specifically from Thangmi communities, have migrated to Darjeeling and Sikkim for seasonal labour and worked as porters within Nepal. Road building thus provided a welcome alternative source of income closer to home. In other cases, however, petty contractors, known as *thekkadar*, may have come from distant districts in other parts of the country and supplied labour from their home districts. For both local and migrant workers, exposure to the construction trades through this work could offer opportunities for labourers to move into petty contracting roles. In Dolakha, these opportunities would prove particularly lucrative in the context of the post-earthquake boom in reconstruction works.

A 'golden wave' for labour?

The anthropologist Michelle Rugh Gamburd (2013) recounts the experience of victims of the Indian Ocean tsunami in *The Golden Wave: Culture and Politics after Sri Lanka's Tsunami Disaster*. The title of her book derives from the ironic phrase 'golden wave' which developed in the local idiom to reflect the politics of humanitarian aid. After the windfall of foreign donations and assistance, the tsunami was dubbed 'merit water', 'golden water', or 'golden wave' to denote at once the easy wealth accruing to those who would seek to benefit and also the moral condemnation directed at widespread practices of taking what one does not deserve. The metaphor of the 'golden wave' thus evokes the paradox of opportunity and devastation brought by a disaster. In this section we describe the post-earthquake coincidence of labour displacement and rising demand before turning to the range of intermediaries working to both govern and benefit from these processes.

After the 2015 earthquakes struck, the construction of the Upper Tamakoshi Hydroelectric Project and its access road ceased immediately. Thousands of people were essentially locked in Lamabagar, not daring to walk out for fear of the landslides triggered by aftershocks. Those trapped included construction labourers, project officials, and security forces, as well as hundreds of temporary residents who had travelled into the northern reaches of the district for the seasonal harvest of *yarsagumba*, the caterpillar fungus valued for its medicinal qualities. A Nepal Army helicopter rescue prioritized project officials and army staff, prompting the construction workers and *yarsagumba* pickers to protest the rescue operation, demanding equal priority for rescue. Eventually, the army evacuated all but the few residents who chose to remain, resulting in a massive displacement of construction labour at the very moment the district was facing unprecedented reconstruction challenges.

The concept of 'reconstruction labour' (*punarnirman ko lagi kamdar*)[8] emerged after the earthquake, constituting a new sector of work that entailed its own set of wage logics, governance processes, and social relations (Figure 4.6). A distinguishing feature of reconstruction labour was the significant presence of international aid and relief organizations, their bureaucratic processes, and the flows of funding under their control. The International Organization for Migration (IOM) was among the first agencies to arrive in Dolakha Bazaar and employ local labour to clear up the debris of collapsed houses. Driven by internal imperatives to quickly mobilize workers to carry out relief operations, and an institutional commitment to fair compensation, the IOM was paying relief workers a rate of NPR 800 (c. USD 7) per day, compared to the pre-existing daily wage rates of NPR 500 (c. USD 4.50) for skilled labour and NPR 400–450 (c. USD 3.60–4.10) for unskilled labour. As such, according to our interlocutors, even during the initial relief phase, local wage rates increased by as much as 100 per cent and were accompanied

---

[8] The term 'reconstruction labour' in English suggests both *punarnirman ko kam* (reconstruction works) and *punarnirman ko lagi kamdar* (the labourers involved in reconstruction works). The Nepali terms for labour used in the region include *kamdar, shramik,* and *jyami* (usually specifically referring to agricultural labour or other domestic work). However, it is also common for people in Dolakha to use the English word 'labour' to describe construction and reconstruction workers. For example, interlocutors would comment 'ahile labour nai paudaina', meaning that construction or reconstruction labour had become hard to find.

Figure 4.6 Reconstruction labourers working on a donor-funded initiative to construct a collection centre for a community dairy in Suspa-Kshamawoti, Dolakha.

Source: Photograph by Bir Bahadur Thami.

by other inflating costs, including those of construction materials. The Vice Chairman of the Contractor Association of Dolakha summarized the situation succinctly:

> The local people were engaged in building temporary shelters, so it was difficult to find labour. Outside labour [from the dam and associated infrastructure] had already departed for their hometowns.... All infrastructure projects were closed; actually, there were [almost] no shelters and a severe food shortage.... [At the same time] the humanitarian organizations needed labour to mobilize for the rescue and relief operations and they paid a high wage; then the labour wage became inflated ... nobody wanted to work for less than one thousand rupees per day in Dolakha.[9]

---

[9]   Personal communication, 23 November 2018.

As relief operations transitioned to long-term reconstruction, new government-issued building regulations also played a part in shaping the emerging sector of reconstruction labour. With the aim of achieving greater resilience to future seismic instability, the National Reconstruction Authority (NRA) issued new building guidelines to govern the 2015 Nepal Earthquake Housing Reconstruction Programme. While significant efforts were made to mobilize local human and material resources, new safety standards required a trained labour force with the requisite knowledge and skills to build in accordance with the new guidelines. The Nepal government's Post-disaster Needs Assessment estimated that around 46 per cent of the workforce needed for reconstruction would have to be 'skilled' and that an estimated 20,000 new mason workers would be required for the housing component alone (NPC 2015a: 15).[10] A key role for donors (working in conjunction with local non-governmental organizations [NGOs]) was the provision of masonry training to residents of earthquake-affected areas to develop a cadre of skilled mason workers (*mistri*) who could be contracted by other residents, the local state, and various non-state institutions to manage the technical aspects of house and building reconstruction (Figure 4.7).[11]

As a result of significant state and donor involvement, reconstruction labour came to be distinguished from infrastructure labour (*ayojanako kamdar*)[12] in a number of important respects. The latter refers to the ongoing work of public infrastructure construction following more or

---

[10] There was also a significant shortage of carpenters because workers migrating from the Tarai often did not possess carpentry skills relevant to the hills (The Asia Foundation 2017: 14).

[11] Trade unions were also actively involved in lobbying for higher wages in the construction sector. In September 2015, trade unions in Nepal organized a solidarity meeting around the theme 'Reconstruction by creating decent jobs!' A proposed roadmap for reconstruction included the creation of at least 200,000 reconstruction jobs, a guarantee of 200 days of employment per year, and a minimum wage of NPR 1,000 (c. USD 9) per day for unskilled workers. See ITUC–NAC (2015) and ILO (2015).

[12] The word *ayojana* literally translates as 'organization', 'plan', or 'scheme', but is commonly used to refer to development projects. The literal translation of 'infrastructure' is *purbadhar*, but this word was not used to distinguish labour for roads, hydropower, and other infrastructure—the word *ayojana* was used instead. The English term 'labour' was also commonly used in place of *kamdar*.

Figure 4.7 Reconstruction labourers working on a private home in Suspa-Kshamawoti, Dolakha.

Source: Photograph by Shyam Kunwar.

less the same techniques and labour management modalities as employed before the earthquakes. Public infrastructure development in Dolakha has continued to involve bidding for contracts by major contractors, who then issue subcontracts for piecemeal work. However, the emergence of the well-funded and closely monitored reconstruction labour market created sizable disparities between the two sectors.

Perhaps the most significant disparity was in pay. Before the earthquakes, according to interviews with key informants and casual conversations with construction workers, daily rates for construction labour averaged NPR 500–600 (c. USD 4.50–5.40). In the wake of the earthquake, daily rates for reconstruction work rose to roughly NPR 1,000 (c. USD 9), while wages in the infrastructure sector did not see the same dramatic increases. At the same time, infrastructure labourers employed by petty contractors faced greater on-the-job risks. One of the appeals of labour subcontracting was that it provided a means to circumvent safety regulations. Regulations require employers to provide accident insurance and safety equipment such as hats and gloves. Workers involved in the large infrastructure projects in which labour recruitment was managed directly by the class A contractor (for example, the Charikot–Singati road expansion) were typically well attired with basic safety equipment and covered by accident insurance. Workers recruited by subcontractors (*thekkadar*), however, tended to lack safety equipment and had been told nothing of accident insurance (Figures 4.8 and 4.9).

Unsurprisingly, such discrepancies led to a variety of efforts by both labourers and contractors to better position themselves within the evolving systems and to take advantage of new opportunities. Because donor- and state-supported employment opportunities and skill training programmes were targeted primarily at local, disaster-affected communities, Dolakha residents dominated the reconstruction labour market at first. The opportunities for local labour created by reconstruction efforts in turn created new incentives to recruit a greater portion of 'infrastructure' labour from outside the district through *thekkadar* networks, from regions where wages had not witnessed similar increases. On road projects in the post-earthquake period, it was not uncommon to encounter labourers from distant districts who had been recruited by lower-level contractors and who were working in Dolakha for the first time.

However, as newly arrived migrant labourers working in infrastructure development became aware of the wage discrepancies, they began to look for opportunities in reconstruction. In fact, as a Dolakha contractor engaged to rebuild the Chief District Office (CDO) building (a 'reconstruction' project)

Figures 4.8 and 4.9 Temporary camp near Swati Bazaar, Kalinchowk Gaunpalika, for infrastructure labourers upgrading the Dolakha–Singati road section after the earthquake (*left*); labourers from western Nepal upgrading the Makaibari–Deurali–Panighat road near Deurali, Dolakha (*right*).

Source: Photographs by Shyam Kunwar.

explained to us, construction workers from other districts who were posted in Dolakha for road building could become a good resource for recruiting labour for reconstruction as well.[13] Some of these former 'infrastructure' workers were subcontracted as labour suppliers (low-level *thekkadar*) who went back to their home districts to recruit labour for reconstruction works. It was similarly reported that a number of locally trained masons in Dolakha also aimed to negotiate a better position within new market relations by becoming labour contractors and hiring their own teams of workers (S. Sangroula 2017; Amnesty International 2017).

The rising demand for labour and practices of recruiting labour from outside the district thus supported the growth of a robust sector of middlemen—labour suppliers who were remunerated by commissions charged both to the contractors and to the workers. The Dolakha contractor for the reconstruction of the CDO building explained that he was paying 'unskilled' labour contracted from outside the district NPR 700 (c. USD 6) per day, and 'skilled' labour (*mistri*) NPR 800–1,000 (c. USD 7–9) per day (in addition to wages, he was also expected to provide daily meals for the labourers). By the time we met him in July 2017, he had employed labour from Bardia, Surkhet, and Rolpa districts. The labour-supplier *thekkadar* was charging NPR 100–150 (c. USD 0.90–1.4) per person per day to the main contractor, while charging a commission or interest on funds advanced as a loan to labourers recruited from outside the district (who generally stay in temporary labour camps while working on contract). Local labour, meanwhile, would reportedly not work for less than NPR 1,000 per day and many local residents were either preoccupied with reconstructing their own homes or had moved away following the earthquakes. Engaging labour suppliers thus ensured the employer a ready supply of labour for the same or a slightly lower total outlay than would have been required to hire increasingly scarce local labour.

While labourers and petty contractors were manoeuvring to take advantage of rising wages, we also found other actors attempting to suppress wage inflation. For example, residents in Dolakha Bazaar, a predominantly Newar community, mounted a vocal campaign to prevent donors from paying higher than average wages to relief workers in the immediate aftermath of the earthquakes. The collective organizing responded to wages

---

[13]   Personal communication, 26 July 2017.

being offered by the IOM for clearing debris from collapsed infrastructure in the Bazaar, which, as we noted above, had doubled pre-earthquake rates. Concerned that these higher rates would set a precedent for the future, Newar residents organized a protest and gathered symbolically at the main gate of the village to refuse entry to the project and its workers. With their collective influence, residents were able to negotiate the wage rate down to NPR 600 (USD 5.5). A retired army captain from the Bazaar explained his frustration with donor organizations' propensity to 'come and go', paying high wages for a short time and then leaving an inflated labour market that 'becomes a burden at the grassroots'.[14]

State actors also exerted some effort to control rising wages, albeit ineffectively, specifically through an official wage rate or *darbhau*. Even as reconstruction works exerted upward pressure on construction sector wages in the years following the earthquakes, the *darbhau*—upon which construction contractors were supposed to base their bids for construction contracts—was kept steady. During our visits in 2016 and 2017, the *darbhau* was set at NPR 460 (c. USD 4) per day for unskilled labour and NPR 640 (c. USD 6) per day for skilled labour, while the daily market rate for unskilled road construction labour was NPR 700 (c. USD 6.5) at a minimum, and the daily rate for reconstruction work was, as noted earlier, closer to NPR 1,000 per day.[15] The state thus failed to account for the impacts of the market for reconstruction labour that it had played a role in creating with the introduction of building codes and masonry trainings. If the *darbhau* was intended to help lower wage rates, it had no bearing on market rates, leaving contractors to reflect real labour costs through other means, including claiming artificially high rates for other aspects of the bid and cutting corners on various expenses, including safety precautions and quality standards.

Within two years of the earthquakes, then, wage rates had increased, driven initially by the relatively high wages offered by donor agencies involved in relief and reconstruction as well as government specifications on reconstruction standards. A differentiated labour market was established,

---

[14]   Personal communication, 3 April 2016.

[15]   As noted earlier, while the rates paid out to labourers brought in from other districts were lower, when the commissions charged by labour contractors are taken into account, the total paid by construction firms was more in line with the NPR 1,000-per-day rate.

which distinguished ongoing public infrastructure construction (especially roads) from post-earthquake reconstruction. The uneven labour market created incentives and opportunities for an emerging sector of labour-supplying middlemen contractors (*thekkadar*) to play increasingly important roles in market making—leveraging commissions from local contractors while mobilizing labour from outside the district through mechanisms that created dependency and built wealth. The local government, meanwhile, was essentially powerless to control the labour market once these dynamics were set in place. An official wage rate for infrastructure construction had little bearing on market rates paid by contractors, driven up first by reconstruction wages and then by demands for commissions from labour suppliers.

Changing labour relations and community dynamics

How were these changing labour relations experienced within the Dolakha communities that had been affected by the earthquakes? As we have seen, the large-scale displacement of labour at the Upper Tamakoshi Hydropower Dam construction site disrupted the lives and livelihoods of members of the massive temporary workforce, as well as those working in the local economy which had grown to serve this workforce. The impact of the new demand for reconstruction labour in other areas of the district, meanwhile, differed significantly, depending on a person's relationship to the labour market. For those who were able to obtain access to reconstruction work, assume roles as labour suppliers, or cater to the needs of the newly emerging population of temporary labour and itinerant experts, the surge in local wage rates aided in the recovery process. However, for many households, the higher labour rates contributed to borrowing or to delays in the reconstruction of homes, as well as to declines in agricultural production, as labour was re-directed to reconstruction efforts. The differentiated impacts and shifts in labour relations in turn contributed to new lines of social tension.

Post-earthquake surveys suggest that the increasing wage rates benefited households and individuals reliant on daily wages. A longitudinal survey by the Asia Foundation over 11 affected districts found steady improvements in daily wage income in the two years following the earthquakes (The Asia Foundation 2017). Similarly, a study by an interdisciplinary team of academics in Dolakha found that wage-dependent families benefited from increased labour demands, alongside cash and food aid distributions, and in a few cases, reported experiencing improved livelihood conditions following the earthquakes (Epstein et al. 2018). Those who were able to move into labour contracting positions were in an even better position to benefit from the construction boom. Skill trainings targeted at women also created opportunities for transgressing gendered labour norms and for increased economic autonomy. However, not all trainees took up *mistri* employment following the trainings (HRRP 2018), and many of those who did so reported increased labour burdens, as they continued to be held responsible for domestic and agricultural duties (Amatya 2019). Meanwhile, as was the case in pre-earthquake Lamabagar, the new influx of labour migrants recruited by labour contractors contributed to the incomes of small hotel owners like Tenzin Sherpa, and the presence of large cadres of aid workers supported local businesses (The Asia Foundation 2017: 19).

In contrast, the rising wage rates posed a challenge for households which depended on hired labour for rebuilding. As was widely reported, the government aid promised to earthquake-affected households only covered a fraction of the total costs of construction, particularly given the demands of the government-approved models (see Shneiderman et al., this volume). Amnesty International, for example, points to 'problematic' assumptions about the availability and cost of labour and materials on the part of government agencies—assumptions that contributed to the significant discrepancies between actual and estimated costs of home reconstruction. In January 2017, a representative of a Netherlands-based relief agency estimated that the cheapest of these models would likely cost around NPR 2–2.5 million (c. USD 18,000–22,000) at going rates, in comparison with the NPR 200,000 (c. USD 18,200) promised for that model (Amnesty International 2017: 31).[16] The shortfalls in government support fell particularly hard on marginalized and low-income groups who were more likely to have stayed in temporary shelters over a longer period of time after the earthquakes (The Asia Foundation 2017: v).

Labour scarcity and rising wages posed additional challenges for those reliant on farming, particularly for those living in more remote, rural areas. The Asia Foundation (2017: vi–vii) found that post-earthquake debt

---

[16] This figure represents a broad-based estimate: exact costs of constructing a given model would vary by location, among other factors.

burdens were higher and incomes were slower to improve in these regions. On the one hand, households in remote, rural areas faced higher costs for transporting materials over long distances—in addition to shortages of trained construction labour—making rebuilding even more difficult and costly (The Asia Foundation 2017: v; Amnesty International 2017: 31). On the other hand, farming households also faced declines in the availability of agricultural labour. Agricultural livelihoods in the region were already in decline prior to the earthquakes; recent years had seen significant outflows of working-age people from rural areas, many of them pursuing the promise of higher incomes in foreign countries. With younger generations moving away, existing practices of labour exchange had also declined, leaving a greater number of labour-scarce households reliant on hired labour. The earthquakes amplified existing labour scarcities, making it increasingly difficult for households to maintain farming operations. An interlocutor in Singati Bazaar described the difficulties that he faced as an aging farmer, saying: 'What is happening is we cannot even touch labour for agriculture work.… As an old man, I cannot walk properly in the villages to search for agricultural labourers and nobody comes [any more] to visit my house for work.'[17]

The transformations in the labour market following the earthquakes 'reduced interest in farming' and prompted shifts to non-agricultural livelihoods, including daily wage work (The Asia Foundation 2017: 18). However, new opportunities were not evenly distributed. Within households, new labour opportunities outside agriculture were primarily filled by men— meaning that women and older children were often left to take on a greater share of agricultural and livestock labour at home (DiCarlo et al. 2018: 799). Between households, Epstein et al. (2018) and DiCarlo et al. (2018) also found that wealthier farming households were better positioned to adapt, and take advantage of government-sponsored agribusiness programmes, by transitioning to labour-saving cash crops such as cardamom (DiCarlo et al. 2018: 802). Such opportunities were, however, not available to lower-income households which lacked sufficient start-up capital, the ability to afford additional agricultural inputs, and the bureaucratic know-how to navigate development programme bureaucracy. These studies' findings align with those of the Asia Foundation survey (2017: 18), which concludes that,

---

[17]   Personal communication, 19 February 2018.

overall, households with the highest pre-earthquake incomes recovered most strongly and quickly.

The differentiated impacts of rising wages, alongside struggles to govern and benefit from labour markets, have also contributed to tensions and conflict in Dolakha. The rising wage rates generated frustration and occasional resistance—as we saw in the case of the campaign against the IOM clean-up by residents of Dolakha Bazaar—among households reliant on labour. Long-time residents, meanwhile, commonly credited migrant labour with perceived increases in looting, prostitution, divorce, and other vices ascribed to social relations in migrants' home districts. We heard numerous, often xenophobic, accounts of how the affective stresses introduced by outside labour compounded the material stresses created by earthquake damage.

Dolakha residents, labourers, contractors, bureaucrats, and humanitarian agencies have all developed critical analyses of labour market dynamics while working to exert control and take advantage of differences between sectors and among labourers. The agency exerted by these actors has also contributed to tensions within communities, and between residents and aid organizations. In our conclusion, we take up the question of how increased recognition of, and deliberate engagement with, these forms of agency in disaster preparedness and response processes could contribute to more effective and just modes of coordination.

Conclusion

The experience in Dolakha illustrates how labour can become a critical arena in which the aftermaths of disasters are created and contested. This chapter tracks two spheres of labour upheaval that have had transformative effects on one of the regions hardest hit by the 2015 earthquakes in Nepal. First, the earthquakes catalysed a massive displacement of labour at the site of a major national infrastructure development project, which disrupted not only construction but also the lives and livelihoods of workers enrolled in construction and ancillary activities. Second, reconstruction emerged as a differentiated labour sector, operating at relatively inflated wages, drawing new rounds of migrant labour to the region, consolidating a cohort of contractor–labour suppliers from around the country and, in turn, rendering labour for agriculture, infrastructure, and reconstruction increasingly scarce. Both scenarios reveal how labour markets are spatially variegated and mediated by the collective agencies of governments, aid organizations, contractors, local residents, and labourers themselves.

Based on this inquiry, our chapter has explored the modes of agency and governance that come into view when labour is taken as a central category of analysis. Attention to the labour dynamics at the Upper Tamakoshi Hydropower Dam construction site at Lamabagar reveals how the earthquakes not only displaced a significant (and soon to be much-needed) labour force, they also dissipated a considerable consolidation of labour power. Prior to their displacement, construction workers exerted their influence over the region's powerful transportation syndicates and interrupted progress on one of the country's prominent National Pride Projects over their demands for a rightful share to ownership in the publicly traded company—an appeal that, though unsuccessful in producing the desired result, demonstrates a burgeoning political awareness of issues of economic democracy.

Consideration of the contradictory dynamics in the local labour market for reconstruction, meanwhile, reveals the significance of wage rates for fragile local economies. Rapid rate increases pose challenges for lower-income households that are facing labour shortages and high costs, while also creating opportunities for both local and new rounds of migrant labour. Aid organizations, state regulatory agencies, and contractor–labour suppliers played a combined role in the making of post-disaster labour markets—donors justified high wages by pointing to conditions of labour shortage and their commitments to just wages, the state's requirements for earthquake-resilient reconstruction demanded higher-skilled labour and more labour time, and a cohort of contractor–labour suppliers pushed costs up by taking commissions on the recruitment of labour and the procurement of supplies. The district administration was ineffectual in its attempts to control labour rates through the *darbhau* (fixed rate) system. And yet, recognizing the processes by which labour markets are produced and instituted offers opportunities for imagining alternative market forms—a much overlooked aspect of earthquake preparedness.

How might greater attention to labour markets, and the agency of the individuals and institutions that shape them, contribute to earthquake preparedness and response? The experience in Dolakha suggests an imperative to anticipate labour shortages for the precarious work of recovery and clean-up, and for the skilled work of reconstruction. In regions with major, ongoing infrastructure development works, such as Dolakha's hydropower dams, plans could be drawn up for deploying existing labour resources for emergency response. Given the extent of infrastructure development throughout Nepal today, ample labour reserves may be available in many regions, and workers' experience, knowledge, and skills could prove critical for timely and effective response. At the same time, effective mobilization of labour in a time of crisis would benefit from a well-organized and secure labour force. Disaster preparedness could thus be understood as going hand in hand with improved labour policies and better enforcement of labour protections to guarantee job security and personal safety.

In disaster aftermaths, the Dolakha experience also suggests the need for policies that could better address the inequities that arise between different labour sectors and between institutions and individuals dependent on labour. Addressing such concerns might entail improved coordination between donors and state actors to ensure that donor priorities—and the large budgets backing these priorities—do not produce significant wage disparities across sectors. An effective and just response might then involve working with labour advocates and organizers to standardize wages across sectors while also ensuring other forms of job security and workplace safety. In the agriculture sector, meanwhile, the post-disaster support systems could prioritize labour-saving technologies and approaches that work with local agro-ecologies and farmers' expertise, rather than relying on expensive capital investments and purchased inputs (A. Bhattarai 2019). Finally, efforts to address the inequities between those who depend on labour in disaster aftermaths could include better accounting for the real costs of labour and materials in relief payments and construction contracts, as well as building standards that prioritize contextualized knowledge and skills, rather than outside expertise (Shneiderman et al., this volume). Ultimately, we suggest that developing more effective anticipatory logics for earthquake preparedness and response hinges crucially on a commitment to economic justice and to valuing and deploying the much-overlooked knowledge and insights of disaster-affected communities and labourers themselves.

5

Disaster, Deceptions, Dislocations

Reflections from an Integrated Settlement Project in Nepal*

Jeevan Baniya

Introduction

Disasters, as well as post-disaster recovery and reconstruction, have sociopolitical implications (Hörhager 2015; Oliver-Smith 1996; Simpson 2013) and flawed or coercive reconstruction strategies can have negative economic, political, and sociocultural impacts (Oliver-Smith 1991). Based on a range of case studies, scholars have argued that for reconstruction and resettlement to be a success, understanding a local context and consulting with and enhancing the participation of an affected community prior to the design and implementation of a rehousing or settlement policy is extremely important (Oliver-Smith 1991; Razani 1984). International frameworks such as the Hyogo Framework for Action 2005–2015 (UNISDR 2005), the Sendai Framework for Disaster Risk Reduction 2015–2030 (UNISDR 2015), and the Sustainable Development Goals (SDGs) 2016–2030 (UN 2016) have also recognized the importance of the involvement, participation, and consultation of affected people and communities in the planning and

* This chapter is based on research conducted as a part of the project 'After the Earth's Violent Sway: The Tangible and Intangible Legacies of a Natural Disaster' funded by the UK's Global Challenges Research Fund through the Arts and Humanities Research Council, grant number AH/P003648/1. The author would like to express sincere gratitude to all the people in the Majhi community for sharing their experiences. Special thanks to Anisha Bhattarai and Kishor Bikram Shah at Social Science Baha for their support in the field.

implementation of policies and strategies for disaster risk reduction and response. This is because it helps not only to increase a sense of ownership of reconstruction, but also to enhance legitimacy and accountability. Reconstruction and resettlement plans and designs that are uniform and imposed from outside, without any consultation or consideration of local and indigenous social systems and cultural contexts, can have adverse impacts on disaster-affected people and communities (Oliver-Smith 1991: 16) and their social articulations (Duyne Barenstein 2006), identity, and traditional lives (Oliver-Smith 1991).

Similarly, providing inadequate space for culturally important ritual practices and for personal privacy (Razani 1984), for sheds, animal pens, and other agricultural needs (Razani 1984; Oliver-Smith 1991) and locating reconstructed dwellings at an excessive distance from kin and neighbours (Razani 1984) also lead to dissatisfaction and the failure of a reconstruction project. Community-led reconstruction processes, based on the framework and principles of rights-based reconstruction, the participation of local people, and owner-driven reconstruction are intrinsic parts of building back better. Owner-driven reconstruction is also more cost-efficient, culturally appropriate, and sustainable as compared with other methods of housing reconstruction (Duyne Barenstein and Iyengar 2009).

This research explores the sociocultural impacts of Nepal's 2015 earthquakes and subsequent reconstruction activity in the context of an integrated settlement development project for a Majhi community in Sindhupalchok district, and is situated in the milieu of the broad and interdisciplinary literature cited earlier. Based on empirical evidence, I argue first that, contrary to what is claimed, the integrated settlement[1] project was not driven by local Majhis, and that external organizations and individuals overlooked the sociocultural and economic sensitivities, indigenous skills, local knowledge, and needs of this community while planning and implementing the reconstruction of their settlement. Second, I demonstrate that the overall settlement plan and design, the individual house designs, and the choice of construction materials and labour seem to have adversely impacted many of the Majhis' long-

---

[1] An 'integrated settlement' is defined as any settlement that is built by integrating in a planned way the available physical, economic, social, and cultural infrastructures (NRA 2074 v.s.).

standing social, cultural, and spiritual practices. Third, delays and a lack of communication from the implementing non-governmental organization (NGO) to the Majhi residents about how the settlement would be reconstructed increased indebtedness and dissatisfaction among the community. Fourth, the reconstruction project contributed to a weakening of pre-existing social capital such as trust, social harmony, and reciprocal relations.

The chapter is based primarily on field research carried out in seven different phases over the period December 2017–March 2020. To understand the reconstruction planning and implementation process as well as people's perception and experiences, a total of 84 qualitative interviews were conducted. Most interviews were carried out with the Majhi residents but the interview sample also included NGO representatives, local leaders, school officials, and technicians. Some key interviewees were interviewed multiple times. Unless supported by citations, the findings are based on empirical research at the study site. The chapter has also benefitted from a review of the relevant literature and field observation at various stages of the ongoing reconstruction.

The Majhis

The Majhis are one of the oldest indigenous groups in Nepal. Traditionally, they have lived in a very close relationship with rivers (Koirala 1968; Majhi 2006). They are also known as 'Bote' in the inner Tarai and 'Kushar' in Chitwan (Bista 2000). Generally, they like to live in clustered settlements, and in joint patrilinear families. They have the tradition of working in groups and communally for fishing and collecting firewood, and they exchange labour for agricultural and construction purposes (Majhi 2006; Gharti Magar and Majhi 2068 v.s.). Of the total population of Majhis (72,614) in the country, 7.02 per cent live in Sindhupalchok district. They have their own language, Majhi or Majhi Kura, which is classified as an endangered language in Nepal. Many of the Majhis' religious practices are similar to those of other Hindus (Koirala 1968; Majhi 2006) but they also consider *tantric* practices as part of their religion (Majhi 2006). Historically and traditionally, boating, fishing, and agriculture have been their major sources of livelihood (Majhi 2006; Koirala 1968).

The Majhi settlement (*basti*) where this study is based is located on the banks of the Indrawati River.[2] There are 53[3] families residing in the settlement with a total of 375 people. Before the 2015 earthquakes, they lived in a more or less clustered settlement with most of the houses made of stones and mud, and roofs made of dry grass (*khar/katus/thakar*) or mud/clay tiles, along with wooden ceilings. The residents kept the images of their ancestors (*kulayan*) covered and separate on the upper floors of their houses or in the corners of particular rooms. In addition to their traditional occupations, Majhis are involved in diverse livelihood activities, including construction (building houses and public facilities and extracting river sand), modern and commercial farming (largely of potatoes and tomatoes), foreign employment, wage work, and yeast (*marcha*) making (Figure 5.1).

Livelihoods based on the manual extraction of sand during autumn and winter are weakening because this work is increasingly done mechanically by contractors. The settlement did not experience any human loss due to the impacts of the earthquakes, except for two persons being injured (one elderly and a child). The area of the community is 9,666.06 square metres (19 *ropani*), and each house has 465 square metres of land for its plot. Until the completion of an un-gravelled road linking the settlement to a highway in 2019, local people had to walk for 3 hours (10 kilometres) to access public transportation. The settlement has a primary school where there are about 40–42 regular students. The school building was destroyed by the earthquakes but has been rebuilt with the support of a German international non-governmental organization (INGO) named Hilfe zur Selbsthilfe (Help for Self Help).

Post-earthquake, the village is being rebuilt under an 'Integrated Settlement Project for the Majhi Community'. Initially, this reconstruction was supposed to be carried out entirely with the support of an individual donor who would raise the necessary funds. However, according to the NRA's NGO mobilization policy (NRA 2072a v.s.) and its policy to identify vulnerable groups (NRA 2074 v.s.), a household would not be eligible to

---

[2]   A tributary of Nepal's largest river system, the Koshi.

[3]   Before the earthquakes the number of families was reported to be about 42 but later in the reconstruction plans, an additional number of houses was included. At the time of the 1934 (1990 v.s.) earthquake, there were only 10 households in this settlement, according to a male Majhi interlocutor in his early 80s.

Figure 5.1 A Majhi woman preparing yeast inside her temporary shelter.
Source: Author.

receive the government grant of NPR 300,000 (c. USD 2,700) if any other individual or organization (including NGOs) supported the reconstruction of their home. This led the individual donor to first register an NGO to facilitate the reconstruction of the settlement. This NGO is said to have been established with the sole purpose of developing this one Majhi settlement (*basti*). It should be noted that an NGO worker had initially introduced the concept of an integrated settlement to the Majhis. Some of the Majhi youth leaders were attracted to the concept because they were promised not only new houses but also the rebuilding of the village as a model settlement with infrastructure, public facilities, and livelihood-related support programmes.

Owner-driven reconstruction: claims and realities

A local community's ownership of and participation in a rebuilding process can have far-reaching consequences; bypassing it can have adverse impacts

(Oliver-Smith 1991: 12–23). Community participation is significant for the planning, design, management, implementation, and evaluation of post-disaster reconstruction activities (Razani 1984) because it provides ownership to the affected people and communities and empowers them, ensures accountability, and makes reconstruction activities more needs-based (Mubyazi and Hutton 2012).

My research has revealed that, while consultations were held with local Majhis prior to the planning of the integrated settlement project, such consultations and meetings were held on grand settlement plans, and no detailed plans and activities were adequately communicated. Also, the external planners and implementers of the project grossly overlooked the sociocultural sensitivities and needs, and the indigenous skills and local knowledge of the Majhi community in the process. The reconstruction of the settlement, the evidence shows, was driven by the organization,[4] not by the affected Majhis. The text on the banner displayed at the project's inauguration programme read 'Integrated Settlement Development Project Run for Majhi Community Living in Indrawati Riverine', indicating that somebody else was reconstructing the settlement *for* the Majhis, and that they were not building it for themselves.

The concept of reconstructing a village as an integrated settlement was introduced to the Majhi community by a former NGO worker (who later became the project manager of the integrated settlement). This person had previously supported a potato farming project among the Majhis and was also familiar with an integrated settlement that had been built by the Dhurmus–Suntali Foundation at another location.[5] The head teacher of the village school, whom the Majhis trusted well, also played a crucial role in facilitating the contact with the president of the current project-implementing organization and in convincing the Majhis to adopt the initial proposal. The NGO worker introduced the concept of the integrated model settlement to the Majhis, explaining that it would entail, in addition to the houses, the development of infrastructure, community buildings, roads,

---

[4] The organization is anonymized and I have avoided using any identifier, including websites linking to it.

[5] The Dhurmus–Suntali foundation (https://dhurmussuntali.com/en/category/social-project), named after two comedian artists of Nepal, has constructed several integrated settlements for earthquake-affected communities and vulnerable groups in Nepal.

toilets, biogas, and so on, and asked them to adopt the integrated settlement. Most Majhis were also in need of external support to build their houses and they accepted the proposal when the president of the organization visited on 6 February 2017 to put forward a proposal for an integrated settlement to the Majhi community.

As will be illuminated throughout this chapter, the settlement plan was declared without a proper study of the potential risks and challenges, which also hindered the reconstruction of the community. Similarly, one of the declared strategies and principles of the integrated settlement development project was to ensure community participation, involving local people at every step of the development process including designing, purchasing, and implementation.[6] For example, some of the key Project Implementation Strategies mentioned on the organization's official website are:

> Community people will be involved as skilled and unskilled manpower for the construction.

> Community participation will be accepted in every step of [the] decision-making process like designing, purchasing, and implementing.

> A public hearing program will be organized every month by the Foundation involving the donors, community people, stakeholders, and government sectors.

In the initial phase, most families were consulted about the integrated settlement, but not every issue was discussed and agreed upon. For instance, a 57-year-old male Majhi said, 'We raised the issue of having cattle and all. This was the design they came up with. They did not show us any alternative options'.[7]

A handful of youths from the Majhi community were involved in consultation and facilitating the reconstruction of the community through one of the major local committees, of which they were members.[8] These

---

6   From the website of the organization.
7   Interview, Majhigaun, 8 October 2018.
8   Other committees were also formed for the purposes of welcoming guests, mobilizing resources and support, organizing cultural performances, and so on.

youths often argued that they always stood for the 'leadership of the people' (*janatako aguwaima*) for the reconstruction activities. Several elderly members expressed their dissatisfaction that they were hardly consulted in the decision-making process and that it was mostly the youth leaders of the committee who were involved. Although this might be seen as locals actively participating throughout the reconstruction process, a closer look at the actual practices suggests that very few affected Majhi families were included or consulted in the key decision-making processes of the project. For example, the organization came up with a pre-fixed master plan for the settlement, including its layout, the designs of the houses and surroundings, the choice of construction materials, and plans for contracting out the reconstruction project, and asked the Majhis to accept it. The community did not see the design of the houses until their foundations were laid.

Some families were not satisfied with the house design. It had only one storey and they were not permitted further extensions; indeed, neither the house design nor the settlement's layout would allow this. There were suggestions that there should be some flexibility in house design and size, but these were ignored. Some families felt coerced into opting for the integrated settlement instead of rebuilding their houses on their own and taking the grant from the government, and they claimed that they were threatened with being ostracized by the community if they did not agree to the project. This is illustrated in the following statement by a young Majhi woman:

> Please do not tell anyone this, but they placed the condition that, if the Majhis did not join together for the construction, they would be discarded from the society and even denied support from other people in the society; they would even be denied construction materials brought for the construction. The young people agreed to this idea but the elderly people would not accept it. We had to sign a paper stating that we accepted the idea of construction of the integrated settlement. People don't say it to your face, but they are not liking the houses.[9]

As per the organization's master plan, the building of the integrated settlement required a layout that was more clustered than the original one,

---

[9]   Interview, Majhigaun, 7 October 2018.

in which houses were scattered over the hillside. This meant land had to be exchanged between members of the community. However, this raised two problems. On the one hand, there were some who were not willing to sell their land to people who did not own land in the settlement project area, or to exchange their land with them. On the other hand, some poor families, who had no land at all to exchange, were worried about being overburdened with debt because, in addition to purchasing a plot for the new building, they also had to invest money in the building of the house.

Even when the reconstruction of the 53 houses was contracted out to a private contractor, it was the organization, not the Majhis, that chose the contracting agency and set the terms and conditions. The Majhis could have reconstructed their houses by using locally available construction materials such as stone, mud, sand, and wood, However, in the name of a model settlement, it was made compulsory in the contract, mainly by the organization and the contracting agency, to use interlocking bricks to build the houses. Hence, the cost of building a house went up to NPR 700,000 (c. USD 6,360).[10] However, the contract did not specify matters such as foundation depth, wall size, room size, and so on.

Accordingly, the organization raised funds; however, the majority of the Majhi residents remained unaware of these funds and their sources, and they did not know anything about whether and how the funds were being or would be utilized in their welfare and interest. Surprisingly, there were no Majhi representatives in any of the committees of the organization.

Majhi perspectives on the new houses

Under the integrated settlement development project, the Majhis were given different types and designs of houses from the ones they had before the 2015 earthquakes. Before the earthquakes, most Majhis had houses of more than one storey. While they used the ground floor for living space and a kitchen, they would store food grains on the upper floor. Most of them were living as joint families of up to 18 people. Those with houses of more than two storeys used their top floor for storing grain, their middle floor as living and eating space, and the ground floor for keeping livestock. A few of them who

---

[10]   The contractor also produces the interlocking bricks.

had one-storey houses with one door and small windows had partitioned sections of the ground floor for use as a kitchen, for living space, and for food grain storage. Most houses had more than one room and their own spacious verandas and balconies. They had yards near their houses, and most had a separate space in the house in which to keep their deities.

The new houses have uniform designs (Figure 5.2). They are single-storey houses with three rooms, a front door, and a couple of windows, and are built of concrete, interlocking bricks, stone, wood, and tin. Most Majhis believe that their houses are stronger and earthquake resilient, and are having their first experience of living inside a modern looking house. They are also glad that the organization has promised to build infrastructure and facilities in the community such as paved roads, drainage systems, drinking water, electricity, sanitation, open spaces, a children- and disabled-friendly community building, a children's park, a water fountain, an open air theatre, water sprinklers, a cultural stage, a temple, a children's learning centre, an integrated livestock shed (*goth*), and so on. However, the houses are not spacious, and there is little space between the walls of the houses to each side. Most of the residents were concerned that they would not be able to keep all their food grain, clothes, and other belongings in the new houses. They were

Figure 5.2 All the houses in the community are of the same size and built of interlocking bricks. Attached to the right is the toilet.

Source: Photograph taken by author on 15 February 2018.

also worried that it would be difficult for them to host and accommodate guests for overnight stays. One of the families which runs a small grocery shop in the community has been looking for land near the settlement on which to build a new house for running the shop, while another has built a two-storey house, using wood, stones, mud, and corrugated galvanized iron (CGI) sheets, and shifted their shop to these premises. This latter family was far happier with the house they have built themselves and expressed their dislike of the house built under the model settlement project. Many members of the community regarded the type of house built in their own way as satisfying their needs.

The usefulness and appropriateness of the new houses was questioned from the very beginning, especially after the first foundations were laid and local people learned that they would not be allowed to use firewood for cooking inside them. Those who relied on agriculture and livestock rearing for their living, and thus needed to use firewood to cook animal food (*kundo*) for their cattle, were especially concerned about this. Several of them informed me that they needed to make another shelter for making *jaand* and *raksi* (traditional alcoholic beverages), while most were of the view that they would need to create kitchens in separate buildings because they would not be able to afford liquefied petroleum gas (LPG) for cooking.

Gradually they were told that they would not be permitted to keep their cattle in sheds near the settlement, in order to prevent the area from getting dirty, although Majhis have traditionally kept livestock such as cows, goats, chickens, and pigs near their houses. They were led to make separate arrangements for cooking and living at one house and cattle and food grains a bit further away from the settlement (Figure 5.3).

Although the residents were told that they would not be allowed to build temporary shelters near their new houses, some had already constructed separate shelters near the settlement, where they had stored grain and other goods; some had even used them for sleeping. Several of them wished that they had the flexibility to build houses of two storeys or more, which would meet their needs. However, the residents could not add a floor to the tops of their new houses or extend the houses sideways, due to the houses' structure and the lack of space. Several of the residents also did not find the new toilets convenient for use because they were very cramped and did not have proper water and sanitation facilities. The septic tanks located right in front of each house were very shallow which meant that they would fill up very quickly (Figure 5.4).

Figure 5.3 Most Majhis had been using these temporary shelters for both keeping their food grains and accommodation for the five years since the earthquakes.

Source: Photograph taken by author on 30 September 2019.

Figure 5.4 Every house has a very small and shallow septic tank such as this without any drainage linked to it.

Source: Photograph taken by author on 30 September 2019.

Likewise, some families were also not so happy to have new neighbours and to find themselves located far away from their previous neighbours, who would often be relatives (*afno santan*). The following statement by a male interlocutor represents how people in the community feel about the new houses:

> People who were previously living freely have been dragged into a small space. I think it is like packing people tightly into the bottom [of something]. This house is only for sleeping in after dinner. It will be merely for showing (*dekhaunako lagi*) and will not be very useful.[11]

People also expressed concern about the heat they felt in the new houses during summer, due to the roofs being made of CGI sheets, and said that it made the houses completely unliveable, while others were not happy to have the main door to the rear of the house. Hence, all families have realized that they have to either build additional houses (of stone and mud) that better serve their needs or keep the currently used temporary shelters (*tahara*) for the storage of food and goods. The majority of them are thinking of building separate sheds to shelter their livestock. They argued that if they had been able to use the NPR 700,000 (c. USD 6,360) themselves, they could have built far more spacious two-storeyed, four-roomed houses with concrete and pillars.

Traditions, culture, and ritual practices

Post-disaster reconstruction has implications for identity, traditional lives, cultural values, and practices (Hörhager 2015; Oliver-Smith 1996, 1991; Simpson 2013). Hence, it is argued that reconstruction plans, approaches, and implementations should be culturally appropriate and sensitive to traditions and cultural needs (Razani 1984). The continuity of rituals, it is emphasized, is instrumental because they have the potential to foster social interactions which can contribute to enhancing solidarity in a community (Dussaillant and Guzmán 2014: 808–32).

---

[11] Interview, Majhigaun, 7 October 2018.

Majhis in Nepal generally carry out various cultural and religious activities and celebrate many feasts and festivals, plus birth-related, marriage-related, and death-related ceremonies and rituals. They offer everything to their ancestors before carrying out the rituals. They perform a range of different rituals in honour of various gods and deities. On one of the major festivals of the Majhis, Koshi Puja, all seven tributaries of Saptakoshi are worshipped: Indrawati, Sunkoshi, Tamakoshi, Dudhkoshi, Likhu, Arun, and Tamor (Majhi 2006). They perform Chipne during the Dashain[12] festival (see later), and carry out rites and rituals such as Pitri Karya (a practice in honour of one's deceased ancestors), a naming ceremony (Nuharan), a weaning ceremony (Pasni), and so on. In many of the feasts and festivals, they sacrifice livestock, prepare and drink *chang*, burn wood fires, and dance all night (in Pitri Puja/Karya) in the courtyards of their houses.[13] They used to keep images of the deities and gods in corners inside their houses, or on the upper floors in multi-storeyed houses. Majhis do not allow other people and outsiders to see their *kul deuta* (lineage deities). It is usually elders, a shaman, a son-in-law, a sister's children, and other knowledgeable people who act as their priests. Offerings are made to ancestors wishing for happiness, good health, and better life for the family, as well as better crops and the safety of livestock.

The impacts of the 2015 earthquakes and the adoption of this reconstruction approach and settlement design have not only hindered Majhis from adequately protecting and worshipping their various gods and deities, but have also required them to compromise on the ways in which they perform their religious and traditional activities and celebrate their feasts and festivals. Since they need a certain configuration and quantity of space for these practices, their continuity in the new houses has been compromised. Some families have stopped carrying out their cultural practices, while the majority have maintained them but in somewhat different ways. It is evident that that the organization defines 'sustainability' in very limited terms, often equating it with materialistic advancement, modern building structures, and economic prosperity while overlooking the

---

12 Dashain, also known as Vijaya Dashami, is a major festival for Hindus in Nepal, and falls during the period of September–October each year. It is celebrated for 10–15 days; however, the first, seventh, eighth, ninth, and tenth days are considered to be the most important ones.

13 See also Music Nepal (2014).

preservation of specific historical, cultural, social, and traditional values. In this regard, the manager of the organization stated in an interview:

> The reconstruction initiative in the settlement involves two parts/ aspects: housing (construction of houses) and other infrastructure development, and other indicators that are essential for any integrated settlement: community building, road, retaining wall, water facility/ fountain, electricity, children's park, septic tank, a community gate, and so on. We asked to make the houses with bricks, mortar, and cement because they are disaster resilient.[14]

Likewise, there appears to be some contradiction in the integrated settlement project's avowed aim of preserving and promoting the identity and culture of the Majhis, while at the same time also encouraging the use of modern materials for house construction and the development of physical infrastructure, one aim of which is to facilitate homestay programmes in the community as also stated elsewhere on the NGO's official website and 3D animation of the Majhi Basti (settlement).

> The integrated settlement will be developed as a home stay destination for national and expatriate guests.[15]

> [The] NGO has a plan to construct [a] Children['s] Park, community hall, auditorium, health post, and stone paving road. After all these facilities, [the] Majhi settlement will be declared as a home stay destination.[16]

In fact, the evidence indicates that the Majhis could be rapidly delinked and dissociated from their past due to the adverse effects of the use of new materials and structures. Indeed, their sense of belonging and ownership of their new homes has already become problematic and weak (Baniya 2018).

Majhis are very protective of their religion, beliefs, and culture, as evidenced in the fact that they discouraged religious groups from introducing and publicizing their religion in the locality after the

---

[14]   Interview, Kathmandu, 18 August 2019.
[15]   'Project Background' section of the website of the organization.
[16]   'Locals Set Example of Integrated Settlement' (website of the organization).

earthquakes. For example, according to some interlocutors, immediately after the earthquakes, some Christian groups visited the community asking to start some religious practices but the Majhis told them that they did not want to convert from their (Hindu) religion and hence the groups went back. People from other castes and even their own daughters married to others are not allowed to enter the house to see their *kul deuta* (lineage deities), which may be covered to prevent outsiders' shadows from falling upon them. Many families said they had kept their god covered and separate, using curtains, in the temporary houses they inhabited after the earthquakes and one Majhi male also said that his family had kept their *kul deuta* in the same old damaged house while their new house was under construction. Some of them were planning to keep their gods in temporary shelters where they felt they could be better protected in the longer term. One 60-year-old male Majhi expressed sentimentally:

> After the earthquake, the gods have also been helpless/deserted (*deutako pani testai bichalli ta ho ni*). Now, the deity is also situated in one place [of temporary shelter]. We have to make a new house for our rituals and worships.[17]

One of the cultural and religious practices most badly affected by the impacts of the earthquakes is Chipne, a ritual performed during the Dashain festival for six days from the day of Astami (the eighth day of Dashain). Using mud, rice flour, and ink made from bean leaves, Majhis write the names of deceased relatives on their house walls, along with images of dead bodies, soldiers and hunters, animals (fish, peacock, elephant, horse, and so on), and trees. On the day of Astami the wall is covered with cow dung and inscribed with these words and images. Songs associated with the images drawn on the walls are sung accordingly. Those who can sing keep singing throughout the night, entreating their ancestors to take all their property (the things written and drawn on the walls, plus various offerings) and leave. After the earthquakes, the loss of their houses and walls made it very difficult to carry out these rituals. While they were living in temporary shelters, some erected makeshift walls of plywood boards for this purpose while others conducted the rituals in the open space outside their temporary shelters. For example, one family inscribed Chipne on a curtain

---

17   Interview, Majhigaun, 15 July 2018.

in 2018 and on a plywood partition inside their temporary shelter in 2019. Many Majhis, especially the more elderly ones, were very much concerned about protecting and worshipping their deities in the new houses because they found the concrete walls culturally inappropriate. Hence, some of them discussed the need to construct a common house for performing such rituals, some considered making a separate temporary shelter for this purpose, and others were thinking about continuing the practice within their new houses, with certain compromises. But some families stopped performing Chipne altogether.

Likewise, the earthquakes also affected the ways in which Majhis worshipped their ancestors during Kul Puja (Kulyan Puja or Pitri Karya). Kul Puja is performed inside the house. It is compulsory that at least one family member from the same *kul* (patrilineage) attends the function and provides the ritual materials; however, *kutumba* members (any male or female members from the maternal side) are not allowed to participate. A separate house is created for the deities, its door is closed, and outsiders are not allowed to enter. Performing these rituals also involves lighting a fire. Once the ritual has been completed, Majhis have to dig a hole in the middle of the floor of the house and bury the materials that have been used. After the earthquakes, it became impossible for these rituals to be carried out properly. Some carried them out in a separate shed built for the purpose outside their temporary shelters, while others returned to their destroyed houses and performed the rituals there. During a discussion about shifting the Pitri Karya to a new community building, which the Majhis would have to build themselves, a 57-year-old local Majhi leader opined:

> We will have to make it and even if they say we cannot, we will
> have to make it. We will have to make a separate house otherwise
> the ancestors will in the future terrorize us and eat our lungs, heart,
> and liver (*natra bholi-parsi kalejo, mutu, phokso khaidinchan*). Our
> ancestors were very strong ... there was no one stronger than our
> ancestors.[18]

Likewise, several Majhis reported that the earthquakes had also affected how they performed the *goth puja*, a ritual dedicated to the deity of the

---

[18]   Interview, Majhigaun, 13 July 2018.

livestock shed. Most Majhis used to perform this by worshipping in a corner of their animal sheds by erecting a stone god or making a hole (*khopcha*) in the wall of the shed. Since the earthquakes, many have lost their permanent sheds, and while some have continued *goth puja* in temporary sheds, others have discontinued this ritual. In this regard, an elderly Majhi male said, 'The earthquake damaged the *goth deuta*. Now I do not know where the gods are, they [referring to the lost residence and the stone statue of the deity] are lost (*deutai harae ani*).'[19]

Interview participants informed us that, due to a lack of space in the temporary shelters, they were not able to celebrate other important feasts and festivals. Not being able to accommodate guests in their temporary houses had also been a great concern; this persists, even in their new houses.

Loan burdens and a sense of deception

Gradually, Majhis became increasingly restless due to the unexpectedly large loan burdens they had incurred for the reconstruction of their houses and also due to the delays in reconstruction. Consequently, as is alluded to in this section, they were unhappy with the overall approach of the construction of the model settlement and with their own youth leaders for facilitating the project.

In addition to the reconstruction grant of NPR 300,000 (c. USD 2,700), each of the eligible households was made to take NPR 400,000 (c. USD 3,600) as a loan and keep their land as collateral at a bank in order to complete the reconstruction of their houses. Those who took out these loans before the government introduced a new guideline in September 2018[20] had to pay NPR 6,000 (c. USD 54) every month for seven years, while those who took them out after the enactment of the guidelines had to pay NPR 7000 (c. USD 64)[21] per month. Many household members informed us that they

---

[19]   Interview, Majhigaun, 15 February 2018.

[20]   *Sauliyatpurna Karjakalagi Byaj Anudan Sambandhi Ekikrit Karyabidhi 2075* (Unified Working Procedure for Interest Subsidy on Subsidized Loans 2075 v.s.)

[21]   According to the new guideline, the interest on the loan was 14 per cent, half of which would be borne by the Government of Nepal while the beneficiaries had to pay the other half, which meant an interest rate at least 5 per cent higher than the initial loan provision.

were reluctant to take out loans; however, they had no choice but to provide their landownership document (*lalpurja*) to proceed for the loan. Most community members were not fully aware of the loan application process or the terms and conditions of the loan; rather, they were just asked to sign the application papers and provide the land documents to the local youth leaders, who undertook to facilitate the process.

According to some interlocutors, leaders threatened to lock up their houses or ostracize them from the community if they did not take out the loan and pay it back with interest. Some of them were compelled to take out the loan because they were notified that they needed to either produce evidence of their house having been built within the deadline stipulated by the government or else return the first tranche of NPR 50,000 (c. USD 450) of the reconstruction grant they had received, which some of them had already spent. During a visit to the community in October 2019, the author discovered that some members had even refused to shift to their new house from their temporary shelter because they felt that they would not be able to pay back the loan.

Most of the Majhis depended on wage incomes and were very much worried about having been burdened by the loan and interest. In this regard, a middle-aged Majhi woman stated, 'People here have never taken even NPR 100,000 as a loan.... They cannot imagine taking NPR 400,000'.[22]

In the beginning, the understanding of most Majhis was that the organization would provide material, technical, and financial support for the reconstruction of their houses so that they would not have to take on the burden of additional costs beyond the reconstruction grant. However, the Majhis were left to reconstruct their houses themselves, using a combination of the reconstruction grant and their own resources. Many of them were also unclear whether the organization was going to pay off the debts (loans and interest) they had incurred. The organization had publicly stated that it would raise funds through various sources, including state and non-state agencies and individuals as well as through various charity shows.[23] Confusion also arose from the fact that at times the Majhis were told that the organization would pay off their loans and sometimes they were told that they would have to contribute their labour to infrastructure construction work in the settlement in order to repay them. This conflicting information

---

[22]   Interview, Majhigaun, 8 October 2019.
[23]   A Nepali language newspaper published on 19 July 2017 (4 Shrawan 2074 v.s.).

seemed to have further fuelled their worries about the incremental growth of the loan and the risk that they would end up greatly indebted.

Several protested that they would have preferred to rebuild their houses themselves and would have already done so if they had been able to take out the loan and use it for this purpose. They were confident that they would have completed these reconstructions on time and at a lower cost (they claimed the government grant of NPR 300,000 would have been sufficient) because they could have used stones, sand, and mud, which were easily available near their community and they would have to have bought only materials such as bricks, cement, and steel elements. They could also have used exchange labour. In addition, individual donors had supported some materials such as CGI sheets and water tanks.

Likewise, local people were mobilized for the construction of the integrated settlement after the first contractor withdrew from the project because it did not receive funds on time (Figure 5.5). Some were carrying out construction activities such as fitting toilet pans and electrification even during the second half of 2019. Some locals worked continuously for two–

Figure 5.5 Local Majhis involved in the reconstruction of their community.
Source: Photograph taken by author on 15 February 2018.

three months. Some were partially paid (at a rate of NPR 1,000–1,200 (c. USD 9–11) per day), some had not received their wages for months, while some had not been paid at all. Many of them had to stop working: some engaged in their own agricultural work while others sought alternative employment. Consequently, this created dissatisfaction among the workers with the committee leaders. Some residents even accused two prominent youth leaders of misappropriating funds and benefitting from the whole settlement project.

The Majhis were also dissatisfied that their complaints and grievances were not being attended to or addressed. An elderly male Majhi fumed and stated, 'We know how difficult it is to run the household, we know our suffering and it is because of this loan that we have not been able to live happily.'[24] Furthermore, as most families found that the new three-room house would not be spacious enough and hence felt the need to build another house or shelter for living or storage space, several of them were also concerned about the likelihood of further financial burdens.

Ramifications for social cohesion and relations

Generally, it is said that social capital, in the form of a leadership's ability to mobilize resources and to provide ownership to community associations, plays a crucial role in developing confidence, trust, understanding, and cooperation among the various actors involved (Coleman 1990; Putnam 1995). It is observed elsewhere that social capital (Aldrich 2011; Murphy 2007; Zhao 2013) also plays an enabling role in recovery and reconstruction. Dussaillant and Guzmán (2014) remind us that disasters promote the construction of social capital and that in the wake of a disaster, a 'trust begets trust' dynamic emerges. In addition, receiving support from the authorities and the promotion of effective modalities in the aftermath of a disaster help to develop positive perceptions of a leadership and may also open up avenues leading towards the promotion of stronger personal and communal trust, further strengthening social capital (Zhang and Wang 2010).

On the other hand, declining social capital due to a deficit of trust and solidarity caused either by a lack of resources or delays in reconstruction

---

[24] Interview, Majhigaun, 7 October 2019.

might also lead to disappointment among those affected (Zhang and Wang 2010), causing further social problems and vulnerabilities. These might also be created by suspicion about newly adopted innovations such as new housing arrangements and new land patterns (Partridge 1989) and doubts about the leadership of the planning and implementation process (Dussaillant and Guzmán 2014).

The Majhis have historically been considered cooperative, and several of them, especially the youths, were very actively supporting their fellow Majhis during the rescue and relief phases of the immediate aftermath of the earthquakes. Fellow Majhi residents placed high trust in them, and external agencies and individuals and state institutions also became interested in engaging with them for relief and rapid-recovery-related activities in the community. Their serious efforts in bringing the organization to support the construction of the model settlement were also greatly praised in the beginning. Similarly, the NGO representative and local head teacher mentioned earlier had also received widespread approval and appreciation from the Majhis. Some youths were of the view that the earthquakes had taught them the lesson that they have to maintain friendly and cordial relationships with everyone in the community and should be cooperating with each other.

However, during the course of the reconstruction of the settlement, it was evident that these forms of social capital weakened due to various reasons. It is impossible to present the causes of this weakening in detail here, for reasons of space, but they included factors such as a lack of support from the government, a lack of adequate information regarding reconstruction-related policies and procedures and grant requirements, changes in government policies, a lack of adequate financial resources to build individual houses, difficulties and delays in receiving government subsidies and loans, the non-availability of and transportation difficulties with construction materials due to the rainy season, land-related disputes and problems, a shortage of skilled labourers, and delays in the inspection and verification of the houses. These hindered the reconstruction process and delayed it for more than two years beyond the promised date for completion.

The findings from the fieldwork elucidated that the delays made the local Majhis increasingly sceptical about the feasibility, benefits, and appropriateness of the whole integrated settlement project. Majhis, including the youths closely associated with the project, learned that the project manager of the organization had joined it after leaving his previous job and that his salary was being paid by the project. His visits to the settlement became more and more infrequent as the reconstruction process was delayed and slowed down. Hence, they became increasingly sceptical of the manager's and the organization's commitment.

Additionally, there were also rifts between and discontentment among some Majhis about issues related to the exchange of land and transfers of landownership, which are still unresolved at the time of writing even though the houses have now been built. Also, families were initially promised that the work on the new houses would include the plastering and painting of the walls. Families felt deceived when they were asked to plaster and paint their own houses and bear the cost of this work themselves. The delays and unmet expectations, as well as the perceptions and experiences discussed in the previous sections, led these youths and some prominent persons like the school head teacher to feel that their social prestige and image were increasingly at stake, as trust among the Majhis weakened.

On one occasion, during parliamentary elections, a local leader affiliated to a Left party was asked by the president of the organization to rally the support of the Majhi community for a candidate belonging to a party other than his own. When most Majhis would not support the idea, he felt he had been put in a difficult situation.

Although it was resolved through negotiation, the Majhis and the party that had entered into a contract with their community had some conflicts. This almost escalated into a legal battle when the contractor refused to continue the reconstruction work without receiving additional funds from the Majhis, which put local Majhis in a predicament as they were one of the parties to the contract.[25] Also, Majhis—both male and female—used to do manual work and skilled work such as carpentry and masonry, and they could exchange labour and help each other in reconstructing their houses. However, after contracting out the reconstruction project to a different contracting agency, the practice of exchange of labour which was common among Majhis was also affected.

The various experiences outlined here led the Majhis to develop a negative perception of the whole concept and approach of an integrated settlement,

---

[25] A signed contract between local Majhis and the contractor company in the presence of a representative of the organization.

of the organization, and of their local leaders, and led to tensions between the youth leaders and the organization. By the time of my most recent visit, the general frustration with the organization and the youth leaders had become more pronounced. The Majhis had become very suspicious that the youth leaders had appropriated some funds through commissions from various reconstruction activities such as contracting out reconstruction and through the purchasing of construction materials. A Majhi man in his late 50s stated:

> Would anyone work without any benefit? Everyone is unhappy about it (*sabaiko man ta phateko chha*).... If the loan is not paid by the organization, it is sure that there will be fighting in the community (*marpit pakkai hunchha hunchha*).[26]

Conclusion

The planning and implementation of the integrated settlement for the Majhis was flawed, ill-prepared, and based on limited perspectives of constructing modern buildings and infrastructure. My findings suggest that a standard design and reconstruction approach does not fulfil the socioeconomic and cultural needs of the affected individuals and communities. Their lack of participation and involvement in the decision-making process, the coercive approach to securing approval of decisions made by a few, the provision of unclear and misleading information, the ignoring of sociocultural aspects, the lack of alternative designs and solutions for reconstruction, and delays in reconstruction, all led to frustration amongst the Majhis. The lack or the limited nature of participation by the affected local community in decision-making and setting objectives and the lack of opportunity to explain their needs and concerns, combined with strict technical restrictions on the design and choice of construction materials, may hinder the construction of affordable and acceptable houses. As recommended by some studies (Duyne Barenstein 2006; Hassenforder, Smajgl, and Ward 2015; Lizarralde et al. 2016), the findings of this study also suggest that enhancing 'owner-driven reconstruction' or 'building back better' requires earthquake-affected people

---

[26] Personal communication, 14 March 2020.

and communities to be involved in reconstructing their houses according to their individual requirements and preferences, which may help to preserve their social fabric, cultural identity, and traditions. A mere emphasis on the technical and compliance imperatives of resilient and safer houses is likely to lead to further vulnerabilities, as people make adjustments or rebuild homes of their own when their sociocultural needs are not met by the house that has not been chosen or constructed by them. My findings also suggest that a sense of ownership on the part of the affected is shaped by a range of factors, including the extent to which the reconstruction of physical structures imparts importance to sociocultural concerns and religious needs, gives them the freedom to make decisions about the reconstruction, and allows them to choose designs, construction materials, their immediate neighbours, and their financial commitments.

If reconstruction plans and their implementation do not meet expectations, it might not only destroy the essence and identity of a people and community, but also generate additional burdens and vulnerabilities among the affected families, weaken pre-existing social ties, and aggravate distrust and conflicts among members of the community, as in the case of the Majhis. Nevertheless, the study also recognizes that affected communities might need technical support and guidance on complying with building codes and rules and regulations for constructing safer houses.

In the context of the construction of integrated settlements, including the relocation of certain unsafe and non-habitable settlements in post-disaster situations, important lessons can be drawn from the findings of this study.

6

Humanitarian Responses of I/NGOs after the 2015 Earthquakes

Empirical Evidence from Gorkha, Sindhupalchok, and Southern Lalitpur*

Amrita Gurung and *Jeevan Baniya*

Introduction

The aftermath of World War II saw a proliferation of non-governmental organizations (NGOs) and international non-governmental organizations (INGOs) worldwide. Like other countries in the Global South, Nepal too saw a rise in the number of I/NGOs after 1990, under institution-building and civil-society-strengthening projects designed to foster participatory democracy, good governance, and development (Frewer 2013; Suleiman 2013, cited in Jones et al. 2014). While some argue that the Nepali term *nagarik samaj* is equivalent to the English term 'civil society' and that the term came into use mainly after 1990 (Shah 2008), M. S. Tamang (2017) notes that the concept of civil society emerged in the context of the struggle against the Panchayat system to protect the rights of people as equal citizens, which *culminated* in the political change of 1990. This 'civil society' comprised a wide array of traditional self-help groups, human rights and professional organizations, ethnic and caste-based advocacy groups, and

* This chapter is based on research conducted by Social Science Baha and supported by the American Jewish World Service (AJWS). The authors would like to thank Sita Nepali, Manju Gurung, Ratna Kambang, Binod Dulal, Swarna Kumar Jha, and Keshav Bashyal for their fieldwork contributions.

collectives of independent individuals aiming to achieve specific goals. In many instances these functioned very similarly to I/NGOs (M. S. Tamang 2017). Furthermore, Heaton-Shrestha and Adhikari (2011) stress that these organizations' everyday works were often evaluated as performances which led to them being perceived as 'political' by state authorities during the struggle against King Gyanendra's direct rule after 2005.

Increasingly, I/NGOs may be seen to be serving as alternatives for government (Lassa 2018), which is typically characterized as 'bureaucratic' and 'elite-centred' (D. Lewis 2014 in Carrasco and O'Brien 2018). In Nepal, NGOs tend to be associated with groups in civil society which lack a broad membership. Some have criticized them for being undemocratic and lacking accountability and transparency (J. Ghimire 2008: 91; Shah 2008; S. Tamang 2005, cited in Baniya 2014); it is alleged that they work under the direction of foreign agents and lack autonomy (Dahal, 2001:113). Panday argues that, because major policies are formulated by foreigners in the headquarters of bilateral and multilateral aid organizations, Nepal's bureaucracy does not have any influence in the process. This not only undermines state institutions, but also distracts the state's attention away from public programmes and services (Panday 1999, 2011, cited in Baniya 2014).

Also, I/NGOs have increasingly taken on development and emergency work, channelling a significant portion of the overall aid budget. Several hundred organizations worked in partnership with local organizations during the humanitarian response to Nepal's 2015 earthquakes. More than 450 aid organizations responded to the emergency (UN OCHA/Nepal 2015). Claimed to be synonymous with or representative of civil society (Benson, Twigg, and Myers 2002, cited in Jones et al., 2014), the number of I/NGOs increased in the aftermath of disasters in Indonesia (Lassa 2018), Japan and the Philippines (Carrasco and O'Brien 2018), China (Lu and Xu, 2014), and Nepal (K. D. Regmi 2016; Jones et al. 2014).

Following the earthquakes, Nepal witnessed a large inflow of new I/NGOs. Meanwhile, the I/NGOs that were already present in the country shifted their previous priorities and programmes to relief, recovery, and reconstruction work. This was because large-scale disasters are known to challenge the normalcy of affected communities, and fragile states like Nepal lack the capacity to cope with their impacts (Tierney 2012; K. D. Regmi 2016; Carrasco and O'Brien 2018; Lassa 2018; Jones et al. 2014). Nepal first institutionalized disaster management with the enactment of the

Natural Disaster Relief Act in 1982; since then this Act has provided a basis for I/NGOs to work in the sector of disaster risk management (Government of Nepal 2013). The work carried out in this sector by I/NGOs prior to 2015 acted as a mere prelude to the overwhelming response the country received in the wake of the 2015 earthquakes (Gaire, Castro Delgado, and Arcos González 2015; Boersma et al. 2016).

Some suggest that such humanitarian support may have comparative advantages, with complementarities in many contexts (Zyck and Krebs 2015), while others critique the 'top-down' development approach for largely dismissing indigenous practices, collective knowledge, and skills (Enns, Bersaglio, and Kepe 2014). Critics of the top-down approach propose a participatory development approach as an alternative to humanitarian responses during times of disaster (K. D. Regmi 2016). Global commitments such as the Sendai Framework on Disaster Risk Reduction 2015–2030 have endorsed the need to localize humanitarian efforts in order to 'build back better', and community participation has been seen to contribute to substantial change when real decision-making powers are given to local people over the different stages of post-disaster rebuilding (UNISDR 2015; Davidson et al. 2007; Lizarralde, Johnson and Davidson 2009; Mubyazi and Hutton 2012). This study is situated in these broader debates. Little is known about how and through which mechanisms and strategies humanitarian responses were delivered in the aftermath of the earthquakes in Nepal, nor do we know what implications they have had for local capacity-building.

Drawing on interviews conducted with representatives of I/NGOs,[1] community-based organizations (CBOs), civil society organizations (CSOs), community leaders, and politicians in three earthquake-affected districts of Nepal (Gimdi in southern Lalitpur, Thuloshirubari in Sindhupalchok, and Fujel in Gorkha) in November and December 2017, this chapter explores the I/NGOs' working modalities, strategies, and roles and their impacts on disaster-affected people and communities. First, we argue that the I/NGOs' response strategies are diverse and shaped by their disaster-related policy frameworks, working-area priorities, and pre-existing networks. Second, although responses from the I/NGOs may play a crucial role in local capacity-building in some cases, the nature of the partnership forged between an

---

[1]   In this chapter, we have treated I/NGOs as entities which provide monetary support to local partners, which implement programmes at the local level.

I/NGO and a local organization seems to be the key factor determining whether it will have positive or negative impacts on local capacity-building and the local ownership of humanitarian activities. Finally, we argue that humanitarian responses based on limited consultation with and limited participation of affected people and communities lead not only to ineffective programmes, but also to the perpetuation of social vulnerabilities and caste-based discrimination. In fact, our research suggests that many people perceive the I/NGOs' work performance as little more than *dekhauna ra bhannalai*, 'in order to show-and-tell'.[2]

Partnership and working modalities

Effective disaster responses and relief and recovery efforts help to build resilience against future disasters (Mustafa 2003). After the 2015 earthquakes, Nepal conducted a Post-disaster Needs Assessment (PDNA) and constructed a Post-disaster Recovery Framework (PDRF) for assessing needs and priorities in recovery planning. These adopted a whole-of-society approach to 'building back better' for recovery and reconstruction activities (NPC 2015a, 2015b; NRA 2016b). The participatory development approach (K. D. Regmi 2016), the 'cooperative approach' (Lu and Xu, 2014), and the decentralization of disaster governance (Daly et al. 2017) are emphasized as effective humanitarian responses in disaster-affected communities. Furthermore, Ward (2011) recognizes that the involvement of local communities can make life-saving differences in strengthening the resilience of an affected population. In line with this, invoking several global commitments, including the Sendai Framework (2015–2030), the Government of Nepal introduced a 'Procedure Relating to Mobilization of Non-governmental Organizations for Reconstruction and Rehabilitation, 2016' (NRA 2016b).[3] In particular, section 7(15) of the Procedure states:

---

[2] Interview no. 25, chairperson, forest group and coffee producer, Gimdi, southern Lalitpur, 26 November 2017.

[3] The Procedure was introduced in pursuance to Section 31 of the 'Act Relating to Reconstruction of the Earthquake Affected Structures, 2015' to mobilize I/NGOs' assistance in the reconstruction and rehabilitation of structures damaged by the 2015 earthquakes in an integrated, collaborative, and justifiable manner.

Any international non-governmental agency shall, while carrying out works, have to do so in partnership with at least one national non-governmental organization which is pertinent to partnerships to be formulated between donor I/NGOs and local level NGOs, community based organizations (CBOs), and other civil society organizations.

In line with the Procedure, the I/NGOs in our study sites worked in partnership with local actors.[4] Locals across the study sites referred to I/NGOs as *maathilo* (upper) donor organizations because they provided funds for most local organizations and they came from outside. Partnerships between centrally located I/NGOs and local organizations were contingent on factors such as programme area, working sector, target population, and prior experience of expending a certain volume of aid. For example, Oxfam Nepal[5] and the Lutheran World Federation[6] (LWF) selected the Environment and Public Health Organization[7] (ENPHO) and the Integrated Community Development Organization[8] (ICDO) respectively as their implementing partners in southern Lalitpur because they were existing local organizations. Similarly, HELP Germany[9] chose Tuki Sangh

---

[4] By 'local actors' we mean CBOs, businesses, industry associations, academic and research entities, religious institutions, government institutions, national societies, and national NGOs.

[5] Oxfam Nepal has been working in Nepal for more than three decades and works in humanitarian response programmes, sustainable development, poverty alleviation, and livelihood programmes in rural communities.

[6] The LWF, a country programme of the LWF World Service, based in Kathmandu, has been working with marginalized and disadvantaged communities in disaster risk reduction, emergency preparedness and response, sustainable livelihoods, and community-led actions for governance and justice since 1984.

[7] The ENPHO is a Kathmandu-based NGO established in 1990 which works in the areas of water, sanitation, and hygiene (WASH), environment, and public health.

[8] The ICDO, established in 2010, is a network of the CBOs of Lalitpur and works in the sectors of sustainable livelihoods, disaster risk response, WASH, Climate Change Adaptation (CCA), CBO development and strengthening, land rights, and good governance.

[9] HELP Germany works in the education sector and funded the reconstruction of schools and livelihoods in Sindhupalchok after the earthquake.

Sunkoshi in Sindhupalchok as its partner to implement programmes related to recovery and reconstruction, and A Drop of Life[10] chose the Community Resource Centre[11] in Fujel, where most works were reconstruction related.

Partnerships also depended on what budget was available. HELP Germany had initially planned to construct a total of 1,734 houses through a particular local NGO partner. This changed as the number of households that needed houses grew, due to an increase in the number of nuclear families.[12] The I/NGO dissolved the earlier partnership and formed a new one with a different district-based organization, Tuki Sangh Sunkoshi.[13] Speculation arose that there had been disagreement over the programme budget with the earlier partner organization, and that this had led to the change.

I/NGOs had also formed new beneficiary groups in our study sites as part of their programme implementation strategies. These groups and committees were formed to undertake programme implementation in livelihood areas such as agriculture, livestock rearing, and reconstruction of private houses and public buildings. For example, in Sindhupalchok, HELP Germany formed a total of 58 different groups[14] and a Majhi community formed a seven-member Locality Improvement Committee to coordinate with an external organization in the building of an integrated settlement, while in southern Lalitpur, Recode Nepal, ENPHO, Poverty Alleviation Organization, Sahas Nepal, and the Icarus Nepal Group formed different beneficiary groups to run agriculture-related programmes and mothers' groups.[15] Similarly, Women for Human Rights (WHR) Nepal and the Association for Dalit Women's Advancement of Nepal (ADWAN) formed

---

[10]   A Drop of Life is based in Hong Kong and works mainly in ensuring water and sanitation in Cambodia, Nepal, and China.

[11]   The Community Resource Centre is based in Chitwan.

[12]   Interview no. 89, ward coordinator, WCF, Thulosirubari, Sindhupalchok, 27 December 2017.

[13]   Interview with members of beneficiary groups of HELP Germany and Tuki Sangh Sunkoshi in Sindhupalchok, December 2017.

[14]   Interview no. 76, chairperson, local CPN-UML (Communist Party of Nepal–Unified Marxist–Leninist) candidate, Thulosirubari, Sindhupalchok, 19 December 2017.

[15]   Interview with local staff members in Gimdi, southern Lalitpur, November 2017.

groups in order to mobilize revolving funds that led many women to undertake vegetable farming and livestock raising in Fujel.[16]

When asked about their tendency to form new groups, I/NGOs explained that existing groups were often non-functioning and that it would require additional time and resources to revive them, whereas forming a new group was much easier. For instance, by forming new mothers' groups in each ward of the village development committee (VDC), Recode Nepal could specifically focus on programmes related to the health and nutrition of new mothers and babies.[17] In contrast, the study also found that Tuki Sangh Sunkoshi, a district-based organization in Thulosirubari, partnered with beneficiary groups previously formed by a micro-finance company, Rural Self-Reliance Development Centre (RSDC),[18] but changed its working modality from saving to income-generating by boosting commercial farming.[19]

Most groups were formed based on various criteria of vulnerability, and included single women, people above 60 years of age, single men, households with more than seven members, and households with no source of income. Despite the I/NGOs' claim to have prioritized vulnerable and marginalized communities, locals were wary of their beneficiary selection processes. Issues of nepotism and favouritism surfaced in I/NGO-led programmes across our study sites. For instance, residents in Fujel claimed that a local NGO employee had diverted WASH-related programmes to his own caste group instead of taking them to the Dalits who were the real intended beneficiaries.[20] Similarly, in Gimdi, locals pointed out that there had been some favouritism at work in recommending participants for mason training by the Ward Citizen Forum (WCF) due to the provision of daily and other allowances for its members.[21]

---

[16] Interview no. 73, social mobilizer, Tuki Sangh Sunkoshi, Thulosirubari, Sindhupalchok, 24 December 2017.

[17] Interview no. 7, field coordinator, Recode Nepal, Gimdi, southern Lalitpur, 26 November 2017.

[18] The RSDC is a micro-finance company that promotes cooperatives (known as *swawalamban sahakari*) in 12 districts.

[19] Interview no. 73, social mobilizer, Tuki Sangh Sunkoshi, Thulosirubari, Sindhupalchok, 24 December 2017.

[20] Interview no. 69, chairperson, school management committee, Fujel, Gorkha, 22 December 2017.

[21] NPR 500 (c. USD 4.5) per day was provided to each mason training participant for the duration of the training. Interview no. 11, programme coordinator, Gimdi, southern Lalitpur, LWF, 24 November 2017.

Challenges and experiences

As noted by Regmi (2016), many NGOs are politically affiliated and they take control of reconstruction. We found that local politicians in Fujel dictated whether or not an organization could carry out its programmes. They demanded a certain percentage of budget share in exchange for allowing I/NGOs to run programmes in their villages. As such, I/NGOs with smaller programme budgets were not given approval. For instance, an NGO had brought a drinking water project to Fujel with a budget of NPR 1,500,000 (c. USD 13,600) but, according to an NRA engineer, 'some people with social and political power told the organization, "only come if you have 22 lakhs [NPR 2.2 million (c. USD 20,000)] budget": so which organization do you think will come if there is bargaining for money even before I/NGOs enter the VDC?'[22] However, there were also other accounts which contrasted with such claims of political interference and bargaining in post-disaster Fujel. A local political leader[23] said:

> [A faith-based organization] wanted to work in Fujel for the long term, but they wanted to do the work of coordination because they did not have a budget. When I found out about this, I immediately told them that if they could not invest money, then they should rather not come to Fujel. What we need is organizations that have long-term and sustainable programmes.

Interviews with organizations that implemented mason training revealed that they could not dismiss participants who had been recommended by VDC officials. These I/NGOs were also disappointed that many of the participants did not actually go on to work as masons after they had received the training. Additionally, these trained masons were considered unqualified to carry out the real reconstruction because they did not have prior experience. Thus, newly trained masons were not given opportunities to carry out reconstruction activities in Gimdi and Fujel. In contrast, people trusted masons in Thulosirubari because they had been trained and hired

---

[22] Interview no. 39, NRA engineer, Fujel, Gorkha, 18 December 2017.
[23] Interview no. 41, political leader, CPN-UML, Fujel, Gorkha, 20 December 2017.

by the Japan International Cooperation Agency (JICA) as mobile masons and largely substituted for VDC engineers and technicians who were not present at most times. The involvement of locals in rebuilding processes as active stakeholders in Thulosirubari validates claims made by Zyck and Krebs (2015) that humanitarian support has a complementary function and facilitates comparative advantages in different contexts. However, women who had taken part in mason training across the sites were not given chances to work as masons due to existing gender norms and prejudices: 'Aaimaaile pani ghar banauna sakchha ra?' (Can women build houses too?)[24]

Other challenges included lack of accessibility. For instance, some I/NGOs lamented not being able to carry out reconstruction programmes in areas where the most vulnerable populations lived: for example, in the higher elevation regions of the study sites which lacked access to roads and transportation. In addition to this, the Government of Nepal's policy was to support housing programmes in compact settlements, which often meant bazaar areas in our study sites.[25] The compact settlements being built by the LWF in Gimdi and the Shweta Shree Foundation in Thulosirubari were cases in point. This suggests a disconnect between policy and response (Hall et al. 2017) because this meant that programmes did not reach those who were living on the margins, often in high-altitude locations that had yet to be connected to the motorable road network.

Likewise, time constraints and the lack of coordination between donor I/NGOs and implementing NGOs, CBOs, and beneficiary groups affected people's day-to-day routines after the earthquake. All the study sites with the exception of Fujel noted a high concentration of I/NGOs that competed for people's time and participation in their programmes. Social mobilizers across the study sites mentioned people being unable to allocate time for all the activities and meetings called by the I/NGOs. It is not surprising that I/NGOs disregarded and circumvented local authority and delivered programmes to their beneficiary groups spread across nine wards of the VDCs. Locals attributed the tendency to what Lu and Xu (2014) describe as

---

[24] Interview no. 51, female mason training participant, Fujel, Gorkha, 26 December 2017.

[25] National Reconstruction Authority, Government of Nepal: 'Procedure relating to Mobilization of Non-governmental Organizations for Reconstruction and Rehabilitation, 2016'.

a 'lack of cooperation' that resulted in a significant waste of resources, time, and energy on the part of both programme implementers and beneficiaries.

The field staff of programme-implementing partners[26] across our study sites complained that they faced increasing pressure from central-level staff. This was particularly evident in the reconstruction of private houses in Gimdi, where central-level staff put pressure on local-level staff to hasten people to build their houses to meet a deadline.[27] In Fujel, I/NGOs were seen to have used local-level staff as per their convenience and to demand work outputs without taking the local situation into consideration. Similarly, a local facilitator of a human rights organization complained that they had to execute what their *mathilo* (upper) donor organization asked them, without much consideration being given to how much money they had to spend to gather people and mobilize them.[28] Inconsistencies and contradictions were observed in some programmes. For example, on the one hand, I/NGOs put pressure on people to finish reconstruction within deadlines, but on the other hand, they provided psychosocial counselling to those same people to deal with the impacts of the earthquake. This vindicates the argument put forward by some scholars (J. Ghimire 2008: 91, 110; Panday 1999 cited in Baniya 2014) that the priorities of the I/NGOs' activities were defined by the donors and elites.

The impact of humanitarian assistance

While acknowledging the positive impacts of humanitarian interventions such as an overall increase in people's awareness, participation in public-infrastructure-building processes, women's involvement in micro-enterprises, and a fair number of employment opportunities, this section reflects on the gaps and limitations of I/NGOs' interventions towards local capacity-building, and the potential risks of this. As in many other disaster contexts, such as India (Sinha 2001), Pakistan (Aijazi 2016), Japan and the

---

[26] Includes national NGOs, district NGOs, CBOs, CSOs, and formal and informal beneficiary groups.

[27] The initial deadline was December 2017 which was then extended for two more months. Derived from interview no. 4, sub-engineer, ICDO, Gimdi, southern Lalitpur, 24 November 2017.

[28] Interview no. 52, facilitator, WHR, Fujel, Gorkha, 27 December 2017.

Philippines (Carrasco and O'Brien 2018), and China (Lu and Xu 2014), our findings indicate that I/NGOs left just as rapidly as they had entered the study sites.

As we have seen, a considerable number of I/NGOs' working modalities involved partnerships with local-level organizations, which included existing groups and newly formed beneficiary groups. The beneficiary groups included mothers' groups, users' groups, agricultural saving and credit groups, and so on. However, the formation of new groups had ramifications insofar as it not only ignored but also disturbed the ecosystem of existing organizations such as CBOs. The chairperson of a local beneficiary group in Gimdi lamented this, saying, 'This organization formed a new beneficiary group with us, taught us a few things, distributed some lemon trees, and left. We haven't heard from them again. The beneficiary group is no longer in existence now.'[29] Similarly, a beneficiary group in Fujel could run health-related training only while they were given money by an I/NGO.[30] Another I/NGO, Help Germany, formed 58 new groups in Thulosirubari to run income-generating programmes, but the groups only functioned as savings groups as opposed to the programme's real objective. I/NGOs also tended to prioritize literate over illiterate populations, regardless of the fact that both were present in the same geographical terrain. This led the latter to view themselves as being excluded from I/NGO support and larger development programmes.[31] For instance, the mostly illiterate Baramu and Majhi people in Thulosirubari claimed that they were not able to get as much relief as their educated counterparts who could 'express and voice' what they wanted. This evidence indicates that many I/NGOs failed to identify the needs of people and to mobilize the existing potential of local organizations in order to build their capacity to respond to a disaster effectively (Bisri and Beniya 2016; K. D. Regmi 2016; Daly et al. 2017).

Misplaced priorities and wasted resources were features of these projects. While some existing savings and credit cooperatives/groups and women's groups did not have the funding to run training programmes even though

---

[29] Interview no. 31, chairperson, Icarus Nepal beneficiary group, Gimdi, southern Lalitpur, 25 November 2017.

[30] Interview no. 53, health assistant, Fujel, Gorkha, 21 December 2017.

[31] Interview no. 48, chairperson, local Baramu organization, Fujel, Gorkha, 25 December 2017.

they had the capacity to do so[32] (which impacted negatively on the overall success of programmes intended to revive livelihood and agriculture), many organizations formed new groups, raised false hopes, and wasted valuable resources and time. Competition between organizations intensified after the earthquakes as they formed new groups and beneficiaries to show that they were doing 'more work than others'.[33] As a consequence, people perceived the programmes as being merely disbursal (*dana chharne*) in nature. This resonates with the argument offered by Jones et al. (2014) that donor assistance can lead to weakening rather than building local institutions and capacities. In southern Lalitpur, this was in parallel with effects that ranged from the slowing down and/or, in the worst cases, disbanding of new beneficiary groups, and to the diminishing interest and participation of locals in the programmes.[34] Complaining about I/NGOs' insensitivities towards existing local capacity, the woman vice-president of a local agricultural group reiterated, 'Villagers think that we are earning so much money but nobody knows about the gastritis we have invited upon ourselves running after I/NGOs on empty stomachs to find programmes and funds after the earthquake.'[35]

People's perceptions and unintended consequences

In line with the claims made by several studies that I/NGOs operate like businesses, contributing to the reproduction of neo-patrimonial networks, class hierarchies, clientelism, corruption, and social inequalities (Frewer 2013; Suleiman 2013; O'Reilly 2010 cited in Jones et al. 2014), the perception of people across the study sites was that I/NGOs had used the bigger chunk of their budgets for transportation, staff salaries, and participants' daily

---

[32] Interview no. 17, vice-chairperson, women's agriculture cooperative, Gimdi, southern Lalitpur, 21 November 2017.

[33] Interview no. 20, social mobilizer, ICDO, Gimdi, southern Lalitpur, 27 November 2017.

[34] Interview with representatives of pre-existing women's beneficiary groups and cooperatives in Gimdi VDC, southern Lalitpur, 21 November 2017.

[35] Interview no. 12, vice-chairperson, women's agriculture cooperative and member of disaster management group, Gimdi, southern Lalitpur, 21 November 2017.

allowances rather than in actual development programmes.[36] Although people did not explicitly mention corruption in the humanitarian assistance, their perceptions hinted at this. Moreover, as the majority of the programmes were 'sealed from above', interviews with local staff revealed that they were unaware of programme budgets and indicated that their participation was limited to programme implementation.[37] Additionally, people in Fujel related an incident in which two influential locals had formed an organization overnight to channel funds from a Chinese organization for the reconstruction of a school[38] which broadly resonates with what some have termed the 'alms bazaar', 'NGO scramble', and 'goodwill bazaar' that surrounds many post-disaster humanitarian responses (Smillie 1995; Cooley and Ron 2002; Aldashev and Verdier 2010 cited in Carrasco and O'Brien 2018). The model of community participation adopted by the I/NGOs shows, in part, a lack of trust between bigger and smaller organizations in which the latter's engagement is only to fulfil the former's interests and agenda. This is very much in line with Arnstein (1969) and Choguill's (1996) use of the concept of the 'ladder of community participation'[39] in which the top of the ladder equates to empowerment and the promotion of community control over projects, whereas the bottom end refers to a form of participation in which people are merely persuaded into taking part in a project and have little or no decision-making power. Furthermore, it is argued that undermining and disregarding the affected communities can have adverse impacts on them (Oliver-Smith 1991; Telford and Cosgrave 2007).

I/NGOs were found to have imposed programmes from above that conflicted with people's day-to-day activities, needs, and time availability. Locals felt that much of their time was being wasted in attending I/NGOs' programmes when they could have easily made NPR 500 per day by doing

---

[36] Interview no. 81, principal, Shree Bhawani Shankar Secondary School, Thulosirubari, Sindhupalchok, 20 December 2017.

[37] Interview, social mobilizer, ENPHO, Gimdi, southern Lalitpur, 25 November 2017.

[38] Interview no. 43, chairperson of road and drinking water committee, Fujel, Gorkha, 21 December 2017.

[39] Originally proposed by Arnstein (1969) and later modified to fit the context of developing countries by Choguill (1996), where the top of the ladder 'empowers' people and the bottom strips people of control over projects.

wage labour.[40] As subsistence farmers, locals across the study sites felt they were not able to carry out farming as they had before the earthquake. I/NGOs failed to take local needs into account and implemented agriculture-related programmes during the off-season, despite people's protests. In the words of a local social mobilizer in Thulosirubari, 'I/NGOs tell one thing to us and do another thing. They don't care about our practical needs; they don't respect our feelings and come only to complete their projects.'[41] A local coffee producer in southern Lalitpur also threw light on the situation:

> People from Oxfam came and told us that their *hakim*s [bosses] were coming and they had to show that we [coffee producers] were preparing beds for sowing coffee seeds. They said they were coming for cross-checking. They forced us to build beds even though we told them that Shrawan [June/July] was not the suitable month to prepare beds. But they just ignored us, saying they knew that. Lately, what I've been feeling is that these organizations are not working for the benefit of people but they just want to show and tell.[42]

Despite good intentions, earthquake responses created unintended consequences. For instance, in Fujel, an association working for Dalits had selectively given relief to Dalits from their own working groups, excluding Biswokarmas (a Dalit sub-group) from a neighbouring village who were greatly in need of support. There were also issues about Dalits overshadowing the needs of other vulnerable groups, such as the Baramu, a Janajati group, in Fujel. A representative of the local Baramu community organization said, 'I/NGOs came with NPR 1,000,000 [c. USD 900] for Dalits and persons with disability (PwDs), but nobody came to bring relief or any support for the Baramu community in Fujel.'[43] Similarly, vegetable-farming training was provided for women of certain wards in Fujel, but excluded Dalit women on the grounds that 'they did not show up

---

[40] Interview no. 5, teacher, Narayani Higher Secondary School, Gimdi, southern Lalitpur, 23 November 2017.

[41] Interview no. 79, social mobilizer, Thuloshirubari VDC office, Sindhupalchok, 25 December 2017.

[42] Interview no. 25, coffee farmer/former forest-users-group member, Gimdi, Ward no. 5, southern Lalitpur, 26 November 2019.

[43] Interview no. 48, chairperson, Baramu Sangh, Fujel, Gorkha, 25 December 2017.

for the training'.[44] Although Dalits were provided with training related to incense- and candlemaking, they were not able to sell their products due to deeply entrenched issues of untouchability and prejudice.[45] Relief, as these illustrations vividly suggest, re-ignited pre-existing caste prejudices and the deep-seated issue of untouchability as well as resentment towards Dalits. The Dalits also repeatedly mentioned having been attacked by non-Dalits due to a perception that they were being prioritized over non-Dalits in earthquake relief and responses. The following quote from a Dalit woman[46] captures the situation:

> Recently, my *kurta* had mistakenly touched a drinking water pipe. Non-Dalits accused me, saying that I had deliberately touched the pipe. It created a big fight in the village. They trample on the pipe as many times as they like when we fill our vessels. They have become angrier with us now after the earthquake. They tell us 'whatever comes in relief, you Dalits take everything, you get all facilities and that's why you have crossed your lines.' They take up the issue of relief and fight with us. They dominate and shame us.

Conclusion

The aftermath of the 2015 earthquakes was marked by a massive humanitarian response, nationally and internationally. Although the post-earthquake context has been described as an opportunity to 'build back better' in its assessment and planning in major documents such as the PDNA and the PDRF, Nepal's policies and practices have often failed to take into consideration the vulnerabilities of people, including geographical difficulties. I/NGOs contributed to the general recovery of the earthquake-affected population through relief, rehabilitation, restoration of livelihoods, and reconstruction. However, there were issues of mismatch in programmes, duplication of beneficiary groups, and lack of cooperation that affected

---

[44] Interview no. 48, chairperson, Baramu Sangh, Fujel, Gorkha, 25 December 2017.

[45] Interview no. 66, retired headmaster, Fujel, Gorkha, 25 December 2017.

[46] Interview no. 54, member, Nagarik Sachetana Kendra, Fujel, Gorkha, December 2017.

the interconnections of local organizations, weakening the pre-existing structures and lowering the participation rate of local people.

People's perceptions inform us that many I/NGOs worked to 'show-and-tell' rather than contributing to sustainable empowerment through local capacity-building. Daly et al. (2017) note that local governments and CBOs can act as an interface between national government institutions, NGOs, international donors, and disaster-affected persons because they have a deeper understanding of the issues at the local level. However, this study reveals that I/NGOs' activities were largely unregulated. Similarly, the I/NGOs' failure to take sociocultural contexts into consideration while delivering a humanitarian response has at times engendered and further entrenched issues of untouchability and caste prejudice.

Therefore, it is necessary to change the basis on which flawed and unequal partnerships are formed between I/NGOs and local-level organizations and groups. In order to prevent that from happening, local-level organizations need to be given equal power in decision making, priority setting, and designing, implementing, monitoring, and evaluating programmes and plans so that they are enabled not only to build back better but also to cope with future disasters.

7

Policies, Politics, and Practices of Landslide Risk Management in Post-earthquake Nepal

Perspectives from Above and Below

Katie Oven, Shubheksha Rana, Gopi K. Basyal, Nick Rosser, and Mark Kincey

Introduction

When an earthquake strikes, the humanitarian response, understandably, focuses on the impacts of the immediate shaking and associated aftershocks. Comparatively less attention is given to secondary hazards including, for example, landslides, which in mountainous countries such as Nepal often present a greater and longer-term risk to the population than the shaking of the earthquake itself. Past earthquakes, including those in Kashmir in 2005 and Wenchuan in China in 2008, have shown that, in addition to the landslides caused by the initial event, mountain communities can expect an increase in landslide activity for decades or longer afterwards, with significant implications for post-disaster recovery and reconstruction. The 2015 earthquake sequence in Nepal is reported to have triggered around 22,000 landslides (Roback et al. 2018), the equivalent of decades of normal monsoon-triggered landsliding. This has resulted in fundamental changes to the landscape: some villages have been destroyed and their population permanently displaced; others are living with a new and ongoing threat of landslides and the uncertainty that this brings. In this chapter, we explore the implications of landsliding for post-earthquake reconstruction from the perspective of scientists, national and local governments, and rural residents living with evolving landslide risk. We draw on our interdisciplinary research undertaken as part of a Department for International Development/ Natural Environment Research Council (DfID/NERC)–funded Science for Humanitarian Emergencies and Resilience project which brings together different analytical and methodological perspectives, including landslide mapping based on satellite imagery, ethnographic work with rural residents, and interviews with government stakeholders and non-governmental organization (NGO) representatives supporting householders impacted by earthquake-induced geohazards. Like Nightingale (2003) in the context of forest management in rural Nepal, we seek to highlight and interrogate the partiality of the different forms of knowledge generated and the implications this has for post-disaster reconstruction and risk management.

Drawing on the work of Oven and Rigg (2015), we begin the discussion by exploring the changing spatiality of hazard, vulnerability, and risk in the earthquake-affected districts of West-Central Nepal, an area described as the 'Tamang epicentre' (Magar 2015),[1] with a particular focus on the Upper Bhote Kosi Valley in Sindhupalchok district. From a landslide perspective, this valley was among the most heavily impacted by the 2015 earthquakes. Here we draw on *ex ante* research, undertaken between 2006 and 2008, that considered the chronic landslide hazard, and *ex post* field studies following the 2015 earthquakes. The chapter goes on to consider the different ways in which risk is experienced, understood, framed, and prioritized by rural residents, the government, NGOs, and scientists, and how these plural understandings have shaped the post-earthquake disaster risk management agenda in Nepal. Consideration is given to the evidence that is used and valued in the identification and delineation of risk, and its subsequent management, both formally and informally, in the post-earthquake space. We conclude by highlighting the value of bringing seemingly incompatible datasets, generated from different epistemological positions, into dialogue for more effective risk management.

---

[1] As noted by Lord and Murton (2017) citing Magar (2015) and Holmberg and March (2015), the earthquakes hit Tamang communities across northern Nepal particularly heavily, compounding everyday vulnerabilities and resulting in significant impacts among this particular ethnic group.

Spatialities of hazard, vulnerability, and risk

Landslides are a frequent hazard in rural mountainous Nepal, most commonly occurring during the monsoon months and resulting in an average of 78 fatalities per year (Petley et al. 2007). These events are highly localized and generally small in scale, usually resulting in less than five fatalities per event. Large-scale impacts from more extensive landsliding are comparatively rare. A notable example was the 2014 Jure landslide in the Sun Kosi Valley in Sindhupalchok district which killed more than 150 people, buried more than 100 houses, and destroyed a section of the strategic highway linking Kathmandu with China (van der Geest 2018). Research prior to the 2015 earthquakes suggested that the number of fatal landslides in Nepal was increasing with time, a trend largely attributed to the proliferation of rural roads, often built with minimal engineering input (Petley et al. 2007; Froude and Petley 2018). The impact of roads on landslides risk is complex: the road construction process itself, which often progresses without technical guidance, can destabilize slopes; while the lure of the road and the opportunities it brings commonly lead to migration, which has been seen to increase the exposure of rural populations to landslide hazard (Oven 2010). Importantly, from a risk management perspective, landslides are incredibly difficult to predict in space and time, and science is not yet able to generate reliable early warnings, rendering landslides a challenging hazard to mitigate and manage (Shroder and Davies 2015). As a result, they are commonly managed in an *ad hoc* fashion as and when they occur, often with a temporary fix.

Landslide disasters arise from the interaction of both geophysical/ hydro-meteorological processes and social vulnerability. However, there is debate around how this interaction is conceptualized and understood. For O'Brien et al. (2007), in the context of climate change, vulnerability may be conceptualized as either outcome-focused or contextual. 'Outcome vulnerability is considered a linear result of the projected impact of climate change on a particular exposure unit (which can be either biophysical or social), offset by adaptation measures' (O'Brien et al. 2007: 75). In contrast, 'contextual vulnerability ... is based on a processual and multidimensional view of climate–society interactions. Both climate variability and change are considered to occur in the context of political, institutional, economic, and social structures and changes, which interact dynamically with contextual conditions associated with a particular "exposure unit'" (O'Brien et al. 2007: 76). We argue that this conceptual understanding is relevant to other hazard contexts such as earthquakes and landslides. Our research has therefore sought to understand how the wider social, political, and economic transformations underway in Nepal have shaped conditions at the household and community levels, and the implications that this has for exposure, vulnerability, and disaster recovery. We therefore take a 'contextual' approach, to use O'Brien et al.'s terms.

Nepal is a low-income country, ranked 147 out of 189 countries in the Human Development Index (UNDP data[2]), with more than 80 per cent of the population classified as rural (World Bank data[3]). Despite money-metric poverty falling in recent years,[4] social inequality remains severe, with wide variations in human development based on caste, ethnicity, and gender (UNDP 2014). Politically, Nepal is undergoing a complex transition following the establishment of multi-party democracy in the 1990s and a decade-long civil war fuelled by severe poverty, socioeconomic inequality, and the marginalization of indigenous groups (Rankin et al. 2018). Nepal adopted a new constitution five months after the 2015 Gorkha earthquake (Hutt 2020) and established a new federal republic, with local elections held for the first time in 20 years in 2017. For some, the constitution is less progressive than had been hoped, particularly regarding the rights of ethnic minority groups and women (Muni 2015; S. Tamang 2018a), with ongoing challenges around representation and accountability at the local level (S. Tamang 2018b).

We focus our research on the community and household where these national level processes are 'ultimately mediated … and turned into action with tangible effects on a given locality' (Wilson 2012: 36). What was clear from the beginning of our research prior to the 2015 earthquakes is that, in order to understand the vulnerability of rural residents to seasonal, monsoon-triggered landslides, it is necessary to look beyond

---

[2] See http://hdr.undp.org/en/data# (accessed 14 May 2020).

[3] See https://data.worldbank.org/indicator/SP.RUR.TOTL.ZS?locations=NP (accessed 14 May 2020).

[4] According to the World Bank, the proportion of Nepal's population living below the international poverty line of USD 1.90 PPP (purchasing power parity) was 49.9 per cent in 2003 and 15 per cent in 2010 (see http://povertydata.worldbank.org/poverty/country/NPL [accessed 14 May 2020]).

the immediate area at risk and beyond a single physical hazard (Oven and Rigg 2015). This, in part, reflects people's 'livelihood footprints' (Rigg, Salamanca, and Parnwell 2012) which are no longer geographically constrained in the way they once were. In the Upper Bhote Kosi Valley in the mid-2000s, landholdings were characteristically small and of low productivity, with less than 10 per cent of surveyed households meeting their subsistence needs from farming alone. Householders therefore relied on non-farm activities, and increasingly remittance income, to meet their livelihood shortfall, including migration to the roadside to set up small shops and hotels, and increasingly overseas to the Gulf States and Malaysia.

Oven (2010) found that within the Upper Bhote Kosi Valley, the landslide hazard itself could be quite precisely delineated in the landscape. The locations of settlements in the hills were often found to be susceptible to large, slow moving landslides that damage, and in some cases destroy, property, infrastructure, and farmland, but usually without loss of human life. By comparison, the roadside settlements located in the valley bottom were often constructed at the foot of steep, unstable slopes or on the only available farmable land, which is commonly colluvial debris flow fans (loose landslide material) or alluvial deposits adjacent to stream channels. Here the landslide hazard was more acute and potentially catastrophic, with accounts of landslides being smaller but more rapid, often sourced from far above. Past events recounted by the residents interviewed as part of Oven's research included a landslide that dammed the Bhairabkunda Khola in 1996 and subsequently breached at night, inundating the roadside village of Larcha and killing more than 50 people.

Importantly, in her *ex ante* study of landslides, Oven (2010) observed that some households exposed to landslides at the roadside were relatively poor, with little choice but to occupy such marginal, exposed land. But there were also households that were occupying these sites by choice, in many instances because the advantages of the roadside location outweighed the risks associated with the landslide hazard. These households were of a variety of caste and ethnic groups, challenging the assumption often made in the literature that such high risk zones are occupied by the most marginalized groups. In some cases it was the accumulated capital from family members working overseas that had made the migration to the roadside possible in the first place. Oven concluded that landslide risk needed to be understood in the context of a wider 'hazard–opportunity' nexus. As summarised by Oven and Rigg (2015), reflecting on Oven's (2010) study:

> For the majority of householders … landslide risk was a low priority concern and immediate, more tangible needs dictated local perceptions of risk. While moving to the roadside might increase landslide exposure, it also increased livelihood and development opportunities that could not easily be realised in the hills.… To the local people interviewed, these risks were hard to compare and weigh: one related to landslides that were considered to be inevitable in such steep terrain; and the other to day-to-day livelihood security that had an immediacy that was generally absent in relation to landslide hazard. (Oven and Rigg 2015: 692)

It could be argued, therefore, that prior to the 2015 earthquakes, householders in the Upper Bhote Kosi Valley were adopting risk avoidance strategies, but only in the context of the everyday risks faced rather than comparatively infrequent geophysical hazards such as extensive landsliding and earthquakes.

It was against this backdrop that the 2015 earthquakes, including the 12 May 7.3 moment magnitude (Mw) event with its epicentre close to the Upper Bhote Kosi Valley, occurred. Residents in a roadside village recounted that on the day of the main shock more than 30 people were killed nearby, mostly by landslides, although the majority were not from the village itself. A bus and a jeep that were transporting, among others, a group of people from outside the valley who had been collecting *yarsagumba*, a valuable Himalayan fungus, in the area were buried by a landslide just south of the village. The 2015 earthquakes have unquestionably transformed space within the valley, with some land completely gone and some no longer habitable.

A study of internally displaced persons in camps across the earthquake-affected districts identified geohazards as one of the primary reasons for migration, including landslides in the respondents' own communities and landslides disrupting roads and footpaths between communities and local services and markets. The same study cited geohazards as the main cause of concern for householders regarding their return to their places of origin (U. Paudel 2017). In the Upper Bhote Kosi Valley, residents were initially evacuated by helicopter to Kathmandu. Some households returned for the Tihar festival in October 2015 to tend their farmland, while others returned several months later. Importantly, many young people have stayed away in order to seek employment, leaving the elderly and young children behind. Indeed, our more recent observations in three hillside villages suggest that nearly two-thirds of the population has left, with many houses remaining shut up or abandoned. This reflects, at least in part, the limited employment opportunities that are now available following the closure of the Arniko Highway due to the earthquakes and ongoing landslides north of the roadside town of Tatopani, and the more recent coronavirus outbreak.[5] Some residents still living in the valley explained that the limited employment opportunities that are now available (for example, labour on 1 of 10 hydropower projects on the northernmost 10 kilometres of the Bhote Kosi River and its tributaries) offer little appeal to those who were previously running hotels and engaged in cross-border trade. As a result, much of the Nepali workforce in the hydropower project in one roadside village reportedly came from Far-West Nepal.

Governing landslide risk in post-earthquake Nepal: the policy context

At the time of the 2015 earthquakes, the Government of Nepal was working with the largely outdated Natural Disaster Relief Act (1982), which was fundamentally oriented towards disaster response, and a more recent National Strategy of Disaster Risk Management (2009).[6] Landslide risk management is the responsibility of multiple technical departments that sit across different government ministries,[7] resulting in notable institutional

---

[5] The Arniko Highway briefly opened in May 2019 following four years of closure due to earthquake-triggered landslides, and was closed again at the beginning of 2020 in the wake of the coronavirus outbreak in China.

[6] See Jones et al. (2014) for a more detailed discussion on the governance struggles and policy processes in relation to disaster risk reduction in Nepal.

[7] At the time of the 2015 earthquakes, responsible ministries and departments included: the Department of Soil Conservation and Watershed Management,

incoherence. In 2005, when our research began, local governments in rural Nepal lacked the resources and expertise at the local level to address landslide risk, and very little has changed in this regard since.[8] As a result, landslides are commonly managed in an *ad hoc* fashion as and when they occur.

Following the earthquakes in 2015, the Government of Nepal took a reasonably proactive stance and began to assess the nature of the landslide hazard and associated risk. This involved initial field assessments by the Department of Mines and Geology of 130 settlements, based on requests from local government officers, and a further assessment of 455 locations across 15 districts by the National Reconstruction Authority, with technical support provided by the United Nations Office for Project Services (UNOPS) in Kathmandu.[9] Combined, these became known as the Geohazard Assessment. The Geohazard Assessment led to a three-tier categorization: Category 1, 'Safer communities/villages where reconstruction can be started any time'; Category 2, 'Communities/ villages under the risk of manageable geohazards. Reconstruction can be started only after applying suitable countermeasures'; and Category 3, 'Unsafe communities/villages due to the existing state of geohazards which are extremely difficult to control technically as well as financially. Reconstruction is not recommended'. The Geohazard Assessment included an approximate number of households requiring relocation, and also oulined recommendations for remedial works and indentified the responsible government agency (namely the Department of Soil

---

Ministry of Forests and Environment (for small, shallow landslides); the Department of Water Induced Disaster Management, Ministry of Irrigation (for large-scale landslides affecting strategic roads and other infrastructure); the Department of Hydrology and Meteorology, Ministry of Water Resources and Energy (for rainfall and flood monitoring); the Department of Mines and Geology, Ministry of Industry, Commerce and Supplies (for earthquake-triggered landslides); the Ministry of Home Affairs (MoHA), with responsibility for disaster response and recovery; and the then Ministry of Federal Affairs and Local Development, with its focus on local disaster risk management.

[8]   We refer here to interviews undertaken with local government representatives in Sindhupalchok district in February 2020.

[9]   See https://hrrpnepal.org/uploads/media/fZHjlOrDyTYid8bF0haK_2017_11_09. pdf (accessed 14 May 2020).

Conservation and Watershed Management or the Department of Water Induced Disaster Management). While this rapid assessment was useful in determining initial levels of hazard and risk at the reported sites, it did so for a snapshot in time only and relied on locally reported information. Further sites have since been visited, and some sites reassessed—in particular, sites where there were concerns that the landslide situation was worsening. As of January 2019, a total of 860 sites had been assessed. Of these sites, 44 per cent (378 sites) were assessed as Category 1, 29 per cent (251 sites) as Category 2, and 27 per cent (231 sites) as Category 3, with more than 3,500 households recommended for relocation.[10]

Category 3 households were eligible for a government subsidy of NPR 200,000 (c. USD 1,800) per family for the acquisition of new land in a safe area. This was in addition to the housing reconstruction assistance worth NPR 300,000 (c. USD 2,700) per family made available as part of the government's nationwide reconstruction plan. Given the concern that landslides would 'further deepen vulnerabilities and put a large number of households at risk of being left behind in the housing reconstruction efforts' (DfID-Nepal 2017: 3), DfID-Nepal were providing a further GBP 375 cash grant to each of the 'highest risk' geohazard affected households and GBP 100 per household for social mobilization and technical assistance (DfID-Nepal 2017: 13).

Unsurprisingly, perhaps, mixed stories in relation to landslide management and relocation were reported. There were reports that some settlements had not been included in the Geohazard Assessment, despite warnings from district geologists and engineers. One such example was Singati Bazaar in Dolakha district, which had seen significant reconstruction in the absence of a relocation plan on the part of the government (Sapkota 2018). A household survey commissioned by the Durable Solutions Consortium also highlighted 'some mismatch between the areas surveyed by the NRA and the place of origin reported by the displaced population living in the temporary camps' (U. Paudel 2017). Some settlements that appeared on the geohazard list, for example, Kerauja VDC in Gorkha district, had not received any support from the Government of Nepal for relocation (Rastriya Samachar Samiti 2016). Others (for example, settlements at risk of

---

[10] Geohazard Assessment Database as of 15 January 2019, Durable Solutions II and People in Need.

landsliding in Kavrepalanchok district), were reported to have been quickly relocated (Sapkota 2018).

Understanding the hazard context: the view from above[11]

Our own mapping work in collaboration with the National Society for Earthquake Technology (NSET)-Nepal (Durham University and NSET data)[12] offers an aerial view of the landslide situation. Using freely available satellite imagery from the United States Geological Survey (USGS) and the European Space Agency (ESA), visible landslides were mapped across the 14 earthquake-affected districts before and after each monsoon from 2014 to November 2019, generating a series of inventories which show the number, size, and location of landslides, how they have changed over time, and the areas at risk of potential future landsliding. Based upon this assessment, we estimated that approximately 13,000 new landslides were triggered by the 2015 earthquakes across West-Central Nepal, an area that had approximately 6,400 active landslides before the earthquake. After the 2015 monsoon season, some six months after the earthquake, this number had increased by about 35 per cent. After the 2019 monsoon, the situation was markedly worse, with the number of landslides about 51 per cent above the level on the day of the earthquake. In terms of landslide numbers, therefore, the situation at the time of writing is far from being back to the pre-earthquake normal.

The mapping work also indicated that the nature of the landslide hazard was changing. Before the first earthquake, landslides were typically either small and perennially recurrent in locations known to be relatively susceptible, and commonly associated with road construction; or were larger, deeper-seated, slow moving landslides that posed a disruptive rather than destructive hazard. After the earthquakes, however, the hazard context was increasingly dominated by debris flows (fast moving masses of soil, rock, and water) which can rapidly travel long distances down valley slopes, and

---

[11] Like Nightingale (2003), and grounded in the work of Haraway (1988), we make the distinction between situated knowledge (the view from below) and the knowledge gained from satellite images (the view from above).

[12] See http://community.dur.ac.uk/nepal.2015eq/ (accessed 30 June 2020).

which are highly sensitive to intense rainfall when saturated. This suggests that the legacy of damage resulting from the shaking means that previously safe levels of rainfall now had the potential to trigger hazardous landsliding. Living with landslide risk after the earthquakes was therefore not simply a case of more of the same, but rather of living with a very different hazard landscape. In Sindhupalchok district, Rosser et al. (2019) estimated that more than 5 per cent of houses were located in the potential runout path of landslides which were still active.

Figure 7.1 shows the spatial distribution of sites assessed through the Geohazard Assessment as of September 2018 (Geohazard Assessment)[13] and the spatial distribution of landslides mapped by the Durham/NSET team (Durham University/NSET data),[14] respectively. While care is needed when making direct comparisons, as the two approaches to identifying at risk locations are quite different, the broad spatial distribution is nonetheless revealing. There were districts (for example, Ramechhap) where the level of reporting through the Geohazard Assessment was perhaps higher than might be expected, given the population density and the number of mapped earthquake-triggered landslides, and there was relative underreporting elsewhere—in northern Sindhupalchok and Dolakha, for example.

Zooming into the municipal or ward level, the maps derived from remotely sensed data identify areas in more distant or hard to reach locations, which may have been missed from other assessments, and bring these into view. An example of such an instance is a remote settlement which administratively sits in the southernmost corner of ward 5 in Bhote Kosi Rural Municipality, despite geographically falling within the neighbouring watershed (Figure 7.2). As far as we are aware, this settlement had not been assessed by the Government of Nepal, despite mapping evidence to suggest that the community was at risk of landslides. Informal discussions with local government officials suggested that this area was not well known to them, or of particular concern.

Aware that this aerial view is just one perspective, and that 'all knowledge is partial and linked to the contexts in which it was created'

---

13   Geohazard Assessment Database as of 15 January 2019, Durable Solutions II and People in Need. https://www.durablesolutionsnepal.org (accessed 30 June 2020).

14   See http://community.dur.ac.uk/nepal.2015eq/ (accessed 30 June 2020).

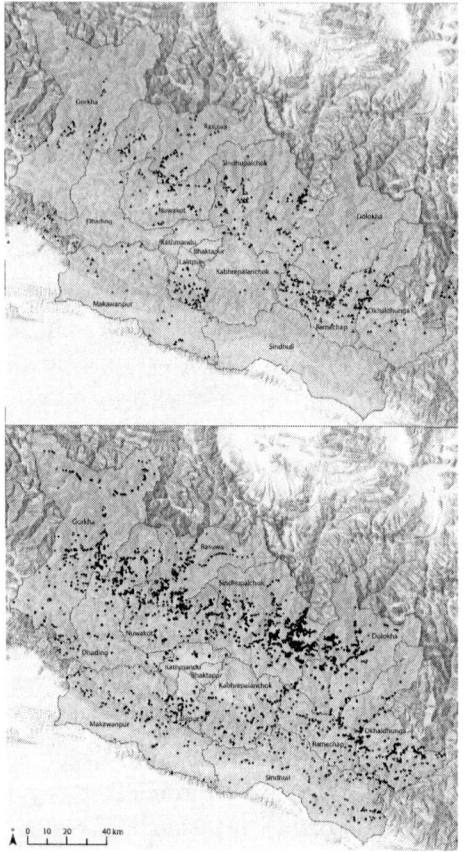

Figure 7.1 Maps showing the location of the sites assessed within the Geohazard Assessment for the 14 most-affected districts as of September 2018 (*top*) and the buildings at risk of landslides following the 2018 monsoon developed by Durham and NSET (*bottom*).

Basemap sources: Esri, Airbus DS, USGS, NGA, NASA, CGIAR, N. Robinson, NCEAS, NLS, OS, NMA, Geodatastyrelsen, Rijkswaterstaat, GSA, Geoland, FEMA, Intermap, and the GIS user community.

(Nightingale 2003: 78), the next section of this chapter seeks to ground these findings in the context of residents' lived experiences of landsliding, relocation, and reconstruction. We focus, in particular, on local perceptions of risk, the importance of an attachment to place, and local politics in decision-making.

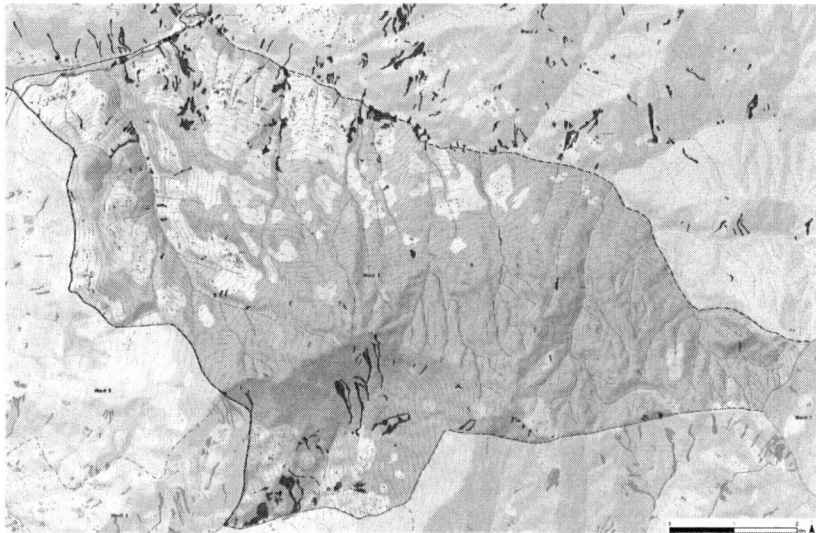

Figure 7.2 Ward 5 in Bhote Kosi Rural Municipality in Sindhupalchok district. The dark grey polygons represent the landslides and the small grey dots the houses. The remote settlements located in the neighbouring watershed, but administratively in ward 5, can be seen in the centre-bottom of the map. The settlements here are approximately three days' walk from the main road in the northwest.

Sources: Landslide data are an output from Durham University and NSET. *Basemap sources*: Esri, Airbus DS, USGS, NGA, NASA, CGIAR, N. Robinson, NCEAS, NLS, OS, NMA, Geodatastyrelsen, Rijkswaterstaat, GSA, Geoland, FEMA, Intermap, and the GIS user community.

Everyday lived experiences of landsliding: the view from below

According to the Geohazard Assessment Database, approximately 145 villages in Sindhupalchok district have been assessed to determine the level of landslide risk faced.[15] Relocation was recommended for 53 of the surveyed settlements, with a further 60 settlements requiring some form of mitigation and management, with recommendations including drainage

---

[15]   Geohazard Assessment Database as of 15 January 2019, Durable Solutions II and People in Need.

and bioengineering, the sealing of cracks to reduce the ingress of water, and the construction of retaining walls. A group interview in March 2019 with social mobilizers based in the district headquarters of Chautara, who were tasked with assisting Category 3 communities with their relocation, suggested that several of the Category 3 settlements had decided not to relocate. According to the social mobilizers, those that had relocated had done so through fear, because they were able to find suitable land nearby that could accommodate all of the displaced households without any negative impacts on their livelihoods, and in situations where the relocation process was managed by local ward leaders. We focus the remainder of our chapter on two of the Category 3 settlements in the Upper Bhote Kosi Valley that had taken the decision not to relocate.

Sketch 1[16]

We focus sketch 1 on a small Tamang settlement comprising approximately 30 households at the time of the earthquake.[17] The majority of the stone houses in the village collapsed during the shaking but, fortunately, no one was killed. Most residents initially fled, temporarily residing in neighbouring villages in the valley or further afield in Kathmandu. They gradually started to return, and as of April 2019 there were 10 households living back in the village, with community members working together to reconnect the water supply and to repair trails. As a village leader who was encouraging the villagers to return and to come together to rebuild the community expounded: 'I am slowly rebuilding the nest, hopefully the birds will come back to their original nest.'[18] His words showed a strong attachment to the land and to the village where he had lived for most of his life.

Landslides were not a new phenomenon here. A village elder recounted a landslide that had occurred approximately 70 years earlier, which impacted

---

[16] We use 'sketch' here, as used by Shneiderman (2015a), to introduce our ethnographic encounters with the two Category 3 villages.

[17] The exact number of households in the village was unclear. This, at least in part, reflects issues around how the household is defined and therefore counted. This has been noted elsewhere in the context of post-earthquake reconstruction (see, for example, Shneiderman et al., this volume).

[18] Interview, Upper Bhote Kosi Valley, 1 April 2019.

the whole village and the surrounding area, killing many people. The village was rebuilt some 15 years later, on the same site. Seasonal, monsoon-triggered landsliding was a common occurrence but the landsliding was exacerbated by the 2015 earthquakes. The shaking itself triggered a landslide in the village, with more landslides occurring in the months and years that followed: 'The 2018 monsoon brought everything down [loose rock and debris perched above the village] one night—around 11:30 pm—burying five Chinese houses [occupied by the hydropower workers] below. We were all sleeping but fortunately no one was hurt.'[19]

Residents in a predominantly male group interview explained that, following an assessment by government engineers approximately one year after the earthquakes, each household received NPR 50,000 (c. USD 450) to start to reconstruct their homes. They were later informed that the village was no longer safe due to landslides and the residents were requested to relocate. There was understandable confusion: 'Why do we need a budget to reconstruct when we are meant to leave?'[20]

According to a local political leader (the chair of the former Ward Citizen Forum [WCF]),[21] the Geohazard Assessment was undertaken following a request by two local NGOs working in the area who approached the district government to raise concerns about the landslide risk in several communities in the Bhote Kosi Rural Municipality. Following the assessment and recommendation for relocation, 'The Displaced and Landless Tol[22] Committee' was formed to represent the views of the community. The head of the committee, a Tamang man living with his family in a temporary shelter in a neighbouring village, explained that the district government provided some support but the relocation process was led by the displaced householders themselves, who were tasked with identifying three to four sites suitable for relocation for all the displaced families wishing to move. This process broadly reflected the procedure

---

[19]   Interview, Upper Bhote Kosi Valley, 1 April 2019.

[20]   Group Interview, Upper Bhote Kosi Valley, 2 April 2019.

[21]   The WCF was a local-level decision-making body created under the Local Governance Community Development Programme, in the absence of a locally elected government.

[22]   A *tol* is a small settlement or community within a ward which shares local resources, for example, a temple, water tap, or community forest. A *tol* is a social rather than a mandatory administrative structure.

set out by the NRA in the 'Procedure for Relocation and Rehabilitation of Hazard Prone Settlements'.[23] The local political leader explained that three options for relocation were identified and the displaced residents decided on a neighbouring village where the land was more reasonably priced and they were not too far from the road. The local political leader facilitated discussions with local landowners and acted as an important intermediary with the local government and the NRA.

The process outlined by both the local political leader and the head of the Displaced and Landless Tol Committee initially appeared fair and transparent. A total of 17 households had agreed to buy land in the neighbouring village, with the NPR 200,000 from the Government of Nepal reportedly buying 4 *aana* (just under 130 square metres) of land per household. The land was subsequently purchased and a *lalpurja* (registration certificate) issued. Further discussions, however, revealed some complex local politics, which led us to question the extent to which the displaced residents had been given a voice in the relocation process.

A resident explained: 'Two ladies [social mobilizers from a local NGO supporting the relocation process] came to [nearby village] and asked us to go to the *gaunpalika* [rural municipality]. We were told that some land had been found for us in [neighbouring village] and that we should move. We initially said yes but when we returned we began to reconsider.'[24] Residents were promised that they would receive help from a local NGO linked to the political leader to construct their houses, install water supply and electricity, and construct a road to provide access to the new site, as well as to establish new livelihood opportunities such as poultry farming. However, according to the residents interviewed, these promises were not kept and a number of issues emerged. The first related to land access, with each household having to pay an additional NPR 100,000 (c. USD 900) to a neighbouring landowner for access to the plot. Second, residents were concerned that the reconstruction grant from the Government of Nepal of NPR 300,000 to which they were entitled would not be enough to construct houses in the new location, forcing them to take out loans.[25] Third, the new plots

---

[23] See https://hrrpnepal.org/uploads/media/fZHjlOrDyTYid8bF0haK_2017_11_09. pdf (accessed 14 May 2020).

[24] Interview, Upper Bhote Kosi Valley, 1 April 2019.

[25] A visit to the neighbouring community (in April 2019) with the local political leader to see the newly purchased land was revealing. An integrated settlement,

of land were considered too small for them to secure a livelihood. As one householder explained: 'Our farmland is here, and in [the new village] we have nothing.… Even if we move there we have just 4 *aana* of land. Where will we put our chickens, goats, buffalos, and where will we collect fodder for them? Nothing!'[26] If they moved they would have to commute to farm their land daily, which would involve crossing a large landslide between the two villages which would be impassable during the monsoon months.

As in Sherry et al.'s (2018) study of Sherpa understandings of glacial lake outburst flood risk in the Rolwaling Valley in neighbouring Dolakha district, the residents we interviewed gave contradictory interpretations of the landslide hazard and associated risk. On the one hand, they showed relatively little concern for the landslide risk they faced as they began to rebuild their houses and repair the trails. On the other, they perceived the hazard to be potentially catastrophic and felt powerless to respond. They rationalized their situation by comparing their village to other landslide-affected locations nearby. For example, participants in a group interview explained how two villages above theirs, which they considered to be at greater risk of landslides, were reconstructing their houses and had received their second payment for reconstruction from the government. Some residents were, therefore, questioning the outcome of the Geohazard Assessment in their own village: 'We feel the previous assessment wasn't very reliable as people came and just observed without using any equipment and were probably guessing.'[27] Some residents stated that there had not been any recent landslides and, as a result, they were not concerned about the risk they faced: '[Over time] we have not found any movement of landslides, and all remains the same, so we are not thinking to move from this place anymore'.[28]

---

in another part of the community, comprising 10 brick houses and following one of the NRA-approved designs, was under construction. Each house was being built with an extra room for use as a homestay at a reported cost of NPR 18 lakh (1,800,000) per house. Other brick houses were being constructed in the same village at a cost of NPR 11 lakh (1,100,000), with homeowners reportedly taking out loans of NPR 8 lakh (800,000) at 14 per cent interest per year to cover the costs of construction.

[26] Interview, Upper Bhote Kosi Valley, 10 December 2018.

[27] Group Interview, Upper Bhote Kosi Valley, 2 April 2019.

[28] Interview, Upper Bhote Kosi Valley, 8 December 2018.

Another householder, who was also deciding not to relocate, did not see the new land in the neighbouring village as a solution. He explained, 'We had arguments in the past [with villagers there]',[29] and he worried that they would not be able to live in the village peacefully. While the neighbouring village was more ethnically diverse with Chhetri, Magar, Tamang, and some Dalit households, the main tensions appeared to be between the displaced residents and the local political leader who was Chhetri, and who, according to some residents, wanted the displaced residents to buy his own land and was making things difficult when they did not.

The processes for support and compensation in relation to the landslide risk were confusing for some householders who were not always sure where to go: 'Sometimes we are told to go to the ward, sometimes the *gaunpalika*, sometimes to the *pradhikaran* [the NRA]. The problems are either seen as too big or too small for the different levels of government.'[30] They tried talking to the ward chair and the rural municipality about their concerns but did not feel they were heard. This perhaps reflects, at least in part, Tamang peoples' 'culturally distanced relationship to the state' symbolizing 'a population marked by centuries of structural violence' (B. Campbell 2018: 111).

> We are invited to meetings in [nearby village] or Chautara [the district headquarters] with other villagers. If they are concerned for us, they should conduct meetings here as we feel comfortable talking here where we feel we are heard.... Our voices wouldn't get mixed with the problems of other villages and some actions or work will actually happen if they focus on us.[31]

There was some discussion about the possibility of requesting a re-assessment by the government, although the reasons for this request were unclear. Other residents expressed concern that more landslides might occur during the coming (2019) monsoon and sought advice from the natural scientists in our team regarding the small-scale mitigation measures that could be put in place. In April 2019 residents were constructing new houses

---

29 Interview, Upper Bhote Kosi Valley, 10 December 2018.
30 Interview, Upper Bhote Kosi Valley, 1 April 2019.
31 Group Interview, Upper Bhote Kosi Valley, 2 April 2019.

in their village using corrugated sheets and simple steel frames. These were still considered temporary houses but were better than the houses they had been living in since the earthquakes. They ultimately planned to rebuild their houses with stone and mud as before, but were hesitating to do so, implying, perhaps, that their decision not to relocate was still to be finalized.

It was thus to our surprise that, upon returning to the valley in February 2020, we were told that a new integrated settlement was being constructed for the displaced Tamang householders and that they were no longer living in their original village. We met with some of the householders at the site of the new settlement, where cement brick houses were being constructed with local NGO support on the land previously purchased collectively using the government payment. This time, however, there was road access to the settlement from the main highway which, we were told, was made possible by the municipal chief who had facilitated the purchasing of the land and provided his excavator to construct the road. Residents were still living in their natal village, with plans to move to the newly constructed houses during the monsoon months when the integrated settlement was finished. As residents explained in a small group discussion, they could reconstruct their houses in their village but the government's recommendation to relocate would not change and they expressed concern that the government would not provide them with any support. Exploring this point further, it became clear that the householders saw the move to the integrated settlement as a sensible financial move; this would be a 'free house' from a government that had provided little if any assistance in the past. Further, the new road had gone some way to alleviating the political tensions between the different communities mentioned earlier. The residents of the settlement in sketch 1 were therefore engaging with the efforts of outsiders to rebuild their lives, but on their own terms. Indeed, to use Liechty and Hutt's words (this volume), they were deciding 'which pasts to rebuild and which futures to claim' (emphasis in the original).

Back in June 2008, Oven interviewed the then Local Development Officer of Sindhupalchok district in Chautara. He explained: 'We say that people directly affected by disasters will be resettled, but it takes years and years to find alternate land and to resettle people. The policy is there but it is difficult to implement because of lack of resource.'[32] But as this sketch has shown,

---

[32] Interview, District Development Committee Office, Chautara, June 2008.

a lack of resources is only part of the problem. It is well documented that caste, ethnicity, gender, income levels, and political party networks intersect to affect vulnerability and resilience to disasters in Nepal (see, for example, Nagoda and Nightingale 2017 and Oven et al. 2019 in the context of drought and flooding, respectively). Indeed, while the Geohazard Assessment may be designed to benefit vulnerable households (in the context of landslides), patronage and power can lead to elite capture, to the detriment of those most in need. While some of these issues appear to have been resolved, the sketch serves to highlight some of the political, cultural, emotional, temporal, and material dynamics at play (Liechty and Hutt, this volume), as residents rebuild their lives.

Sketch 2

The second sketch is from a village in the hills above the Arniko Highway. The settlement comprised approximately 90 households across five *tols*, the majority of which were Sherpa and Dalit (60 and 25 households, respectively), interspersed with a small number of Chhetri households. The Sherpa householders, many of whom were Lama (religious practitioners of Sherpa ethnicity), had strong social ties, reflecting a shared ancestry. As our host explained, 'All the Lamas here belong to the same clan. We are all relatives of each other.'[33] The Lama householders were mainly concentrated in two of the five *tols*, near to the *gumba* (monastery), which, according to one elder, had been in the village for more than 20 generations.

Unsurprisingly, then, residents had a strong attachment to the place. A new *gumba*, built to replace the previous, very old, monastery, was completed shortly before the earthquakes in 2015. Sadly, during the first earthquake, the bottom storey of the new monastery collapsed, and was damaged beyond repair. Residents were, understandably, keen to rebuild the *gumba*, a symbol of their shared culture, ethnicity, and religion.[34] Our second visit, in March 2017, coincided with a visit from a *lama* from India. Many young people who had migrated to Kathmandu for employment following the

---

[33] Interview, Upper Bhote Kosi Valley, 29 March 2019.

[34] See Sherry et al. (2018) for a related discussion on cultural landscapes of risk among the Sherpa peoples of Nepal.

earthquakes had returned to the village for the ceremony. Afterwards, we were invited to a small building which was being used to store the statues recovered from the *gumba*. There we were asked many questions about the earthquakes and landslides and, most importantly, if it was safe to rebuild the *gumba*. As noted by Campbell, in a Tamang community in neighbouring Rasuwa district, residents 'made it their collective priority to rebuild their Buddhist temple, accommodate their fragile family of statues and, thereby, restore their internal communicative order for recognising the recovering citizenship of household dharma, from which blessings and power can circulate' (B. Campbell 2018: 122). Rebuilding was about 'gather[ing] the whole village together, raising general esteem, and providing a sense of recovery' (B. Campbell 2018: 114).

A formal assessment of the landslide risk, undertaken following the 2015 earthquakes by the Department of Mines and Geology, resulted in the recommendation that the whole village should relocate. This recommendation reflected a concern that the downward movement of the land, observed by the residents themselves at the time of the earthquakes, and the cracks that had developed across the hillside, could indicate the potential for a large landslide. However, as discussed in the context of sketch 1, residents received their initial housing grants before they were informed of this recommendation, so people had already started to rebuild their homes: 'The government hasn't said anything about the relocation after they came for [the housing] assessment. And even the *pradhikaran* [NRA] has also provided the tranches of support that means we think [the village] is not a dangerous place, otherwise there should be information.'[35] According to a representative from UNOPS, which provided technical support to the NRA for the Geohazard Assessment, this was deliberate. If the government was seen to be withholding the housing reconstruction grants from householders in Category 3 communities, it would be viewed as forced relocation. However, as noted by the lead social mobilizer in Chautara, the reconstruction payments for Category 3 communities were halted in other districts to 'indirectly pressurize householders to relocate'[36] but this was not the case in Sindhupalchok. There was some concern amongst residents that if they rebuilt on a Category 3 site where relocation had been recommended,

---

[35] Interview, Upper Bhote Kosi Valley, 26 November 2018.
[36] Interview, Chautara, Sindhupalchok, 28 March 2019.

the Government of Nepal could refuse to provide services, in particular, electricity, as well as birth and citizenship registration, although there was no evidence to suggest that this would actually be the case.[37]

Rather than viewing the Geohazard Assessment as an opportunity to 'bolster previous state-territorialising stances' (B. Campbell 2017: 73), our own experience of engaging with the NRA Executive Committee over a three-year period suggests that they were more concerned about their case load of Category 3 communities increasing, and managing the expectations of earthquake victims. However, when asked directly if relocation was a recommendation or a requirement, one NRA official noted that 'Category 3 means you must [relocate].... In formal terms it may have been [a] recommendation, but it is [a] must. Nobody in Category 3 land [should] live there. They have to vacate that land'.[38] The 'sensitivities' associated with this were, at the same time, acknowledged. From a

> vulnerability [to the hazard] point of view ... it is sensible but the social sensitivities are there because there are *gumbas*, monasteries there and their ancestral burial location is somewhere there, they grew up there and would like to live there, so this type of human feeling[s] are there.... It has to be voluntary, it cannot be forceful.... People have to be absolutely convinced. If not, we cannot touch, the government will not touch because it would trigger a huge amount of resentment.[39]

In June 2018, the residents wrote to the NRA to confirm that the community would not be relocating. They were deciding to rebuild their lives in the village, against the recommendation of the outsiders who had come to assist. This decision reflected a number of factors. First, their own perceptions of risk. As members of the mothers' group explained, they were scared at the time of the earthquakes and did not know where to go but 'it's been a long time now so it [the sinking of the land] probably won't happen again'.[40] The

---

[37]　Such rumoured threats were also noted by Limbu et al. (2019) in their study of post-earthquake reconstruction in Bhaktapur, Dhading, and Sindhupalchok.

[38]　Interview, Kathmandu, 26 February 2020.

[39]　Interview, Kathmandu, 26 February 2020.

[40]　Interview, Upper Bhote Kosi Valley, 30 March 2019.

risks no longer seemed urgent, at least for the residents in the main *tol* near the monastery. Second, and as outlined earlier, the importance of the site's symbolic and cultural value, and the clan's tie to their ancestral land. Third, financial concerns: 'We have considered relocating but the Government of Nepal only gives us 2 lakh [200,000] rupees and this is not enough as the land in [a neighbouring village, where they would consider moving] is 12 lakh [1,200,000].'[41]

Importantly, the decision to remain in the village and not relocate was not shared by all residents. As a householder displaced by landslides explained, 'The people near the monastery [the influential Lamas] and in the neighbouring village make the decisions.'[42] Indeed, a number of residents felt disconnected from the decision-makers within the community: 'The political party representatives make the decisions here. They are all in Kathmandu so the issues here don't really matter for them. Big people are not concerned with petty things.'[43] The small number of households that were directly impacted by landslides, or that live below active landslides in two of the five *tols* in particular, were more positive about the idea of relocation. As a young Sherpa man who lost his house and three goats to a debris flow explained, 'People [living near the monastery (*gumba*)] don't want to go, but if we had the option we would have gone.'[44] He had heard from the government that he would be relocated to a neighbouring village but he had not heard anything further. Indeed, he did not sign the letter saying that the community would not be relocating, although it was unclear whether or not he had been given the opportunity to do so. He noted, 'Only specific *tols* in [the village] are our community. All political leaders are from [near the monastery] and they face a different set of issues.'[45] Importantly, however, for those households impacted by landslides, relocation was not seen as the answer outright. 'We are scared about relocating too. Will the land be big enough? What about the impact on our livelihoods? We need to keep our original land so we can continue to farm.'[46]

[41] Interview, Upper Bhote Kosi Valley, 30 March 2019.
[42] Interview, Upper Bhote Kosi Valley, 30 March 2019.
[43] Interview, Upper Bhote Kosi Valley, 30 March 2019.
[44] Interview, Upper Bhote Kosi Valley, 30 March 2019.
[45] Interview, Upper Bhote Kosi Valley, 30 March 2019.
[46] Interview, Upper Bhote Kosi Valley, 30 March 2019.

Sketch 2 highlights three significant issues in the context of relocation. First, we were dealing with complex landscape change and incomplete knowledge of the landslide risk and how this would change over time. Residents were looking for concrete answers to their questions and concerns which scientists were unable to give. Second, it is essential to recognize the 'dynamic, complex relationship between communities and their land' (Nightingale 2003: 80). For the Sherpa people living in the village, their ancestral history and the presence of the Buddhist *gumba*, which is important for their own cultural practice, tied them to this particular place. These semiotic dimensions cannot be ignored by scientists, governments, or NGOs in the context of landslide risk management. Third, there was a political element to the decision-making processes underway, which were being led by, and in the interests of, particular members of the Sherpa community. The situation and views of other residents living in the immediate path of active debris flow channels were not being seen or heard. This is where the ward-level landslide maps offer significant potential as a micro-scale hazard assessment tool, providing householders, local leaders (including the local government), and the NRA with a more nuanced understanding of risk across a given community. In the case of sketch 2, the mapping suggests that not all houses were at equal risk and it may have been unnecessary, from a landslide exposure perspective, for the whole community to be designated as Category 3.[47]

Conclusion

The 2015 earthquakes have transformed the physical landscape and have, as a result, created a new risk environment. It is therefore necessary to consider the question of reconstruction not just from the perspective of housing design and earthquake-safe construction practices, but from the land and the landscape itself. The experience of the earthquakes showed vividly that whilst an earthquake-resistant building may withstand the shaking, the location matters too. Of course, rural residents have been living with

---

[47] According to the NGO supporting displaced households with relocation, interviewed in February 2020, the community in sketch 2 was revisited by members of the NRA executive and technical specialists before the monsoon in 2019. The site was reassessed, and the settlement was downgraded to Category 2.

landslides for generations, and have developed their own understandings and management practices, which are widely documented (see, for example, Johnson, Olson, and Manandhar 1982; Bjønness 1986; Smadja 2009). However, what happens when the hazard context changes completely, as was the case after April 2015, with landslides occurring in new locations not previously at risk, and the nature of the landslide hazard itself also altering?

In this chapter, we have viewed the landscape from two very different perspectives: First, from above—the view mapped from space, detached from the local context and devoid of local meaning. Second, from below—the situated account, which begins to unpack the local politics at play and the cultural and personal meaning attached to place in this post-earthquake context. In so doing, we recognize that the knowledges generated 'are partial and that [the] different vantage points ... produce different views of particular processes and events' (Nightingale 2003: 80).

Wary of the claims commonly made by users of remote sensing data of its 'objectivity and neutrality' (Nightingale 2003: 79), the mapping work has the potential to challenge the politicized perspective from below, which relies largely on local government reporting of landslide-affected settlements requiring a site visit and assessment. Indeed, as Ghale (2019) reminds us, the seniormost official in any district across Nepal is likely to be a high-caste man with little or no understanding of local language or culture, which raises genuine concerns about representation. While the elections for local mayors offered some hope for representation and accountability, this was not always the outcome.[48] The view from above also renders more geographically (and commonly politically) remote areas visible and as equally represented as others, which may not otherwise be so. The mapping has the potential to provide a different perspective for residents themselves, which they can explore, question, and challenge, and layer with their own local knowledge and situated understandings. Used in this way, the maps are not simply a 'blunt instrument', to use Campbell's (2017) term, but a potential tool for empowerment which could enable residents to make more informed decisions and, if necessary, make a case for their own relocation, or indeed their own decision to stay. Importantly here, unlike the Geohazard

---

[48] For the *Nepali Times*, in their article on model mayors, '[m]ost [mayors] are good-for-nothing puppets of their political masters, many are corrupt construction contractors behaving like foxes guarding the chicken coup, while a few who want to improve their cities or villages have no idea how to do it' (*Nepali Times* 2018).

Assessment, which provides a single risk categorization for a settlement, the satellite mapping can provide a more detailed relative risk assessment at the household level.

There are, of course, caveats. As soon as a map is drawn it is outdated, particularly in a rapidly evolving environmental and reconstruction context. There is also potential for the maps to 'perpetuate rather than alleviate the conditions that create differential vulnerability patterns at village level' (Nagoda and Nightingale 2017: 85). Maps delineating land or individual houses at risk could drive down land prices, either through what they show or how they are correctly or incorrectly interpreted to stigmatize particular households, or the reverse, likely in favour of particular beneficiaries. They could be used to make a case for forced relocation, or to force a cartographic delineation of a community in a context where space is defined or understood in very different ways. Reconstruction may require relocation, but what happens when relocation is impossible due to a lack of land or money, or because it is culturally undesirable? For sure, some places are more straightforward to relocate, but some places made meaningful through cultural practice—for example, the Buddhist *gumba*—are not. This semiotic dimension cannot be ignored by scientists, governments, or NGOs in post-disaster reconstruction. This, we argue, is where exploring landslide risk from different methodological and analytical perspectives offers real value and insight.

PART III

Rebuilding Structures

8

The Politics of Participatory Disaster Governance in Nepal's Post-earthquake Reconstruction

Nimesh Dhungana

Introduction

The 2015 Nepal earthquakes were not only an epicentre of human suffering, they also invigorated various forms of citizen- and civil-society-driven initiatives that brought both the Government of Nepal and the humanitarian community under close public scrutiny and criticism (Dhungana 2019). Amid these criticisms, the government adopted the globally circulated vision to 'build back better' Nepal, with a focus on the 'owner-led reconstruction' of damaged houses that also pledged a participatory and accountable governance of reconstruction. The 'Nepal Earthquake 2015: Post-disaster Needs Assessment' (PDNA) report, a major policy document published in June 2015, less than two months after the first earthquake, articulated the government's commitment to the participatory governance of reconstruction as follows:

> The GoN [Government of Nepal] will work to strengthen governance systems more broadly in line with the Good Governance Act of 2006 [*sic*]. This will include strengthening accountability processes, working collaboratively with civil society, strengthening citizen service centres and rule of law processes, and ensuring the participation of the most vulnerable, affected populations in decision-making processes. (NPC 2015b: 255)

The National Reconstruction Act, promulgated in December 2015, reiterated the government's vision of 'prompt completion of the reconstruction works', coupled with a sustainable, resilient, and social-justice-based approach to longer term reconstruction (Government of Nepal, Ministry of Law, Justice and Parliamentary Affairs 2015). The Act also laid the foundation for a central body, the National Reconstruction Authority (NRA), which would be responsible for overseeing and coordinating post-disaster reconstruction.

Using Nepal's post-earthquake environment as an empirical context, this chapter engages with the hitherto little understood topic of the politics of participatory disaster governance within post-disaster reconstruction efforts. Drawing on the concept of spaces of participation (Gaventa 2006), and using an ethnographic mode of inquiry, the chapter critically investigates the interface between the policy and practice of participatory governance in Nepal's post-earthquake housing reconstruction. Specifically, it aims to locate the politics of participatory governance of disasters within state–society relations and explores the potential and limitations of such politics in enabling disaster-affected citizens to influence the policy and practice of housing reconstruction.

The participatory governance of disaster

Disaster scholars have long called for a participatory and accountable mode of disaster recovery that gives primacy to the voices and rights of disaster-affected communities (Cuny 1983). Since the mid-1990s, in response to the growing criticism of a performance deficit with which both state and non-state agencies working in humanitarian disasters were faced, varied forms of international standards and procedures of accountability and participation have proliferated in the disaster sector. All of these initiatives claim, explicitly or implicitly, to make disaster reconstruction community-centric, participatory, and accountable (The Sphere Project 2011; CHS Alliance 2014; UNISDR 2015).

Given the growing complexity of disasters and disaster responses, the conceptual and practical boundaries of participation have also expanded. The practice of disaster governance is increasingly seen as polycentric, involving the participation of and collaboration between variously located state and non-state humanitarian agencies, communities, and experts. These are expected to hold different roles and responsibilities in the task of making disaster recovery responsive to the needs of those affected (Tierney 2012; Bakkour et al. 2015; Bae, Joo, and Won 2016). While primarily focused on disaster risk reduction, the recently introduced Sendai Framework calls for 'mutual outreach, partnership, complementarity in roles and accountability, and follow-up' among state and non-state actors (UNISDR 2015:13). Despite these global policy initiatives, Raju and da Costa (2018) argue that both the conceptualization and implementation of participatory and accountable governance of disasters remain relatively misunderstood.

The politics of participatory governance

Despite the growing normative and policy appeal of participatory governance in disaster contexts, the critical literature reminds us that power and politics often impinge on its practices and outcomes. Scholars of critical participatory development have noted that participation is embedded in, intertwined with, and shaped by politics and power dynamics, which often reproduce power inequalities instead of empowering local communities (White 1996; Cooke and Kothari 2001; Mansuri and Rao 2012).

As an empirical context for this study, Nepal's experience with community-based natural resource management serves as testimony to the unpredictable and often unintended outcomes associated with participatory governance. Hailed as an international success story in the 1990s for its unique approach to participatory resource governance, Nepal's community-based natural resource governance has in recent years come under scholarly criticism for failing to overcome the unequal nature of benefit sharing and resource allocation (Shrestha and McManus 2008). Nepal's experience also underscores deep-seated social inequalities that impinge on the deliberative and democratic ethos which underpins localized participatory spaces (Ojha, Cameron, and Kumar 2009). Moreover, in aid-recipient societies, the rhetoric of participation and related notions of empowerment and accountability tend to be used to realize previously determined agendas, not to democratize the structuring and execution of aid programmes (Cornwall and Brock 2005). Donors' emphasis on professionalism, effectiveness, and expertise often outweighs the demands for participation, accountability, and justice in aid-recipient communities (Barnett 2013).

Given the critical evidence, a plural outlook on the potential and pitfalls of participatory governance is warranted. As an analytical entry point, this chapter uses John Gaventa's conceptualization of 'spaces of participation', which encourages a complex and heterogeneous understanding of participatory spaces (Gaventa 2006).[1] Gaventa argues that in response to the growing criticism of 'governance deficit' in the public sector, state agencies have actively promoted varied forms of participatory spaces of governance, or 'invited spaces' such as consultation meetings between citizens and authorities, to improve the quality of public sector performance. Citizens, on the other hand, continue to invent independent forms of participatory mechanisms or 'claimed spaces' such as advocacy initiatives, social movements, and community associations, to challenge and contest the state's decisions and public sector performance (Gaventa 2006: 26–27). Despite the availability of invited and claimed spaces, according to Gaventa, actual decision-making processes may still take place within the narrow realm of powerholders (closed spaces), highlighting the risk that the transformative potential of participatory spaces will be compromised, co-opted, or neglected.

The politics and complexity of participatory governance in a disaster context

While the debates mentioned above mostly pertain to everyday development contexts, the processes and outcomes of citizen participation and accountability become even more unpredictable in post-disaster contexts. While calls for participation and accountability are common in the wake of disasters, scholars also argue that in the longer run state actors often prove adept at deflecting such calls for policy or institutional changes (Olson 2000; Boin, McConnell, and Hart 2008; Pelling and Dill 2010; Venugopal and Yasir 2017). When faced with major pressure to save lives, state actors are also skilled at promoting and mobilizing voluntary efforts by citizens, but such efforts may be neglected, or even considered as a deterrent towards longer-term reconstruction (Hayward 2014). It is also observed that citizen-driven reconstruction activities often falter in the face of a government's indifference and neglect (Davidson et al. 2007; Cho 2014). The transformative potential of participation in a post-

---

[1]   Gaventa's version of 'spaces of participation' here builds on the works of other social and participatory scholars, notably Andrea Cornwall (2002), who, in turn, drew inspiration from Henri Lefebvre's (1991) work on the social production of space.

disaster context can also be hampered by issues inherent to participatory mechanisms. The absence of a strong civil society, systems of patronage, and the existence of partisan politics may further limit the interest and ability of disaster-affected communities to engage with and influence local authorities (Pelling 1998).

Yet this should not lead us to discount the potential of citizen participation in post-disaster contexts. Efforts to make disaster recovery participatory and deliberative have been seen to emerge alongside state-driven modes of disaster recovery and reconstruction (Cho 2014; Cretney 2018). Curato (2018), in her ethnographic study of post–Typhoon Haiyan Philippines, found that the practices of post-disaster governance there ranged across authoritarian, communitarian, and deliberative modes, evoking the possibility for different forms of participatory spaces and struggles that disasters can spark. Cretney (2018) provides similar evidence, suggesting that a mixture of community-driven participatory initiatives, including local hearings, emerged in the aftermath of the 2010 Canterbury earthquake, which served as a countervailing force against the top-down, state-led recovery processes.

This chapter draws on these emerging debates to explore the nature and implications of the politics of participatory disaster governance that played out in Nepal's post-earthquake housing reconstruction efforts. The study was conducted in a context where the Government of Nepal had made an explicit commitment to give primacy to participation and accountability in the disaster reconstruction (National Planning Commission 2015a). My main aim is to challenge the normative underpinning of participatory disaster governance, which views participation by local communities as a precondition for effective disaster recovery, on the one hand, and their democratic right, on the other. The chapter locates disaster governance, and within it participation and accountability, beyond the managerial and administrative logics of disaster recovery but within the complex state–society politics that tend to both influence the response to a disaster and, in turn, be influenced by that disaster (Hilhorst 2004: 60). It assumes that while participatory ideals and practices run the risk of falling prey to the state's technical and managerial logics of disaster response, citizens may simultaneously use such spaces to pursue 'a new form of [disaster] citizenship for a new era of governance', foregrounded in the values of rights, entitlements, and solidarity (Remes 2016: 20).

Methodology

Methodologically, this study draws inspiration from and contributes to contemporary forms of ethnography of development (Mosse 2004; Lewis and Mosse 2006; Cornish et al. 2012) and ethnography of disaster response (Klinenberg 2003; Andersson 2014; Curato 2018). Specifically, it is informed by 'interface analysis', in which ethnographers seek to bring variously situated actors and activities (for example, beneficiaries, local implementers, state officials, donors) 'into one analytical frame' (Lewis and Mosse 2006; Andersson 2014: 285). The aim is to examine the contradictions and complexities of policy interventions, that is, 'the relation of policy and practice not as instrumental or scripted translation of ideas into reality, but as a messy free-for-all in which processes are often uncontrollable and results uncertain' (Lewis and Mosse 2006: 9). As an exploratory study, it also seeks to reveal political contestation and the possibilities that permeate invited and claimed spaces of participation (Gaventa 2006). For analytical purposes, the term 'invited spaces' here refers to state-mandated, formalized modes of participatory spaces (for example, public hearings, consultative meetings), while 'claimed spaces' include citizen- or civil-society-led initiatives (for example, community meetings, local advocacy, and monitoring activities), primarily geared at challenging the state's policies and plans for bringing improvement in the delivery of public services.

Fieldwork, data sources, and analysis

Ethnographic fieldwork was conducted for three months from March to May 2016, spanning two sites: Sankharapur Municipality (Sankhu), a peri-urban community on the outskirts of Kathmandu, and Kathmandu, the centre of policy-making.

Sankhu is a traditional Newar[2] settlement, with an estimated population of 28,854 (as of 2016), located in the northeast of the Kathmandu Valley.

---

[2]   Newars are the original inhabitants of Kathmandu Valley. Famous for their indigenous culture and craftmanship, most of the Newar communities within Kathmandu operate through community-based organizations (CBOs) called *guthis*. Many such *guthis* also exist in Sankhu and played a critical role in early response and recovery.

With 98 deaths, 6,452 houses fully destroyed, and 587 houses partially destroyed, the April 2015 earthquakes and the subsequent aftershocks had a devastating effect on Sankhu.[3] In the aftermath of the earthquakes, Sankhu saw an influx of national and international non-governmental organizations (NGOs), volunteers, and citizen groups, to join the local rescue and relief efforts. As a site of historical and cultural significance, it also garnered attention for longer-term conservation and recovery, making it a suitable site for ethnographic investigation.

The ethnographic inquiry was also conducted in Kathmandu. As the nation's capital, Kathmandu represented the site of a polycentric post-disaster governance system (Tierney 2012), with varied forms of interactions among state and non-state actors involved in the recovery and reconstruction. One such site of interactions was the Housing Recovery and Reconstruction Platform (HRRP), an internationally recognized and government-mandated collaborative disaster governance forum. Participant observation of HRRP meetings helped to reveal the governance expectations of various actors, including the NRA and other relevant government units, and humanitarian NGOs. Fieldwork in Kathmandu was also supplemented by my observation of a district-level public hearing[4] and a policy dissemination meeting focused on longer-term reconstruction.

My ethnographic evidence consisted of field notes from participant observation at a total of nine meetings—community meetings, public hearings, reconstruction-related meetings, and policy dissemination meetings—that represented a mix of invited and claimed spaces of participation. The research also involved regular field trips to Sankhu, where I observed the status of the reconstruction and conducted interviews

---

[3]   These figures were generated as part of the ethnographic fieldwork/interviews with the officials at the Sankharapur Municipality Office.

[4]   According to the Good Governance Act 2008, local bodies in Nepal are required to organize public hearings with the purpose of 'making the activities of the office fair, transparent, and objective and addressing the lawful concerns of general people and stakeholders' (Government of Nepal 2008: 24). Since these public hearings are organized on a trimester basis and their organization is entirely dependent on the government, I managed to attend only one during my fieldwork. It nevertheless served as a major lens through which to understand the general functioning of such meetings, the kinds of issues that are raised, and the government officials' reactions and conduct in such meetings.

with local communities and officials. In addition, my analysis also involved 21 semi-structured interviews with 13 policy-makers, high-level public officials, and politicians in Kathmandu, and 8 local-level officials and community members from Sankhu. Interviewees were purposively selected given their knowledge of and experiences in responding to the earthquakes. Data analysis was complemented by a review of key documentary evidence, including recovery- and reconstruction-related policy and legislative measures, minutes from selected HRRP meetings, and documents retrieved from the local government bodies.

Ethical approval for the study was granted by the LSE Research Ethics Committee, and interviews were conducted after securing informed consent from participants. The identities of the individual interviewees are either anonymized or replaced with pseudonyms in the findings. Most of the participant observation data came from attendance of meetings that were, in principle, open to the public. As far as possible, the organizers were informed of my identity and aims, but informed consent was not sought from individual participants of such meetings. Although the identity of a few individuals may be traceable due to the nature of their professional status, their words were spoken in a public setting and the findings presented here possess no significant professional risk to such individuals.

It is widely acknowledged that there is no single or linear approach to ethnographic analysis. Nor is the analytical process independent of the ethnographer's presumptions, biography, and hunches (Hammersley and Atkinson 2007). Data analysis followed coding of the ethnographic data, aided by the NVivo11 software. Special attention was given to specific vignettes or 'snapshots or short descriptions of events', which provided a representative account of the phenomenon in question (LeCompte and Schensul 2013: 269). Additionally, data analysis was also supplemented by the author's positionality and reflexivity as a native of Nepal, former development practitioner, and observer of the Nepal earthquake response, albeit from a distance.

In pursuit of owner-led reconstruction

In the weeks following the earthquakes, adhering to international standards for post-disaster reconstruction, the government conducted a rapid assessment of the socioeconomic effects of the disaster. Its PDNA report

(National Planning Commission 2015a, 2015b) estimated 498,852 houses as 'fully damaged' and in need of reconstruction assistance. The government also adopted the term 'owner-led reconstruction'. A donor conference was held in June 2015 to coincide with the launch of the PDNA, in which the international donor community pledged aid of over USD 4 billion to 'build back better' Nepal.

The topic of governance, and within it, participation and accountability, was given special consideration in the PDNA. A member of a multilateral aid agency, who contributed to the planning and execution of the PDNA, remarked that prioritizing governance within long-term reconstruction meant an emphasis 'not on what forms of aid are delivered and how much [aid], but how recovery activities are delivered'.[5] Establishing the necessary standards for 'how' the recovery and reconstruction was to be pursued became a major priority of the post-disaster reconstruction.

Eight months after the April earthquake, in December 2015, the NRA was launched, establishing two conditions for 'owner-led reconstruction': (*a*) verification of eligible individual house-owners for housing assistance and (*b*) establishment of monitoring mechanisms to ensure the proper utilization of the individual housing grants.

This was accompanied by the establishment of the 'Multidoor Basket Fund' involving the key bilateral and multilateral donors that were supporting housing reconstruction. The process involved eligibility determination of the affected households/house-owners through a comprehensive household census, called the Nepal—Household Registration for Housing Reconstruction, across the 14 most affected districts. The census sought to capture information about damaged houses, together with demographic information about their owners. The analysis of this data would result in the verification of eligible grantees and the setting up of formal 'Participation Agreements' between individual grantees and their local government unit.

While an assessment of damaged households had already been conducted for the PDNA, the new census sought to make the reconstruction more 'scientific' and 'evidence-based'. The donor community was of the view that the original estimate of the number of damaged houses was 'inflated' at the local level. It was also determined that the original cash assistance of NPR 15,000 (c. USD 136) per household, given as a 'relief fund' to build

---

[5]   Personal communication, 9 May 2016.

temporary shelters to those with 'fully damaged' houses, had been widely misused by the affected households. The reassessment, therefore, was also focused at minimizing wastage in the deployment of housing assistance.

The eligible house-owners were entitled to NPR 200,000 (c. USD 1,800)[6] in housing grants, which were to be disbursed in three separate instalments. Part of the terms of the 'Participation Agreement' was that the individual grantees were required to hold or otherwise set up a bank account in which this financial assistance would be deposited. This was to ensure the proper monitoring of the usage of housing grants and hence avert the risk that the cash assistance would be misused. Despite the term 'owner-led', which evoked a notion that individual house-owners had the ultimate power to determine the nature of the reconstruction, it hardly gave citizens any role in or ownership of decisions regarding the course of the reconstruction. Instead, it devolved the responsibility for self-regulation, monitoring, and financial risk management to individual house-owners.

Conditional participation

The policy of state-led 'owner-led reconstruction', as indicated above, provided little space for local participation. What is noteworthy, however, is that the possibility of house-owner participation was not completely discarded. Rather, the participation of and accountability to local communities were conceived and integrated as contingent upon the completion of the eligibility determination process, with those failing to make it to the eligibility list being given the opportunity to appeal, or to lodge formal complaints with the relevant local government unit. In other words, the voice of the affected communities was to be given consideration through a locally available Grievance Handling Mechanism.

The model was problematic for two reasons. First, the state's promised housing entitlement of NPR 200,000 and the criteria associated with its disbursal were determined without meaningful citizen engagement. Despite the policy rhetoric, this already undermined the inherent right of the individual house-owners to shape the course of the post-disaster reconstruction. Second, the administration of the eligibility determination process produced

---

6   The amount was later increased to NPR 300,000 (c. USD 2,700).

an uncertainty for local communities awaiting reconstruction assistance. The effect of this was evident at the local level. By the time I completed my fieldwork in May 2016, 13 months after the first earthquake, there was no clear sign of the census starting in urban communities, including Sankhu. As a result, local communities' participation in the reconstruction was dependent upon the effective completion of expert-led regulatory processes. But those very processes were slow or non-existent, and were directed from the top, which meant that they were at odds with the democratic underpinning of participatory disaster governance.

Standardizing NGOs' participation and a partnership of convenience

In the immediate aftermath of the 25 April earthquake, the Nepal government made a special appeal to the international community to support the recovery and reconstruction effort, and many domestic and international humanitarian agencies responded to this appeal. But the growing involvement of the NGO sector soon became a concern for the government. Sagar, a senior official in charge of coordinating and planning the emergency response, alleged that the NGO sector 'systematically bypassed the government'. The NGOs were also accused of not consulting the local authorities, and of competing with one another, leading to fragmented and uncoordinated recovery efforts.[7]

A major goal of the NRA was therefore to ensure that the longer-term reconstruction took place in a standardized and coordinated manner. Its participation in meetings with NGOs was primarily geared at realizing this goal. This was mostly evident through my observation of HRRP meetings.

The HRRP was established in December 2015, coinciding with the establishment of the NRA. Together with the NRA, the platform sought to cultivate a dialogue among widely dispersed domestic and international humanitarian and development NGOs or 'partner organizations'.

While this fieldwork was being conducted, humanitarian NGOs were instructed by the NRA to suspend their reconstruction activities, raising confusion regarding their future role in Nepal's post-disaster reconstruction.

---

[7]   Interview with Sagar, 15 March 2016.

The HRRP meetings, in principle, were an opportunity for these NGOs to have a dialogue with the NRA regarding such policy decisions. Yet my observation of HRRP meetings did not reveal any major opposition to the NRA's decision, or any serious engagement between state and non-state actors. Rather, such meetings were used by the NRA officials to justify the launch of the census, to reassert the NRA's policy decisions, and to seek cooperation from the humanitarian sector to make the ongoing housing survey and subsequent 'enrolment' of local communities in the housing agreement a success. Consider this comment made by the Chief Executive Officer (CEO) of the NRA in one of the HRRP meetings:

> We would like to get your [NGOs'] feedback on the policies, but before that I would like to emphasize on [the beneficiary] enrolment support. I know many organizations are willing to provide housing grant[s] to the affected populations. But we have asked them to stop this for the time being until we streamline the overall approach. It has to be within the policy framework and, as you know, at the moment we have the survey going on, and on the basis of the survey we will be in the position to identify the poorest populations, marginalized populations to give extra level of support.[8]

While these meetings saw the NRA officials attempting to legitimize their decisions and use the humanitarian sector to realize their goal of 'owner-led reconstruction', they were attended only irregularly and intermittently by senior NRA officials, raising questions over the participatory and collaborative rhetoric that underpinned such meetings. The frustration of participants at these meetings would be palpable when senior-level NRA officials failed to show up, or simply sought cooperation from the NGOs, rather than engaging with them on policy issues. In one such meeting, a participant told me 'there is no point in attending these meetings'. On another occasion, while the senior NRA officials were themselves absent, their agenda was indirectly endorsed by a major donor official who, while defending the NRA's absence, also encouraged NGO actors to cooperate and become 'forthcoming' in making the 'beneficiary enrolment' process a success.

---

[8]   Department of Urban Development and Building Construction (DUBDC) building, Kathmandu, 17 March 2016.

The 'weak capacity' and uncertain role of government-induced participatory mechanisms

When the earthquake struck, the central government became anxious about the local government bodies' capacity to respond to the disaster. Besides the 'capacity crisis', Nepal had not had local elections for almost two decades and local governments were managed by bureaucrats. This further compounded the issue of coordination and representation at the local level. To address this problem, in the immediate aftermath of the earthquake, the Ministry of Federal Affairs and Local Development instructed local bodies to mobilize local community-based structures and activists to facilitate emergency aid distribution. The involvement of such local communities was considered central, in view of the 'weak capacity' of the local bodies in responding to the disaster.

In Sankhu too, the government sought the active participation of local community-based structures in coordinating emergency needs. One such community-based structure, the Ward Citizen Forum (WCF), was quickly mobilized, primarily to facilitate local-level coordination. WCFs are community-based structures set up under the government's broader plans to institutionalize and uphold the agenda of 'good governance' at the local level, particularly through the planning, monitoring, and evaluation of development projects.[9] A member of one such WCF mentioned having actively supported the government in its relief and recovery efforts. Another mentioned having collected data about the victims/households on his own, which was later used by the local government to develop a household-level 'beneficiary list' and to deliver relief funds of NPR 15,000 (c. USD 136) per household.

However, as the emergency phase of the earthquake relief made way for the longer-term recovery, these community organizers did not merely find their involvement diminishing but also expressed a sense of abandonment

---

[9] These structures were launched in 2005 against the backdrop of the attempted royal coup, and the brief suspension of democracy until the monarchy was overthrown in 2006 through a popular movement. Their origin and activity, therefore, were not uncontroversial. Because these were not elected bodies and worked under the guidelines set by the Ministry of Federal Affairs and Local Development, their claim of 'independence' was hotly contested by locals. In particular, local politicians considered them illegitimate and claimed they needed to be scrapped as and when local elections were held.

by the government. Bhanu, who spearheaded local relief efforts as a WCF coordinator, described his frustrations over the tendency of the government to instrumentalize participatory structures and local actors as per its convenience:

> The government put the WCFs in a trap. We are the ones who were directly responsible to the affected people. We are the ones who had to deal with the people in the emergency response. Even for the policy issue, we were expected to coordinate with affected people. We didn't get any incentive, no salary. We haven't received a single rupee in the name of incentive. We are not even given any money to have snacks. But we had to do so much work.... Now we have to listen to people's complaints and scoldings. The government officials and members of the political parties are sitting in their chairs, and they decide for us. And we are the ones who are expected to take their decisions to the local level.[10]

Local community actors such as Bhanu were also subject to 'people's complaints and scoldings' because the government-mandated spaces of participation proved to be increasingly removed from handling local concerns related to reconstruction. An excerpt from my field notes from a public hearing that was organized in Sankhu illustrates this point:

> During the whole public hearing that lasted for about 2 hours, only one question, towards the end, was raised concerning the earthquake recovery and relief. A participant stated that there are still some families who haven't received the [NPR] 15,000 assistance. He asked, 'Can you clarify, why is that?' He further asked, 'What is happening to the further [housing] assistance, and what initiative is being taken by the municipality'? The Executive Director of the Municipality responded by saying 'the Central Bureau of Statistics' under the direction of [the] NRA will soon be sending enumerators to assess the detailed damage of the houses. After that the real victims will be re-identified and assistance distributed. Beyond that even we also don't know much. We haven't been given a specific budget nor instructions by the NRA, despite our repeated efforts for the same.[11]

---

[10]   Interview with Bhanu, Sankhu, 4 May 2016.

[11]   Sankhu, 15 March 2016.

The above observation is telling for two reasons. First, in a meeting of over two hours, only one question was raised that directly pertained to earthquake relief and the reconstruction of Sankhu. Instead, the meeting appeared as a ritual, in which local administrators and politicians delivered speeches that were only remotely linked to reconstruction. Second, when questions were raised by the community, they mostly related to local water projects, the management and reconstruction of local roads, and the structuring of school management committees, among other topics, which had little connection to the housing reconstruction assistance promised by the government.

The lack of questions concerning the housing reconstruction in such forums, however, did not mean that such concerns did not afflict the locals. My fieldwork in the local communities provided ample evidence that it was a major, if not the sole concern, facing local communities. Consider this remark from Sapana, an active member of a local women's group:

> In my neighbourhood, many families are still living in temporary shelters. Three families had their roofs blown away by the wind. You know this is such a windy season, people don't feel secure. So the main problem is reconstruction [of houses]. Yes, people [in Sankhu] have everyday livelihood problems but people will eat whatever they find, they will manage, but building a house is a different thing. Even for middle class people like me, it is difficult. For poor families this is impossible.... The government has only promised [NPR] 2 lakhs [that is, 200,000] per household, but that is too little to build a house. How will people manage the rest?[12]

Sapana, given her status and role in the community, mentioned having to routinely confront such questions from local communities. This was corroborated by my fieldwork in the area. Almost a year after the earthquakes, very few houses had been reconstructed. Although the government had not explicitly prohibited the reconstruction of new houses, there was no dedicated mechanism for communicating this message to the communities, which meant that even those who were capable of rebuilding their houses without government assistance were discouraged from doing so. Government-induced public hearings like the one above were deficient in addressing local-

---

[12] Interview with Sapna, Sankhu, 20 May 2016.

level concerns and anxiety, let alone inviting citizen inputs concerning the reconstruction of Sankhu. Such events, as Suresh, an NGO activist, put it, 'are organized by the local government in haste because they are required to organize them',[13] meaning that this was part of the government's bureaucratic obligation, but was devoid of the political will to give the locals control over decisions surrounding the so-called owner-led reconstruction.

Episodic participatory spaces, uncertain outcomes

Despite the growing uncertainty, local communities and civil society activists were insistent on organizing alternative spaces in which to pursue a vision of locally driven reconstruction. The fact that the census had not started in urban communities like Sankhu was also seen as a window of opportunity for them to alter the course of reconstruction.

Such alternative spaces took the form of local meetings that allowed local communities to demand answers regarding delayed housing assistance and challenge the New Buildings Regulation introduced after the earthquakes. They also brought to the fore pre-existing concerns facing local communities, ranging across small and fragmented landholdings, the depleted socioeconomic opportunities facing local youth, and disregard for the cultural and religious heritage of Sankhu.

Others used such meetings to raise more deep-seated issues related to power inequalities between Kathmandu and Sankhu. In one of the meetings, a participant claimed that Sankhu, despite being in close proximity to the power centre, Kathmandu, had been systematically marginalized in the past. Another local activist accused the local government of neglect for not controlling illegal sand mining from a nearby river of cultural importance, which he claimed had intensified since the earthquakes. Locals also used the opportunity to express their feeling that the promised cash assistance for reconstruction was meagre, given the rising cost of building materials.

Despite such varied voices, the possibility that such meetings would lead to meaningful and substantial changes in the process of reconstruction appeared slim. Consider these proceedings from one of the meetings I observed. Termed 'Community-led, Community-based Reconstruction Meeting for Regeneration

---

[13]   Interview with Suresh, Kathmandu, 29 March 2016.

of Sankhu', the meeting was attended by the NRA's CEO, along with the local Member of Parliament and the Executive Director of Shankharapur (Sankhu) Municipality. The meeting started with some local activists making a case for the unique reconstruction needs of Sankhu town. A local activist highlighted the need for a distinct model of reconstruction for Sankhu, given its historical and cultural significance, while also ensuring that the new houses were equipped with state-of-the-art infrastructure. The CEO listened to the presentation. But the meeting showed a similar pattern of behaviour to that observed at central-level meetings. For the CEO, the meeting was yet another opportunity to communicate the expert-driven, evidence-oriented activities of the NRA, update people on the ongoing census and enrolment status, and express regret over the slow start of the reconstruction assistance in Sankhu. He mentioned '1,600 engineers have been mobilized to do reassessment of damaged houses. They will soon be starting the assessment in Sankhu'. Among other issues, the CEO also mentioned that the reconstruction of Sankhu would take local needs and priorities into account. Crucially, the onus was put on the affected communities to come up with a plan for reconstruction. The CEO stated, 'Give final shape to the master plan and I will make sure it gets supported.' A subsequent speaker, a political leader, echoed the CEO's remarks, asking the local communities to become more proactive in coming to a consensus about the specific agenda for Sankhu's reconstruction. After addressing the meeting, the CEO left the so-called interaction programme. Chaos ensued in the meeting hall with many following the CEO out with their unresolved questions, while others left the meeting shortly afterwards, in a visible sign of displeasure over the CEO's fleeting presence, and the lack of any opportunity for a meaningful interaction.[14]

One interviewee claimed that the phenomenon of participatory spaces turning into scenes of high-level officials visiting Sankhu, making conciliatory remarks, and offering a vague vision for the future recovery had happened several times during the year that had passed since the earthquakes. 'People come to the meeting to know what the government's plan is for Sankhu? How long do we have to wait?... All we know now is from the media, the news, but nobody [from the government] has told us what is happening for Sankhu.'[15]

---

[14]   Local school, Sankhu, 15 April 2016.
[15]   Sankhu, 4 May 2016.

Instances of such participatory forums failing to generate meaningful engagement between powerholders and locals were also observed at the central level. In one of the HRRP meetings in Kathmandu, local civil society/ NGO activists were invited to present their perspectives on the reconstruction issues facing urban communities within Kathmandu Valley. The idea of including local representation gained traction when in one of the earlier meetings, concerns were raised that local NGOs and local activists were given little space in such meetings. A civil society actor from Sankhu was also invited to share his ideas, in another infrequent opportunity to represent Sankhu. During his presentation, he made an impassioned appeal for special attention to be given to the unique reconstruction needs of Sankhu. Among other things, he criticized the tendency of government actors to overlook the role of local civil society, while also demanding more meaningful engagement between the communities and the local government:

> We are the local civil society organization, and we are here not to wait, but for raising our voice and action for rapid assistance for reconstruction..... We need more and more access to the local government, the Municipality, because that is our primary point of contact.[16]

However, government officials, including those from the NRA, who were ostensibly supposed to listen and respond to such voices, were not even present at this meeting. The facilitator of the meeting, representing a multilateral aid agency, reassured those present that the meeting minutes would be prepared, and circulated to the NRA leadership. Yet for the local activist it was a moment of missed opportunity.

'Don't ask the way to the village you are not travelling to'

The ethnographic evidence shows that the earthquakes reinvigorated interest among local communities and local civil society actors to forge a new vision for Sankhu. But it also suggests that such spaces may have stimulated

---

16   DUBDC building, Kathmandu, 26 May 2016.

a sense of mistrust and suspicion of the actors involved in reconstruction. One issue that was raised by several interviewees is that outmigration had been historically increasing in Sankhu. Prior to the earthquakes, many sociopolitically active members of the community had abandoned Sankhu to pursue a better quality of life in Kathmandu. Yet, claimed some, the earthquakes brought those people, and others, back to Sankhu, calling themselves 'locals'.

In one of the community meetings I asked a local political activist, Badri, how he came to know about the meeting and what his expectations were. He expressed a sense of doubt over the aims of the meeting and actors involved in it. Upon further probing, he mentioned that although one of the main organizers of the meeting had an ancestral home in Sankhu that had been destroyed by the earthquakes, his family had long left Sankhu and had lost touch with the local realities. However, as a successful engineer he could leverage his 'connections', and after the earthquakes he started representing Sankhu 'in the name of reconstruction'. 'These people know the donor community well. They know people in the NRA. They know how to bring money and they do things their way. It is a local event and I was invited, so I had to come, but I don't have much hope', he further added.[17]

Thus, while the transformative outcomes of the participatory spaces were far from clear, such spaces enabled locals to see the influx and intermingling of donors and state and non-state actors. Locals were prompted to question the organizers' claims to be representative and made them wary of exclusionary relations that were likely to take root under the banner of locally induced reconstruction. While scepticisms and doubts over the broader aims of such local meetings were widely echoed by many interviewees, for many participation in local meetings, at the minimum, meant being informed about or reconfirming their understanding of the sources of delay in housing reconstruction, and the growing weakness of local authorities in responding to local concerns.

A telling comment was made by a community activist, Navin, who recounted his experiences of surviving the earthquakes, losing his house, and facing a major psychological trauma for a few days, only to recover and join the local rescue and relief effort. He said that the early days of the earthquake aftermath were marked by a sense of communion and solidarity.

---

[17] Local school, Sankhu, 15 April 2016.

The outpouring of national and international support was described as something that elevated the sociocultural and historical profile of Sankhu. Governmental efforts were slow and sluggish but they were supplemented by spontaneous local efforts. Interactions between government officials and local activists like him were more frequent, with the latter providing much-needed support to the government in identifying victims and coordinating responses. But for him, those moments of citizen invigoration were long gone. When asked if he had recently attended any of the community meetings or consulted with the local officials from the ward office or the municipality to apply pressure for reconstruction, he poignantly replied with a Nepali proverb, 'Najane gaunko bato nasodhnu'—'Don't ask the way to the village you are not travelling to'—reiterating a sense of futility in engaging with the local authorities regarding everyday questions related to reconstruction.[18]

Conclusion

By examining the politics of participatory governance in Nepal's post-earthquake housing reconstruction, I bring out three issues for discussion: first, the gap between the policy and practice of participatory reconstruction; second, the bureaucratic governance context of Nepal and its influence on participatory disaster governance; and third, the potential for disaster-induced participatory spaces to shape longer-term state–society relations.

First, I have shown that, despite the initial policy commitment of the government to a participatory and accountable governance of reconstruction, the affected communities were actually marginalized under the government-driven programme of 'owner-led reconstruction'. The finding is consistent with emerging evidence from the Nepal earthquake that reveals the practical deficiencies in the government's stated claims for the participatory mode of longer-term reconstruction (Daly et al. 2017). My research also shows how the notion of participation and associated ideas of voice were distinctively conceptualized and integrated as conditional upon the disaster-affected communities proving their eligibility for housing assistance. Such a mode of conditional participation is far removed from

---

[18] Sankhu, 15 May 2016.

and contradicts the democratic underpinnings of participatory governance of disasters in which disaster-affected populations have the 'right to determine and influence' decisions concerning post-disaster reconstruction (Cuny 1983: 128). My research shows that in reality the state actors' narrow framing of 'owner-driven reconstruction' was merely aimed at turning disaster-affected citizens into target beneficiaries of the housing reconstruction programme (Krause 2010), while negating their rights as citizens to participate in and influence the course of reconstruction.

While spaces of participation existed in post-earthquake Nepal, my study shows that they tended to be co-opted by the state actors to pursue their predetermined vision of post-disaster governance. At the central level, the NRA was found to be adept at using spaces such as the HRRP to justify its vision of 'owner-led reconstruction', communicate its regulatory decisions, and, in the process, ensure compliance on the part of the humanitarian NGOs. Although such spaces were framed as promoting a participatory and collaborative mode of disaster governance, my study exposes the risk of such spaces being instrumentalized by powerholders merely to justify expert-driven decisions and escape public scrutiny.

Second, the study adds to previous scholarship on disaster politics that draws attention to the larger political context and state–societal relations of the disaster-hit society as a major determinant of post-disaster reconstruction (Dynes 1999). Disasters are usually identified as having occurred at a particular time and place, but they also occur at a particular time in human history and within a specific social and cultural context. While the NRA failed to ensure the wider participation of affected communities, the power and performance of the NRA itself have to be understood within Nepal's contested climate of political and bureaucratic reforms. The NRA came into existence eight months after the earthquakes in controversial circumstances. Reflecting an intense power struggle among major political parties to wield control over how the post-earthquake reconstruction was to be governed, the first CEO of the NRA, under whose leadership the original ideas of owner-led reconstruction and participatory governance were adopted, was replaced just two weeks after he took up his job. The NRA also assumed a complex organizational structure, spanning actors and experts from different government agencies, political parties, and donor agencies. By the time the NRA had become fully operational, the national reconstruction agenda that had garnered major national and international attention in the aftermath of the earthquakes had already been eclipsed. The overall reconstruction process was further marginalized after the fast-tracked promulgation of the constitution in September 2015, which sparked protests in the southern plains of Nepal and subsequently an economic blockade of basic goods flowing in from India.

Additionally, the mandate of the NRA, which was not an executive body but a coordinating and overseeing one, meant that it had to constantly manage its role in relation to other state and non-state actors associated with post-earthquake recovery and reconstruction. Specifically, the NRA was expected to build on and adhere to pre-existing policy and practical experiments designed to bring 'good governance' to the aid sector. Mobilizing expertise and 'streamlining' post-disaster reconstruction thus became a major objective for the NRA, at the cost of local community participation. On the one hand, the situation is reminiscent of the previous history of disaster management in Nepal in which the national-level disaster preparedness and recovery organization faltered amidst the varied expectations of pre- and post-disaster governance (Jones et al. 2014). On the other hand, it also underscores that the potential for public participation in a post-disaster context is not independent of the disaster-hit country's wider political context. In the present case, the progress of reconstruction more generally, and the participatory governance of reconstruction in particular, were closely intertwined with Nepal's ongoing contentious politics, with the old structures of governance being dismantled, and bureaucratic and power relations in a state of flux (Nightingale et al. 2018).

The role of the NRA and the broader questions of 'success' or 'failure' in reconstruction also have to be viewed within the intellectual and methodological limits of this research. Intellectually, it is beyond the immediate scope of the research to determine whether, or to what extent, the promises of 'owner-led reconstruction' were realized in practice. Rather, my main concern has been to explore the inconsistencies between the idealized world of participatory disaster governance and the real world of implementation in Sankhu. Relatedly, the methodological aim of this chapter is contextually and temporally bounded. That ethnographic research is never a complete or absolute portrayal of the phenomenon under investigation but, at best, a 'selective representation of reality' is well acknowledged (Hammersley 1992: 78). The selective representation of reality is even more central in disaster research, given the fluid nature of reality that permeates a disaster context. As Simpson (2013) argues in his ethnographic account of post-earthquake Gujarat, what constitutes knowledge of the sociopolitical realities of a post-disaster context is ever-evolving, variously constructed, and subject to continual contestation.

Since the completion of my fieldwork in May 2016, much has evolved at the level of politics, policy, and practice in Nepal's reconstruction. Two issues merit further consideration. First, some more recent media reports have claimed that Sankhu has made major strides in housing reconstruction (Lama 2019). Although encouraging, such an assessment needs to be viewed with caution because the reconstruction of physical houses does not necessarily mean that they reflect the voices and demands of the concerned homeowners. This calls for further inquiry into the role and expectations of homeowners in Sankhu's 'owner-driven reconstruction'. Second, two years after the earthquakes, and after a gap of almost two decades, Nepal held elections in 2017 to local bodies in which housing reconstruction featured as a major electoral issue. To what extent the change in the local democratic context and the reinstatement of elected representatives have shaped the process of participatory reconstruction is another area for further inquiry. Although I plan to pursue these lines of inquiry, the present discussion is limited in its ability to empirically engage with these questions.

Finally, while my research shows that state officials are adept at instrumentalizing participatory spaces, it also reveals, almost paradoxically, that such spaces have the potential to redefine post-disaster state–society politics. Although the instrumental value of such spaces in altering the course of reconstruction remains open to investigation, it can be argued that they did help local community activists and affected communities to build a better understanding of the larger functioning of the state-led reconstruction, and to develop critical perspectives on the wider assemblage of state and non-state actors that make up or reinforce the massive undertaking of providing housing assistance to nearly 500,000 house-owners.[19] Disaster-induced participatory spaces enabled local communities to witness the intermingling of state and non-state actors, which in turn prompted critical reflection about the aims and actors behind the so-called locally induced pressures for Sankhu-specific reconstruction. Local community workers who participated in the relief efforts, in turn, became aware of both the instrumentalizing and neglectful tendencies of the local

---

[19] As one example of the changing context of disaster response and reconstruction, the number of houses requiring reconstruction assistance was later increased to 800,000 upon the completion of the housing census.

state actors. This evidence shows that disaster-induced participatory spaces have an intrinsic value, enabling disaster-affected citizens to 'see the state' and become critical of the workings of the government bureaucracy at the local level of service delivery (Corbridge et al. 2005: 7; Bukenya 2016).

One clear 'sighting' that the local communities have developed is of the 'weak capacity' of the local authorities to respond to pressing local demands. Despite years of effort in public and local governance reforms, the low level of responsiveness of local bodies in Nepal is hardly a new insight (Pandeya 2015). Yet, as my findings from Sankhu show, the post-disaster meetings prompted the local communities to become further aware of the entrenched power inequalities that characterize Nepal's central–local bureaucratic relations. Although episodic and uncertain, the unfolding of the local spaces of participation encouraged community members to develop a specific understanding of the NRA as a body that was becoming increasingly top-down, expert-driven, and remote from the everyday concerns of local communities. The local authorities, on the other hand, were seen by the local communities as politically unequipped to negotiate the terms of reconstruction in line with their aspirations.

Although a sense of cynicism was observed among community members who questioned the immediate value of participatory spaces, I tentatively conclude that such cynicism is not to be misunderstood as a sign of disempowerment. Indeed, in contexts characterized by socioeconomic inequalities and entrenched political neglect, participatory forums represent an ongoing struggle by ordinary citizens to make their everyday claims for improved public services visible and recognized by powerholders (Rao and Sanyal 2010). The present study highlights that even when the powerholders sought to tighten their grip on the participatory spaces, or to co-opt them, they prompted the local communities to become conscious of the increasingly homogenized mode of longer-term housing reconstruction, while also reimagining an alternative mode of post-disaster governance that would give primacy to the long-standing local needs and voices of the affected citizens (Remes 2016). Participatory governance in general and participatory spaces in particular, in this regard, served as 'interrogative encounters', with the potential to reshape unequal state–society power relations.

9

Changing Perspectives on International Aid in Nepal since the 2015 Earthquakes[*]

Shobhit Shakya

Introduction

The 2015 earthquakes tested the resilience of Nepali society and the Nepali state to its limits. A fragile regime that was going through a transition from a democratic monarchy to a federal republic and trying to put 10 years of civil war behind it was handed down the mammoth tasks of immediate response and long-term rehabilitation (Hachhethu 2009; Lawoti 2003; Upreti 2006). As expected, Nepal had very little choice other than to turn to its neighbours, friends, and the international community in general for assistance. Help, mostly in the form of relief materials, did arrive, and in large quantities too. But Nepali officials were overwhelmed, and chaos ensued in Nepal's only international airport (PTI 2015). While the government desperately needed aid and assistance from the international community, it also needed to assert control over the situation. Many reports accused the government of creating bureaucratic obstacles which slowed down the flow of aid, and some also alleged corruption (Burke and Rauniyar 2015; Francis 2015), but the other side of the story was that the government also needed to keep checks on potential illegal or inappropriate activities and could not be too lenient with its protocols. As an article published in the *Huffington Post* (Alfred 2015) pointed out, it was necessary for the government to stay in control and this the government

[*] Funding for facilities used in this research was provided by the core infrastructure support IUT (19-13) of the Estonian Ministry of Education and Research.

was trying to do. A similar situation continued in the longer term as well, with the government struggling to collaborate efficiently with the non-governmental organizations (NGOs) and international non-governmental organizations (INGOs) which were the recipients of a large percentage of the international aid that was coming into the country. As a step towards controlling the situation, the government eventually introduced a single channel policy for the incoming aid by establishing the Prime Minister's Disaster Relief Fund (Mahatara 2017).

In the longer run, it looked as if the government's and the people's general perception of NGOs and aid agencies was gradually changing after the earthquakes. Discontentment on the part of the government, and changing public views of the activities of I/NGOs and aid agencies, eventually led to the drafting of the National Integrity Policy (NIP) in 2018 (*The Himalayan Times* 2018b). This policy was widely criticized and, as of late 2019, it looked as if a revised version would be tabled sooner or later, with the Ministry of Home Affairs (MOHA) being authorized to draft a new law in November of that year (P. M. Shrestha 2019). The decision from the government was claimed by some to be evidence of the government 'flexing its muscles' towards the establishment of an authoritarian regime, or a populist step taken with consideration of the growing sentiment amongst the people (S. Manandhar 2018). The authoritarian tendencies of the K. P. Oli–led government that was elected with a huge majority in 2017 have been well discussed (D. Adhikari 2018; S. Manandhar 2018; Paudyal and Koirala 2018). Yet this cannot be the only reason for the government's steps, because local governments led by other parties have also been seen to move away from international aid, as the case of the heritage reconstruction process in Bhaktapur Municipality has shown (*The Himalayan Times* 2018a).

This chapter presents some key aspects of the increasing disapproval of I/NGOs and aid agencies in Nepal. In the first section, I identify some of the key discourses, based on media reports and secondary literature. I mostly base this section on desktop research but also on my own experience of the earthquakes in the field, and on contemporaneous media reports. Further on, building on my ongoing research on post-earthquake heritage restoration in relation to traditional governance mechanisms, I discuss the case of heritage reconstruction in Bhaktapur and how user committees have been instrumental in the post-earthquake heritage reconstruction process. I investigate the characteristics of these user committees and compare them to the traditional *guthi*s. I also consider some issues that have arisen in respect of aid-based development in general and discuss the relevance of the self-funding principles of the traditional institution of the *guthi*.

Discourses in the aftermath

The 2015 earthquakes received a high level of coverage in national and international media. The open call for assistance made by the Nepal government resulted in multiple governments sending their teams to conduct rescue operations; this was followed by NGOs/INGOs and independent groups of all sorts initiating their own operations and relief campaigns. The situation was overwhelming for the government whose bureaucratic competencies were tested to the fullest. It was already a challenge to coordinate with the several rescue teams with equipment and military vehicles that were coming in. In addition, an unprecedented amount of relief material was arriving at the airport (*BBC News* 2015). While NGOs and aid agencies were criticizing the government for imposing unnecessary bureaucratic procedures, the government was denying allegations that it was slowing down the distribution of aid material. There were two sides to the initial discourse: first from the perspective of the NGOs, which pointed out the strictness of the bureaucratic process and made accusations of corruption against the government; the second being from the perspective of the government, which saw a need for control and better accountability. In addition to the initial discourse, other discourses relating to foreign aid followed as the rebuilding process went forward. While there was insecurity on the part of the government due to the increasing activities of Christian evangelists, from the people's perspective there was a question of dignity when the government was relying excessively on foreign aid, specifically for the restoration of heritage monuments. The key aspects of the earthquake aftermath which might have shaped the discourse concerning foreign aid will be summarized in the subsections that follow.

Immediate relief efforts

Nepal has witnessed extensive NGO activity, with 50,358 NGOs registered with the Social Welfare Council as of July 2019 (Social Welfare Council

Nepal n.d.). As such, it is predictable that in a situation of disaster, the level of activity from the non-government sector will be immensely high, and this was exactly the case in the aftermath of the 2015 earthquakes. With all NGOs and INGOs, regardless of their primary sector of operation, getting involved on the ground as first responders, it was evidently an overwhelming task for the government to coordinate these activities, and this was made even worse by the lack of anticipation and preparedness on the part of the government. As a *New York Times* article (G. Harris 2015) pointed out, quoting the United Nations resident coordinator, the United States (US) ambassador, and several Nepali officials, the immediate response was slow due to bureaucratic processes not being efficient. As aid workers became increasingly frustrated, accusations of corruption and the intentional blocking of aid flows were levelled at the government (Burke and Rauniyar 2015; Francis 2015). The government's failure to send relief materials to remote areas even several days after the earthquake made this claim stronger, as there were protests and widespread criticism of the government's relief efforts (P. Adhikari 2015; Poudel 2015).

The government's policy of discouraging 'unofficial' channels was blamed for its failure to ease the inflow and distribution of aid (Burke and Rauniyar 2015). It set up the Prime Minister's Relief Fund in an attempt to keep track of the inflow of funds (Mahatara 2017). But the government's perception was that smaller NGOs, most of which did not have any expertise in disaster response, did not have the capacity to distribute aid on their own, and that coordinating with these smaller NGOs was creating an administrative burden. There was also the question of the reliability and transparency of the different funding campaigns that were being initiated by independent groups and smaller NGOs. As an article in *The Diplomat* pointed out, it was certainly not the case that Nepal was unwilling to accept international aid or was not trying to coordinate with aid agencies and I/NGOs (Claire 2015). It was also necessary for the government to check on the inflow of goods for substandard or superfluous materials; completely avoiding any kind of paperwork or checks would not have been the best step. This certainly was a probable scenario, as was evident from an incident of distribution of rotten rice by the World Food Programme (WFP) in Gorkha, which was taken back after the government intervened (*The Kathmandu Post* 2015b). This was certainly not an isolated case and more incidents followed, prompting the Prime Minister's Office to direct the authorities to distribute edible relief material to the earthquake victims only after laboratory tests (*The Kathmandu Post* 2015a).

It was not just the distribution of material goods that was perceived as a problem by the government. Funds collected individually or through smaller NGOs could not be accounted for in many instances. There was no means by which to ensure that funds collected by all NGOs, independent groups, and individuals reached the earthquake victims. The government's mistrust of NGOs grew further, and in 2017, when the country was being affected by floods, the government made the use of 'official' channels mandatory and tried to curtail the independent activities of NGOs by barring collection of funds by NGOs and individuals (*The Himalayan Times* 2017a).

A perceived threat of proselytization through aid

In the immediate aftermath, and in the overall recovery process after the earthquake, the topic of religious conversion came to the media's attention, and even scholarly discussions included the topic in some instances (Bennike 2017; Suhag 2015). A number of media outlets published articles with headings such as 'Bread Not Bibles for Nepal' and 'Nepal Earthquake: How Religious Groups Prey on the Victims of Natural Disasters'. A discourse which held that NGOs in Nepal were luring underprivileged communities towards conversion through financial promises was reaching the mainstream (Hamad 2015; Suhag 2015).

Historically, Nepal has tended to show insecurity towards foreign influences in matters of religious belief. The majority of the population, and especially the Hindu Brahmin and Chhetri ruling classes in the country, have been excessively protective of the religious status of the country, as was also seen recently during the drafting process of the 2015 constitution (*The Himalayan Times* 2015).[1] During the earlier period of the Shah monarchy, it is clear that the regime was not only unsupportive of Christians coming into Nepal but was suspicious of any kind of foreign activity in the country (Liechty 1997). As the country transitioned into democracy over the years that followed, there has been a gradual increase in the acceptance of religious

---

[1]   See also Sen (2015).

heterogeneity from the perspective of the state and law (K. B. Thapa 2010). Still, a large portion of the country's population was wary of the rapidly growing Christian community and foreign involvement in Christian evangelism; this has led many to support Nepal being reinstated as a Hindu nation (*The Week* 2019; *The Himalayan Times* 2015). With an ongoing debate on secularism and laws on religious freedom, the earthquake might have helped to garner support for laws that would be more restrictive of proselytization. Thus, the constitution subsequently promulgated in September 2015 and the Criminal Code Bill that was enacted in 2017 placed restrictions on religious conversion (*Spotlight* 2017). As per the new law, while conversion was not illegal in itself, proselytizing was illegal and so was speaking against another person's religion. Nonetheless, the reaction to the new law from the Christian community was predictably negative (World Watch Monitor 2018).[2] The *International Religious Freedom Report* for 2016 from the United States Department of State, Bureau of Democracy, Human Rights and Labor had acknowledged the growing anti-Christian sentiment in the country with incidents of arrests for proselytizing. But the same report also mentioned that Christian missionary hospitals and welfare organizations continued to operate without government interference.[3]

Heritage and public sentiment

The important and complex task of restoring heritage monuments, which included the restoration of 753 monuments that were affected by the earthquake (Satyal 2018), lay before the government in the aftermath. The significance of these historical monuments meant that aid and assistance for their restoration were readily promised from various sides. Specifically, two key projects immediately started with direct assistance from the international community. In Kathmandu's historic Hanuman Dhoka heritage site, a project to restore the Gaddi Baithak, a building built in 1908 by the Rana Prime Minister Chandra Shamsher, started with US assistance, and the

---

[2] See also Janssen (2016) and Khadka (2017).
[3] See United States Department of State, Bureau of Democracy, Human Rights and Labor (2016).

older Malla-era Newar-style nine-storeyed Basantpur Durbar began to be rebuilt by the Chinese (*My Republica* 2017).[4]

Given that the Kathmandu Durbar Square was a listed World Heritage Site, it is understandable that the government felt immense pressure to make arrangements that would ensure the swift renovation of these structures. The pressure understandably would have come from both within and outside the country, because the situation with the heritage monuments was already starting to receive international attention soon after the earthquake (Bell 2016; Sengupta 2015; Theophile and Newman 2016). Furthermore, the incapacity of the local government was evident in several cases and this was turning into a national embarrassment (AFP 2017; Mathema 2017; Ojha 2017). At this point in time, it was easier for the government to go ahead by accepting foreign assistance in heritage restoration projects. However, this certainly was not the only possible approach: a variety of models were utilized in parallel across different projects (Lekakis, Shakya, and Kostakis 2018).

For the government it was a case of pressure to get these World Heritage monuments rebuilt, but for the local Newar population this came with the sense of a loss of dignity. Most heritage monuments in the Kathmandu Valley were built during the Malla period (c. 1201–1779 CE) and the local Newar population has the strongest cultural and emotional connections with them. The Newars are considered the original inhabitants of the Kathmandu Valley and the trading towns that surround it. Most of the heritage monuments were built by the Newars during the Malla or Licchavi (c. 400–750 CE) dynasties at a time when 'Nepal' meant mainly the Kathmandu Valley and the people living there were called the Newar (or Newa in the local dialect) (Nepali 2015; P. R. Sharma 2015; B. G. Shrestha 1999). For this reason, handing over the nine-storeyed Durbar within the Hanuman Dhoka complex, which was the traditional seat of the Newar Malla Kings of Kathmandu, to the Chinese government (Government of Nepal, Ministry of Culture, Tourism and Civil Aviation, Department of Archaeology 2018) was seen as hurtful to the sentiments of the local population.

---

[4] Gaddi Baithak Restoration Project, http://miyamotointernational.com/gaddi-baithak-restoration-project-us-embassy/ (accessed 22 January 2018).

During my research on heritage restoration in Nepal (Lekakis, Shakya, and Kostakis 2018), it came to light that activists who were promoting the restoration of heritage monuments through community initiatives were highly disapproving of the restoration process being handed out through direct agreements with foreign governments. These 'heritage activists' have been critical of the use of foreign aid in heritage restoration because they feel that rebuilding these monuments through local initiatives would make a powerful statement of capacity and resilience. Their narrative was that these monuments were built and maintained by their ancestors without any foreign technical help, using native technology and traditional mechanisms which involved the community organizations that were native to the local Newar population—the *guthis* (Khaniya 2005; Lekakis, Shakya, and Kostakis 2018; Maharjan and Barata 2017; Pradhananga, Shrestha, and Dee 2010; Quigley 1985; Toffin 2005). Several incidents occurred which clearly showed the discontentment of the local activists: for example, it was reported that protests by local activists were a key reason for the United Nations Educational, Scientific and Cultural Organization (UNESCO) withdrawing from projects to reconstruct two other temples in the Kathmandu Durbar Square complex (Satyal 2019a; see also Lotter, this volume).

There were also the questions of building techniques and materials. The activists' emphasis was on promoting local skills and providing employment for local artisans. When rebuilding through foreign assistance, there was uncertainty whether the architectural integrity would be maintained, or local skilled resources used. The concept of intangible heritage was also an angle through which several questions were raised. The mechanism through which construction was managed by traditional organizations such as the *guthis*, which used to oversee most of these historical monuments, was also considered intangible heritage (Diwasa, Bandu, and Nepal 2007; C. KC 2016; Lekakis, Shakya, and Kostakis 2018; Pradhananga, Shrestha, and Dee 2010). With restoration projects being handed out to INGOs and foreign experts, questions were raised about the impact of these actions on the intangibles.

The National Integrity Policy

The NIP was proposed by the MOHA during the Sher Bahadur Deuba–led government (June 2017–February 2018) and the draft was prepared by former secretaries Mohan Banjade and Sharada Prasad Trital (*The Kathmandu Post* 2018b). The policy was first formulated in 2017 and eventually the draft was presented by the Prime Minister's Office in 2018 (*The Himalayan Times* 2018b).

The draft policy contained several clauses relating to NGOs and INGOs. Some of the regulatory requirements for INGOs and NGOs were clearly aimed at enabling the government to control their activities. As per the draft, INGOs would not be allowed to send reports to their parent organizations outside the country without the consent of the government, their annual budget was to be approved by the Finance Ministry, and they would not be allowed to implement projects without the government's consent (*The Himalayan Times* 2018b; *The Kathmandu Post* 2018b). For local NGOs, the regulations were even stricter, requiring them to get permission from the government to receive any donation from donor agencies, and to inform the authorities within seven days of receiving these donations (*The Kathmandu Post* 2018b).

Due to these extremely restrictive rules, it was certain that the draft would be met with sharp criticisms from I/NGOs and the civil society in the country, and there was active criticism from the NGO Federation of Nepal and also several diplomatic missions (*Northeast Now* 2018). According to the non-government sector, the draft was even more worrying when considering other evidence for the changing scenario as well. In 2018, the government came up with the Foreign Nationals Monitoring Directive which was supposedly aimed at making the activities of foreign nationals in Nepal more 'transparent and ethical'. Later on, there were also reports that the government was mulling over regulations to make it mandatory for Nepalis to get clearance from local bodies before leaving for foreign destinations on a tourist visa (*The Himalayan Times* 2018d). This series of steps from the government that showed tendencies towards an authoritarian approach caused anxiety among international agencies. But the government seems to have tried to downplay these policy changes by calling them 'internal matters'. According to a news report published by *My Republica*, the Prime Minister was agitated by the 'unwarranted interest' from several international agencies (*My Republica* 2018b). Eventually the government relented under the pressure (*The Kathmandu Post* 2018a).[5] Despite this initial

---

[5]   See also A. Giri (2018).

backtracking, as of late 2019 there were still indications that the government would pursue the policy direction, with the MOHA being authorized to draft a new law concerning the non-government sector in November 2019 (P. M. Shrestha 2019).

It can be understood that the NIP was the continuation of a chain of events that subscribed to the discourse of INGOs and NGOs being responsible for proselytizing and trying to interfere in the internal matters of Nepal. Nepal has always been considered friendly towards its foreign partners in general, both Western and regional. The recent development does not necessarily reflect an increase in anti-West sentiment in general but is probably related to an increasingly nationalistic politics, which needs further study and inferencing. The earthquakes in 2015 might have acted as a catalyst for such politics.[6] This does seem highly paradoxical because after the earthquakes the government had to depend on international aid and secured pledges of USD 4.4 billion for earthquake rehabilitation. However, these and other events that followed the earthquakes also gave rise to a strong national discourse against foreign aid and foreign-aid-driven I/NGOs.

The case of heritage restoration in Bhaktapur

The discourses discussed above provide grounds for us to hypothesize that the Nepal government was becoming less inclined to accept international aid as a result of a particular chain of events that followed the 2015 earthquakes, these events having varied backdrops and maybe direct or indirect effects on the changing perspective. As part of my ongoing research on the relevance of *guthi*s in post-earthquake heritage reconstruction (Lekakis, Shakya, and Kostakis 2018), I closely studied the heritage reconstruction process in Bhaktapur, where disagreements between the German side (the German Embassy and the German development bank KfW) and Bhaktapur Municipality regarding the modality of the restoration process eventually caused the German side to withdraw from the project. This case

---

[6]   The continuation of this perspective seems to be reflected in the controversy surrounding the United States' Millennium Challenge Corporation's Nepal Compact (B. Ghimire 2020).

can provide some insights into the perspective on aid in Nepal concerning heritage restoration in the aftermath of the 2015 earthquakes.

Immediately after the 2015 earthquakes, the Germans stepped up for the reconstruction efforts, and were probably drawn to Bhaktapur by earlier German involvement in heritage restoration there (Kawan 2015). The Durbar Square in Bhaktapur Municipality is one of the seven sites within the Kathmandu Valley listed in UNESCO's World Heritage List (UNESCO n.d.), and needed to be restored with urgency. By April 2016, the reconstruction had commenced, through a three-party agreement between KfW, the Government of Nepal, and Bhaktapur Municipality (*The Himalayan Times* 2016). In total, 10 structures were planned to be reconstructed through this arrangement, including the Pujari Math at Dattatreya Square, the National Arts Museum, Fasidega temple at Bhaktapur Durbar Square, the old building of Bhaktapur Municipality, Bhairav Dyo Chhe, Chyasimandap at Bhailukhel, Nyatapola temple, Hada Chhe at Nasamana and the buildings of the Bidyarthi Niketan Higher Secondary School and Shreepadya Higher Secondary School (*The Kathmandu Post* 2016a). All of these structures were historical buildings in the Durbar Square and were prioritized not only for swift reconstruction but also for archaeological investigation, in order to get clearer information on their historical significance. However, due to some opposing voices from within the Municipality, the project largely stalled.

The political transformation expedited by the earthquakes of 2015 also had effects on local politics. Nepal successfully conducted local elections in 2017 for the first time in almost two decades (*World Politics Review* 2017). This brought new local representatives to the municipalities who had a different vision from that of the central government for their respective municipalities. The Nepal Majdoor Kisan Party (NMKP) had always been strong in Bhaktapur Municipality and this party won the election there with a convincing majority. The newly elected local leadership had a clear vision regarding the reconstruction of the heritage structures and wanted to employ local skilled resources and technology through a model based on local 'user committees'. The Municipality issued calls for community representatives to come forward to take part in reconstruction projects: groups that would have been formed through grassroots initiatives would come forward and take responsibility on the basis of agreements with the residents of the relevant area. A noticeable influence of the NMKP in the case of most user committees in Bhaktapur was claimed by some respondents. This was understandable, given the overwhelming influence of the party within the city. According to the Deputy Mayor, Rajani Joshi, the Municipality did not give any preference based on party affiliation when handing over projects to user committees. Still, political influence in community activities in any field cannot be ruled out.

The participation of the local community in the maintenance of religious and social structures within the Kathmandu Valley was not an entirely new concept. Historically, *guthi* organizations had been providing the function in a very similar fashion. *Guthi*s were community organizations that were either instated by the ruling monarch (*raj guthi*) or formed through the grassroots initiatives of local communities (*niji guthi*) and looked after physical infrastructure, social welfare, or religious/cultural activities (Khaniya 2005; Quigley 1985; B. G. Shrestha 2012; Toffin 2005). The 'user committee' in the current context of Bhaktapur replaces the traditional *guthi* organizations that used to be responsible for the upkeep of these historical public structures, but the modality is similar, if not the same. These organizations display the same spirit of community initiative, as discussed elsewhere (Lekakis, Shakya, and Kostakis 2018). According to the information provided by the Deputy Mayor, smaller projects were already having success in restoration through this model and the Municipality wanted to use the same model for larger projects as well.

In April 2018, KfW formally withdrew from the project. This was reported by the national news agency in Nepal as KfW pulling out from its commitment (*The Himalayan Times* 2018a). The Mayor of Bhaktapur Municipality, Sunil Prajapati, in an interview published by *Nepali Times* in June 2018, used strong words such as 'sovereignty' and 'self-respect' while clarifying the reason for KfW eventually stepping back (Bhattarai 2018a). He mentioned that Bhaktapur already had two engineering colleges and a large pool of skilled resources and was thus able to rebuild these structures using the resources that were locally available. However, the conditions laid down by KfW meant that the Municipality did not have an absolute say in the techniques and materials used in the reconstruction process or in the process of selecting contractors.

From the perspective of the German side, a complete handover of control to the Municipality without conditions, as per the usual process, would not have been acceptable because of their own standards and rules. In an interview included in the same report, the German Ambassador Roland Schäfer focused on the relationship Bhaktapur Municipality had had with KfW, explaining that 'KfW had to defend modalities for a reconstruction grant because of its general mandate, and that this could not be adapted to where Bhaktapur's leadership saw the city moving between 2015 and 2017'. In my communications with the German Embassy, Claudia Hiepe, Head of Development Cooperation, pointed out the three key points from the perspective of the German side which led to the failure of the cooperation attempt, as follows:

1. Use of local materials: Bhaktapur Municipality was of the opinion that the project should exclusively use local (traditional) materials. The German side suggested that while the use of local materials needed to be encouraged, the emphasis needed to be on having earthquake resilient structures which could also make prudent (internationally accepted) use of modern materials if required.

2. Exclusive utilization of user committees: Bhaktapur Municipality wanted to ensure that all activities were done through user committees. While the German side accepted this for most of the work, it was not able to accept a blanket use. The German side suggested going through a tendering process for the high-ticket items like the Old Municipality Building and schools, in line with the German Financial Cooperation regulations.

3. Use of international consultants: Bhaktapur Municipality felt that it had the internal capacity to implement the project and duly monitor construction work, even without the assistance of an international consultant, in this case a construction engineer. However, this did not comply with German financial cooperation regulations.

To my question as to whether the German side had doubts about the accountability and transparency of the Municipality's preferred model of working through user committees, Hiepe answered with a firm 'no'. In fact, for smaller projects the German side was already willing to utilize user committees, which would have not been the case if there were any concerns about accountability and transparency. Taking this into account, it can be understood that the conditions placed on the use of German financial support were not considered appropriate by Bhaktapur Municipality and, due to their requirements, the German side could not become more flexible. Thus, the two sides mutually agreed to part ways, with the allocated funds being redirected for other purposes within Nepal.

Even with the Municipality leadership's commitment to use local skilled resources and funds for the reconstruction, it is doubtful that the Municipality had the financial capacity to fund the projects. Bhaktapur is the smallest of the three major old cities in the Kathmandu Valley and has a much smaller annual budget in comparison with Kathmandu and Lalitpur (Patan)—just NPR 1.73 billion (c. USD 15.7 million) for the fiscal year 2017–18 (*Setopati* 2018). Given this scenario, it is certain that the Municipality does not have the capacity to fund some of the major reconstruction projects. For this reason, in October the Mayor had a meeting with the National Reconstruction Authority (NRA) regarding the funding of the heritage restoration projects. According to the official social media page of the Municipality, there was a positive response from the NRA.

In my interview with her, the Deputy Mayor seemed to reiterate the stance of the Municipality that the reconstruction work on the heritage monuments needed to be done using local skills and techniques. The failure of the Rani Pokhari project (Ojha 2017) and other restoration projects in Kathmandu seemed to be one of the main influences on the decisions of the leadership in Bhaktapur. Coincidentally, as per the developments that followed, Rani Pokhari started to be cleaned and readied for reconstruction with the help of a team of women sent by Bhaktapur Municipality under the supervision of a user committee (Ojha 2019b). This happened as reconstruction of Bhajya Pokhari, another pond like Rani Pokhari, with a temple at its centre, was taken forward by Bhaktapur Municipality with notable success, using the same model (Phuyal 2018). Similar prior success with a model using local user committees was a strong reason for the added confidence of the Municipality leadership in the continued use of this model. In addition, as explained by the Deputy Mayor, having an engineering college (Khwopa Engineering College, run by the Municipality itself) added to the list of reasons why it was justifiable for the Municipality to reject the conditions put forward by the German side as far as the need to have an international consultant was concerned. Moreover, the condition that the projects were to use a bidding process did not go well with the Municipality, with the bidding process already detested by most stakeholders (AFP. 2017; S. K. Shrestha 2014). For heritage structures to be constructed through native technology was a priority for the Municipality. Thus, it believed that it would be more appropriate for locally trained engineers rather than international consultants to oversee the reconstruction of the structures. The Department of Architecture in

Khwopa College of Engineering had run courses in traditional architecture and was believed by the Municipality to have suitable expertise in heritage architecture and building techniques.

Despite the firm stance of the Municipality that the reconstruction should be done through the involvement of the local community and local skills, it seems that the larger project cannot be self-funded by the Municipality and that eventually the funding will come from the NRA. The NRA and the pre-existing strategy of the government for post-disaster management were heavily dependent upon international aid, despite criticisms of how international funds were being funnelled into the country (Claire 2015; Jones et al. 2014) and concerns about transparency and accountability in the use of these funds (Deen 2015). Given the predisposition of the international community towards the possibility of misuse of the aid funds, modalities that differ from internationally accepted standards are sure to be questioned. This posed a challenge to the Municipality to stick with its stance. Yet the partial success the Municipality achieved in the restoration process had been portrayed in a positive light (Prajapati 2018) and this provided grounds for the Municipality to push on with its agenda. There were other municipalities that were also showing a willingness to follow this model, with the Lalitpur Municipality deciding that the Bhimsen temple in Patan would be rebuilt with a user committee in charge (*The Himalayan Times* 2019b). However, with the project only partially funded by the Municipality, the committee responsible for the reconstruction of the temple also went ahead with crowdsourcing activities (*My Republica* 2019). Some projects, like the Kasthamandap, which faced initial hurdles too, made progress through local participation (Lekakis, Shakya, and Kostakis 2018; *The Himalayan Times* 2019a). Other projects which already utilized user committees and even involved traditional *guthi*s have also achieved appreciable progress (Shakya and Drechsler 2019). For technical assistance, the efforts of the Department of Archaeology, UNESCO, and the NGO Kathmandu Valley Preservation Trust (KVPT) have been effective (*Spotlight* 2020), in addition to the expertise accumulated by the municipalities themselves. Although the model of reconstruction through community participation in the heritage field was showing good prospects, it was evident that financing would be the biggest challenge if foreign aid were to be completely rejected. This was especially true for fringe projects where interest from central government agencies may be minimal. There is also the question of the longer run, when organizations like the NRA may be dissolved and funding through them would not be a possibility for the municipalities.

Discussion

User committees and guthis

The concept of user committees and community participation has been used extensively in Nepal in the implementation of policies to govern natural resources such as water and forests (K. P. Acharya 2002; Chakraborty 2001; H. K. Shrestha 2018). The reasoning and influencing factors behind the policy implementation are something that would require a separate study, but the available literature shows that the Panchayat system, which used territorially based politico-administrative units (K. P. Acharya 2002), and the National Forestry Plan (NFP) of 1976, plus other rules that subsequently followed, provided for the formal recognition of villagers' management of forest resources through user committees (K. P. Acharya 2002). Since then, the concept of community participation, grassroots initiatives, and the employment of user committees for providing various functions of local governance has become a favoured model in the country (Harris et al. 2003; Mateo 2014; H. K. Shrestha 2018). There has been significant interest in studying this aspect of governance in Nepal from international scholars, notably Elinor Ostrom (Agrawal and Ostrom 2001; Varughese and Ostrom 2001). User committees have a more *ad hoc* manner of formation and in the case of Bhaktapur they are likely influenced by the NMKP, which raises questions about how party politics and the popularity of one party or another will affect the stability of these user committees.

The *guthi*, in contrast to user committees, is an institution with a history of at least 1,600 years, as it was a part of a system of state administration that was prevalent from the Licchavi period (c. 400 CE) onwards (D. Vajracharya 1973). According to the available inscriptions, *guthi* organizations were formed by the monarchs of the time with the goal of maintaining water resources, roads, *pati* (wayside shelters for travellers, the homeless, or other purposes), and so on. Despite the historical importance of the institution, *guthi*s have diminished and have been largely sidelined from governance, beyond matters of cultural significance among the Newar community (Shakya and Drechsler 2019; Toffin 2005). Yet the assumption that *guthi*s are nearly obsolete and merely relics of the past is something which can be argued against. Especially since the 2015 earthquakes, *guthi*s have re-emerged to some extent, either in discussion or in practice (C. KC 2016; Lekakis, Shakya, and Kostakis 2018; Gellner 2019). Given that user committees are formal institutions that are supported better by the legal mechanisms in Nepal, and that *guthi*s are defined primarily as religious trusts (as per the definition provided by the Guthi Sansthan Act, 1964), it is clear why user committees are preferred. There are even legal complexities in registering a new *guthi* at the current time (P. Sangroula 2020). However, the definition of *guthi*s as merely religious trusts is flawed. Especially within the Newar community in the Kathmandu Valley, it is unarguably the case that *guthi*s have a wide range of social functions (Gellner 1992: 236; Nepali 2015; B. G. Shrestha 2012; Toffin 2005, 2008). The traditional Newar lifestyle is greatly intertwined with this socioeconomic institution (Toffin 2005, 2019) and it is for precisely this reason that, when the Government in 2019 attempted to introduce a Guthi Act Amendment Bill, it was primarily Newars who took to the streets in a protest that was said to be the largest since the revolution of 2006 (referred to as the Jan Andolan II) that ended the direct rule of monarchy (Ojha 2019a; Satyal 2019b; Toffin 2019). But, despite the legal roadblocks which prevent *guthi*s from actively taking control of reconstruction efforts, as shown by my ongoing study of Maitripur Mahavihara (Lekakis, Shakya, and Kostakis 2018; Pradhananga, Shrestha, and Dee 2010; Shakya and Drechsler 2019), *guthi* members have still been resourceful in finding ways to get involved in the reconstruction of their monuments. At Maitripur Mahavihara, a committee was registered with members of the *mahavihara* and its *guthi* for running the reconstruction project. Thus, the *guthi*s can legally be interpreted as community-based organizations (CBOs). Of late, several *guthi*s have registered as NGOs as well (Social Welfare Council Nepal n.d.). This largely blurs the line between *guthi*s and user committees in practice, regardless of what the legal arrangements in the country may assert.

As an informal institution, a *guthi* is much more mature and established than a user committee because *guthi*s are an integral part of the Newar lifestyle (Gellner 2019; Nepali 2015; B. G. Shrestha 2012; Toffin 2005). While user committees have a more or less *ad hoc* nature as to how they are formed and there seems to be little ground for arguing that these groups would continue to function in the longer run, *guthi*s are, by design, intended to last for generations and the responsibility of a *guthi* member is passed down from father to son. Having been formed based on kinship (Toffin 2005) there is a social stigma in not fulfilling one's duties in a *guthi*, which keeps members from discontinuing their affiliation to a *guthi*. *Guthi*s, considering those that are still existing, have the capacity to deliver their functions, although most of the functions of existing *guthi*s are confined within the religious and cultural spheres. For instance, there are numerous religio-cultural festivals known as *jatra* that take place in the Valley, which are significant as tourist attractions as well as for their cultural value, and these are all organized by the *guthi*s (T. T. Lewis 1993; Maharjan and Barata 2017; B. G. Shrestha 2012; Toffin 2007). Some of these *jatra*s are elaborate celebrations which extend over days or weeks and involve thousands of participants and spectators and are thus testament to the organizational capacity still retained by the *guthi*s. But the functions of *guthi*s have always extended beyond the religio-cultural sphere, with several social functions such as maintenance of water supplies and schools, and provision of funeral services, among others, being ensured through their involvement (*My Republica* 2018a).[7] An added advantage that *guthi*s have over user committees is their ability, albeit only in principle in many cases as of now, to self-fund most of their activities. Historically, most *guthi*s were usually provided with landholdings and other immovables in the form of endowments by either the ruling monarch or wealthy patrons (M. C. Regmi 1977, 1965). The rent produced by these holdings funded the activities of the *guthi*. Some percentage of the land in the Valley is still owned by *guthi*s (J. Adhikari 2008). However, the level of revenue generated by the use of these plots of land will probably not be as high as previously, because farmers in the Valley have largely moved away from their profession, and examples of diversifying the means of generating income through the optimal use of these properties are scarce.

While *guthi*s have a strong historical connection with the lifestyle of the Kathmandu Valley, which suggests that they have clear advantages over user committees, the reason for their dwindling popularity is largely unfavourable state policy (Lekakis, Shakya, and Kostakis 2018; Maharjan 2013; Pradhananga, Shrestha, and Dee 2010; Shakya and Drechsler 2019) and the failure to reform this institution to fit the present context. Having been sidelined and not subjected to reforms that would adapt them to new contexts, many of the *guthi*s and their routines may seem outdated and

---

[7]   See also Khaniya (2005), Quigley (1985), and Toffin (2005).

impractical at times. As organizations with centuries of history, with many of them functioning in a more or less unchanged manner, most *guthis* are patriarchal, and are criticized for being so (Dangol 2010). Many lack the capacity for proper accounts keeping and administrative capability, as not all members have higher education. Some of these issues that may be identified as problems surrounding the *guthi* institution are general societal problems, whose imprint falls onto the *guthi* institution as well (Shrestha and Mamta 2010).

Issues with aid-based development

The level of trust of I/NGOs amongst much of the population and within the government certainly appears to be decreasing, as the case of Bhaktapur and the media discourses discussed above suggest, and there are signs that government policy will pose difficulties for their activities. The changing government policies do not come just from the incumbent party but also reflect the general sentiment amongst the population; this claim is reinforced by the case of heritage restoration in Bhaktapur. This is not something that has not been witnessed by members of the international community before. Former US Ambassador Alaina B. Teplitz observed that the community had the right to 'ask tough questions' about foreign assistance (Teplitz 2018) and went on to suggest that the government, the media, and the people should ask questions like—'Is that project really in Nepal's national interest? Does it provide jobs or convey skills to Nepalis? Does it put us in debt, and how much? Is this project sustainable? Is the community or government engaged? Does that project align with Nepal's national priorities?' She further mentioned that Nepal should 'insist on community involvement'. It can be understood that the article was written by Teplitz based on her reflections on the sentiments of the people in the country. The case of Bhaktapur does bear similarity to the suggestion from Teplitz in insisting on community involvement as well as in many other aspects.

The case of heritage restoration projects in Bhaktapur and the drafting of the NIP might both be looked at from a similar angle as far as their implications are concerned. However, the two have rather different underlying causes. The NIP stems from the increasingly negative attitude towards I/NGOs and aid agencies amongst a section of the population and the government in the country. This negative attitude towards I/NGOs and aid agencies has been further fuelled by the fear of proselytizing. It seems that the NIP itself was highly contentious within the government, and what the government will come up with regarding the new law concerning I/NGOs is still largely uncertain. The Bhaktapur case, on the other hand, is not in itself a display of a local government being opposed to all forms of foreign aid. Rather, the emphasis of Bhaktapur Municipality was on local capacity-building and using local resources and skills, an emphasis which created an incompatibility with the requirements of the German side.

The Bhaktapur case shows that the processes and institutions in place are often a major cause of the ineffectiveness of aid in development. Bureaucratic arrangements are designed more for the disbursement of aid and maintaining transparency about where the aid goes, rather than the ultimate goal that the aid is supposed to achieve. Easterly (2002) explains that 'aid bureaucracy' is more focused on the aid disbursed than the delivery of a service. The relationship between donors and aid recipients usually develops in such a way that the recipient government becomes primarily accountable to the donor agencies and less citizen-oriented, thus making it difficult for a social contract to be developed between the government and citizens (Moss, Pettersson, and van de Walle 2006). Using the principal–agent theory to describe this phenomenon, Castel-Branco (2008) argues that if strong institutions are not in place within the recipient country, the recipient country or the agent will be more accountable to the donor than to its own constituency. Owing to this, the donor agencies are often more influential in policy building within the recipient country; meanwhile, the aid recipient does not have active ownership of the projects that are in place.

There are concerns about the dignity of a recipient nation when it comes to development assistance. Often aid comes as development assistance that is tied with advice and conditions provided by richer nations and international institutions (Easterly 2007). Advice in the form of what is 'good for you' comes as a subjective idea that is highly influenced by values and traditions external to the society for whom it is supposed to be good. The question 'good for whom?' can be asked when terms such as 'good governance' are discussed (Drechsler 2004). Often, the conditions put forward may even hurt the dignity of the recipient. Policies from the donor countries come from a macro-level policy perspective that may not always take cultural sensitivities into consideration. In Bhaktapur, the standardized policy of the German side did not suit the particular case. Moreover, the case of Bhaktapur is not an isolated one: there is an increasingly clear body of public opinion that is opposed to using foreign aid when strict conditions that are felt to be unfavourable to the country are included. There is also an increasing tendency towards aid agreements being more widely scrutinized. The controversy surrounding the Nepal Compact of the Millennium Challenge Corporation (MCC) of the US exhibits this tendency. The MCC's Nepal Compact (which was signed in 2017) was to provide Nepal with USD 500 million in grants. However, as confusion grew over linkages between the MCC and the US Indo-Pacific Strategy and a clause that the Compact would prevail over Nepal's existing laws in case of conflict, there were widespread criticisms of the Compact (B. Ghimire 2020). There is a question of geopolitical influence surrounding the controversy; however, the level of public interest in the matter does show that Nepal can be wary of the conditions sought to be imposed. The Kasthamandap reconstruction is also a good example of a project which largely sought non-involvement of international donors or foreign contractors (Lekakis, Shakya, and Kostakis 2018; Tuladhar 2018; *The Kathmandu Post* 2017). The people involved in the restoration processes believed that the non-involvement of foreign donors and consultants would help to keep intact the dignity of the local community and also the state, by exhibiting indigenous capacity.

Questions of dignity, and alternatives to aid

A keyword that one comes across when considering the case of post-earthquake reconstruction in Nepal is 'dignity'. Whether considering the national discourses that have developed in the aftermath of the earthquake, or in a local context such as that of Bhaktapur, there is a realization that what the country was searching for was self-sufficiency and within that a sense of dignity. Dignity is a key aspect of development, as acknowledged by the United Nations' Agenda for Sustainable Development (United Nations 2015). Dignity means much more than adequate healthcare, proper nutrition, clean drinking water, and other such necessities. In a Buddhist economy, dignity directly associates with happiness and happiness in turn is the goal of Buddhist Economics (Bodhi 2010; Drechsler 2019). Dignity also concerns the equal treatment of all cultures, and equality has been considered a crucial element of happiness (UNESCO 1982). Autonomy is largely associated with dignity. Self-control or self-mastery, according to Buddhist values, is a crucial part of the notion of dignity and happiness

(Bodhi 2010). International aid often comes with too many strings attached; it has been argued that this reduces the liberty of developing countries to plan their own course of development and creates a dependency on aid (Tandon 2008). Some writers have even likened development aid to 'neocolonialism' (Buba 2018; Palacios 2010).

Several nuanced aspects of the aid mobilization in Nepal after the 2015 earthquakes raised the question of whether the government in Nepal, at the national and local levels, views development with dignity as possible through aid, or whether an alternative is required. Whether it be due to nationalistic policies or the desire of the general population to be self-sufficient, as the case of Bhaktapur showed, Nepal may not have the same level of activities involving international aid in the future. The country certainly cannot avoid accepting international aid as a whole, and will need to tread carefully. In the longer run, the alternative will certainly involve indigenous capacity-building in fiscal governance. The short-term interests of governments often give way to aid-funded short-term projects and these tend to help legitimize the government's performance. However, they fail to provide long-term strategic approaches for development. For developing countries the approaches needed are balanced across various essential aspects, including fiscal capacity-building (Drechsler 2009; Lin 2012). Taking Nurkse's view on fiscal administration for low-income countries, the goal should be always to push for improvement in domestic capacity, just as in techniques of physical production (Nurkse 1958: 264–65). In heritage governance in Nepal, traditional *guthi* institutions not only provided the human capital for the restoration of heritage structures but also served the function of sourcing the funds for the maintenance of these structures (Khaniya 2005; Lekakis, Shakya, and Kostakis 2018; Pradhananga, Shrestha, and Dee 2010; B. G. Shrestha 2012).

It would be overly ambitious to say that a potential rejuvenation of the *guthi* institution is the answer to the funding dilemma faced by heritage restoration or other infrastructure projects, but smaller projects can certainly be executed through funding received from rent sources still available to the municipality or local *guthis*. In the longer run, tackling larger projects by developing similar models further can certainly be a possibility. Funding infrastructure projects (religious or not) through land endowments and community-based fund sourcing is not a concept unique to *guthis*. *Waqf* practice in the Islamic world endorses similar concepts (Latif et al. 2018). In Europe, elaborate cathedrals have been built using community-based funding (Brichta 2014; Wolff 1999). Notre-Dame cathedral in Paris, which burned down in 2019, is largely being rebuilt through donations coming in from the community (Sansom 2019). If the economy overall is healthy, heritage structures of high sentimental value can easily be locally funded, which is more dignified than looking towards foreign aid that may come with stringent conditions. The *guthi* principle of self-funding resource-intensive activities through community involvement can be argued to have significant potential. It is necessary to acknowledge that even though the user committees that have effectively taken over the restoration projects in Bhaktapur are not very different from *guthi*s in essence, a vital aspect—the capability to self-fund their operations—is missing. Furthermore, user committees have a far more temporary nature, compared to *guthi*s. It is worth considering whether the Bhaktapur and other local governments can learn from the *guthi* institution as they seek to develop self-funding capacity.

10

Reclaiming Heritage

The Politics and Poetics of Newar Urbanism

Sabin Ninglekhu, Patrick Daly, and *Pia Hollenbach*

Introduction

The reconstruction and restoration of cultural heritage sites has become a common concern following conflicts and disasters. Most conservation efforts focus on communal heritage in the form of prominent religious sites, cultural monuments, museums, and archaeological sites. In Nepal, large religious complexes and prominent cultural monuments, including the Kathmandu Valley's UNESCO World Heritage Sites, experienced extensive damage due to the earthquakes of 2015. Many historical urban settlements in the Kathmandu Valley, such as Harisiddhi, Thecho, Khokana, and Bungamati, also saw significant destruction of communal heritage. In the immediate aftermath, the importance of such heritage sites for local cultural identity and ritual practices, as well as their economic value as attractions within the tourism economy, led to urgent calls from a wide range of international and local stakeholders to repair, preserve, and rebuild these sites as a core part of the post-disaster reconstruction process. Against this backdrop, this chapter takes up the 'household'—vis-à-vis heritage preservation—as the primary unit of analysis to focus on the historic urban landscapes in the Kathmandu Valley that include large numbers of private commercial and residential spaces and structures. The key question that the chapter addresses is this: If heritage is embodied within the layout, form, and aesthetic of private residential and commercial spaces, how do residents, NGOs, and governments prioritize cultural preservation against the need to rebuild quickly, efficiently, and safely while adhering to the norms and standards of architectural aesthetics and cultural authenticity?

The earthquake of 25 April triggered a major humanitarian response, including support from international emergency response teams, relief and reconstruction advisors, and over USD 4.1 billion pledged by international donors (National Planning Commission 2015b). In December 2015, the National Reconstruction Authority (NRA) was formed and issued a national plan for rebuilding that advocated 'owner-driven' reconstruction and a fair distribution of housing aid (National Planning Commission 2015a). The NRA's plan explicitly advocated the empowerment of affected persons, and their right to participate in the design, planning, and construction of their homes and commercial properties. It also promoted hazard mitigation through new seismic resistant building codes and by-laws, and the need to promote community-level economic development.

As discussed in more detail later, the initial building codes and by-laws endorsed by the NRA were criticized by stakeholders in historic urban settlements because many of the new building specifications were incompatible with traditional architectural forms and land use patterns. This created tension and exposed an inherent contradiction within the NRA's plans— strict adherence to what the government determined were safe building practices limited the possibility to rebuild historic urban neighbourhoods, and prevented local stakeholders' cultural expression. In response to concerned stakeholders, and recognizing the importance of historic neighbourhoods in Kathmandu for the image of Nepal and the tourism industry, the government subsequently issued a new set of building codes and by-laws designed specifically for urban heritage areas. However, these new by-laws subsequently imposed a top-down mandate, which provided an official statement about which aspects of heritage were most essential and therefore needed to be conserved, but also effectively limited the right of affected persons and households to determine how best to proceed with rebuilding.

In this chapter, we will analyse the tensions that have emerged during the reconstruction of historic urban settlements in the Kathmandu Valley following the 2015 earthquakes. We focus on two core issues. First, we investigate how rebuilding an 'ideal' historic town, as defined by the by-laws for historic neighbourhoods, presented homeowners with practical challenges such as additional costs and bureaucratic burdens, and limited their freedom to build their houses according to their personal means and aspirations. This raises questions about how the rights of individual families to adequate housing and the rhetorical emphasis on 'bottom up' and participatory humanitarianism should be weighed against parallel arguments for the importance of identity and cultural heritage. Second, we unpack the reconstruction plans of several historic urban neighbourhoods to show how the plans to 'conserve' heritage and the associated sociocultural life can be seen as transformative and, as such, shift community dynamics and the use of space at least partially away from long-held traditions, and more towards modern uses of heritage architecture for primarily economic purposes such as tourism.

Heritage, reconstruction, and identity

Scholars of heritage studies have long argued that cultural heritage (both tangible, physical things and intangible cultural expressions and practices) is a fundamental aspect of cultural identity, and thus a core part of what it means to be human. Cultural heritage includes a complex range of often interconnected places and practices that are critical for socializing, worshipping, commemorating the past, and reproducing and transferring cultural values and knowledge. The destruction of cultural heritage, therefore, can have a profoundly negative impact upon individuals and communities (Waterton and Smith 2010). An extreme illustration of this is the intentional targeting of cultural heritage during conflicts, when armed groups try to inflict emotional and psychological trauma, to at least deprive their targets of critical social infrastructure, and, in some cases, to eradicate all traces of a group's historic claims and presence in a particular location (Daly and Rahmayati 2012; Daly and Winter 2012). There has been an increasing recognition that the destruction of cultural heritage by disasters, while not intentional, can also undermine the cultural identity of affected communities. Additionally, research has also shown that the destruction of vernacular forms of cultural heritage can disorient disaster-affected persons and impede reconstruction efforts, because local rituals and a communal infrastructure provide residents with the venues and facilities necessary for commiseration and the carrying out of practical rebuilding functions such as community meetings (Daly and Chan 2016).

Therefore, any approach to post-disaster reconstruction needs to consider the historical, and not only the cultural implications of damage to the built environment but also the potential ruptures to cultural and social practices that might accompany rebuilding plans. To do so, it is imperative to map out the cultural heritage of disaster-affected areas as part of post-disaster damage assessment and reconstruction plans, and consider the implications of any proposed changes upon the underlying social fabric of disaster-affected communities. Accordingly, the preservation and reconstruction of cultural heritage has become a common part of post-disaster rebuilding plans—especially when the disaster has impacted areas of prominent cultural significance (Daly and Rahmayati 2012). For the most part, reference to cultural heritage in post-disaster situations emphasizes communal structures such as places of worship, museums, and archaeological sites. In practical terms, it is common for some combination of national agencies, local stakeholders, and (in cases where resources are lacking) external donors and 'experts' to undertake careful restoration and preservation of specifically selected, highly visible sites (Crooke 2010).

Newar urbanism

'Newar urbanism' is a term that returned to the popular lexicon in the aftermath of the 2015 earthquakes. Sudarshan Raj Tiwari, a prominent scholar of Newar architecture, culture, and history in the Kathmandu Valley, likens Newar urbanism to a theatre or a stage on which the drama of the everyday life of the Newar unfolds (Tiwari 2015). Tiwari's use of the words 'stage' and 'drama' alludes to the ways in which the tangible structure of the Newars' heritage, such as courtyards, rest houses, temples, monasteries, ponds, and water spouts, as well as houses with vernacular designs, are inextricably intertwined with the intangible rituals of culture, ethnicity, and everyday life. This mode of urbanism is filled with a 'dramatic display of marked symbolism' to borrow Levy's (1992: 2) description of a Newar town, Bhaktapur, in the Kathmandu Valley. Spatial divisions and demarcations are symbolic markers—'stones, shrines, temples, roads, and pathways'— which guide and regulate 'symbolical enactments' that allow for the city's endless civic dance to unfold (Levy 1992: 157). Together, the tangible and intangible structures and rituals of heritage imbue the place with social meanings and an emotional orientation. This rendering of Newar urbanism, however, is not intended to promote Newar urbanism as an ideal, for there is a risk of such a romanticization glossing over the deep hierarchies and stark divisions along caste and gender lines within a very diverse Newar society.

Gopal Singh Nepali, a foundational scholar in the study of the Newars, argues that the origin of the Newars is a controversial question. He suggests that their histories of migration and their cultural affinities reveal that they have Tibeto-Burman as well as Indo-Aryan origins. As such, the present Newar population is a complex of many ethnic groups (Nepali 2015). In the years since Nepali's ethnographic research on Newars was first published, other scholars have examined and exposed their complexity further. While most of the contemporary architectural urban form that is now called Newar urbanism may have been set in stone during the time of the Malla dynasty, it would be an over simplification to claim that Newar society is '… a direct legacy of the mediaeval Malla Period' (Toffin 2008: 18). Instead, Newars are an ethnic group that is deeply divided along lines of caste, religion, dialect, and locality (Gellner and Quigley 1995). They have highly regulated and differentiated gender roles, and economies that are rooted in myriad ways of life and livelihood, including specialized trading, farming, and handicrafts (Levy 1992). The *guthi* system, a form of 'associational life' that is central to organizing and regulating the cultural and religious lives of the Newars through multifarious rituals, divides as well as binds the Newar people along lines of kinship, caste, and gender. There are several *guthi*s in every Newar town, each with its own kinship-based members and its own deity. Each *guthi* organizes its own ceremonies and rituals. For certain rituals, members from one *guthi* are not allowed to be a part of a ritual held by a different *guthi*. 'For this one day, our town becomes a place filled with different countries. One cannot enter the territory of the other', says one resident when describing a guthi ritual.[1] In other words, the hierarchy incipient within the Newar diversity is also spatial in nature and is performed and reproduced through spatial practices of heritage.

In the wake of the 2015 earthquakes, Sudarshan Raj Tiwari proclaimed, 'more than monuments and buildings, the earthquake has destroyed urbanism itself' (Tiwari 2015).[2] It is clear that Tiwari was alluding to the architectural ruins that filled the alleyways and inner roads of major traditional urban centres of the Kathmandu Valley such as Sankhu, Bhaktapur, Bungamati, Harisiddhi, and Patan. Tiwari also lamented the loss, as temporary as it may be, of the intangible matters of everyday

---

[1] Hari Maharjan, personal communication, 12 May 2019.
[2] Excerpt from a presentation that Tiwari gave in 2015 at Martin Chautari.

practices and rituals that are the heritage of the Newars. What is also clear is that for the purveyors, proponents, and preservationists of Newar urbanism, the primary focus is architectural, in which culture is a matter of aesthetics present in the rituals and the festivals. For many, reclaiming Newar urbanism, in principle, is to excavate the Newar way of life from under the rubble, and the re-erection of physical structures representing heritage. The actual practice of such a process is, however, filled with everyday critical challenges at the household level that can only be excavated through ethnography. Such an endeavour may bring to light social struggles that are incipient in the Newar way of life that is to be restored—struggles that are laid bare as the invocation of individual rights rooted in the practice of everyday life encounters the aspirations of aesthetics and authenticity that the project of reclaiming 'Newar urbanism' carries.

After the 2015 earthquakes in Nepal, images of beautiful historic structures in ruins or propped up with make-shift braces were widely circulated and drew attention to the depth of the cultural loss caused by the disaster. They remind us that the effects of disaster extend far beyond the present—reducing aspects of the past, and creating cultural ruptures that shape the longer-term future. The destruction of cultural heritage, from temples and palaces to the narrow winding alleys and courtyards of residential areas, creates a set of unique challenges in terms of reconstruction. It is against this backdrop that our research in Nepal has focused on four urban neighbourhoods in the Kathmandu Valley: Bungamati, Harisiddhi, Thecho, and Patan. The ongoing research is ethnographic, and primarily led by qualitative interviews. In each settlement, households affected by the earthquakes were divided into three different groups: 'rebuilding', including households still rebuilding at the time of the interview; 'complete', households that have completed the rebuilding and moved in; and 'vacant', households with houses that either continue to lie dilapidated after the earthquake or whose rubble has been cleared and now exists as a vacant plot waiting for rebuilding. Each group consisted of 20 households. Therefore, in each settlement, over 60 households were selected for interview. Over the past three years, we have been meeting with the members of these households at different intervals for interviews and informal conversations. Together, these regularly updated accounts of the households' experience of the rebuilding became a basis for framing what James Holston calls the 'ethnographic present': '... the realm of the present that is rooted in the heterogeneity of the lived experience, which is to say, in the ethnographic present and not in the utopian futures' (1999: 48).

The research project also uses a quantitative research method. All of the households in the core areas of the settlement, affected in different degrees by the earthquakes, were selected for quantitative survey. The survey provides a comprehensive and substantive overview of the general livelihood, income standards, family size, access to social capital and financial capital, and landholding, including the general vernacular detail of their house, before and after the earthquakes. The set of data collected through the survey provides a robust context for the research in which to locate the 'ethnographic present'. In addition, we have been conducting extensive surveys and reviews of critical planning documents since the 1990s. The 1990s marked the beginning of the major thrust of the Nepali state towards liberalization and decentralization, inserting discourses such as 'self-help', 'public private partnership', and 'user committee' into the public lexicon around planning and governance (Ninglekhu and Rankin 2008). As such, the current permutations vis-à-vis post-earthquake disaster governance have to be located in this particular history, which may provide antecedents for the post-earthquake frameworks for governance, such as the promotion of community-led reconstruction committees in the urban areas of the Kathmandu Valley.

In the months following the earthquakes, in each of these neighbourhoods, groups of stakeholders banded together to start mapping out reconstruction plans. This was done through community reconstruction committees and collaborations between local parties, non-governmental organizations (NGOs), and the Nepal government. Here, we focus on Bungamati. Bungamati's population of 6,000 people is comprised predominantly of 'high-caste' Newar groups, such as Tuladhar, Bajracharya, and Shakya, followed by Mali and Maharjan. The Mali and Maharjan, traditionally, are gardeners and farmers, and the latter are considered the backbone of Newar society. Bajracharya and Shakya are high-caste priests, while Tuladhar are merchants whose livelihood is traditionally based on wooden handicrafts. The 2015 earthquakes destroyed over 550 houses in the Bungamati core. Four traditional ponds, four temples, and more than ten rest houses were also destroyed.

In the wake of the earthquakes, Bungamati was able to draw significant interest and attention from nationally and internationally based organizations. This was due to a number of important factors. It was the severity of the destruction of private homes as well as public monuments that drew immediate attention. But, more critically, the inherent social and cultural capital of the place that has been influential in wielding substantive institutional interest is due to the centrality of Bungamati in the Kathmandu Valley's landscape of heritage. For example, the Rato Machhindranath Jatra is a month-long chariot procession and one of the major festivals of Nepal that honours the Buddhist deity of compassion. To the deity, Bungamati is home, as it is the Rato Machhindranath temple in Bungamati that houses it. Such is the importance of the chariot festival that the historian Sudarshan Tiwari has made a romantic gesture to it vis-à-vis Newar urbanism: 'Newar urbanism is agricultural. It is pedestrian and truly wheel-less. Only the very god of gods travelled in wheeled chariots. Its characteristic charms and expressions were all laid and happened on its streets and squares at the crossroads. All this now lies under the rubble of the 2072 Earthquake' (Tiwari 2015). There have been attempts in the past to institutionalize this centrality of Bungamati internationally. For example, in 1995, a few years after the reinstatement of the multiparty democratic system in Nepal, a collective of locally based preservationists and leaders of Bungamati pushed forward a plan to nominate Bungamati as a potential UNESCO World Heritage Site. However, after more than two decades, Bungamati is yet to be enlisted. In the words of a local architect and preservationist:

(U)nlike in other historic settlements, very few initiatives have been taken by local leaders to persistently push for Bungamati's nomination as a World Heritage Site. Doing so requires a regular documentation of the status of local tangible and intangible heritage structures in Bungamati, as well as actively lobbying and liaising with key stakeholders within the heritage fields at the municipal and national scales. This form of proactive organizing has not been taking place in Bungamati, before as well as after the 2015 earthquakes.[3]

The earthquakes of 2015, however, provided a reactive impetus for a group of architects, preservationists, and local leaders of Bungamati to push forward the project of heritage with a renewed zeal—and this time to promote it as the heart and centre of post-earthquake Newar urbanism. Subsequently,

---

[3]   Anil Tuladhar, personal communication, 7 August 2019. Our discussion around the nomination of Bungamati as a UNESCO World Heritage Site relies largely on anecdotal accounts taken from interviews and informal conversations that shed light on locally based initiatives that have taken place in the past. No written or published account of this initiative is publicly accessible.

the Government of Nepal and the United Nations Human Settlements Programme (UN-Habitat) positioned Bungamati as the most significant historic urban settlement that required reconstruction, and which would serve as a model for approaching all historic urban neighbourhoods in Nepal. The section below traces the coalition of key local, national, and international stakeholders and the concretization of the multifarious interests around reclaiming the Newari heritage.

Heritage as placemaking

In the wake of the 2015 earthquakes, an *ad hoc* collection of organizations, under the loose auspices of UN-Habitat, conducted damage and needs assessments, compiled research on the historic background of the settlement and its ancient Newar town layout and architectural forms, and drafted a number of parallel proposals for rebuilding Bungamati. Here we briefly discuss three such initiatives, in order to illustrate how expressions of interest in preserving cultural heritage were merged with concerns about urban planning and economic development and effectively appeared to value transformation over preservation.

Researchers and students from K. U. Leuven University's MA programmes in Human Settlement and Urbanism and Strategic Planning used Bungamati as part of a project that was a combination of student practical assignment and humanitarian mission. This project was made possible via a long-term association between UN-Habitat and K. U. Leuven University globally. Through field visits and extensive studio time, the researchers drafted a report in which they situated Bungamati within the past 50 years of urban development in the Kathmandu Valley. They argued for using the 'opportunity' created by the earthquake to address some of the failings of Bungamati, by changing the density of the settlement, modifying traditional structures to make them seismic resistant, and leveraging cultural heritage to encourage tourism (a common theme in all the Bungamati reconstruction plans).

As a strategic next step, UN-Habitat brought Architect's Design Associates (ADA), a group of Nepali architects that included some Bungamati residents, into the fold with the very specific remit of translating K. U. Leuven's report into a medium that would be legible to the local community. ADA integrated its expertise and knowledge of architecture and heritage with the key components of the K. U. Leuven report to prepare a 3-D presentation for the local community, with the following aims at the core of its message:

- To support rebuilding traditional settlements of Kathmandu Valley that are damaged by the earthquake keeping the urban fabrics intact and enhanced;
- To support rebuilding of traditional houses robust, safe and that conserve heritage values;
- To support rebuilding of the economy of the people by promoting compatible businesses and trades to heritage conservation. (Amaya et al. 2016)

As part of this, they identified numerous improvements that they wanted to make to traditional architecture to increase seismic safety and also to enhance the liveability of buildings: these included increasing natural ventilation and light, and accommodating modern infrastructure such as plumbing, utilities, and internet connections. They drafted numerous architectural models for mixed-use commercial and residential spaces that utilized some aspects of traditional Newar architecture and use of space, while adding in new components that would support cultural tourism, such as homestays, cafes, and souvenir shops (Figure 10.1).

Perhaps the most ambitious rebuilding plans were those proposed by ARCADIS, a global design and consultancy firm. Using an existing global partnership programme with UN-Habitat, called SHELTER, ARCADIS was asked to prepare a master plan for Bungamati. Under this partnership, ARCADIS' mission statement was to 'demonstrate how traditional settlements of Kathmandu Valley can be revitalized and made into livable and vibrant townships through people's "processes"' (Smolders 2015: 8). While adopting an ostensibly heritage-centric approach, their plan envisioned a fundamental transformation of Bungamati, both in terms of its built environment and local economy. They proposed enhancing the infrastructure to provide better public transportation, environmentally friendly waste management systems, and open green spaces. To improve the tourist experience, they recommended a large visitor centre, a lighted night time heritage walk, an earthquake memorial park, and 'pop-up' public art installations. In addition to increasing heritage tourism, they recommended establishing a vocational training centre that would focus on traditional crafts. Finally, they proposed to turn Bungamati into a

Figure 10.1 Heritage home, as envisioned by Shelter Program, UN-Habitat.
Source: UN-Habitat.

'digital city' through high speed internet connections and training courses in computer literacy.

The final document as a guideline for rebuilding Bungamati that was eventually drafted after ARCADIS' iteration had to be converted into a 'Citizens' Charter' first, if it were to have any tangible effect on the rebuilding—as was originally envisioned when UN-Habitat first collaborated with K. U. Leuven. As such, UN-Habitat worked collaboratively with the municipality to convert the document into a 'Citizens' Charter'. While this exercise was taking place, the NRA was formed. Following this, UN-Habitat presented the document to the NRA, which was sufficiently impressed to suggest that the document, which was originally meant for Bungamati alone, should be converted into a national document for the governance of rebuilding in traditional settlements. This suggestion from the NRA was important because it opened an avenue for UN-Habitat to work with the Ministry of Urban Development, specifically with two key objectives: first, to address a few concerns around the provisions contained in an existing national document called the 'Basic Building Guideline for Settlement Development, Urban Planning and Building Construction 2015', which were not compatible with recreating the built form, or whatever remained of it, of the Newar settlements; and, second, to insert the Bungamati document as a key component of the 'Basic Building Guideline'.

The Ministry of Urban Development revised the aforementioned 'Basic Building Guideline' after the 2015 earthquakes to regulate rebuilding practices in the earthquake-affected districts of Nepal. However, the Guideline included a set of provisions that failed to take into consideration the unique built form of the Newar towns in the Kathmandu Valley.[4] The following provisions were deemed to be impractical. First, it stated that row-houses would not be allowed building permits; and, second, that neighbourhood roads were required to maintain a minimum width of 6 metres. If they were narrower, the government would apply 'eminent domain' to dismantle houses to make way for street-widening.[5] These provisions posed a major threat to the envisioned restoration of Newar urbanism, as identified by UN-Habitat in collaboration with the three sets of actors mentioned earlier. If, as P. S. Joshi of UN-Habitat pointed out, these conditions were to be applied to the traditional towns, almost all the row houses would have to be dismantled, because most streets and alleyways in the inner parts of the settlements were less than 6 metres wide. In addition, the average landholding of a Newar family in these towns, excluding farmlands on the periphery, is no more than 400 square feet (based on a quantitative survey of the Newar settlements). Street-widening would leave the houses bereft of any sizable plots on which to rebuild a liveable house.

To address the potentially destructive contents of the 'Basic Building Guideline', UN-Habitat initiated the drafting of a separate by-law that

---

4   P. S. Joshi, UN-Habitat, personal communication, 13 November 2018.
5   'Eminent domain' refers to the power of the state to stake claims over private property for public use.

would provide a guideline for, as well as regulate, reconstruction in the historic towns, while warding off the threat to Bungamati's urbanism. An ad hoc committee of three individuals—a local head of UN-Habitat, a senior-level policy expert, and a retired bureaucrat—worked on this by-law. The by-law, thus prepared, was, on the one hand, meant to preserve the Newar vernacular character of the place, while, on the other hand, it was also to provide less stringent and more flexible grounds for households to rebuild their homes. After much lobbying and negotiating through the competing institutional interests of the NRA and the Department of Urban Development and Building Construction (DUDBC), the heritage by-law was inserted as a separate chapter in the 'Basic Building Guideline', which, over time, took on a life of its own and became a legally binding national document to guide the rebuilding of all traditional towns in Nepal. Thus, it was guaranteed that historic urban settlements would be exempted from complying with the provisions that non-traditional, relatively modern settlements had to comply with—that the streets in the Newar towns could remain as they were and that rebuilding could restore row-housing. This particular by-law provided relief to the residents, while also preventing the complete annihilation of the Newar urban landscape. The new chapter included the following provisions that focused on the reconstruction of private houses and public monuments, and also aimed to maintain the integrity of the public spaces:

1. The house's façade is to have a Newari design, with wooden door and window frames of specified size and number.
2. The interior of the house can be decorated according to one's will, but the exterior is to display bricks.
3. The vertical limit of the house is not to exceed 32 feet.
4. Only one-third of the terrace can be an open space; the rest has to be covered under a slanted roof.

It is hard to find fault with calls to build stronger, more robust structures capable of withstanding future earthquakes, to address long-standing concerns about the ills of unplanned urban sprawl, and to encourage economic development. However, in the case of Bungamati, all of these reconstruction plans were explicitly framed around the importance of preserving cultural heritage, citing how the unique cultural identity of the inhabitants was embodied within traditional architectural forms. The plans, produced by experts with the endorsement of UN-Habitat, are more realistically seen as a form of placemaking, where Newar heritage—usually limited to the aesthetics of the façades of buildings—was to be selectively appropriated to carry out a development agenda. The types of changes needed to address the ambitious goals of the various parties involved in the planning would have reconfigured both the built environment, and also the social fabric and social practices of Bungamati.

Furthermore, the calls by the organizations involved for 'bottom-up' and participatory reconstruction were undermined by the imposition of externally drafted plans that emphasized some non-local concerns. The reports were filled with idyllic renderings of clean rebuilt spaces populated by well-dressed locals and obvious foreigners. The examples used to illustrate the new components of Bungamati were largely drawn from European cities. The plans seemed to merge a European view of liveability, including green spaces, cycle paths, and lighted heritage walks, with a tourist perspective of what a heritage city should be, and tried to pass that off as a locally constructed heritage preservation plan.

In Asian countries more generally, the broader conversation around heritage is concerned with the preservation of historic urban landscapes, which largely comes out of efforts to preserve entire neighbourhoods. The premise for this is that in urban historic neighbourhoods it does not make sense to view heritage in terms of individual structures. This logic treats heritage as a composite which contains different constituent parts. As such, any efforts towards the preservation of heritage cannot divorce an individual structure as a heritage site from the milieu of which it is a part. The value of heritage comes from the collective, not the individual (Daly and Winter 2012). It can be argued that it is this logic that underlines UN-Habitat's vision of heritage preservation in the Newar towns in Nepal, because it promotes a more holistic plan that treats each and every house in the town as part of a wider tapestry. On the one hand, the formation of this particular by-law has enabled the key policy stakeholders to institutionalize their call for the preservation of cultural heritage and the commercial plan contained in the vision. On the other, our ongoing ethnographic work reveals that most of the provisions in the by-law have, directly or indirectly, created major challenges and obstacles for households with regard to balancing their practical limitations and personal aspirations with the mandates of the heritage by-law.

Heritage and everyday life

Architectural integrity, according to the mandates of the heritage by-law, is to be reflected in the façade and the roof of the house: wooden door and window frames with particular dimensions; no balcony on the front face; ceiling height to be no more than 8 feet; and only one-third of the terrace to be left open, with the rest covered by a separate terrace roof. Together, these propositions create conditions that are financially challenging and filled with multiple nodes of bureaucratic entanglement that tend to trample upon one's agentive capacity to decide for one's own sake.

The intangible cost of heritage

Considered central to Bungamati's identity as a heritage town, the Rato Machhindranath temple, completely destroyed by the earthquake, is now undergoing a slow and gradual reconstruction process (Figure 10.2). Jointly funded by the Embassy of Sri Lanka and the Government of Nepal's Department of Archaeology, the reconstruction of the temple was halted for a long period, beginning in the summer of 2017, after the foundation was dug and filled with brick and cement mortar. The contractor, to whom the rebuilding was contracted out, was caught unawares when local leaders pointed out that the bricks that had been used to build the foundation were 'inauthentic' because of the Roman script letters that were inscribed on them. The locals demanded that the foundation work had to be reversed and redone with bricks using Newar characters. After a long stand-off between the contractor, the local leaders, and the funding authorities, a decision was made to redo the foundation work with Newar-inscribed bricks, and the reconstruction was resumed soon afterwards. This incident is worth noting because it highlights the importance of the idea of 'authenticity' that building materials are supposed to contain, specifically in relation to the reconstruction of Newar heritage. In order to maintain the 'authenticity' of the design, households are encouraged to use 'authentic' bricks, which are more expensive than 'normal' bricks, for the walls and the façade of the houses that are being rebuilt. And once the reconstruction is complete, households are asked to cover the pillars on the outside of the house in order to maintain the 'authenticity' of the house.

Figure 10.2 A *puja* held to mark the reconstruction of the Rato Machhindranath temple.

Source: Photograph by Sabin Ninglekhu.

It is the doors and windows, however, that add most to the overall cost of a Newar house. The majority of Newar households in Bungamati have intimated that, had they been free to use aluminium instead of timber for doors and windows, they would always opt for aluminium, like many residents in the non-traditional 'modern' neighbourhoods in the city. A wooden window would cost almost three times as much as an aluminium window of similar size. Some households felt the 'peer pressure' to opt for more elaborate and intricate carvings on doors and window frames, either because an adjoining house had done so, or because their house stood in front of an expensively and elaborately assembled heritage structure such as a temple or a museum. Further, because the stipulations of the by-laws about the design and size of the door and window frames are quite specific, households often struggled to meet the standards because they were not

Figure 10.3 Row of houses at the main Bungamati 'Bus Stand'. None of these adheres strictly to the heritage by-law.

Source: Photograph by Sabin Ninglekhu.

feasible on financial or practical grounds.[6] In addition, many were unaware of the specifications because not everyone had access to the provisions of the by-laws and certainly not in a language that was comprehensible to them. In the absence of a clear understanding of the specifications for doors and windows, it is common in places like Bungamati to come across many households which have had to constantly revise the heritage-centric design in the hope that it will be endorsed by the architects and engineers when they come to vet it (Figure 10.3). In many cases, the households have had to take out window frames after they had been installed because they were found not to comply with the heritage mandates in the aftermath.

---

[6]   For example, a door or a window has to be 'odd-bay'—meaning, the number of window or door frames on a façade has to be odd, not even. Likewise, a window frame cannot be more than 5 feet 6 inches high and 2 feet 6 inches wide. Similar conditions apply for door frames.

When the houses fell apart, they exposed the complex nature of the pattern of home- and land-ownership that had been passed down informally through the generations. Over the past four years, many joint families have disbanded and converted into nuclear families. One of the key factors pushing this break from the concept of joint family is the nature of landownership and tenure; the other factor is a provision in the heritage by-law that puts a cap on building height. The average landholding per family or house in the core Bungamati area is around 400 square feet—barely enough to accommodate one room per floor. If a house were to be rebuilt in the same old location, it could not be more than 32 feet in height, as mandated by the heritage by-laws. This means that, given the limit imposed on the height of a house and the average landholding per household in the core area, an ancestral house that would accommodate two to four families before the earthquake, if and when it was rebuilt, could only have three to four rooms: just enough for one family, which, typically, comprises anywhere from four to eight family members. As such, families have no choice but to break away. There are many households in the traditional settlements that lament that the current limit on the building height is not 'practical', simply because it is not able to accommodate the number of members in a family. It is equally important to note that the majority of Newar families are self-employed or have home-based entrepreneurship. That is, they run a Newar restaurant, a handicraft workshop, or a general shop on the first floor at the ground or street level, already congesting the living space further up. We do not intend to suggest that the changing family structure—from joint to nuclear—within the Newar settlements and cultural life is instigated solely by the limits set by the heritage by-laws. Far from it. Rather, as the respondents have intimated themselves, the by-law is just one of several factors that is pushing many Newar families away from the joint system.

According to the heritage by-law, only one-third of a house terrace may be left open, while the rest has to be covered by a roof, which has to be slanted at 25 to 30 degrees. For many households, a terrace with a narrow space is problematic, primarily because it leaves no room for them to dry their grains. The majority of Newars in Bungamati continue to farm; produce from the farm, such as rice and maize, can last for three–six months, depending on family size. Others complained that the limited terrace leaves little room for the elderly people of the house to sit out in the sun. They say that there is no open public space in the town for the grain and the elderly anymore like there used to be. The number of houses has increased, while the roads have widened, gradually eating away at the open spaces that used to exist. The terrace that the by-laws demand, as such, would leave little room to offer continuity in the contemporaneous practice of everyday life, rooted in Newar culture and tradition.

While some local residents in Bungamati saw the heritage by-laws and building codes as an opportunity to not only systematize the tenuous and informal nature of landownership but also to reclaim the heritage that is gradually lost over time, to the majority the heritage-centric by-laws trampled on an individual's right to manage life on his or her own terms and conditions. Getting the Newar design right, moreover, was, in and of itself, a fraught endeavour, a long drawn-out bureaucratic process. Often, an engineer, usually a government representative, would find faults in the size of the window frames, the number of window frames on the façade of the house, the size and design of the roof of the terrace, or the terrace itself, and so on. This led to further delays. In a majority of cases, the households either decided to start rebuilding without the design approval because waiting for it would seem like an unending process, or the government experts found technical faults in the design half-way through the construction process, which left the households in a state of limbo. The shortcut route to a guaranteed shelter, as such, would be to build without the permit. In Bungamati, it is very rare to find a household that is rebuilding or has completed rebuilding after obtaining a building permit. Outside of the obstacles that are created by the technicalities of the design mandates, the design itself is not inclusive enough to accommodate the lived realities and experiences of everyday life that may have very little to do with 'heritage' itself. As one resident reasoned, 'If heritage-centric rebuilding is for tourism, tell me how will I benefit from it? I am not into the handicraft business, I don't have a shop to sell anything to the tourists, and they are not interested in talking to me, so it is not like I will make new friends. So, what is in it for me, really?'[7]

The long road to recovery

The provisions contained in the by-law require the Newars to bear the responsibility of preserving the Newar identity of a place as bearers or

---

[7]   Sushil Tuladhar, personal communication, 25 July 2018.

custodians of culture and heritage. While many Newars see the rationale behind the need to preserve heritage, and its attendant economic benefits in the future, the exigencies of contemporaneous everyday circumstances also push them to question the practicality of the imperative of heritage on the grounds of rights and justice rooted in private property, summarized succinctly in a question that an interviewee posed, quite animatedly, 'This is my land and I am building my house on this land. So, should I not have the primary right over what kind of house I want to build?'[8]

This frustration, which filled the course of almost every interview we conducted in Bungamati, is primarily of a financial nature, in that the rising cost of building materials, combined with the growing quantity of building materials needed to rebuild, have made reconstruction in general, and heritage-centric reconstruction in particular, an expensive proposition. The financial demand adds more to the overall reconstruction cost, which is already soaring due to seismic safety standards.[9]

Most of the Newars in Bungamati, as in other traditional settlements in the Kathmandu Valley, own farmlands in the peripheries of the core areas in which they live. These are ancestral properties that have been passed down through the generations. The majority of the landowning Newars, therefore, have sold some portion of their land in order to fund most of the rebuilding cost. For the small section of the Bungamati population without surplus land, rebuilding is an insurmountable task, simply because without any land to sell, there are no resources for rebuilding. As such, these are the households that are gradually losing faith, as well as 'resilience', under the weight of waiting for a house that may never be rebuilt. However, in relation to those who sell land to rebuild, the loss of land has some major implications with respect to heritage—both tangible and intangible.

It is common to hear the Newars lament the loss of land. To many, it is linked with the ancestor's *chino*—a gift, a mark, a symbol, and a legacy.

---

[8] Gyanendra Tuladhar, personal communication, 20 August 2018.

[9] Although discussion of seismic safety standards vis-à-vis reconstruction is outside the scope of this chapter, which is heritage-centric, it is worth noting, in brief, that the mandates of seismic safety standards have put major financial pressure on households. The building codes require thicker pillars, a 'double tie beam', and a foundation that is at least 5 feet deep, meaning new structures require a higher quantity of cement, bricks, and iron rods, compared to the structures prior to the earthquake.

The loss of land, therefore, is also a loss of 'heritage'—a very tangible heritage. 'What will remain of the Newar identity if we sell our ancestral *chino* to be occupied later by non-Newars from elsewhere?' said one of the residents.[10] The loss of land also signals the loss of a traditional life rooted in farming. Even though Bungamati is referred to as a 'town' in common parlance, and is in close proximity, geographically, to the urban areas of the Kathmandu Valley, it retains many rural characteristics because many Newar families continue to rely on agriculture to support their subsistence. The loss of land, whether complete or partial, also means a complete or partial loss of farming as a lifestyle and livelihood. As a result, a Newar family that relied on seasonal grains and vegetables for a few months every year would now have to increase its dependency on the market to meet its daily needs. The loss of land would also mean that the Newars are left to find work outside of the agricultural field to support their subsistence needs. Together, these would mean a gradual transformation of everyday Newar life. This is not to claim that the earthquake was the sole rupture, or sole instigator, that changed the course of Newar everyday life. Rather, it is to suggest that the earthquake expedited certain futurities of the Newar everyday life that would, otherwise, have still unfolded, albeit at a more gradual pace. The transition to consumerism is made possible in large part through the commodification of land, the selling of which allows for assembling things that represent 'prestige' and 'modernity'—for 'doing' the middle class identity (Liechty 2003). Based on our ongoing ethnographic research, it may be argued that the earthquake has expedited the process of commodification of land, albeit to fund the project aimed at 'preserving tradition' via rebuilding heritage.

A majority of the Newar households rely on their existing stock of social capital for loans. A dense network of social relationships and family ties allows the Newars to mobilize their social capital to gain financial capital. It is common to come across families who have borrowed money from friends and family members. This is an informal loan arrangement, free of interest and with a flexible repayment plan. However, 'social capital' exists in a field of power, re-entrenching social differences and class divide (Ninglekhu and Rankin 2008). In other words, access to social capital and the ability to mobilize it are unevenly distributed among the households. As such, some

---

[10]   Hari Gopal Maharjan, personal communication, 9 January 2018.

of these households, already without surplus land to sell, are also not in a position to participate in social networks to access other forms of capital necessary to fund rebuilding. Whereas there are other households with access to dense family networks and kinship ties that find ways to access finance from different financial institutions, ranging from women's cooperatives to private banks.[11] These loans from friends or cooperatives offer the recipients some relief, because there is money now to inject into completing the homes whose construction has had to take pauses from time to time during the different phases of rebuilding, due to a lack of cash. However, they also invite elements of uncertainty into the futures of these families. In the absence of formal and regular sources of monthly income, for example, many are unsure how long the repayment of their loans will take.

As tactics and strategies around selling land and securing loans unfold, the concept of 'recovery' takes on new meanings over time. Many equate recovery with the reclaiming of land that was sold to finance a rebuilding: 'We feel like we will "recover" once we have been able to reclaim [purchase back] the land that we had to sell'.[12] However, such casual statements are also underlined by an acceptance that the land will of course never come back. Likewise, even if loans are interest-free and with no formal repayment structure, they still may take several years, or even a generation, to repay. That is why, 'for Bungamati to get back to the stage it was at before the earthquake, it may take at least 10 years', says another resident.[13] Another says:

> Recovery is a broad thing. Rebuilding a house is not recovery. I am in debt long before the house is complete. After it is complete, one moves into the new house. This movement is not recovery. A family has shifted to a new, more secure, location. That is all. There are many more things left to do, including repaying loans.[14]

The resident points at the trade-offs that people are making to build their new homes—taking loans and selling land. In doing so, the resident brings

---

[11] The much-publicized 'subsidized housing loan' from the government, which is different from the housing grant, has so far remained a chimera that has only brought frustration after initially offering hope in the wake of the earthquakes.

[12] Chiri Mai Tuladhar, personal communication, 12 May 2018.

[13] Anil Tuladhar, personal communication, 12 February 2018.

[14] Manoj Shrestha, personal communication, 17 August 2018.

to light the consequences of the trade-offs that extend far into the future, signalling that the pursuit of 'recovery' may be an endless process.

For the residents of Bungamati, preservation of cultural life is secondary. The primal necessities come down to the basic need to preserve biological life. However, if the conditions are such that preserving biological life hinges on the preservation of a cultural life, in the manner that is imposed through the by-law, households show a willingness to either bypass or subvert the bureaucratic upheavals. These upheavals are raised as a result of the regulatory frames devised as part of the post-disaster governance of the Newar towns. Given the stringent regulatory measures of the heritage by-law, the households have no other option but to ultimately comply with the provisions to be able to build a house. As such, the households end up pursuing a series of actions and strategies that will ultimately pave the way to building a house, albeit after suppressing their own agency, articulated succinctly in this quote, a response to a question about adhering to the heritage by-law: *Rahar le hoina kar le*—'out of compulsion, not desire'.[15]

Conclusion: aesthetics, authenticity, and everyday life

The anthropologist Veena Das (2006) foregrounds the dual nature of everyday life in her work on the everyday practices of the urban poor in India. She contends that the cure for myriad struggles inherent in everyday life is to be found within the everyday itself. The insights of Henri Lefebvre (2003) may be brought to bear on Das's account of both the struggles and the possibilities incipient in the everyday: 'There is no thought without utopia, without an exploration of the possible, of the elsewhere; there is no thought without reference to practice' (Lefebvre 2003: 182). If utopia is to be broadly understood as the egalitarian pursuit of the good life, the 'elsewhere' that Lefebvre mentions may have a counterintuitive meaning—it is the practice of the here and now. As such, following Lefebvre, the 'elsewhere' may be explored—and found—in the here and now: in the 'ethnographic present'. If Newar urbanism can be considered a form of utopia that UN-Habitat envisions will be attained through the application of the heritage by-law,

---

[15] Bekha Tuladhar, personal communication, 21 December 2019.

the 'ethnographic present' encountered through our research in Bungamati reveals the messy realities incipient in the everyday. These realities have critical implications for planning thought if the ongoing project of reconstruction in Bungamati is to address the struggles that mark the everyday practice of rebuilding at household level. However, in the ensemble of planning documents put forward to guide and regulate Bungamati's rebuilding, the 'everyday' continues to be the 'elsewhere' to which Lefebvre alludes.

In the nostalgic pursuit of what may be called the 'authentic' Bungamati, the heritage by-law advances a certain aesthetic and architectural standard as a mandatory logic for reclaiming the authentic place. The envisioned future for the contemporary project of Newar urbanism is not based on the here and now, the existing 'lived realities' of households enduring rebuilding. Rather, the future is conjured by putting together a hybrid and liminal ensemble which combines European aesthetics of liveability, touristic imagery of a heritage city, and a purportedly 'community-led' desire for the preservation of culture and identity (Figure 10.4). However, this politics of aesthetics and authenticity hinges on an idea of 'preservation' that in reality is of a transformative nature. As an unintended consequence, the project of preservation has transformed social relations in Bungamati so that land and everyday life become secondary to culture, as if tangible and intangible matters of heritage are not contained in land and everyday life.

It is in this everyday, not in the master plan, that a messy politics of rebuilding is actually unfolding in concrete terms. Most have started rebuilding their homes through the sheer force of subversion, aided by rumour, among other tools, such as 'hope', and, maybe, 'resilience', that much-vaunted aphorism. In light of these challenges facing the NRA, one of the next critical steps might be to make sincere attempts to locate the unfolding 'elsewhere', that is, the everyday, closer to the heart of its master plan. The content of the by-law, its partial basis in different plans and projections designed by international students and different other civil society bodies, and the kind of future that is promised, indicate that the by-law was informed in part by nostalgia, and in part ambition: nostalgia for the city that was, driving the ambition to create the city that is yet to come. However, the 'ethnographic present' shows that the heritage preservation project could eventually invite a future into Bungamati in which the built form could merely be an urgently assembled simulacrum of a place that was

Figure 10.4 An advertisement that marks the opening of 'Bungamati Home Stay'. *Source*: Photograph by Sabin Ninglekhu.

originally built organically and incrementally over decades.[16] In the process, such a project, instead of 'preserving' the historical *continuities* of space and

---

16   A foreboding may be found in the work of Simpson (2013)—an anthropological account of the aftermath of the 2001 earthquake in Gujarat. Simpson discusses the rebuilding of a Gujarati village that sacrifices the functional value inherent in the traditional architecture in the name of authenticity, to eventually rebuild a place

time, would instead transform and orient towards an uncertain direction not just the urban landscapes, but also the intertwined practices of everyday life itself.

By way of conclusion, we would like to end this chapter with our recollection of a meeting involving a policy-maker, a local architect, and a local community member. The architect organized the meeting with the policy maker to address community grievances regarding the challenges that the heritage by-law posed. In other words, for the local community, the by-law prioritized aesthetics and 'authenticity' over use and function of the house deemed critical to meet their everyday needs. After hearing both long and short stories about the challenges, the policy-maker's proposal was as follows:

> There is a partial solution if we imagine the Bungamati core as spatially organized in three concentric circles with the Rato Macchindranath temple as the centre of the circle. If so, the circle of households next to the temple have no option but to adhere to the heritage by-laws as they are right at the heart of the heritage. The secondary circle may be exempted from certain requirements. The tertiary circle, or the third circle, because it is further away from the centre, may be accorded the benefit of their location with looser regulation.

In probing the boundaries of the by-law, the policy-maker may have recognized the impediment in the by-law, while revealing something equally crucial: The higher one works up the structure of governance and bureaucracy, the less likely it is that one will interact closely with the lived experience of the everyday life of the ordinary, and the more likely it is that one will encounter a statistical and stereotypical representation (Gupta 2012)—in this case, in the form of concentric circles. Such interactions only happen through the optics of master plans and by-laws. As such, the practice of the everyday life of the ordinary, much of which is filled with conditions of emotional duress and material drudgery, ends up being normalized, and in some cases unfairly misrepresented, leading to unjust outcomes.

The plethora of paper work and the multi-layered channels of government staff which form the different nodes of the post-disaster governance that was assembled urgently in 2015, coupled with the committees of elected representatives at local and municipal levels after the 2017 elections, have

---

'conceived of as a "drive-in" for tourists in search of handicrafts and traditional rural life' (2013: 92).

conjured up a bureaucratic edifice that citizens find hard to navigate. When a householder goes to the local ward office or the municipal office to enquire about the reason for their absence from the list of recipients of the housing grant (despite being 'earthquake victims'), or how far their file for design approval has travelled up the bureaucratic ladder since it was submitted, or their eligibility for the subsidized housing loan, the edifice very soon turns into a vortex of non-information. On the one hand, this vortex leaves such ordinary people in a state of limbo amidst the urgency of their need to build a house before Dashain, or before the next monsoon, or the winter, or, in many cases, before they are due to host a deity at their house for an upcoming festival. On the other hand, the frontline state representatives, who often operate at the behest of higher level bureaucracy, work with limited agency and time horizons, and, as such, have their own politics of urgency to contend with. Given this uncertainty, incipient in the everyday life of the ordinary, how might we call on planners and bureaucrats who work higher up the field of the everyday to pay attention to the 'ethnographic present' that reveals the complex spatial and temporal realities?

11

Kathmandu Durbar Square

Heritage Reconstruction as a Political Process of Negotiating Ownership and Authority*

Stefanie Lotter

> The modern disaster is anything but natural in its constitution; it is a deeply political, moral, and cultural phenomenon.
>
> —Kristian Cedervall Lauta (2018: 43)

Introduction

In order to understand a disaster, we must study differences between its preconditions (Oliver-Smith and Hoffman 1999: 4) and its aftermath, along political, ethical, and cultural lines. Since the 2015 earthquakes, heritage preservation in multicultural Kathmandu has emerged as a discursive space in which political, ethical, and cultural issues such as claims to the ownership of sites and authority over the past are navigated. This chapter concentrates on the re-negotiation of power relations in a single site: the

---

* This chapter is based upon research conducted as a part of the project 'After the Earth's Violent Sway: The Tangible and Intangible Legacies of a Natural Disaster' funded by the UK's Global Challenges Research Fund through the Arts and Humanities Research Council; grant number AH/P003648/1. It would not have been possible without the help, encouragement, and support of Abhas Rajopadhyaya, Anatta Shresthacharya, Anie Joshi, Alok Tuladhar, Binita Magaiya, Kai Weise, Michael Hutt, Sanjay Adhikari, Shailesh Rajbhandari, Suman Shrestha, and Sumana Shrestha. Any mistakes that remain in the chapter are, however, solely my responsibility.

centrally located temple district and former royal palace of Hanuman Dhoka, technically known as the Kathmandu Durbar Square Protected Monument Zone. With a diameter of approximately 300 metres, the site offers a microcosm of Kathmandu's heritage negotiations involving an array of local, national, and international stakeholders. The examples chosen for the purposes of this discussion indicate a paradigm shift: the authoritative government-led approach established in 2016 was challenged by a community-led participatory approach in 2019. As such, this research constitutes a critical heritage study which contributes to our understanding of the political and ethical factors at play in the disaster aftermath.

The temples and palace courtyards that constitute the Kathmandu Durbar Square Protected Monument Zone were built between the 7th and 19th centuries, with the majority of the monuments dating from the 17th century. These were severely damaged by the 2015 earthquakes which reduced many of them to little more than a plinth or a set of foundations. In the immediate aftermath, when all hopes of finding any more survivors had died, several things happened simultaneously. Using heavy machinery, the Kathmandu Metropolitan City (KMC) removed what it considered to be merely 'rubble' at the time, in order to reduce hazards and clear public space. Meanwhile, citizens became volunteers, working together with the military and the police to guard the area and to retrieve and secure wood, stone, and metal elements from the temple sites. This was the moment when future political leaders were identified amongst those who volunteered, and territorial boundaries were established by fencing and locking up heritage sites. At the same time, international solidarity was expressed and foreign countries pledged to rebuild rural infrastructure as well as the country's heritage sites, showing little concern for local dynamics.

In the years that followed the earthquakes, the initial themes of site access and safety, ownership and authority, and value and authenticity developed further along rationales of political mandate as well as cultural obligations and indigenous rights. The competence of authorities such as the KMC, the Department of Archaeology (DoA), the United Nations Educational, Scientific and Cultural Organization (UNESCO), and donor organizations with regard to heritage reconstruction was questioned at various stages, and public concern over the process and quality of reconstruction expanded into criticisms of institutional stakeholders in the heritage reconstruction process. Concerned citizens began to take an interest in the concept of community rebuilding as an alternative to tendering out reconstruction work to commercial companies, and local municipalities warmed slowly to the idea of a more publicly endorsed reconstruction process, especially when they could be given credit for it as a positive example of basic democratic processes.

The move towards community-led rebuilding was facilitated both by the international discourse on heritage, which had shifted its emphasis towards protecting intangible heritage, and the local discourse of heritage activists who initially campaigned against the use of non-traditional materials and techniques but soon began to advocate a rights-based approach. Through a combination of democratic instruments, such as the use of social media, writing petitions and letters, and registering court cases, heritage activists inserted a new dimension into the protective framework laid out in national and international charters and the guidelines initiated by the DoA and UNESCO.

Due to this opening of a new field of civil society activity, traditional stakeholders were forced to rethink their practices. A general paradigm shift that rejects authoritative approaches in favour of participatory approaches in reconstruction can be identified over the period, while the risk that the approach would be co-opted also becomes apparent. I argue here that heritage reconstruction goes beyond restorative coping strategies in which 'heritage provides community [with] the familiarity that helps them to cope' and to 'readjust their lives after [sic] earthquake' (KC, Karuppannan, and Sivam 2019: 430). Instead, I argue that heritage activism, whether as critical observer or new custodian, is framed within a larger decolonizing agenda. Ideally, heritage activism enables civil society when it asks for transparency in local and state decision making, and forces authorities to follow due process. However, heritage activism can also be purposed to articulate nationalist feeling against the backdrop of history, or in resistance to international soft power influence, or to reposition ethnic claims to specific places, which sit uneasily within a self-proclaimed 'inclusive' society.

From ritual (dis)continuity to hurt national pride

After the 25 April earthquake, large banners with the flags of various nations were attached to fences and scaffolding at reconstruction sites to indicate the involvement of donors. The signage advertised foreign donor agencies as if they were demarcating conquered territories (Figure 11.1).

Figure 11.1 Gaddi Baithak during its reconstruction, with a prominent US flag attached.

Source: Photograph by author.

The flags were locally interpreted as soft power influence (O. A. Rai 2018) and emerging signs of a new neocolonialism. Chinese, American, and Japanese donor agencies were criticized for politically insensitive displays such as announcements of reconstruction work on large multilingual signboards that crucially omitted to include any text in Nepali (Figure 11.2).

Outsiders' offers to assist financially conflicted with the need to reaffirm ownership over heritage through a process of community-based, or at least national, rebuilding. Interestingly, however, the debate over the inappropriateness of foreign national flags at Nepal's heritage sites was also projected back into the historical past.

Example 1   Gaddi Baithak

The relatively young Gaddi Baithak, a neoclassical wing added to the Hanuman Dhoka Palace by the then prime minister Chandra Shamsher J. B. Rana in 1908, is central to the Kathmandu Durbar Square Protected

Figure 11.2 One of several Chinese and English language signs at Hanuman Dhoka.

Source: Photograph by author.

Monument Zone. The Ranas, whose family autocracy ruled Nepal from 1846 to 1951, went to great lengths to both express their admiration for the colonial force across the border and to internationally declare Nepal's independence. Today, the Rana era is read as a dark age of Nepali history, and with the rise of nationalism Rana-era neoclassical buildings are increasingly being edited out of the cityscape.[1] Where this is not possible, as in the case of the Gaddi Baithak,[2] alternative means are sought for expressing discomfort with the structural reminders of an oppressive regime and its international ties.

---

[1] Several of the neoclassical buildings of the Rana era, such as Bagh Durbar and the National Art Museum in Bhaktapur, have been earmarked for demolition; equally, Rana-era temple designs are being replaced after the earthquake with designs that predated them, as in the cases of Rani Pokhari in Kathmandu, Bhai Dega in Patan, and Fasi Dega temple in Bhaktapur.

[2] No images or architectural drawings exist of the monument that predated the Gaddi Baithak at this location.

Figure 11.3 Gaddi Baithak: before the renovation.
Source: Photograph by Binita Magaiya.

Before the earthquake, the balustrade of the balcony terrace of the Gaddi
Baithak displayed a lattice design in which two crosses were superimposed,
not unlike in the national flag of the United Kingdom where the layering of
St Patrick's, St Andrew's, and St George's crosses results in a similar outline
(Figure 11.3). During the process of post-earthquake reconstruction, the
United States (US) flag was displayed on top of the scaffolding as part of
a signboard announcing US-sponsored reconstruction work. At the same
time, the design of the balustrade was modified by filling in part of the
lattice design (Figure 11.4). This minor modification, while going against
the principle of authentic reconstruction, conforms politically with a newly
discovered national pride that does not allow the display of foreign flags at
key heritage sites, whether as temporary banners, sponsors' plaques, or as
part of the original architectural design.

The removal of this supposed Union Flag was noticed and discussed in
the Nepali media (S. Giri 2018) and equally amongst heritage specialists,
and was widely seen as a politically loaded act. When I asked Suman
Shrestha, a heritage activist and entrepreneur, about it, he laughed: 'Well,
what do you expect? The Americans have renovated the place and left their

Figure 11.4 Gaddi Baithak: after the renovation.
Source: Photograph by Binita Magaiya.

mark, destroying the Union Jack that had been there before, because of the Ranas' love for them [the British]. Everyone leaves their mark here.'[3] In his statement, Shrestha relates the funding agency for the reconstruction of Gaddi Baithak, the US Ambassador's Fund for Cultural Preservation, to the removal of the presumed 'British flag' at the site, as if one flag was being lowered in order to hoist another to mark a transition of political influence. What is implicit here is a popular conflation of political power, soft power, and historical design choice. The removal serves to distance Nepal visually from its own unwanted past and from the visual association with the perceived (neo)colonialism of foreign development agencies. By stating that 'such "minor" issues should not be used to hurt relations between the two countries' (quoted in S. Giri 2018), in an attempt to downplay the inauthentic alteration, Bhesh Narayan Dahal, the Director General of the DoA, rather emphasized the neocolonial argument and its foreign policy dimension.

---

[3]   Personal communication, Kathmandu, 28 March 2019.

Since the earthquake, heritage reconstruction has become increasingly a matter of national pride and an opportunity to demonstrate independence; thus, outsiders' offers to assist conflict with a need to reaffirm ownership over heritage. As caretakership, and therefore ownership, lies for heritage activists in Nepal in the communal practice of crafting, maintaining, worshipping, and celebrating, partaking in the process of care through reconstruction can be interpreted as a claim to authority and ownership. In a similar sentiment of growing national pride, further heritage reconstruction sites at Hanuman Dhoka are being 'reclaimed' by community groups, to be rebuilt without international help. The complex example of the Agam Che will serve here to provide an emic interpretation of foreign cultural insensitivity in heritage reconstruction.

Example 2   The Agam Che

After the 2015 earthquakes, the Agam Che, one of the last vestiges of the transition from the Malla to the Shah dynasty (*The Himalayan Times* 2018c), stirred up a conflict over reconstruction practices that involved both the absence of a ritual and an earthquake-damaged monument. From the very beginning of Prithvi Narayan Shah's rule in the late 18th century, the king carefully crafted a realignment of religious powers[4] to legitimize his new dynasty, bringing the tutelary deities of conquered monarchies under his realm (Burghart 1996: 233). In addition to the tutelary deities Taleju and Kumari, the Malla kings who had ruled over the Kathmandu Valley since the 12th century also worshipped their lineage deity as a private source of power. The worship of lineage deities (Newari: *digu deo*; Nepali: *kul devata*) is common in Nepal, and by their very nature, lineage deities cannot be brought under the realm of a new dynasty. Lineage deities are worshipped periodically by initiated members of a particular ancestral line, in a designated ritual space. In high ranking families, worship takes place under the guidance of a priest, who in Nepal is usually a tantric practitioner. Lineage deity rituals are

---

[4]   The arrival of the Shah dynasty clearly promoted a more Indic celebration of festivals (Baltutis 2018: 1388), which Baltutis sees as an adaptation, 'a politically-charged signal of innovation' indicating change to the degree of a 'seismic shift in religious ideology and performance' (Baltutis 2018: 1429).

secret and neither the ritual practice nor the name of the deity is revealed to the non-initiate, for fear of this leading to a calamity.[5]

From the perspective of required ritual continuity, the discontinuation of a regular ancestral *puja* is extremely unusual, because 'the puja ensures a healthy and prosperous life of the lineage members' (T. Manandhar 2014: 36). After the arrival of the Shahs, the Mallas' ancestral worship was discontinued due to the murder of the Malla king; however, the Agam Che shrine room, the consecrated site of the ritual, was closed rather than de-sanctified, and remains to this day an unused and locked-up sacred space.[6] The Agam Che is located above the Hanuman statue next to the entrance to the former palace (Figure 11.5), which today accommodates the Hanuman Dhoka Museum, a national museum administered by the DoA. The whole of the wing within which the shrine is located[7] was damaged in the 2015 earthquakes and its renovation was assigned to the Japanese development agency the Japan International Cooperation Agency (JICA), which was not made aware of the ritual significance of the closed sacred space.

It is in principle possible to relocate a lineage deity and thereby de-sanctify a site. This is done in the case of orderly migration when a *dyah saray yayegu*, a Newar ritual, is performed during which 'the priest uses a mantra to incorporate the god, while he [the deity] is being moved, within his body' (Toffin 1995: 200). It is commonly understood that such a ritual did not take place at the Malla king's Agam Che and that therefore the room should still be treated as the sacred seat of a deity[8] which nobody except the family priest of the Mallas or an initiated family member should

---

5 The Shahs' lineage goddess was never worshipped on the palace grounds and hence there is no second Agam Che on the site. Whitmarsh (2018: 50), drawing on Burghart (1996: 233), states that the Shahs exchanged their *kul devi* Kalika for Taleju after they had conquered Kathmandu. I am not convinced of this, and suspect that Taleju became merely the Shahs' *ista devata*, 'most-favoured deity'.

6 Aruna Nakarmi, the head of the Hanuman Dhoka Museum, confirmed this in an interview on 11 April 2019.

7 The transition from the Malla dynasty to the Shah dynasty was marked architecturally at this site by an expansion of the palace in size and height (Korn 1976: 60), with the living quarters of the Shahs moving from the palace wing to the left of the entrance to the newly built Nautale ('nine-storeyed') Durbar after 1770.

8 Stiller confirms that this sentiment existed 40 years ago. He explains, 'Except for necessary repairs from time to time, no one may now enter it [the Agam Che], and

Figure 11.5 The entrance to Hanuman Dhoka Palace with scaffolding after the 2015 earthquake.

Source: Photograph by author.

enter.[9] As it stands, this suspended ritual situation complicates the physical reconstruction of the Agam Che and requires a ritual intervention to appease the deity and prevent calamity.

---

its sanctity remains inviolate even though the Malla kings themselves have ceased to rule in Kathmandu for several hundred years' (1975: 21).

[9]   Bist (2012) states, 'Strangely, members of the Malla royal family were forbidden from entering it.' This is perhaps unusual but Uddhav Man Karmacharya, a priest of the Taleju Bhawani temple, confirms it (see *The Himalayan Times* 2018c) while Stiller earlier stated that, in line with general Newar practice, 'entrance to the Agam Che was always restricted to the members of the Malla royal family' (1975: 21) without referring to restrictions regarding gender and initiation.

At present there is no tantric priest specifically associated with the worship of the Mallas' lineage deity at Hanuman Dhoka, and a new interaction at the Agam Che would require a new beginning. According to the journalist, heritage activist, and priest Abhas Rajopadhyaya, any tantric priest who took on duties at the site, whether to conduct a ritual or to conduct necessary repairs, would have to study the material evidence first, in order to understand the discontinued ritual and keep the sanctity of the shrine intact.[10] In the likely absence of any written texts to guide such a priest, he would have to work out the qualities and attributes of the lineage deity from the features of the shrine,[11] such as the iconography of the roof struts and the artefacts inside it. Once this knowledge had been recovered, the deity could be temporarily moved to allow repairs at the shrine to take place or, as has been undertaken in other places, the by now initiated priest could undertake the necessary repairs himself.

In the aftermath of the 2015 earthquakes, JICA initiated inspections to be carried out to assess the damage, compare site measurements and architectural drawings, and create a differentiated, technocratic plan for reconstruction. The JICA team included an experienced Japanese restoration architect and it began its work with a budget of USD 3 million. However, when the team demanded access to the Agam Che to take measurements in September 2018, quite predictably perhaps, a storm broke out. Uddhav Man Karmacharya, a tantric priest working at the Taleju temple of Hanuman Dhoka, walked across the Kathmandu Durbar Square to the police office, which temporarily hosts the wood workshop and site office of the Kasthamandap Reconstruction Committee (KRC), knowing that he would find politicians and heritage activists there who might sympathize with his concerns regarding the disturbance of a sacred site by non-initiates.

Versed in the registers of modern activism that uses all democratic instruments available to concerned citizens, members of the KRC took up the case and wrote a petition to stop the work at the heritage site immediately. The petition was signed swiftly and sent to the Parliamentary

---

[10] Based on an interview with Abhas Rajopadhyaya, Kathmandu, 10 July 2019. As the Malla kings in Patan, Bhaktapur, and Kathmandu were related to one another, it is most likely that they followed the same lineage deity. Patan Museum has dismantled the former Agam Che at its site and some secret and sacred artefacts have even been displayed.

[11] See, for comparison, Chapagain and Tiwari (2018: 136) and von Rospatt (2011).

Commission of External Affairs, which approved it instantly and forbade any foreigner from entering the site (see also Pun 2018). The Parliamentary Commission perhaps went further than it needed to when it ordered the DoA to immediately stop all work at *all* religiously significant heritage sites in which foreign authorities were involved. As a result of the order, work was indeed stopped at the Agam Che site for the next six months, until February 2019 (*Osnepal* 2019). By that time, high-level mediation through the National Reconstruction Authority (NRA) had produced a workable solution. A local user group and advisory team was to be formed for the Agam Che reconstruction that would monitor and advise on culturally sensitive issues such as access to the sacred site. This was considered a more effective safeguarding procedure than the previous plan to involve the DoA, which had failed to halt the work and instruct JICA.

There is a consensus that citizen participation is an inherently positive cornerstone of democracy (Arnstein 1969). For Arnstein, participative involvement varies in intensity—from low-level manipulated participants to tokenistic involvement through opinion polls, at one end of the scale, to empowered citizens who execute delegated powers or even take control of management and decision making, at the other. Arnstein's model would rank the intervention at the Agam Che, with its interplay of political, heritage, and religious interest groups, at the highest end of her scale of citizen power in which citizens take control of the process. However, Arnstein does not specify a process by which established authority can be replaced, nor does her model envisage conflict amongst different citizen participants who all claim authority. This omission is crucial, as Hurlbert and Gupta (2015) have shown. The case of the Agam Che complicates Arnstein's model further as neither custodianship nor ownership is obvious at the site. A participatory approach to heritage preservation would require us to identify communities which can demonstrate their continuous use of the heritage site or other vested intangible links to the site. As users of the shrine have been absent for centuries, the formation of a 'user group' relies on (self-)appointed guardians of the past. Such appointed or self-appointed 'user group' members are mostly well-known members of society. They are not necessarily members of a vested community, but are considered prime custodians due to the subject knowledge they hold, the good intentions they have demonstrated elsewhere in the past, or due to the political or financial influence they wield. As inheritance is thereby replaced by a more distant concept of care, the connection between site and custodian becomes more remote. With greater cultural distance, the term 'user group' tends to be obscured and the method of forming a user group and an advisory team is, in the absence of a basic democratic process, open to an exercise of political negotiation that will tend to favour authority over inclusion. The composition of heritage advisory groups across the Kathmandu Valley is, with regard to gender, ethnicity, age, and origin, rather homogenous, which may indicate a flaw in the process of empowerment. The ideal of citizen participation that heritage activists promoted after the earthquake was based on the ideal of volunteerism but has so far resulted less in genuine community-led reconstruction and rather more in the insertion of a new group of heritage functionaries whose presence satisfies the far-reaching request for a more participatory process of reconstruction.

The Agam Che case has become a precedent for the guidance of future foreign involvement at heritage sites of religious significance. Future projects will now have to consider including local living heritage expertise at steering level if they are to avoid repercussions. The speed and force of the reaction to JICA's request for the key to the shrine, as well as the absence of a direct low-level mediation attempt, suggest that this case had been identified early on by activists and politicians as a potential precedence case for direct foreign involvement at religious heritage sites in the future. One could argue that the blanket accusation of cultural incompetence and ritual illiteracy, levelled at all foreign agencies, was based on a larger political concern over autonomy and self-reliance. However, given that there is no workable mechanism that would assess cultural competence and sensitivity in foreign agents, and given the nature of the quick staff turnaround in this sector, a more sustainable work model had to be found to guarantee effective site monitoring. Whether appointed user and advisory groups will serve the purpose of safeguarding heritage well is yet to be seen.

Example 3   The Jagannath temple

On 9 June 2019, the UNESCO office in Kathmandu stated in a press release that UNESCO would officially withdraw from the reconstruction of the Jagannath and Gopinath temples, which it had started on 10 December 2018. The reconstruction had been suspended on 23 December, due to the order of the Parliamentary Commission that had stopped work at all religious sites following the Agam Che petition. UNESCO had then begun a mediation process with community members, the NRA, the Ministry of Culture, Tourism, and Civil Aviation, the DoA, and the local and provincial governments. As a result of this, it was able to resume work on 15 May 2019. However, following 'threats made by some locals a few days later to the restoration workers on-site' (UNESCO 2019), UNESCO withdrew from both projects and handed all documentation over to the DoA. The DoA's Director General, Damodar Gautam, criticized the threats that had been uttered saying, 'Although it's good for locals and stakeholders to take ownership of heritage sites, we cannot welcome the move of the locals of issuing threats to the workers after UNESCO started the construction work' (Satyal 2019). Both the UNESCO press release and the DoA Director General were trying to limit the damage that had been done to the agreed procedure and the integrity of UNESCO. It is not quite clear why Rajesh Shakya (a Provincial Assembly member of Constituency 8) had shouted at a worker on site: 'I will break your bones if you do not get off this scaffolding right now!'[12] Despite having been part of the mediation process, it seems that Shakya was making use of a high-level politician's unwritten right to veto an agreed process.

As a result of such interventions, the Government of Nepal will eventually need to establish rules by which the paradigm shift towards greater self-reliance in heritage reconstruction can be achieved. If Nepal establishes expert and user group authority to determine the future of its heritage through culturally linked custodianship, the funding body of projects may even be secondary.

However, if heritage reconstruction is developing further into a project of national pride, the new paradigm will have to categorically prevent foreign agencies, including international authorities such as UNESCO, from working in Nepal. Whichever path is taken, citizen participation in projects depends not just on the level of engagement but also on the ability to achieve consensus amongst different groups. It requires the ability to plan, take joint decisions, manage, and act upon an agreed plan in which even veto rights will have to be considered. When inheritance is replaced by a more distant concept of care, whether the ideal of UNESCO world heritage or that of an expert and user-accredited Newar heritage, custodianship must build authority through its ability to reconsider, negotiate, and build trust with authorities as well as within communities.

---

[12]   Reliable but undisclosable source, information has been cross-checked.

From the examples of the Gaddi Baithak, the Agam Che, and the Jagannath temple, it emerges that heritage authority is highly negotiable. While foreign involvement through development agencies is increasingly seen as cultural interference, the local claim to authority is emerging from various fields, including politics, ritual specialists, and modern heritage activism. Post-earthquake heritage activism referenced decolonization and independence to regulate foreign involvement while, as will emerge from the following, it also requested local authorities to increase transparency and accountability.

Watchdogs and custodians: the varying roles of heritage activists

When the first earthquake struck on 25 April 2015, Kasthamandap, a large three-storeyed wooden rest house at the southern end of the Durbar Square, tilted and fell to the ground, crushing 12 people to death. Kasthamandap, locally also known as Maru Sattal, had been dated through textual references to 1135 CE (Allinger and Melzer 2010), but post-earthquake carbon dating of its foundations now dates part of the structure to the 7th century (Coningham et al. 2016). According to local legend, the origin of Kasthamandap goes back to Lila Vajra, a powerful tantric priest who bound a tree deity (*briksha devata*) to the site, which enabled the construction of the wooden structure of Kasthamandap from a single tree. The original tree must have been rather enormous, considering that wood procurement for the structure was one of the more difficult issues in the post-earthquake reconstruction.

It is summer 2017 and Amit Bajracharya, an architect from the KMC, is certain that the Campaign to Rebuild Kasthamandap (CRK) will be just a temporary phase. 'How will they get wood of that size if they do not go through the government? They will not get the *sal* wood anywhere but through the Forest Ministry and the Timber Corporation of Nepal.'[13] Two years later, in summer 2019, Binita Magaiya, an architect and a member of both the Kasthamandap Reconstruction Committee[14] (KRC) and the earlier

---

[13] Personal communication, Kathmandu, 29 June 2017.

[14] Also known as Kasthamandap Punarnirman Samiti, established 6 May 2018; see https://kasthamandapnepal.org.np/.

Figure 11.6 Wood stored at the office of the Kasthamandap Reconstruction
Committee.

Source: Photograph by author.

CRK, awaits a wood delivery for Kasthamandap at 4 a.m. Magaiya agrees
that timber procurement remains one of the more challenging parts of the
reconstruction (Figure 11.6); indeed, the aforementioned politician Rajesh
Shakya had helped on several occasions by speaking directly to the Timber
Corporation. Without political leverage, procurement is difficult and time
consuming.

It is July 2019, and I ask Suman Shrestha, a heritage activist: 'What would
have been different if, back in summer 2017, the Kathmandu Metropolitan
City (KMC) had been given the sole authority to reconstruct Kasthamandap?'
He shrugs, 'Well, Kasthamandap as a structure would be finished now.'
Having studied the work of both organizations, the CRK and the later KRC, I
understand this to be a well-formulated critique of the KMC. Shrestha makes
a point we had discussed many times before. There is a difference between
reconstructing a monument and rebuilding living heritage. For the CRK,

this was the defining difference, between the government tendering out a construction site of historical importance to a commercial company, on the one hand, and a community group rebuilding heritage while fostering its cultural, social, and religious relations, on the other.

Yagya Man Pati Bajracharya, the 43rd descendant of Lila Vajra, the tantric priest who bound the tree deity and constructed Kasthamandap, emphasizes the importance of intangible heritage, whose absence turns living heritage into a lifeless monument:

> Contractors hired through the KMC are people who are trained in foreign techniques such as tie beams and concrete. They cannot build it [Kasthamandap] in the traditional way and if they cannot do it, they should not rebuild Kasthamandap at all. Then one could preserve what is left as a reminder of old times: have a monument instead.[15]

For Yagya Man Bajracharya, it is fundamental to understand the difference between lifeless structural preservation—'reconstruction'—and the invigorating concept of *rebuilding*, which includes the revival and performance of all intangible elements associated with a site. In his understanding, rebuilding requires active community involvement if it is to be effective. He does not believe that technocrats, whether foreign or Nepali, are able to accomplish the rebuilding of living heritage; this is why he suggests that it would perhaps be more apt for them to preserve the lifeless monument of a Kasthamandap ruin, to serve as an earthquake memorial.

Given the stark contrast between the technocratic and activist approaches to reconstruction and rebuilding, it is not surprising that activities at the site of Kasthamandap began rather slowly. In November 2015, the compilation of an inventory for Hanuman Dhoka was started by the DoA, UNESCO, and the International Council on Monuments and Sites (ICOMOS), assessing architectural elements of wood, stone, and brick stored in 23 different locations, amounting to an enormous puzzle and a report of over 500 pages (Aryal and Shrestha 2016).

The KMC was meanwhile preparing to invite tenders for the reconstruction of Kasthamandap. For the architectural drawings (the basis of the tender), the DoA had employed Manohar Rajbhandari, a

---

[15] Personal communication, Kathmandu, 5 July 2018.

structural engineer from MRB & Associates. The first drawings by MRB went public before they were accepted by the KMC, which had already noted that they did not comply with UNESCO guidelines with regard to material authenticity and technique. Heritage experts began to be seriously alarmed by the plans, and also by the proposed process of tendering out the reconstruction, which meant that the government would have to accept the lowest bidder, regardless of their experience or the quality of their previous work. Around September 2016, a newly formed group named the Campaign to Rebuild Kasthamandap (CRK) began to oppose the plans and also the process of reconstruction proposed by the government and offered to rebuild Kasthamandap through community involvement instead. The KMC's conservation architect, Amit Bajracharya, explained that the government tender process could have been modified to include a pre-selection process to eliminate incompetent contenders. He thought that the CRK would be best placed as a monitoring body that would inspect and advise the KMC: 'As a government body, that was what we were able to offer them.'[16] This non-binding monitoring role was rejected by the CRK group. For the young heritage activists, such a proposal did not go far enough. It did not guarantee citizens the right to have an impact and risked, according to Arnstein's (1969) ladder of participation, becoming an empty non-binding tokenistic ritual instead of an empowering civil society process.

Over the course of 2017, the CRK grew into an impressive 120-member group with a wide range of skills. These were mostly young professionals from Kathmandu with training in heritage documentation, museum studies, social work, heritage conservation, architecture, engineering, and law. The CRK met regularly and Birendra Bhakta Shrestha, a local elder, was made chairperson in the hope that he would draw in more local residents. From the beginning CRK members were aware that the residents of Maru, the local area to the west of Kasthamandap, were related through various intangible links to the site, and the group explored these links through oral history interviews. Over time, and as annual festivals took place, a more detailed network of involvements and obligations of various neighbourhoods emerged and the 'user group' list at the CRK grew to involve around 40 different communities and neighbourhood groups. Heritage activist meetings were held regularly,

---

[16]   Personal communication, Kathmandu, 29 June 2017.

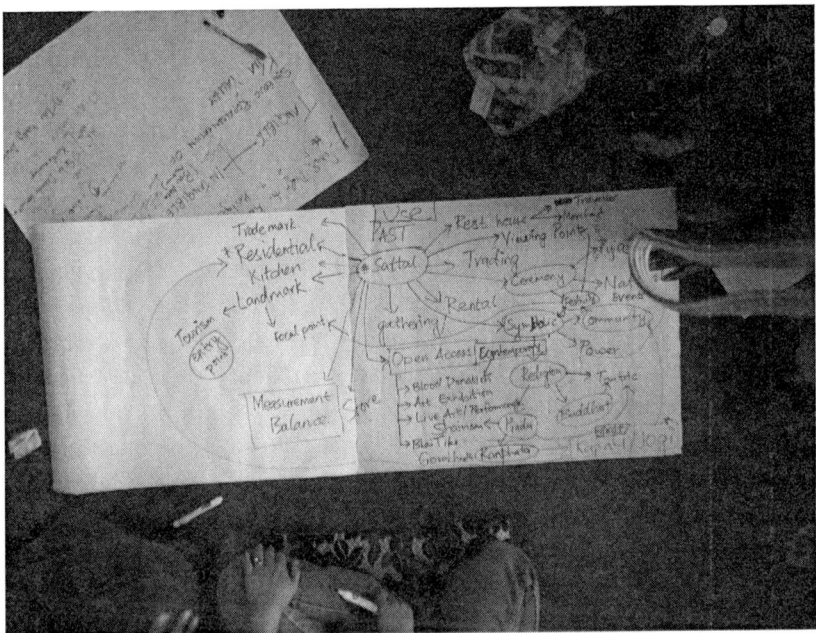

Figure 11.7 Activists at the Campaign to Rebuild Kasthamandap using creative techniques to explore the potential uses of a restored heritage site.
Source: Photograph by author.

at times inviting local leaders, and the group discussed various ideas for an inclusive Kasthamandap heritage site (Figure 11.7).

Group members began to refer to themselves as 'heritage activists' and started a well-planned social media campaign to draw attention to the controversial architectural plan and the tendering process. On 12 May 2017, two days before local government elections commenced all across Nepal,[17] the CRK managed (after considerable lobbying) to get all of the relevant authorities around a negotiating table to propose a community-led alternative to the KMC's proposals. As changes within the power structure of the city were pending due to the elections, and the KMC had not made much progress over the last two years, the authorities were temporarily

---

[17] These elections were conducted in three phases, on 14 May, 28 June, and 18 September 2017.

inclined to champion change—perhaps only in the gleeful knowledge that, upon losing the election as predicted, the opposition would have to resolve any repercussions.

A four-way agreement was signed between the following parties: the NRA, the DoA, the KMC and the CRK. This official memorandum of understanding (MOU) [18] detailed that the CRK would now have the legal authority and responsibility for rebuilding Kasthamandap or, in Arnstein's (1969) words, citizens would take direct control of the process. Initially, the new plan was endorsed, with the NRA's Chief Executive Officer, Govinda Raj Pokharel, praising the CRK as a 'model project' that would 'safeguard the originality of Nepali architecture, and the history and culture of the community' (Pradhananga 2017).

The group had promised in this formal agreement to raise all the necessary funds from the community, but soon it became entangled in discussions over ethical principles with regard to the nationalities of donors, exposing the heterogeneity of visions within the CRK. Questions were also being asked about how representative the CRK was of the wider local community. As a group of mainly young professionals, everyone was aware that they did not represent the full range of the society in question. The group had identified and connected with the traditional cultural and religious groups (*guthis*) of the area and were in touch with several elders through the oral history project they were running to explore traditional intangible connections. However, the CRK overlooked the importance of other organizations in the area, including the youth clubs, which were a legacy of Nepal's Panchayat era (1962–90). Youth clubs are part-financed by the KMC, their historical ally. They usually promote sports activities and help the KMC by providing security at festivals. The CRK also did not engage with local business associations and the representatives of various political parties at the ward level. The KMC architect Amit Bajracharya explained in 2017 that the absence of a more inclusive approach was a mistake: 'They [the CRK] are some part of the community of course, but they may not be the most experienced people in the field.' [19]

---

[18]   The agreement was signed by Yamalal Bhusal (Joint Secretary of the NRA), Bhesh Narayan Dahal (Director General of the DoA), Ishwor Raj Poudel (Executive Officer of the KMC), and Birendra Bhakta Shrestha (Chairman of the CRK).

[19]   Personal communication, Kathmandu, 29 July 2017.

After the local elections, the new mayor of Kathmandu, Bidya Sundar Shakya, was not interested in the existing MOU and signalled that he was not committed to it. At the same time, it was clear that he needed Kasthamandap to be rebuilt quickly in order to prove his leadership to the electorate, as he had done during the immediate aftermath of the earthquake when he was instrumental in the rescue process at the Kathmandu Durbar Square. The CRK became vulnerable under these new conditions and the authorities were waiting for an opportunity that would allow the city to take back control.

In June 2017, this opportunity presented itself. The monsoon rains were approaching and the foundations of the site were unprotected. CRK members were aware of the problem, and organized bamboo scaffolding and tarpaulins to erect a roof above the site. As there was not yet a fundraising campaign in place, the members paid for these materials themselves and called via social media for volunteers to help in setting up the roof. Things did not go well and the few volunteers who pitched up on the day struggled with the task. By the end of the day the vulnerable sections of the enormous site were barely covered (Figure 11.8).

And then, due to a communication error, the key to the site ended up with the police, who delivered it to the KMC instead of the CRK, which

Figure 11.8 The initial protection of Kasthamandap in June 2017.
Source: Photograph by Binita Magaiya.

at that time was the official key holder. In addition, a youth group came to complain to the KMC that the tarpaulin had not been put up properly. This community complaint allowed the KMC to take matters back into its own hands by using the key without asking for permission to access the site, and by setting up a sturdy roof, using the bamboo the CRK had bought. And this is where Amit Bajracharya becomes a little angry: 'Yesterday [the CRK] posted, "KMC has vandalized the site" instead of saying "KMC put it [the tarpaulin] up properly".' Bajracharya is at a loss: 'Our relationship with Rebuild Kasthamandap is messed up. I don't have a personal cold war with them, I work for the government. But I also have a little bit of knowledge!'[20] The tarpaulin incident, however well intended or planned by the KMC, was instrumentalized by the mayor Bidya Sundar Shakya who now declared the MOU to be invalid, arguing that it had been a mistake to give an unprofessional group such authority.

In spring 2018, the CRK had its own internal conflict that had been growing over months. Its chairman, Birendra Bhakta Shrestha, and Sumana Shrestha, one of its most articulate young leaders, fell out. Birendra Bhakta Shrestha stuck to the ideal of community financing and insisted on the legality of the MOU. Sumana Shrestha, on the other hand, noted the change in the political climate and was ready to compromise as long as the community rebuilding approach could be retained to some degree. Even if managerial authority was transferred back to the KMC, community involvement should be at the core of the structure to form a collaborative partnership. For Sumana Shrestha, avoiding the tender process, agreeing on binding local expert advice, and paying higher daily rates to local craftsmen were cornerstones of their negotiation with the city.

When I revisited the site in June 2018, there was a banner hanging at Singha Sattal, the office space of the newly formed 'Kasthamandap Reconstruction Committee' (KRC) while the banner of the CRK was still hanging a few metres away at the familiar office which was now almost deserted. Excluded from the CRK, Sumana Shrestha had worked with a handful of volunteers on an elaborate organizational structure for the new KRC which fell into two areas: an implementation group and a policy, coordination, and supervisory group. While the former was where she envisaged the erstwhile CRK volunteers and community

---

[20] Personal communication, Kathmandu, 29 June 2017.

members contributing in sub-committees, the latter would become the space for politicians and authorities to contribute and be affiliated. The mayor, Bidya Sundar Shakya, would be given the prestigious position of the chairperson of the steering committee and Rajesh Shakya too was roped into the steering committee to gain a maximum of political support from all sides. Technical advice would be provided by Kai Weise, an experienced conservation architect; documentation would be conducted by Anie Joshi who had previously worked in documentation at Gaddi Baithak; and noted heritage experts such as Sudarshan Tiwari would contribute their knowledge through the expert committee. On 10 May 2018, the mayor announced that since the community had formed a new committee, obstacles had been removed and smooth progress at the site was guaranteed. Rajesh Shakya echoed his statement and invited the public to volunteer and participate in the sub-committees.

The CRK split, and while one part of the group saw itself taking up the role of a watchdog, the other group was involved in the site office which had now moved to the courtyard of the Metropolitan Police Range. For the time being, the KMC was advising the Hanuman Dhoka Durbar Adda (Hanumandhoka palace management and conservation office) to administer state funding to rebuild Kasthamandap. However, volunteers at the KRC retained a dwindling hope that part of Kasthamandap could still be community financed through donations. Sumana Shrestha did not see the community financing as being as essential as before ('After all, it is tax money that is spent on the site'), but she was proud that Kasthamandap had not been tendered out and that a highly experienced team of wood workers was being paid a decent salary at the site.

Heritage activists started with the stark ideological contrast between rebuilding a living heritage and reconstructing a lifeless monument, disconnected from its community. Now, in collaboration with the KMC, some of their former ideals such as community financing have had to be dropped, while the ideal of community involvement is retained in parts, and volunteers are called upon whenever timber has to be moved or rituals have to be organized. The example of Kasthamandap makes it clear that state authority can be challenged through civil society initiatives. However, local community organizations have to be based on diversity and inclusion in order to be effective in the long term. Post-earthquake heritage activism managed to increase transparency and accountability, and influenced the managerial structure at the site of Kasthamandap. The fact that ultimately the city stepped in and political support was needed should not detract from the evaluation of this achievement.

Conclusion

Since the 2015 earthquakes, heritage has proven to be a contested field at the intersection of culture, politics, and society. With an array of stakeholders at any one location, the Hanuman Dhoka Monument Preservation Zone has had its fair share of the wider debate over ownership and authority. Beyond the creative moment of perceived openness to change that the disaster instilled in heritage activists, it is their insistence on community ownership that will remain their legacy.

Across these examples, three themes have emerged. First, there is the rejection of 'outsiders' in the field of heritage, whether as project leads, contractors, or even financial contributors. This had been justified by the outsiders' proven incomprehension of managing secret and sacred spaces. The fact that the terms 'outsiders' or 'technocrats' were used to refer to Western-educated Nepali architects and engineers, as well as to international professionals, suggests that the 'outsider' is identified ultimately on the basis of cultural competence and belonging, not ethnicity. Also connected to the idea of the outsider is the question of who might be identified as an 'insider' and speak with authority within the discourse of heritage reconstruction. Aside from craftspeople and experts, it is the institution of the 'user group' whose membership is somewhat malleable. Belonging to a place over generations creates authority, as does partaking in intangible heritage through activities such as celebrating or rebuilding. However, not everyone's participation is locally desired and the CRK's claim to take part in the reconstruction was ultimately rejected at the local level. Young Nepali professionals from a variety of more or less local backgrounds were perhaps considered not 'local' enough to be trusted with the important task of rebuilding Kasthamandap. Both the lack of political support and the lack of local neighbourhood support resulted in the termination of the CRK's leading role.

Second, these examples show the use of coercion as a measure to achieve politically motivated heritage decisions. The authorities of the NRA, the DoA, and the KMC along with the mayor and Provincial Assembly members have supported projects or opposed them, according to the wider political context at a particular time and place. Co-opting 'user groups' through political appointments and playing community groups off against each other are new strategies for retaining hard-won political powers. Finally, it should be highlighted that heritage activism has, after all, fundamentally and sustainably changed the field of heritage reconstruction by introducing civil society into the discourse. As watchdogs, activists will continue to send petitions and initiate court cases to effectively limit the powers of the state or international organizations through ethical and cultural arguments and rigorous monitoring.

PART IV

Building Memory

12

Cultural Heritage Display after the 2015 Earthquakes in Nepal

The Architecture Galleries, Patan Museum

Katharina Weiler

Aftermath

From loss to rebuilding

In the Kathmandu Valley, the earthquake of 25 April 2015 destroyed or damaged hundreds of ancient living monuments, including temples in the three historic town squares (Nepali [Nep.] *darbar*) of the cities of Kathmandu (Kantipur), Patan (Lalitpur), and Bhaktapur. These sites are considered to be of outstanding universal value and have been on UNESCO's World Heritage List since 1979. They have not only become key elements of the national pride and identity of Nepal but are also the basis for a growing heritage tourism industry. Soon after the destruction, voices were raised in newspapers bemoaning a 'sense of an ending' and 'a new sense of loss' (Karki 2015) while claiming a future for Nepal's architectural heritage. In the aftermath, for many involved, controversies over rebuilding became a debate about cultural identity and cultural values, presenting new alliances and frictions in the process of re-evaluating cultural heritage (A. Bhattarai 2018).

This chapter focuses on the Architecture Galleries that constitute a section of the Patan Museum, housed inside the ancient Royal Palace at the Patan Durbar Square (Figure 12.1).

In the wake of the earthquake, the exhibition introduced some of the prevailing cross-disciplinary cultural–historical discussions around conservation and post-earthquake reconstruction or rebuilding and applied them to the field of museology. The following analysis thus contributes

Figure 12.1 Patan Durbar Square: aerial view looking north, showing the architectural ensemble before the 2015 earthquake destroyed and damaged major temples and parts of the palace (*right*) with its three courtyards—Keshav Narayan Chok (*back*), Mul Chok (*centre*), and Sundari Chok (*front*).

Source: Photograph by M. Bista, August 2004.

to the field of heritage studies and also museum studies, an emerging interdisciplinary area that has increased in popularity since the 1980s. So far, there is hardly any study of Nepal's museums (Whitmarsh [2017] is a rare example) or of museums of Newar material culture or cultural heritage. Here, an exploration of the museum space raises questions about the production of cultural heritage in the aftermath. How did the exhibition address the earthquake? What history was being told? Who were the people involved in the reassessment of the site, the actual 'authors' of this post-disaster narrative? At the same time, the Architecture Galleries' exhibits challenged the museum visitor to contemplate contested concepts that had been affected by the earthquake and were now being projected onto certain cultural goods through different agents (local and international): for example, 'cultural heritage' (Nep. *samskritik sampada*), 'value' (for example, historic value, memorial value, spirit of place, authenticity), and 'identity' (for example, national/international heritage, memory, loss, recovery).

Destruction and response

The Patan Museum is housed inside the ancient Royal Palace with its three courtyards (Nep. *chok*, Newari [New.] *chuka*) flanking the Patan Durbar Square in the northeast: the Keshav Narayan Chok; the Mul Chok, the main courtyard of the palace; and the Sundari Chok. Prior to the earthquake, the square was occupied by a number of monuments including two arcaded platforms (Sanskrit [Skt.] *mandapa*, New. *madu*) dating back to the 14th (South Manimandapa) and early 17th centuries (North Manimandapa), the Charnarayana temple (consecrated in 1565), and the Harishankara temple (consecrated in 1706). From an architectural historian's perspective, the ensemble of buildings boasted Nepal's most intact Malla-period architecture, containing a wealth of history in its architectural details from the 14th to the 18th centuries. Beyond this, the two temple buildings served as mantles hosting a powerful centre: an iconic stone block with the four manifestations (*chaturvyuha*) of Vishnu, and a sculpture of Harishankara, a manifestation of Vishnu (Hari) and Shiva (Shankara). The historic architecture on the ground has thus been densely interwoven with Newar living religious traditions and has functioned as a public cultural space for many Nepalis. What was left of this seemingly immovable architectural heritage after the strong shaking on 25 April 2015 was a heap of rubble consisting of thousands of movable fragments. By a wonder, nobody died in the debris on this site. The palace's Keshav Narayan Chok and the Mul Chok survived the earthquake, though they were slightly damaged, as did two other temples on the square: the Vishveshvara temple (consecrated in 1627) and the Krishna temple (consecrated in 1637). But in the Sundari Chok, with its ancient Tusa Hiti step-well at its centre, the east wing that was in the process of being restored collapsed entirely.

While the Patan Museum was closed for a short period immediately after the earthquake, the Kathmandu Valley Preservation Trust (KVPT)—the first international charity dedicated to safeguarding architectural heritage in Nepal—coordinated the rescue and protection of thousands of historic architectural fragments directly after the collapse of the buildings on the Patan Durbar Square. Founded in 1991 and with a track record of more than 50 building projects, the Trust's presence on the ground during the earthquake allowed its team to spearhead this recovery effort. Hundreds of local volunteers, the Nepal Army, and the Nepal Police helped to store remnants of a disrupted past linked to daily rituals in the palace courtyards. The Patan Museum thus became the repository of the salvaged fragments (Figure 12.2).

The KVPT's intention was to return the collapsed structures to their original state. For this intervention, the Trust initiated the Patan Darbar Earthquake Response Campaign, with significant financial support from international stakeholders (KVPT 2016). The rebuilding initiative was thus launched and enabled by the concentrated efforts of an international private non-profit organization supported entirely by donations. Most of the funds required to ensure the revival of the buildings on the square came from foreign donors. Nevertheless, the Trust exchanged experiences with Nepali agencies such as the National Reconstruction Authority (NRA), the Department of Archaeology (DoA), and the National Society for Earthquake Technology (NSET), and cooperated with local priests. The communication between these agents resulted in the shaping of a

Figure 12.2 Keshav Narayan Chok: the Patan Museum's courtyard in its use as the interim repository of thousands of salvaged timber fragments from the Patan Durbar Square, immediately after the earthquake of 25 April 2015.

Source: Photograph by R. Ranjitkar, 29 April 2015.

multi-perspective conservation approach that responded to the site-specific challenges (Weiler 2017a: 383). In this regard, Rohit Ranjitkar, the KVPT's Country Director, had already emphasized in late 2015 that it was 'important to preserve tangible history, as well as the intangible' (Lewsley 2015).

Authenticity

The tangible

The conservation approach was based on the KVPT's attitude towards the preservation of original material at all costs. This conception of the authenticity of architectural heritage was developed in Europe towards the end of the 19th century and was largely guided by ideas about aesthetic and historical value, age value, and materiality. The notion has had a global impact on conservation efforts ever since (Weiler 2017b: xviif), and inevitably informed the rebuilding efforts at the Patan Durbar Square. From 2015 to 2019, interim storerooms were set up in the palace garden, as was a workshop for the cleaning, repair, and restoration of a vast number of architectural elements and the identification of constituent parts. With the indispensable skill of Newar craftspeople, the monuments on the square were faithfully rehabilitated, while the KVPT's conservation approach of maintaining as much of the original material as possible in order to ensure material authenticity was closely connected to a paradigm that turned Nepali heritage into a projection screen for global desires. This approach was recognized by the Trust as a tribute to the unique accomplishment of the Kathmandu Valley's endangered architectural heritage. However, it contrasted with the Nepali building tradition's cyclical concept of time, which venerates the place rather than the built structure itself. It is linked to building practices in which the demolition of consecrated buildings by natural or human agents and their subsequent replacement may not necessarily be considered as harming the value and meaning of that space, which may itself continue to serve as a place of worship (Gutschow 2017: 17–23). Here, the Sanskrit term *jirnoddhara* means anything from maintenance to major renewal to total replacement, while rebuilding only (re)uses undamaged historical or new building components.

The intangible

Thus, the Patan Darbar Earthquake Response Campaign opposed the Venice Charter's universalizing invocations. These privilege an 'original' over a 'replica' by preaching 'a contemporary stamp' (ICOMOS 1965, Article 9) on any extra work, and were laid down with a European bias and advocated by professional monument conservators. As Niels Gutschow, the KVPT's technical advisor, has explained elsewhere:

> Replacing a carved strut (with or without documentation of its predecessor) of a temple in Nepal was ruled out by the principles of the Venice Charter, because it never occurred to the authors of the charter that replicas of deities would be carved by carpenters whose ancestors had carved the originals. It was also beyond their experience and imagination that a carved roof strut should be turned into a deity by means of a ritual act. In fact, in a Newar context, a carefully repaired historic strut supports the value of material authenticity as advocated by international professionals. In contrast, a newly carved strut with an open-eyed deity stands for a process authenticated by the hereditary carpenter. (Gutschow 2017: 45)

In this regard, the local tradition of replacing elements that are deemed to be beyond repair with copies of those same elements was instrumental in authenticating craftsmen's creations in the framework of the rebuilding process at the Patan Durbar Square. The master carpenters (New. *shilpakar*), wood carvers (New. *kijyami*), masons (New. *avah*), and metal workers (New. *nakahmi*) from Bhaktapur as well as stone carvers (New. *lvahankahmi*) from Patan who engaged in the rebuilding of the Patan Durbar Square's monuments under the KVPT's stewardship are descendants of the craftsmen of the Malla period (13th–18th century CE) who once built the elaborate palace wings and the temples at the Patan Durbar Square. They have inherited their professions down to the present day. In this sense, the local craftsmanship—Nepal's 'intangible cultural heritage'—touched upon notions of immaterial authenticity in the rebuilding of the living monuments at the Patan Durbar Square. To some extent, the workshop could even be perceived as an open-air museum, with the working craftsmen on display transformed into an intangible heritage as a mode of cultural production in the present (Kirshenblatt-Gimblett 1998: 7).

Cultural heritage display

The Patan Museum and its Architecture Galleries

The Patan Museum is one of approximately 15 museums in the Kathmandu Valley, many of which suffered severe damage from the 2015 earthquakes. The restoration of the Keshav Narayan Chok, which had fallen into decay, was initiated by the architect Eduard Sekler and work began in 1982. It was made possible by the joint efforts of His Majesty's Government of Nepal and the Austrian Government and led finally to the transformation to a museum by the Austrian architect Götz Hagmüller, with the mission to preserve the sacred art, culture, and iconography of Hinduism and Buddhism (Hagmüller 2003). In 1997, the Patan Museum was inaugurated by the late King Birendra Bir Bikram Shah. Most of the exhibits are antique cast bronzes and gilt copper repoussé works, as well as stone sculptures that were once stolen from shrines or temples and later recovered and stored by the authorities (Dixit 2003: 99–101). The museum has become a key historical and cultural centre and one of Patan's major attractions for both Nepali and international tourists. It holds a semi-autonomous status, unlike other state museums of Nepal, and is managed by its own board of directors, while the DoA, the custodian of all tangible 'national heritage', retains its legal authority over collection and conservation control.

The idea of developing galleries to showcase and explicate the particulars of historic Newar building craft and philosophy, along with the presentation of the restored structures themselves, dates back to discussions that took place in the 1990s (Gutschow and Roka 2017: 7). In the meantime, the ambitious Patan Royal Palace Restoration and Conservation Project under the stewardship of the KVPT started its work in 2006. The intention was to restore and rehabilitate the entire palace complex, including its Mul Chok and Sundari Chok courtyards. In 2011, the restored Mul Chok finally offered the opportunity for an architecture museum: The Architecture Galleries housed inside the Mul Chok opened in 2013 as an extension of the Patan Museum. These galleries were initially dedicated to the great architectural traditions of the Kathmandu Valley and were under the curatorial leadership of Niels Gutschow, the author of an encyclopaedic study of Newar architecture (Gutschow 2011). Historical

windows, columns, struts, and tympana collected in the Kathmandu
Valley were displayed in a typological order. By early 2015, the final
component of the Patan Royal Palace Restoration and Conservation
Project—the Sundari Chok's east wing—had been stabilized and was
awaiting funding for restoration (KVPT 2016: 12). After the earthquake
of 25 April 2015 reduced this rear wing to a heap of rubble, it was rebuilt
with the financial help of the German Embassy. This work was completed
in 2016 (Figure 12.3).

The lengthy restoration process of the Sundari Chok, from inception
in 2006 to completion in December 2016, and its transformation into
a museum was documented in a comprehensive report (Gutschow and
Roka 2017: 7). The Sundari Chok complex is now another addition to the
Architecture Galleries.

Figure 12.3 East Wing, Sundari Chok: the early 18th century east wing, of which
only the ground floor arcade withstood the 2015 earthquake damage, after
rebuilding was completed in late 2016; behind the façade, the 'Grey Box' breaks
with the norms of Newar interior space.

Source: Photograph by A. Rajbansh, 11 December 2016.

Towards a new approach

The devastation of the 2015 earthquakes and the subsequent conservation efforts in the Patan Durbar Square have had a significant impact on the KVPT's approach to the display of cultural heritage, and on curatorial decision-making within the Architecture Galleries (curated by the Trust's international team of architects, who also directed the rebuilding: Erich Theophile, Executive Director, Rohit Ranjitkar, Country Director, and Niels Gutschow, Chief Technical Advisor). The curators were challenged to rethink the museum as a meeting place and platform for transcultural exchange, so that it would convey to Nepali museum visitors and international tourists some of the prevailing discussions around cultural–historical significance, conservation, and rebuilding in post-earthquake Nepal, and their relationship to change.

The post-earthquake permanent exhibition presented the KVPT's multi-perspective and site-specific conservation approaches, both with the help of well-tried museal documentation (for example, architectural fragments, descriptive panels, and documental photography) and by integrating 'innovative' forms of exhibition design such as audio-visual display, contemporary architectural design, assemblage, and multimedia installation. In the Sundari Chok space, moreover, the KVPT's original aim, which was to present the exhibition rooms as documents of Newar interior design and to display exhibits 'as additions to the historical structure' (Gutschow and Roka 2017: 23), was revisited in order to integrate the 2015 earthquakes' legacy.

'Post-earthquake' permanent exhibition

Documentation: conservation, restoration, reconstruction

With the help of museal documentation of architectural preservation after the earthquake, the KVPT told the building history of the seriously damaged or collapsed historical structures on the site that ranked among Nepal's most significant architectural monuments. The documentation mainly shed light on the Patan Durbar rebuilding project's negotiations about 'authenticity', and on the KVPT's methods and techniques. The following examples are listed in the chronological order of their initial building dates, rather than in their museum tour order.

Figure 12.4 Manimandapa room, Mul Chok: exhibition space dedicated to the conservation of the two 'Pavilions of Jewels' (Manimandapa) that collapsed on 25 April 2015, with poster documenting the repair of the South Manimandapa's twelve timber columns, illustrated descriptive panel, original full-scale draft of a replicated column by Bijay Basukala, and selection of fragments of the South Manimandapa's wooden building elements beyond repair (*left to right*).

Source: Photograph by B. Basukala, 24 June 2019.

The 'Jewel Pavilions' (Manimandapa)

An exhibition room in the Mul Chok complex was dedicated to the rebuilding of the communal arcaded platforms known as 'Jewel Pavilions', or Manimandapa—two 16-pillared, arcaded halls flanking the stairway to Mangahiti, an ancient step well (Figure 12.4).[1]

---

[1] The rebuilding of the Manimandapa was funded by the German Foreign Ministry; Prince Claus Fund, the Netherlands; The Embassy of Japan in Nepal; South Asia Institute, Heidelberg University; Himal Initiative Deutschland e.V., Bamberg; Himalayan Bank Ltd.; and Mangal Tole Sudhar Samiti.

An illustrated descriptive panel introduced the museum visitor to the history of the Manimandapa and highlighted the historical and social meaning of this key Nepali building type:

> The southern Mandapa ranks among the most important edifices in Newar architectural history: it is the elaborate pot motif at the bottom of the 12 surrounding pillars and the peculiar moldings of the 4 high interior pillars that makes it a landmark in history.

Furthermore, the visitor was informed that the pillared hall, datable to the early 14th century, in its reconstructed form 'appears as a miniature version of the much [more] famous iconic Kasthamandapa of Kathmandu'. The northern Manimandapa was established by King Yoganarendra Malla (r. 1684–1705) in 1701, in place of an earlier structure, as a royal council house and coronation site.

The exhibition text stated that, in the wake of the tremor, 'the failure of the column's tenons largely caused the collapse' that was followed by the rescue of all pillars, windows, and struts from the rubble of the two completely destroyed structures. According to the panel which explained the rebuilding techniques, 'the replaced tenons are encased in stainless steel sleeves to improve the future seismic performance.... Major and minor damages of the remaining columns were faithfully restored'. In this way, it explained the KVPT's mode of reconstruction, which even accepted so-called modern material where its use ensured (seismic) strengthening and was considered necessary.

In the same room, a poster documented the repair of the South Manimandapa's 12 timber columns. Along one of the walls was arranged a selection of fragments of the building's wooden elements, imparting the power of the earthquake's destruction. The column displayed in this room was too weathered and had suffered severe damage during a previous utilization of the building, so it was replaced by a new one. An original full-scale draft of the newly created column-design by the eminent draughtsman and (re)construction supervisor Bijay Basukala from Bhaktapur, that served as a model for the Newar craftsmen who carved the 'replica', was thus exhibited here. Since Basukala copied various elements from the remaining columns to design the replacement, the curators seemed to be conveying their commitment to the intangible Nepali tradition of copying elements as part of the process of rebuilding.

The Charnarayana temple

An illustrated descriptive panel inside an exhibition room in the Sundari Chok introduced the Charnarayana temple as the oldest temple on the Patan Durbar Square. Its construction was initiated by a member of the city's nobility in 1563, at a time when the Malla kings had lost their power. Set on a massive plinth, the 'red brick core structure with its carved timber tripartite portals and its two pyramidal roofs', according to the text, 'represent[s] the earliest tradition of Newar temple architecture, which evolved in the Kathmandu Valley fifteen hundred years ago'. The panel informed the museum visitor that the temple

> was partly damaged in the 1833 and 1934 earthquakes but retained almost all of its exquisite historic carved timber portals, tympana, windows, and struts. The earthquake in 2015, however, caused a catastrophic collapse of the entire structure, down to the plinth.

Furthermore, it informed the reader that most of the temple's original veneer bricks (New. *daci apa*) and carved elements were salvaged from the rubble, and that five broken struts could be reconstituted. The salvage, and the earlier photo documentation as well, were said to have 'set the stage' for what was described here as the 'faithful restoration and replication of carved broken parts'. As described here, these efforts were the precondition for the KVPT's 'exact rebuilding' of the temple.[2]

The Krishna Mandir

The history and design of the Krishna Mandir at the Patan Durbar Square, an octagonal stone temple that only devotees are allowed to enter or ascend, were introduced by a descriptive panel inside the Sundari Chok: the temple,

---

[2]   The rebuilding of the Charnarayana temple was funded by the United States Ambassador's Fund for Cultural Preservation; South Asia Institute, Heidelberg University; Gerda Henkel Foundation, Düsseldorf; Embassy of Japan in Nepal; World Monuments Fund through support from American Express; John Eskenazi Foundation; Bonhams; Manju and Jharendra S. J. B. Rana; Nepal Investment Bank Ltd.; the German Foreign Ministry; and Himalayan Bank Ltd.

which has a towering central core and a palatial enclosure of 16 airy pavilions topped by 21 gilded pinnacles, was built by King Siddhinarasimha Malla (r. 1619–1661) and consecrated in February 1637. Readers of the panel text were informed that it had suffered from the major earthquakes of the last centuries and even withstood the tremors of the 2015 earthquakes. However, the text showed the results of the recent damage assessment by the KVPT, stating that

> careful study has revealed just how close the structure was this time to collapse. Cracks on the second floor, dating from the 1833 and 1934 earthquakes, widened in 2015, and a number of additional structural stone members were damaged, including base stones at the corners, several keystones, and dislodged columns.

The panel also commemorated the Trust's conservation works conducted from October 2015 to August 2018 thus:[3]

> The Trust brought in the technical expertise of Neeta Das, a stone conservator from Kolkata, who worked with Newar stonemasons to replace the damaged corner stones. Conservation faculty and students from the University of Applied Arts Vienna, who had already supported a number of KVPT's arts conservation projects, rehabilitated all of the building's stone joints with an Italian lime product imported via Delhi. It is notable that all of the damaged historic stone elements of the temple were able to be consolidated, with the exception of only one column and one column fragment.

As if to evidence the earthquake destruction and the irreparableness of the original structural stones that, in the eyes of the KVPT, justified their replacement, the museum displayed the dilapidated base stones from the second floor next to the panel.

---

[3]   The conservation of the Krishna Mandir was funded by the Gerda Henkel Foundation, Düsseldorf; The Embassy of Japan in Nepal; University of Applied Arts Vienna; Nepal Investment Bank Ltd.; and Himalayan Bank Ltd.

The Harishankara temple

The Sundari Chok also provided space for a descriptive panel that related the building and reconstruction history of the Harishankara temple,[4] built by Yogamati in memory of her father, King Yoganarendra Malla, in 1706. With three tiers of stepped, pyramidal roofs above a triple-stepped plinth, this monumental structure reached 'a new level of architectural sophistication', according to the text, as it was built with a timber pillared colonnade of 'heretofore unseen intricacy and beauty'.

According to the documentation, the 20 timber columns wrapped around the ground floor failed structurally in the earthquake of 25 April 2015, causing the temple's total collapse; the 20 semicircular carved tympana of the ground floor colonnade came to rest unharmed on top of the massive heap of debris. The panel recorded the rescue and recovery of all historical doorways, pillars, windows, and struts: 'In the end, more than 90 percent of the historical carved elements were able to be preserved and have been reused in the temple's rebuilding.' The exceptions to this included one ground floor column and several timber elements, which were beyond repair and were exhibited next to the panel. They were 'faithfully remade by the hands of carpenters, many of whose ancestors created these marvels 300 years ago'. The rebuilding of the historical structure, 'faithfully restored to the centimeter', included seismic reinforcements, for example 'connecting the timber columns to base stones below and beams above with concealed stainless steel-pins'.

The museal documentation of these examples clearly characterized the collapse and destruction of the historic buildings caused by the earthquake as an outright 'catastrophe'. In view of the aftermath, in fact, the curators highlighted the project's commitment to the historical fabric that extended to all broken or fragmentary components as well. It underlined the value ascribed to anything original which could possibly be reconstituted into the rebuilding to maximize the material authenticity of the buildings, even if they required significant repair or structural consolidation. At the same time, the exhibition showed the KVPT's approach to differing notions

---

[4] The rebuilding of the Harishankara temple was funded by the Gerda Henkel Foundation, Düsseldorf; the German Foreign Ministry; and University of Applied Arts, Vienna. For a detailed documentation of the preservation of the temple, see Gutschow (2019).

of what was described in the exhibition as 'faithful' cultural heritage preservation, and declared them to be compatible with each other. In the Newar context, for example, in previous centuries, post-earthquake rebuilding would have reused only undamaged building components. As documented in the Architecture Galleries, examples of a basically 'inventive' Newar craftsmanship included the repair of wood and stone carvings, combining both the original fabric and recent additions, and using 'traditional' and 'modern' material, but employing historical methods and techniques wherever possible.

Monochrome photographs (2015): the temporary storerooms

The passageway between the Mul Chok and the Sundari Chok was turned into a picture gallery with monochrome photographs taken by Kathmandu photographer Ashesh Rajbansh in 2015 on behalf of the KVPT. The pictures were initially taken to document the temporary storerooms. They showed the KVPT's attempt to reduce the havoc caused by the destruction of 25 April 2015—the basis of all rebuilding: a shelf, loaded with hundreds of timber beams with stylized ends (New. *dhalikva*) in the shape of a Newar mythical animal's face (New. *kusuru*); a hall filled with elements of windows and portals; a heap of timber hands, broken off from the early-18th-century Harishankara temple's figurative roof struts (Figure 12.5). A text explained that

> these photographs document a phase of the earthquake response which might otherwise be forgotten. Within days of the quake, hundreds of police, army, and locals were rallied to collect thousands of artifacts and building components from fallen monuments. KVPT subsequently erected storage sheds and racks to allow careful review and sorting.

In other words, these pictures found their way into the Architecture Galleries' permanent exhibition as 'reminders', capturing a timeless aesthetic of order and moments of a bygone past at once. Moreover, they also documented the KVPT's endeavour to save as much of the historical fabric as possible.

Figure 12.5 Storeroom, Patan Royal Palace garden: monochrome picture of a shelf loaded with hundreds of timber beams with stylized ends (New. *dhalīkva*) in the shape of a Newar mythical animal's face (New. *kūsuru*), exhibit in the Architecture Galleries.

Source: Photograph by A. Rajbansh, 6 October 2015.

Audio-visual display: 'KVPT [stories]'

An audio and visual tour shown on a monitor in a room in the Sundari Chok collected the voices of KVPT staff and other (local) people involved in the Patan Durbar rebuilding project.[5] In different illustrated 'chapters', they shared their thoughts on the history, relevance, and future of the project as well as the purpose and determination to rebuild. The museum visitor was invited to listen to personal stories of culture and living heritage. In the chapter 'The Temple', for example, Rohit Ranjitkar and Erich Theophile talked about the history of the Charnarayana temple and explained how, in their eyes, the spirit of the place as a religious site of ongoing devotion and the architectural significance of the historic monument lived on through the people whose living heritage propelled its future, and those who were

---

[5]   This digital presentation is also accessible under http://kvptstories.org/.

rebuilding it with the original pieces that had been rescued: 'authenticity is overused, but it's pretty clear: this is what authenticity is', said Theophile. In another chapter, 'The Architect', Rohit Ranjitkar explained why he had devoted his life to conserving the extraordinary monuments that define his home city, to which he had 'a very close sentimental attachment'. In 'The Activist', Kanak Mani Dixit, writer, journalist, and a strong voice of cultural preservation in the Kathmandu Valley, described the cultural and religious value of the temples for Hindu and Buddhist devotees and explained that, from his point of view, 'the places of their obeisance, the temples, must be preserved, because that adds value and texture to our lives'. Last but not least, Niels Gutschow and Bijay Basukala introduced themselves as 'The Theorist and The Artist' who document the historic temples of the Kathmandu Valley. Whereas Gutschow described his practice as an 'obsession', Basukala explained how he was able to apply his passion for 'learning the details of the temples' by drawing them. Through face-to-face encounters with these and other protagonists, the museum audience was made aware of the entanglement of built heritage and local living traditions and the (rebuilt) site's cultural value and authenticity, both material and immaterial. The various views and shifts in perspective conveyed to the museum visitor that the reconstruction approach on-site fitted into international norms, but that the overall endeavour was 'hybrid' because of the many aspects of local practice which were also integrated into it.

The 'Grey Box': adaptive reuse with contemporary design

To the curators, the post-2015 earthquake rebuilding efforts offered an opportunity to rethink the Sundari Chok east wing's interior. Already in 2014, the first-floor joists had been removed to create a two-storeyed space for the exhibition of architectural drawings: 'the removal of the joists represents a severe intervention that changed the historical configuration of the east wing considerably' (Gutschow and Roka 2017: 274). Thereupon, a 'mock-up of the interior space, with lights imported from New York and plywood covering provisionally the wall surfaces, was set up in November 2014' (Gutschow and Roka 2017: 275). The new vertical space contrasted with the narrow spaces of the Sundari Chok's other wings, which had clay plastered walls and a pisé floor that were treated as major exhibits in themselves, where visitors were asked to take off their shoes to experience the original Newar flooring. Up to this time the architectural drawings and an original ivory window had constituted the only conventional exhibits. Despite the earthquake, which had caused the upper two storeys to totally collapse, a new double-storeyed space was rebuilt and finalized in late 2016 (Figure 12.6).

The earthquake brought into debate the opportunity to install four vertical square pipes tied to each of the rebuilt walls to reinforce the façade's long wall and its counterpart. Cement boards were screwed to aluminium profiles to create a smooth surface across both walls. It was this recreation of the two-storeyed space, the 'Grey Box', that was seen by the three curators as the 'most critical intervention of the entire Patan Palace Conservation Project' (Gutschow and Roka 2017: 275). However, as in pre-earthquake times, Theophile's, Ranjitkar's, and Gutschow's arguments in favour of this ahistoric change were based on an international practice

Figure 12.6 'Grey Box', Sundari Chok: the east wing's interior, transformed into a two-storeyed gallery; the ahistorical vertical space showcases architectural drawings.

Source: Photograph by R. Roka, 2019.

that 'propagates adaptive reuse' (Gutschow and Roka 2017: 274) and encourages the transformation of historic buildings into museums as a contemporary design process. The hall housed architectural drawings by Bijay Basukala and Anil Basukala from Bhaktapur and townscapes by a German architect, the late Andreas Brandt, from the private collection of Niels Gutschow, on loan to the museum. According to Gutschow, the drawings

> suggest the temporality of architectural heritage which faces loss, either by an earthquake or by neglect, and the impulse to create new structures. Documentation drawings represent a treasure house of memory. Ultimately, architecture is preserved by drawings. To highlight this contrast, the gallery in the east wing breaks norms of interior space of Newar architecture with a ceiling height of rarely more than six feet. Enlarging the interior space allowed presenting large drawings in a space adapted to the needs of a museum.[6]

Assemblage: the transformation of timber fragments

Inside the Sundari Chok complex, the vulnerability of Patan's monuments and the limits of conservation were brought to the foreground through the display of 'dismembered arms'[7] that once belonged to the figurative roof struts of the three-tiered Harishankara temple and the two-tiered Charnarayana temple.

The collapse of these structures mutilated the multi-armed goddesses and gods of these temples. Of the original 286 forearms fixed by iron nails to the Harishankara temple struts, according to a descriptive panel, only 6 were preserved at the lower-roof level. Also, only 6 of the Charnarayana temple struts' original 62 forearms survived the earthquake damage. A text explained that 'from the rubble of the two collapsed temples 162 arms were salvaged. The process of disappearance began, however, in the 19th century.

---

[6] Niels Gutschow in an e-mail of 21 June 2019.

[7] Descriptive panel titled 'Dismembered Deities: 102 Arms, Separated from the Struts of the Harishankara and Char Narayana Temples'.

Hands were often damaged and their attributes lost'. Although the hands hold various objects with iconographical meanings, for example, thunder bolt (Skt. *vajra*), mace (Skt. *gada*), conch shell (Skt. *shankha*), or sword (Skt. *khadga*), 'it is impossible to assign the preserved arms to a specific strut and to design the missing ones'.[8]

Here, the leading architects decided not to restore based on speculative conjecture. While the struts with their figures, even if partly mutilated, were reconstituted in their original location under the tiered roofs of the temples, the curators displayed a selection of 90 arms to 'demonstrate the variety of the dismembered arms'. The delicate forearms were screwed onto wooden strips and presented within a square alongside an interior wall (Figure 12.7). The transformation of the ancient temple's timber fragments into an assemblage or piece of art appeared as a unique way for the architect–curators to reuse parts of Newar architectural heritage, and a means of ascribing new value to them. The installation bridged the gap between the actual temple site and the respective exhibits, keeping both parts in their damaged state, as an associative reminder of the destructive nature of the earthquake of 25 April 2015.

Multimedia installation: a tribute to craftsmanship

During the four years of conservation work, the lively activity of the woodcarvers, masons, and metal workers temporarily engaged in the interim workshop (2015–19) in the backyard of the palace offered visitors to the Patan Museum a unique behind-the-scenes insight into the actual process of rebuilding and preservation: a view of the craftsmen at work with a continuous soundscape that filled the museum compound.

---

[8] In the case of the Harishankara temple, it was impossible to pair up these fragments with the figures (free-spirited representations of Shiva or Vishnu) to which they originally belonged, due to the lack of any documentation. Adalbert Gail delivered photographic documentation of the Charnarayana temple's figurative roof struts—unique representations of Krishna, however, identifiable through their labels—that enabled construction supervisor Bijay Basukala to assign at least some of the hands that broke away in the wake of the collapse in 2015. For a detailed documentation of the struts, see Gutschow (2019: 101–48).

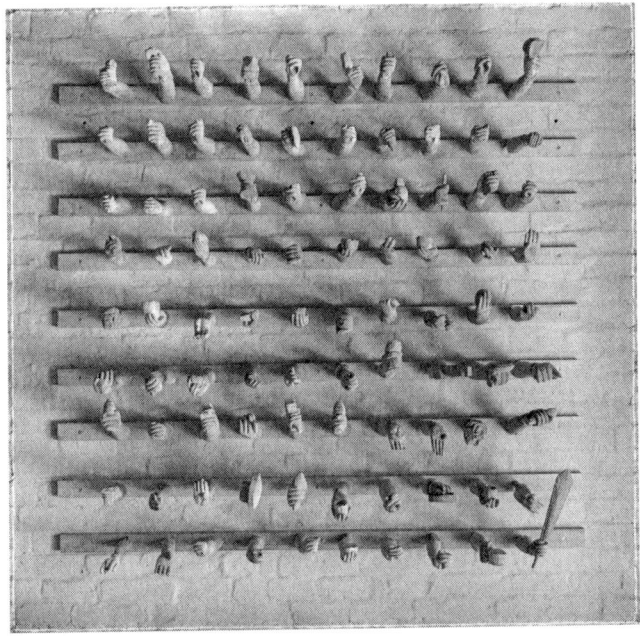

Figure 12.7 Assemblage, Sundari Chok: the curators' selection of 90 arms originating from the figurative roof struts of the Harishankara temple transforms the fragments into artwork; the assemblage bridges the gap between the rebuilt temple site and the respective exhibits, keeping both parts in their earthquake damaged state.

Source: Photograph by A. Rajbansh, March 2019.

A video, shown in a curated 'storeroom' in the Mul Chok among a collection of wooden fragments salvaged from the rubble, but beyond repair, memorialized the spirit of the temporary workshop (Figure 12.8).

The video 'Close Up: A Set of Resonating Carving Chisels' (2019) by the German multimedia artist Britt Hatzius presented an encounter with two woodcarvers (Pushpa Lal Shilpakar and Hari Prasad Shilpakar) from Bhaktapur engaged in the restoration and rebuilding of the Harishankara temple.[9] The artist chose to use various recording techniques to visually

9   Britt Hatzius, 'Close Up: A Set of Resonating Carving Chisels', single channel HD video with sound, 07:45 min, 2019, https://vimeo.com/346481793 (accessed 20 May 2020).

Figure 12.8 Multimedia installation, Mul Chok: 'Storeroom' with video 'Close up: A set of resonating carving chisels', single channel HD video with sound, 07:45 min, by Britt Hatzius.

Source: Photograph by K. Weiler, 11 September 2019.

and aurally convey the tactility involved in this woodcraft. The panel text explained:

> Attaching a microphone to the surface of the wood, the sound of the carvers' hammering is heard traveling through the material itself, the way a medical doctors' stethoscope picks up a heartbeat. Drawing the listener into the repetitive thumping sound of each beat, the camera gets close too, almost touching the wood carvings and ritually-imbued chisels.

With an acute attention to detail, the artist captured an intangible cultural heritage, including its rhythmic sound, that had been passed from one generation to the next, dating back to when the temple was first built. From the curatorial point of view, the video paid tribute to the re-evaluation of living traditions that justified the KVPT's monumental rebuilding approach and the visual continuity of fragments and replicas at the Patan Durbar Square. It contributed to an experiential engagement with Nepal's cultural heritage, both material and immaterial, the sound of chisels still resonating in the museum space. Also, it challenged the museum visitor to take into account the binary facets of carpentry and woodcarving as both craft and joinery.

Temple versus museum: the custody of the Harishankara image

The future of Harishankara, the god who dwelled inside the eponymous temple, in a way addressed the KVPT's preservationists, the DoA (taking on the former role of the *guthi sansthan*), the Municipality, the Mangal Tole

Figure 12.9 Image of Harishankara, stone, c. 1706: Harishankara (*centre*), a manifestation of Vishnu (Hari), *proper left*, and Shiva (Shankara), *proper right*; on 25 April 2015 the god who dwelled inside the respective temple broke into two pieces—Parvati's head (*left*), Vishnu's mace, Garuda's hands (*bottom, left*) and a part of the aureole broke off.

Source: Photograph by S. M. Lakhe, 2015.

Sudhar Samiti (the local association), and the Brahmin priest in charge of the temple, Gurudatta Mishra, as well. The original Harishankara image dates back to the early 18th century (Figure 12.9). It used to be firmly situated inside, at the centre of the temple building. It was the living monument's centre of worship and would be covered with layers of ritual offerings such as rice, butter, and vermillion, as signs of continuous religious worship. On 25 April 2015, the image was buried under the debris. It was salvaged from the rubble but was found to have broken into two pieces. Parvati's head, Vishnu's mace, Garuda's hands, and a part of the aureole had also broken away.

From a ritual perspective, Harishankara was declared void. In late 2015, a team of conservators from the Institute of Conservation at the University of Applied Arts, Vienna, was able to restore the sculpture so carefully that the cracks were almost invisible. From a conservational point of view, the sculpture's restoration reinstated Harishankara's visual integrity. But the question was whether the restored sculpture could be revitalized through a ritual and reinstalled inside the rebuilt temple, or whether the idol had forever lost its spiritual significance and had become an archaeological object, or even a museum exhibit which should be assigned to the Architecture Galleries.

The restored Harishankara thus exemplified ambiguous perceptions: to some (to the priest, for example), it was an inanimate and meritless sculpture. To others (to the professional conservators and curators of the Architecture Galleries, for example), it was an antique worth maintaining for its historical and artistic value. The differing notions evoked diverse solutions. Should the original image be reinstalled inside the sanctum of the temple? Or should the temple be home to a new idol, which would take the place of the original and be ritually animated by a priest? And should the restored image be displayed inside the Architecture Galleries?

In early September 2019, a replica which was much smaller than the original was finally ordered by the Municipality with the participation of the Mangal Tole Sudhar Samiti (but in the absence of the authority of the *guthi sansthan*) from Amar Shakya, a stone carver from the Bhīnchēbaha quarter in Patan (Gutschow 2019: 464). On 3 October, the 5th day of the Dashain festival, which celebrates the victory of the mother goddess Durga over the buffalo demon Mahishasura, and was also the day of the temple's original consecration, the rebuilt temple was re-consecrated, and the restored statue left its temporary shelter inside the museum compound of the Keshav Narayan Chok to return to its original location. On the same day, the replica was also delivered to the same site. While the 'original' image was re-installed in its original place inside the sanctum, the replica was set on a pedestal placed in front of the restored statue. Kirtinath Mishra, a priest engaged by the actual temple priest and assisted by Abhishek Mishra, performed the consecration ritual (Skt. *nyasa*) for the replica, while the restored image remained inanimate. In this way, the future of the antique was claimed right at the living monument's centre of worship rather than inside the museum space.

Patan's heritage tourism industry

While, even in the aftermath, the Patan Durbar Square has uninterruptedly been representing a core area of Newar culture, the consecration ceremony for the rebuilt Charnarayana temple was finally performed on 29 January 2020. After all, the preserved living monuments will continuously be revived by religious traditions and local cultural use. At the same time, the Patan Darbar Earthquake Response Campaign's endeavour revived the concept of a 'World Heritage Site' and responded to the demands of Patan's tourism industry. Since before the earthquake and also during its aftermath, international tourists have paid separate entrance fees to the Durbar Square and to the Patan Museum. However, reduced to ruins, the square, and the museum as well, had lost their relevance as tourist spots in the immediate aftermath of the earthquake.[10] In the fiscal year 2014–15 (2071–72 v.s.), 72,670 visitors came to the museum.[11] Their number had dropped to 46,583 in the fiscal year 2015–16 (2072–73 v.s.) that followed the tremor and destruction.[12] In September 2016, the Lalitpur Sub-metropolitan City and the Patan Museum changed their ticketing system to offer a combined ticket. Under this new regime, tourists coming from the countries belonging to the South Asian Association for Regional Cooperation (SAARC) were charged NPR 250 (c. USD 2.25), and 'third-country' tourists were charged NPR 1,000 (c. USD 9). In the

---

[10] Source: http://www.patanmuseum.gov.np/content.php?id=180 (accessed 15 April 2020).

[11] 48,409 Nepali visitors including students, 6,998 visitors from SAARC countries and China, and 17,263 'foreigners'.

[12] 32,868 Nepali visitors including students, 3,515 visitors from SAARC countries and China, and 10,200 'foreigners'.

fiscal year 2016–17 (2073–74 v.s.), the square and the museum, though still undergoing reconstruction, regained their relevance as tourist attractions. According to a museum officer, the incorporation of the museum entrance fee into the Patan Durbar Square ticket 'has helped to increase the flow of tourists into the museum' (A. Shrestha 2017) as the museum welcomed 176,904 visitors.[13] The number of people who visited the museum reached a peak of 232,594 visitors in the fiscal year 2017–18 (2074–75 v.s.) while the inflow of domestic tourists was also on the rise.[14] The ('World Heritage') site including the Patan Museum thus attracted more Nepali and international visitors than ever before. In 2017–18, the tickets sold on site brought a total of NPR 142.81 million (c. USD 1.3 million), of which around NPR 132.49 million (c. USD 1.2 million) were collected through the sale of combined tickets to foreign tourists alone (Kafle 2019). Even though Nepali tourists did not have to pay for entrance to the square, the Patan Museum Development Committee charged domestic visitors NPR 30 (c. USD 0.27) and Nepali students NPR 15 (c. USD 0.14). Of the proceeds generated by the tickets, 75 per cent was allocated to the Lalitpur Sub-metropolitan City, 15 per cent to the Patan Museum Development Committee, 5 per cent to the maintenance of the Patan Durbar Square, and 5 per cent to the promotion of tourism and administrative expenses.[15]

Legacy: a memorial to loss and recovery

With the earthquake destruction on the Patan Durbar Square giving way to the active rewriting of its history and the recontextualization of its architectural past in the post-disaster context, the loss of historic yet living monuments and their rebuilding clearly had an impact on the KVPT's curatorial practice. In this regard, the Architecture Galleries bore testimony to the approaches of cultural heritage conservation in the framework of the rehabilitation on the site, as substantial parts of the exhibition communicated

---

[13] 68,076 Nepali visitors including students, 17,110 visitors from SAARC countries and China, and 91,718 'foreigners'.

[14] 93,428 Nepali visitors including students, 22,389 visitors from SAARC countries and China, and 116,777 'foreigners'.

[15] See http://lalitpurmun.gov.np/en/content/unidoor-system-tourist-entrance-fee-collection-notice (accessed 15 April 2020).

the Patan Durbar Square's history of destruction and rebuilding. In a way, the exhibits took on the role of testimonies to the KVPT's efforts to reclaim and reinvent Patan's tangible and intangible cultural heritage, and highlighted the leading architects' thoughts on diverse aspects of authenticity, especially in respect of historical fabric, methods and techniques, and form.

The growing number of international and domestic visitors to the Architecture Galleries, including their earthquake-related permanent exhibition, were introduced to the KVPT's rebuilding efforts as a joint heritage production. This was launched and enabled by an outside intervention, under the stewardship of a team of international experts and primarily with financial support from abroad, rather than through any national or communal efforts, but it was implemented by a team of Nepali architects, engineers, craftspeople, and scholars, based on concentrated negotiations. The exhibition thus emphasized not only intersections between apparently opposed poles such as 'global' institutions and 'local' communities, or 'shared heritage' and 'local inheritance', but also the boundaries cutting across them—after all, certain conservation approaches practised on site provoked a clash of cultural values. This highlighted the need for a careful use of concepts related to cultural heritage in order not to push academic research towards a specific, already well-established, narrative (Brosius 2017b: 377).

Above all, the Architecture Galleries underlined the role of display in the production of and belief in Patan's cultural heritage and cultural identity in the aftermath of the 2015 earthquakes. As Erich Theophile remarked in 2019 with reference to the diminutive 'pile of leftovers' from the rubble of 2015, 'those are going into the museum as a new kind of installation to show people: "so, that's what is left over!"' (E. Theophile 2019). In this sense, the exhibition, and the rebuilt monuments on the square as well, mediated a 'new sense of future for the past' and bore testimony to a process of cultural heritage formation in a time of crisis, with the rebuilding effort a hitherto unparalleled way of valuing historic fabric and reviving original fragments in Nepal and a novel way of coping with loss. More than that, the Architecture Galleries told an ambiguous story of cultural heritage as both a victim and a survivor, a story of loss and recovery.

13

Working on Disaster

Nepali Artists' Engagement in Post-earthquake Kathmandu Valley

Christiane Brosius

In the aftermath of the 2015 earthquakes in Nepal, local artists were at the forefront of responding to the event through art practice as well as helping those in need. This chapter explores ways in which the disaster produced particular responses from artist-activists based in Kathmandu. In responding to the disaster, they developed strategies and tactics for coping with, and working on, the event and its consequences for people's everyday lives (see Liechty and Hutt, this volume). In this way, a temporal solidaric community emerged, both digitally and through on-site art events that, as Liechty and Hutt (this volume) propose, aimed at rebuilding 'lives, meaning, memory, and social relations', thus 'actively crafting a future'. This crafting, or aesthetic formation (Meyer 2009), could be traced across various levels, from individual initiatives on Facebook to on-site collective curations and exhibitions, including engagements with very particular local concerns and conditions as well as international strategies of artistic relief work (for example, the Tōhoku Earthquake in Japan [2011] from where the art project Camp.Hub in Bhaktapur received inspiration by learning how solidaric relief work helped aged people and tried to use traditional and simple ways of socializing to allow for coping strategies in disaster regions to evolve and nurture social fabrics). One of the key aspirations of the artists whose work I shall discuss in this context was, I propose, to shape moments of bottom-up solidarity that helped earthquake victims to consider themselves as survivors who could generate hope and confidence while also recognizing despair and crisis. The social networks that were thus appealed to were clearly based on the idea of transgressing caste, ethnic, and class boundaries rather than reifying essentialized boundaries. However, they also did so by paying attention to local particularities, such as specific terminologies, preferences and values, and cultural patterns.

This chapter will consider the photographic series 'Meanwhile in My Neighbourhood: Earthquake Diary' by the artist Sanjeev Maharjan. This set of several dozen photographs, taken with a mobile phone camera immediately after the 25 April earthquake and uploaded onto the artist's Facebook page, revolves around the dominant presence of the disaster as a media spectacle, against which the artist composes a subtle visual narrative of 'ordinary' everyday lives. These images show how the earthquake event intensified an already existing artistic engagement with urban and social transformation that has now, in the dramatic aftermath, developed even further. The second case I will describe is the community-art project '12 Baisakh' (the Bikram calendar date of the 25 April earthquake). The Kathmandu-based artist collective ArTree Nepal spent six months in one of the worst affected neighbourhoods in the Kathmandu Valley: Thulo Byasi, in Bhaktapur. Its members' aim was to engage in humanitarian aid, help to build shelters, and provide psychological and humanitarian support for survivors. The ethnographic research I conducted on the earthquake's aftermath asked the following questions: How does one respond to disaster through artistic practices without simply aestheticizing tragedy? How can art become an intervention and provide a space for reflection? How has the earthquake contributed to an ongoing engagement with community-based art, with themes of urban neighbourhood, heritage, and civil society, but also inequality and belonging? Finally, what chronology have the artworks produced in 2015 developed and how have artists continued to engage with the disaster? The chapter is inspired by the concept of 'commoning' that has been discussed in the context of space utilization in post-earthquake New Zealand (Dombroski, Diprose, and Boles 2019). Here, commoning is seen as a form of socio-spatial resource through which ideas of a common wealth can be temporarily created and addressed.[1] This includes the readiness of a particular group to release a closely defined 'good' to be shared with others, even risking its negotiation and transformation in the process. This readiness to share requires trust, care, and responsibility, which are to be learnt while commoning.

---

[1] I thank Stefanie Lotter for bringing my attention to the concept of 'commoning' as a resource for disaster management.

Old ties, new formations

The 2015 earthquakes generated a wave of creative energy and collaborative action among Nepal's artists. I suggest that engaging in post-disaster reconstruction and relief work enabled a collaborative contemplation of how artists can facilitate the shaping of a Nepali society that would recognize local particularities and cultural heritages and promote the idea of a society that was not confined within ethnic boundaries. The aftermath, one could argue, became a laboratory for new societal ideals which hoped to overcome a very difficult challenge: to recognize the need of small communities, often ethnic and caste-based, to sustain their way of life, and yet also to invite these to become part of an open society, based on a sense of sharing while at the same time deviating from state-based visions of national identity and cohesion. Instead, the fabric for civil society and the public sphere would be co-produced dynamically.

'Aesthetic formation' seems an appropriate label for the artists' engagement with and in the disaster. Birgit Meyer, who coined the term, points to the relevance of aesthetics for creative knowledge production and socialization. Aesthetics, beyond Kantian enlightenment and taste, is then a form that generates and shapes the world, and contributes to the making of places and social relations. 'Formation', rather than community, proposes a rethinking of community 'as a fixed, bounded social group', to underline the temporality and oscillating nature of social groups (Meyer 2009: 6–7). In their reflections on millennial globalized protest movements, Werbner, Webb, and Spellman-Poots reiterate that 'all politics is aesthetic' and consider 'architectural and spatial forms and organizational principles that animate the political' (2014: 2). The examples that follow offer a better understanding of how different members of the art scene in the Kathmandu Valley 'worked on the event' of the earthquake to come to 'terms' with possibilities of social change and the role of art therein. In this context, memory work as 'repair work' becomes 'future work' (see also Lord and Bradley, this volume).

Against spectacle: aesthetic formations
of the everyday

All photos are memento mori. To take a photograph is to participate in another person's (or thing's) mortality, vulnerability, mutability.

> Precisely by slicing out this moment and freezing it, all photographs
> testify to time's relentless melt.
>
> —Sontag (2001 [1973]: 21)

Sontag's precise observations bring the intimate interplay of visual representation and social practice to the fore. They also chime with the art historian Gennifer Weisenfeld's thoughts on imaging the 1923 earthquake in Japan: 'Such representations are a vivid reminder of the constructed nature of disaster imagery, whose producers had a vested interest in spectacle and aesthetic impact while providing visible evidence of the event' (Weisenfeld 2012: 83). Focusing on disaster as spectacle, Weisenfeld goes on to say that spectacle is 'a form of pathic image targeted to force viewers to look and to hold their attention.... Spectacle produces spectators who are distinct from participants' (2012: 83; see also Lord and Bradley, this volume).

For many young Nepali artists, there was a persistent tension between engaging with their art in social projects and becoming eyewitnesses of the disaster as they tried to work on and through the event itself by engaging actively, emphatically, and humanistically in regeneration, reconstruction, and transformation. Instead of paralysing the viewer through voyeuristic spectacle and so commodifying both viewer and viewed, the art practice, so many of them hoped, would encourage a participatory encounter that might lead to social action. This momentum of art as social engagement stands in opposition to the often sensationalist standardized representations of Nepal in mainstream, and mainly foreign, media. In the aftermath of the 2015 earthquakes, many Nepalis were critical of foreign correspondents, and particularly Indian photographers and filmmakers, who hunted for sensational images and stories. These images allegedly failed to (re)present the self-perception of many Nepalis, especially the young, who were actively involved in relief work and who coined the slogan 'we will rise again' as a cry of self-empowerment and confidence. Sanjeev Maharjan's photographs speak of a search for alternative narratives of a disaster situation, implicitly critiquing the language and imagery of disaster spectacles. Maharjan's pen-and-ink trilogy 'We Will Rise Again' (Figure 13.1) connects not only to the slogans that circulated on social media in May and June 2015 (for example, 'We are not suffering victims but active, solidaric, and hopeful survivors') but also to local media reports of a 'new generation' of Nepalis who were investing their time and energy in social participation and relief work. Indeed, in the months after the earthquake, an energetic commitment and

Figure 13.1 'We Will Rise Again': ink drawing depicting the post-earthquake scenario in Kathmandu by Sanjeev Maharjan, part of a trilogy, Kathmandu, 2015.

Source: Screenshot by Christiane Brosius, from Sanjeev Maharjan's Facebook page, May 2015.

a palpable vitality characterized the city, despite ongoing personal traumas and the many losses.

The gaze we encounter here is one that translates the unspeakable into art. The impulse to share and communicate goes beyond the mere visualization of an event and instead becomes a careful annotation of, and in, space and time, laid out like an experiential landscape: a personal memento mori, to cite Sontag again. Maharjan's photo-diary entries on Facebook carried captions such as 'Things are getting normal in my neighbourhood' (8 May 2015) or were anchored by hashtags such as #Wewillriseagain, thereby providing a frame that reflected both his own reading of the situation and the experiences of the citizens with whom he interacted during his walks through the streets of the wounded city. It is almost as if we are walking with the photographer: he takes us to small shops that have just re-opened, or past a barber wearing a yellow helmet for protection whilst he works, surrounded by patient customers awaiting their turn (Figure 13.2). We see flower vendors on the street, or peep into one of the countless temporary shelters to see children cheerfully smiling at the photographer, for they recognize their next-door neighbour (Figures 13.3 and 13.4). An old woman folds her hands in prayer in front of a temple. We are led through narrow alleys punctuated by struts and joists; we look down from Maharjan's multi-storey concrete house into the courtyard and see that neighbours have returned to their everyday activities, be they reading the newspaper in the morning sun, washing clothes at the community tap, or gathering for a family ritual (Figures 13.5–13.7). The camera as the eye and sensorium of

Figure 13.2 Barber shop in Kathmandu on 20 May 2015, illustrating the reopening of shops after the April 2015 earthquake.

Source: Facebook posting and photograph by Sanjeev Maharjan, part of the Earthquake Diary series.

Figure 13.3 Flower vendor among the rubble, Basantapur, Kathmandu, 9 May 2015.

Source: Facebook posting and photograph by Sanjeev Maharjan, part of the Earthquake Diary series.

Figure 13.4 Children in a post-earthquake shelter, Basantapur, Kathmandu, 9 May 2015.

Source: Facebook posting and photograph by Sanjeev Maharjan, part of the Earthquake Diary series.

the participant observer takes note of resting cats and people, of household items rescued from damaged homes and now lined up in front of deserted houses, of people collecting reusable items from the rubble on the street (Figure 13.8).

This practice of stock-taking and archiving a catastrophe is Maharjan's personal response to the much more sensational images in the mainstream media. It is a cautious and humble reaction to fragility—both the photographer's own and what he sees around him. But in that fragility is a stern, even stoic, will to return to normal life. Although Maharjan's photographs of his walks, which he uploaded on Facebook almost instantly alongside hashtags and spare annotations, subsume the itinerary as 'Meanwhile in My Neighbourhood', there is little sense of a community, beyond family, individual couples, and persons engaged in everyday activities. In conversation, Maharjan revealed that the act of walking and taking photographic stock of the return of everyday life among the remains and rubble of the earthquake helped him to ground himself. Against the

Figure 13.5 Hanuman Dhoka, Kathmandu Durbar Square.

Source: Facebook posting and photograph by Sanjeev Maharjan, part of the Earthquake Diary series.

Sanjeev Maharjan
12 May 2015 · Kathmandu, Nepal · ☺ · ℮

Today is my grandmother 12th days death ritual. We all family members were having prasad after puja when earthquake struck. We are all safe in my neighborhood and community.
#Wewillriseagain #nepalearthquake2015 #7.4afterquake

Figure 13.6 Death ritual in the artist's courtyard, 12 May 2015.

Source: Facebook posting and photograph by Sanjeev Maharjan, part of the Earthquake Diary series.

👍 Like   💬 Comment   ↗ Share

Figure 13.7 'Things are getting normal in my neighbourhood', 8 May 2015.

Source: Photograph by Sanjeev Maharjan, from the Earthquake Diary series.

Figure 13.8 Man collecting objects from the rubble of a collapsed house, Bhaktapur, 22 May 2015.
Source: Photograph by Sanjeev Maharjan, from the Earthquake Diary series.

high-speed news imagery of the disaster, these images, then, generated an inert, alternative ephemeral landscape of witnessing.

Taking photographs was only one means of engaging with the event of the earthquake by making it tangible. Maharjan also collected oral histories which were sometimes merely short snippets of narrative about the moment when the earthquake struck. Community-based engagements and an emphasis on dialogue and participation became prominent features of Nepali art activism after the earthquake (see Naidu-Silverman 2015). This evinces an aspiration to construct or frame the meaning of the disaster-event in a way that—most importantly—involves human agency (see Liechty and Hutt, this volume). The event is thus not cast as something that just happened and has passed, but rather as something that lingers on and, despite its dramatic effects, allows itself to be worked on.

Neighbourhood as urban belonging

Beyond the instant response to the earthquake, many artists used the disaster as a catalyst for reflecting on other, broader themes that surfaced in this liminal moment. They opened up the discourse to previously hidden or less articulated but nevertheless relevant social, political, and cultural domains. While ArTree engages with the themes of 'community' and 'neighbourhood' from a political and cultural angle, Maharjan's approach is more personal and subjective: it relates the urban transformation that he experiences, which becomes more evident with the earthquake, to the Newar heritage, and more specifically to the farming community of Maharjans, including his own family and their farmland. The photographs he took during walks through his neighbourhood speak a more intimate, poetic language of belonging to the city. A variety of relationships with places and people are tied into this tender web of Maharjan's placemaking, including the barber, the flower vendor, or the man selling chickens. His photographs of these shared spaces, even the temporary shelters, exude a sense of intimate solitude and solidarity as social and physical havens.

Maharjan's work on the earthquake also allowed him to dig deeper into the fabric of the city as a modern and rapidly changing social space and to address issues that were brought to the fore by the earthquake, such as the notorious lack of open spaces or the uncontrolled hunger to build houses and ignore safety measures.[2] We see this when his camera looks down into a courtyard to see a woman washing, a man reading the newspaper (#WeWillriseagain: 'Things are getting normal in my neighbourhood'), and when he engages intensely with his *aji*'s (grandmother's) memories of the earthquake of 1934 and of growing up in Kathmandu, by interviewing her just a few days before she dies. He mourns her death and documents the

---

[2]   For more details, see Khazai et al. (2015) and Kathmandu Living Labs, at http:// www.kathmandulivinglabs.org/.

Newar funerary rites; he also grieves the loss of traditional landmarks in the city due to their collapse. When he annotates his photographs of modern houses, questioning how long they might stand before they too collapse, this is also related to a growing interest in the relationship between built spaces, everyday life, and heritage. In loss and grief, something new is gained.

In the wake of the earthquake, the consciousness of humans' dependency on their surroundings grew, increasing the potential for further placemaking. The dependency on securely built houses and also on modern infrastructure such as roads, electricity, and water supplies became more than obvious. The earthquake ushered in a ghostly fear: the sense of being trapped among houses that could collapse in an instant at any moment. Earthquakes do not recognize caste or class (though the vulnerability of the poor is most evident); thus, even if only temporarily (see Hutt, this volume), a shared sense of community emerged (Figure 13.9).

The city and the perception of continuity and change in this 'laboratory' of civil society play a crucial role in Sanjeev Maharjan's work. It is not surprising that the city features centrally in many Nepali artists' work because it is their immediate habitat. But this interest in urban everyday microspaces is not only a critical response to the mainstream media's representations of Nepal as picturesque. It is also a distancing from earlier canons of classical art education in which the modern city was largely marginalized and seen as inauthentic. Earlier Nepali pictorial art was dominated by nostalgic rural countryside scenes, manicured pastoral scenes, or small-town vignettes, situated in mountainscapes outside, or portrayals of the rustic past of the Kathmandu Valley. 'Heritage' was part of a salvage paradigm rhetoric, opposed to the splintering urbanism that was covering the valley with a patchwork of brick houses.

In the 2000s, Nepali artists started to perceive the city as their studio, their field of research-based art production, and their work inevitably reflects their lifeworlds. Pre-earthquake photographs by Maharjan capture the new architecture of modern buildings, made of concrete, 4–5 storeys high (see Figure 13.9)—as opposed to the 2–3-storey brick houses with wooden carved windows and hip roofs laid with clay tiles. But instead of creating a dichotomy that freezes the 'traditional' in time and opposes it to the 'modern', Maharjan invites the synchronicity of both as facets of diversity and inclusion in contemporary Nepal. Hence his ethnographic vignettes of urban life are also a way of participating in and making the new city, including intangible and tangible forms of cultural heritage.

Figure 13.9 Impression of houses that survived the earthquake, 15 May 2015.
Source: Photograph by Sanjeev Maharjan, from the Earthquake Diary series.

Maharjan's photographic diary of the city also reflects the rapid changes taking place across Nepal, and in a particularly condensed form in the Kathmandu Valley, that are often addressed in contemporary artists' work. Here the city also stands for a diversity of lifeworlds, including national and transnational migration; democratization processes and ethno-political tensions and contestations; asymmetries of access to education and work, and of wealth and poverty; and the landless or homeless populations that have gathered in the Kathmandu Valley since the civil war of 1996–2006.

The many struts that attempt to stabilize not only the earthquake-damaged houses in the narrow alleys but also the Rana mansions and palaces are here an allegorical representation of citizens' lack of trust in government structures. Maharjan's photographs trigger several possible associations with the city: they include not only a longing for an intimate neighbourhood in which Newar rituals and relations are functioning, and a deep appreciation of the history and cultural heritage of the city of Kathmandu (though the relationship to the Rana period is more than ambivalent), but also an embrace of the new open spaces and forms of collectivity that are possible through ethnic and social diversity. Maharjan's triptych 'We Will Rise Again' shows traditional pagodas as well as modern high-rises (see detail of Figure 13.1), reflecting the idea of a multi-temporal and diverse city. It remains unclear whether 'neighbourhood' in such a context is a magic emblem for nostalgia, or the utopian hope of a new civil society in a 'New Nepal'.

Neighbourhood as civil society

Another theme that surfaces in post-disaster Nepali art works is that of the fabric of community and society. The 2015 earthquakes struck a country that was still struggling to write a new constitution that would represent all ethnic and regional groups alike, a society affected by poverty and inequality, strong ethnic and caste ties, and corruption, with fresh memories of civil war. The earthquake catalysed debates on the role of the state and foreign agents, civil society, and community. I argue that this reflects an increased search for social and political—but also aesthetic—formations that could facilitate alternatives to monolithic narratives of national identity, development, and modernity. Maharjan's search for an urban neighbourhood could be seen as a reflection of this (see Figures 13.6 and 13.8). In the earthquake context, one could argue that communities become shelters and shelters become new communal sites. This invisible potential is emphatically felt and thought in Maharjan's photographs.

Especially after the first earthquake of 25 April, and against the notion of being passive victims, remarkable social energies were set free and bundled together in collective action across ethnic and social strata with the idea of having survived and being resilient. But besides the question of survival, questions about the loss of urban heritage and its future role came to the fore: What should be preserved, and how and why? In what kind of a city can and do we want to live, and can there be a 'Nepali' city? Moreover, questions about post-ethnic solidarity became prominent: Can we use this event to shape a 'better' society? How can Nepali citizens become responsible caretakers of this? One such example was Rebuilding Bungamati, an art-driven relief initiative by the faculty and students of Kathmandu University's Department of Art and Design. Sujan Chitrakar, artist, curator, and head of the department, described the earthquake as 'a kind of a turning point for Nepal' (Brosius and Maharjan 2017: 111). Although the student volunteers involved in this project encountered frustrations (such as the local population's expectation that they would take over full responsibility and find solutions to problems such as structural violence and depression), certain sustainable structures of exchange could be built.

Many of the emerging Nepali artists today are Newars from the cities of the Kathmandu Valley. Some, but not all, come from artist families such as the Chitrakars, while others come from different regional, caste, and ethnic backgrounds. While the cities of the Kathmandu Valley largely stand for a particular form of ownership and tradition of placemaking (that of the Newars, as traders, craftsmen, artists), Kathmandu and Patan in particular offer the potential for the shaping of a more ethnically and socially diverse space. Many of the artists involved in post-earthquake relief work also aspired to an active involvement in the democratic structures of their country.

Younger artists increasingly consider societal challenges, frictions, and tensions as their field of art production, and increasingly adopt collaborative or participatory and research-based methods. This change is also connected to a realization that there is a gap between art curricula and everyday lifeworlds. According to Hitman Gurung, ArTree co-founder, artist, and curator, speaking of his group's engagement in disaster-artivism in the city of Bhaktapur:

> Looking back, it is really that inability to understand each other that led us down this path. 12 Baisakh became an attempt to reshape how contemporary artists look at issues facing our communities.... Their stories are varied and each one uniquely personal. However, the incident has pervasively unsettled the relationship cultivated by individuals to their surroundings. (ArTree Nepal 2016)

This observation resonates with demands in early anthropology to move from 'armchair anthropology' to doing fieldwork, thus to 'unlearn' in order to 'learn'. Its turn towards community-based art is visible in Maharjan's walk-alongs, which weave together the loose network of a vulnerable community, but also highlight its resilience and determination to cope. Maharjan's fellow artists insist that caste, class, and ethnicity do not matter to them. Yet there is a deep interest in and concern for traditional lifestyles, which seems likely to create tension at some stage because it coincides with ethnic and caste-based identifications. Nonetheless, this vision of a 'communitas' unleashes new potentials for solidarity and collective action. My next example, too, underlines artivists' commitment to overcome reified identities and yet search for the possibilities of a specifically 'Nepali' way. This becomes evident in the constitution of the artist collective ArTree Nepal, which is made up of members of different ethnic and caste communities. The artists respond to pressing questions about how Nepal can retain its rich heritage by becoming an open society, but still recognize the rights and aspirations of ethnic groups without fixing and politicizing them.

This aspiration to contribute to a more inclusive civil society comes in tandem with the increased interest and reflexivity of a younger generation of Nepalis in ethnicity and ethnic heritage as central elements of a new sociality. The artists find no clear answer to this apparent contradiction. Instead, they aim to throw it open, so that it can be tackled by civil society, rather than by the state or political parties. The earthquake has aroused an interest among artists in what seems to be at stake, and how this can be made visible and discussed. Maharjan's own interest in his Newar culture and Jyapu heritage has grown. His childhood and youth were partly spent in his grandparents' fields, witnessing the agricultural cycle and its rituals. His membership of this lineage shapes his view of the earthquake experience as he engages with his grandmother Hakalani, as well as with disaster memories of Newars from Bhaktapur, and his post-disaster work has provoked him to think more about issues of belonging and its relation to heritage and inheritance.

New spaces, constellations, and formats
for post-disaster artivism

The carefully connected network of oral and visual stories also speaks of a motivation to be artists in a society whose economic and cultural infrastructure is precarious: Maharjan's fellow artists underline time and again that for them, caste, class, and ethnicity do not matter. At the heart of the young artists' work is a search for and commitment to unbound solidarity, an idea of connectivity beyond partial and politicized identities.

The late Dina Bangdel noted that 'the 2015 Nepal earthquakes radically transformed contemporary art practices, as contemporary Nepali artists responded to the conditions of devastation and trauma' (2017: 59; on art and activism in South Asia, see also Achar and Panikkar 2012). She argued that this could be seen as a reflection of the artists' growing desire to connect with everyday life in Nepal and to be able to respond to internationally available art formats, such as site-specific installations, artistic research, or community-based art and interdisciplinary collaborations. Hitman Gurung argues that artists want to overcome the divide between their art and the everyday life of people, in order to better understand them and share this knowledge. Rather than seeing such a community-based approach as appropriated from the international art field, ArTree Nepal believes that art has 'deep roots in social practice'; that is, it requires 'strategic grassroots interventions and a goal of shaping emerging communities' (ArTree Nepal 2018: 4) through which an egalitarian society is imagined.

This pushes art works out from the confines of the so-called white cube (the gallery and museum space, and also the artist's studio), onto the street or other outdoor sites, the 'field'. The works by Sanjeev Maharjan and Camp. Hub, and those curated by ArTree, did not come out of the blue, but were a consequence of a systematic search by these young artists for new spaces for art production, exhibition, social embeddedness, and activism. The urgency to respond was both personal and collective, and it became, as Bangdel argues, 'a rediscovery of their roots and heritage that this generation of young artists had often taken for granted' (2017: 60); it became a form of collecting and archiving data, and thinking about the ethics of artistic response.

Since the 1990s, and especially for the generation born during the 1990s, a new type of artist has emerged in Nepal. S/he is both a global nomad and a local activist, equally aware of the potential offered by international art events (for example, biennales, art fairs) as of the potential for using art to open up spaces and communication forums that can empower neighbourhoods and civil society. Artists such as Hitman Gurung and Sheelasha Rajbhandari, the co-founders of ArTree, are multi-taskers—they curate, produce art, create institutions. In Nepal, they do this despite a dearth of funding, collectors, and gallery spaces, even in Kathmandu.

The role of art in times of disaster gives this a different, possibly more urgent, quality. Rooting themselves in art as social practice, and inspired by international models of community art, as in the case of the US-based Centre for the Study of Art and Community,[3] ArTree's founders see their

---

[3] See https://www.artandcommunity.com/csac/who-we-are.html (accessed 16 June 2019).

work as facilitating social justice and informal education, 'sustainable working and living contexts … strongly linked to environmental and urban revitalization work' (ArTree Nepal 2016: 17). Cat Powell names four aspects of the purpose of art in times of disaster. These are: to resist apathy, blind anger, or fatalism; to remember alternate histories—especially of marginalized groups—but also ways of coping with disaster and to learn from this; to salvage by enforcing immediate action, but also recognizing and understanding; and last, to help others to survive, by offering art as 'a bulwark against despair' (Powell 2016). All four purposes are mirrored in the ways in which Nepali artists responded to the earthquakes. This brings us to the second case study in Bhaktapur: the 12 Baisakh Post-Earthquake Community Art Project, which then turned into a multi-sited event entitled Camp.Hub in September 2015.

Camp.Hub: out there and close-by

In the summer of 2015, Maharjan joined Camp.Hub and developed the community-based installation work 'Stories from Thulo Byasi' that, as its title suggests, is intricately entangled with the life of people from the eponymous neighbourhood. Maharjan's installation of a wall, made from bricks salvaged from the destroyed houses and dedicated to the residents of Thulo Byasi, was the result of several interviews with local residents during the summer of 2015 (see Brosius 2017a and Figures 13.10 and 13.11). Recordings of these interviews were accessible via headphones installed in front of the U-shaped brick wall at the Camp.Hub site in Thulo Byasi. Photos of the interviewees and quotes from conversations about their experience of the earthquakes, in Newari or English, were inlaid into some of the bricks.

Even though Maharjan developed and conducted the project on his own, it formed part of a collective artist engagement, including joint meetings in Thulo Byasi. It could also be read as an approach comparable to 'memory work', a mode of sensemaking and a social technology of collective repair (Lord and Bradley, this volume). However, a demanding (because complicated) sense of shaping a new society that could sustain 'old foundations' (for instance, Newar rituals and sites of gathering) also played a role in this. Camp.Hub thus became another 'laboratory' for testing new aesthetic formations.

A key feature of this project, which ran from May to October 2015, was that its directors, Gurung and Rajbhandari, wanted to take responsibility

Figure 13.10 Wall installation 'Stories from Thulo Byasi', by Sanjeev Maharjan, part of the Camp.Hub exhibition in Thulo Byasi, Bhaktapur, September 2015.

Source: Photograph by Christiane Brosius.

Figure 13.11 Detail of the wall installation 'Stories from Thulo Byasi', by Sanjeev Maharjan, part of the Camp.Hub exhibition in Thulo Byasi, Bhaktapur, September 2015.

Source: Photograph by Christiane Brosius.

through strategic and continuous dialogue with community members. The site was selected quickly: by 28 April 2015, they had already decided to focus their attention on Thulo Byasi, a Newar quarter of the UNESCO–World Heritage city of Bhaktapur, where the population was largely agriculturalist, but also ran small businesses, with some involvement in the service industry. Around two-thirds of the 700 residential buildings were heavily damaged or had collapsed, 11 deaths had been confirmed, with many more injured, and 500 people were living in temporary shelters on nearby fields made available by neighbours. Along with instant humanitarian help, Hitman Gurung defines the desire to engage in humanitarian relief work for a time after the earthquake as a significant attitude among artists: 'memorizing details, collecting stories became a process.... Devastation and death, numbers and statistics, from the city and beyond occupied our thoughts for hours on end' (ArTree 2016). The context is strongly reminiscent of an ethnographer's planning, and of the challenges of fieldwork as well as the burden of representation (Foster 1995). Trust had to be gained, for many locals suspected that the artists would only collect data and were uncertain what relief work could look like in such a state of emergency. Contemplating the fact that their research would include a 'survey'-like collection of data to understand the fabric of the neighbourhood, because of a lack of available existing data, Gurung and Rajbhandari observe:

> We introduced ourselves as an artist collective willing to help the community. But it was very difficult for them to understand us. They were only used to being contacted by media persons or NGO workers. We were often questioned about our motives, who was funding us and giving us money, what was the camera for. (ArTree Nepal 2016: 3)

These are classical issues for an ethnographer, but to find them reflected in artists' research-based work was a surprise for me. Moreover, the challenge was to find a 'gate-keeper' who would be willing to introduce and yet still allow for multiple forms of access to the diverse groups. One such gate-keeper was the local badminton club that managed the temporary shelter. The co-directors write that each programme and activity only began after consultation with local stakeholders, so as to create trust and multiple ownership: for instance, for evening screenings of films in the camp, an office-cum-socializing space was opened at the outskirts of the affected neighbourhood.

With 12 Baisakh, ArTree tried to capture traditional practices and places in order to restore faith in the future, and to use everyday practices and knowledge as social glue and sources of hope and belonging. Traditional gatherings to play devotional music (*bhajan*) were used as means of creating social events, such as the opening event of the group exhibition where a large evening concert with musicians seated in festively lit-up *patis* (arcaded platforms) attracted a large crowd of locals and visitors from other towns in the Valley. Potters, mask-makers, musicians, brick-makers, and knitters were invited to participate in the event, not only to use their skills as resources for regeneration and healing but also to present the rich Newar culture to outsiders.

Camp.Hub worked through a series of so-called hubs—meeting points for community-building, communication, play, and leisurely engagement located within and outside the Thulo Byasi area (Figures 13.12–13.13). These included temporary shelters and camps. ArTree aimed to create a different character for each hub, knowing that different sets of people would frequent them over the day with different expectations and experiences to be shared. Beyond instant humanitarian help, ArTree built up a multi-sited set of

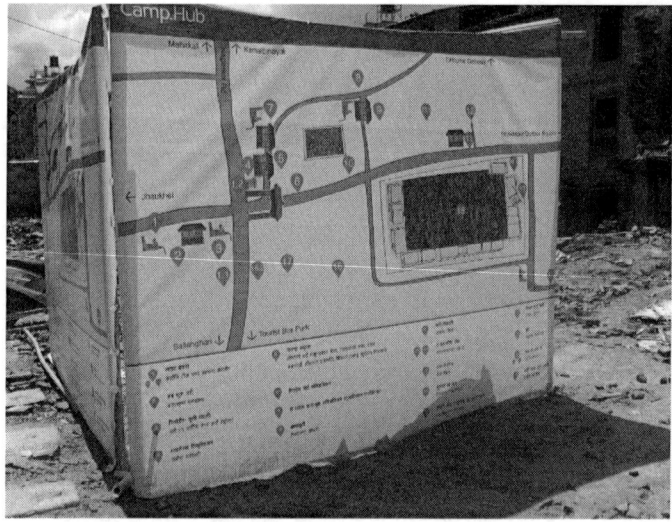

Figure 13.12 Wall showing the map of the Camp.Hub sites, Thulo Byasi, Bhaktapur, September 2015.

Source: Photograph by Christiane Brosius.

Figure 13.13 Camp.Hub site, September 2015.
Source: Photograph by Christiane Brosius.

diverse activities to engage with communities at different times of the day and for specific reasons. They roped in therapists for trauma-related work (mainly women), an anthropologist to consult artists on research-based methods, and an educator to develop didactic tools for engaging women and children in activities such as story-telling and informal learning. In this way, Camp.Hub became a 'shared space', with places for reciprocal exchange and learning from and with each other.[4] Harles and Rajbhandari

---

4   Handouts were compiled to help artists who wanted to work with Camp.Hub to familiarize themselves with basic organizational skills. In July 2015, a manual helped artists to reflect upon the concepts, methodology, materiality, and aesthetics of their project, following a University of Kansas overview of community-based public research (ArTree Nepal 2016: 20–21). Artists were even asked to write a progress report (handout 2 August 2019, by Nischal Oli). Preparations for the multi-sited community art project began with three weeks of artistic research, community meetings, and a deadline for final concepts. One month was provided

claim that 'vernacular heritage' played a central role as a 'form of belonging, of attachment to place, expressed through the daily rituals, memories and community life' (2017: 387). A handout on research methodologies was prepared by the anthropologist Abhas Rajopadhyaya who offered a three-hour workshop on how to develop a research-based art project that seriously considered community contexts, such as the Newar 'water life-cycle'—how rituals connect with a pond and everyday life in a neighbourhood—and included instruction on how to conduct interviews (ArTree Nepal 2016: 27–30). In this way, the community would be engaged in something familiar, whilst outsiders' knowledge of Newar rituals could be enriched.

ArTree faced not only practical obstacles such as flooding of the tents during the monsoon rains, a lack of toilets, and hygiene issues, but also incidences of depression and domestic violence. To translate their status as strangers into that of companions was one of the biggest challenges, as ArTree members have stressed in my interviews with them. These 'strangers' from the neighbouring city also became aware of the fact that a rural community such as Thulo Byasi worked differently from their own: not only was its Newari dialect so different that even Newars from Kathmandu or Lalitpur had difficulties in understanding it, but its lifestyles were also distinct and there was a certain suspicion of outsiders.

ArTree Nepal produced a report on the 12 Baisakh project which included local feedback. Some local people were appreciative of 12 Baisakh's activities and the fact that the team of activists did not just parachute in and drop goods or help build infrastructure without engaging more deeply. One local teacher is quoted as saying, 'You people came before the government officials, you did lots of programs … you stayed in the community all day long, from morning to night. Unlike people from other organisations you stayed with us, ate the same food we ate' (ArTree Nepal 2016: 7). Another resident appreciated that

we did new things together, it helped us to shift our focus, to forget our grief. It created excitement among us, also we learned a lot. You transformed our earthquake affected place and made it more delightful. Lots of people came to visit Byasi. I was part of Basibyalo project. I felt very strange to express my sad story and look at myself

for the production of the work, and a week in September for the installation of the art works, with the exhibition opening on 18 September 2015.

but later everybody praised me, they said everybody has their own pain, you have yours, and you share it with others and this technique of sharing is very interesting.... Byasi became popular because of the project. (ArTree Nepal 2016: 8)

The Basibyalo project that is referred to here was an installation by artist Subas Tamang from the ArTree collective, who called it 'Basibyalo: A Sharing Space'. The installation dealt with a public arcaded resthouse (New. *phalcha*, Nep. *pati*) in which three people were killed when it collapsed during the earthquake. Tamang's art intervention was to video-record oral histories with local people and exhibit these in the remains of that site. Tamang's hope was that this would not only encourage interaction in public space and raise a sense of collective ownership and belonging in the community, but also encourage community members to stay in Thulo Byasi. He also built a makeshift *phalcha* in the temporary tent camp so that people had a place to hang out and talk to each other or just relax away from the sometimes crowded, dark, hot, and uncomfortable shelters. In conversations, and through his participant observation, Tamang found that other people would avoid being indoors because they feared another earthquake or strong aftershock, and that many felt lonely and isolated. The building of familiar and open places was an initiative to provide recreation resources to people who were suffering from stress and trauma: 'Familiar places have now become faraway memories that incite anxiety and fear among people.... Camp.Hub aims to function as a memory plane where people feel comfortable and artworks reflect healing processes' (from *Camp. Hub Handout*). Here, cultural heritage and the built environment came to be seen as crucial pillars of social resilience and urban regeneration, a process of creating common wealth.

The community art project did not automatically turn strangers into friends. But it facilitated a key aspiration of ArTree Nepal's underlying agenda: to learn more about the society that is still a stranger to itself, because so many groups operate in compartments shaped by ethnicity, caste, or region. The 12 Baisakh report states:

We had come as outsiders attempting to understand their plight and help them. We had to build an intimate relationship with the community even if it meant repeating our motives and our work to many individuals. They knew very little or nothing about art or the Nepali contemporary arts scene. (ArTree Nepal 2016: 4)

Rajbhandari reflects on another aspect of relief work, that of emotional attachment: 'We have built such a deep relationship and it is difficult to leave and go, it is almost like a family.'[5] She also remarks that the local women had not known each other well before; they hardly used the streets, and there were not many reasons to spend free time together, if indeed there was such time at all. There was also substantial competition among them for access to resources. The post-disaster context had opened up space for new social relations to be tied and strengthened.

Besides Sanjeev Maharjan's installation 'Stories from Thulo Byasi', which consisted of over a dozen oral histories of the earthquake event and photographs of the interlocutors, and Subas Tamang's work, some other community art projects should also be mentioned. For 'Vadakuti' (Dolls' House), ArTree member Lavkant Chaudhary mentored children's art productions over several months, engaging them in making dolls' houses and learning how to make paper clay figures from a local mask-maker. In the dolls' houses, the children then restaged scenes from what they remembered from the time the earthquakes struck, thus enabling them to articulate what they would otherwise possibly not be able to express, and to engage in a creative and intimate process of self-reflection and indirect dialogue. ArTree member Mekh Limbu gave several children aged between 8 and 12 sketchbooks and asked them to draw and tell their stories. The volunteers working with 12 Baisakh found that children were particularly affected by the earthquake. With their schools closed and parents and other adults engaged in harvesting or reconstruction work, children were often left alone to themselves with hardly any opportunity to articulate their needs and feelings. 12 Baisakh tried to use engagement not just for regeneration but also for informal learning.

In the context of the Camp.Hub exhibition project, ArTree co-founder Sheelasha Rajbhandari engaged with women from Thulo Byasi who had previously earned their living as home-based workers producing knitwear for the tourism and export industries. These women, aged from their late teens to their mid-forties, had suffered a loss of income (because many workshops had closed down after the earthquake) as well as depression or loneliness. Rajbhandari wanted to tap into knitting as a resource for personal and social regeneration, pride, and creativity. By bringing 10 women together on a daily basis and encouraging them to knit their own portraits, the artist

5   Personal communication, September 2015.

learned about their everyday conditions as well as opened up a space for them to socialize (Figures 13.14 and 13.15). According to Rajbhandari's artist statement on this project, 'having them use an existing skill for a new purpose engaged them and helped them cope with the stress of managing a household in the aftermath of the quake' (ArTree Nepal 2018). For several weeks over the summer, Rajbhandari met with these women in a shelter located in a courtyard of demolished houses.[6] To portray themselves on the basis of a digital photograph (with one stitch for each pixel) was challenging for many, and required them to overcome a certain shyness. Increasingly, and especially during the exhibition in Thulo Byasi, they experienced an attention that placed them in a new light, something that also went beyond the immediate disaster context: it gave them a new position and recognition in a predominantly conservative patriarchal society.[7] Rajbhandari had used the same format of collaborative craftsmanship-cum-story-telling in an earlier community art project in south India in 2014. There she had worked with embroiderers and women from a factory producing sanitary pads. The pads were quilted onto a large embroidered and figurative work. In the Bhaktapur case, the empowering practice of collaborative art production and the sharing of otherwise often tabooized emotions, such as longing or (in the Bhaktapur case) mourning the losses from the earthquake, were relevant. Over the course of the project weeks, Rajbhandari was able to learn about the working conditions and labour networks the women were involved in. For some time, a psychotherapist was also invited to join the sessions and listen to the women's narratives. The women were encouraged to think of themselves as creative producers, to perceive their work as something that could be shaped and even improvised by them. One of the participants stated:

> After doing it [knitting] I felt that whatever I was feeling inside, I could express it, and I felt good. The things that I was unable to tell anyone and it felt like [once] I had spoken to someone I was more

---

6   Most of the women from the neighbourhood had to move to temporary shelters around a water tank, and had to cope with very basic living conditions, sometimes sharing a room with other families. In September 2015, some of them had still not been able to return to their damaged houses to gather some of their belongings, says Rajbhandari (personal communication, September 2015).

7   Rajbhandari, personal communication, September 2015.

Figure 13.14 Exhibition space from 'Weaving the Story of My Heart',
collaborative project by Sheelasha Rajbhandari, 2015.
Source: Photograph by Mekh Limbu, ArTree.

relaxed.... I was just angry. The earthquake had just struck and
wherever you looked you saw dead and injured people lying around,
blood, and then black because black is dark.

One local of Thulo Byasi adds: 'I am really happy because I made something
that I had never thought of. I am proud that I can make my own face
[laughs]. It is like you make all these hats and you don't know where they
go'[8] (see Figure 13.14).

Artists such as Limbu, Tamang, and Rajbhandari signalled the
potential of coping with a personally and collectively traumatic experience
in a new way. They devised new forms of articulating emotions through
the creation of safe and open spaces for meeting, such as the *phalcha* in
the camp or the knitting workshop in a shelter. This also provided the
necessary time and attention for exchanges and did not further position
the survivors as victims, but rather as human agents. The fact that the

---

[8]   Personal communication, September 2019.

Figure 13.15 Sheelasha Rajbhandari, co-director and curator of Camp.Hub (*third from right*), with women who participated in the community-based project 'Weaving the Story of My Heart', September 2015.

Source: Photograph by Christiane Brosius.

members of ArTree were outsiders meant that trust had to be gained: this required time and patience, and in some cases it failed. But it also created the possibility of ignoring certain otherwise restrictive social boundaries, such as caste, or family conflicts, and introducing new formats for social engagement and articulation that opened up the residents of the Thulo Byasi neighbourhood to each other in new and unanticipated ways. Words were found where silence would have dominated; mourning was allowed where it is often stigmatized as inappropriate.

So the post-earthquake context also opened up space for new social relations. Social encounters came to the fore and working on the event primarily meant working on the idea of community and society, on creating social ties. The ArTree artivists' focus on heritage as a cultural and social resource emphasized working on an event: using it as a moment of reflection about what is possibly at risk and what can still be prevented from disappearing. Heritage was not seen as something static that can just be handed on, but as a discursive and dynamic form of knowledge production too (Labadi and Logan 2016; Hall 2007). The aim was to see this not only as a particular group's property, or something that must be protected and conserved, but also as something that could be shared and used to generate something new, possibly even with new stakeholders. That cultural heritage as a process can help to facilitate social relations across communities is one of the major results that emerged from this initiative. This underlines the fact that the earthquake and its aftermath triggered new energies for co-production as a process of managing social and cultural resources (see also Lekakis, Shakya, and Kostakis 2018: 2).

Taking the event beyond time and space

The final part of this chapter focuses briefly on two interrelated issues with respect to the artists working on the event and also the ways in which the event impacted the art works and their circulation in the long run. They allow us to contemplate how a disaster lives on, not only in often less articulated personal and group memories but also in art works and exhibition formats.

Nepal's English-language news media paid some attention to the artistic responses to the earthquake, underlining the social engagement of artists with respect to Rebuilding Bungamati or Camp.Hub.[9] Local responses to the earthquake also featured centrally in the International Photo Kathmandu festivals of 2015, 2016, and 2018. Some coverage of artists' activities appeared in international news media. Camp.Hub received some attention from abroad because of its compact format of combining long-term community- and research-based art activities in Bhaktapur with public outreach, with its conceptual narrative and good visibility. Hitman Gurung and Sheelasha Rajbhandari were invited to Seoul city to visit South Korea in September 2015 to report on their experiences of using art for conflict and crisis management in traumatized localities; they also presented their project in Jakarta in November 2015 and at the Dhaka Art Summit in 2020.

---

[9]   See Pande (2016) and Kunwar (2015a, 2015b); S. Bhattarai (2018b). Coverage of contemporary artists seemed less frequent in Nepali newspapers, which requires more exploration elsewhere.

Some art works created in the context of these post-disaster community activities received international attention. Rajbhandari exhibited the collaborative work 'Weaving the Story of My Heart' at the India Art Fair 2016, initiated and curated by the late Dina Bangdel. The same work also travelled to Denmark in 2016, along with Sanjeev Maharjan's installation wall 'Stories from Thulo Byasi' in the exhibition 'Nepal: Parallel Realities', curated by Sangeeta Thapa and Ditte Seeberg at the Moesgaard Museum (Figures 13.16a and b). Tamang and Maharjan were invited to partake in a workshop on oral history with their works from Camp.Hub in Bangalore, India, 2016. In 2019, Hitman Gurung's large post-earthquake canvas 'We Are in War without Enemies' from the series 'This Is My Home, My Land, and My Country...' was exhibited at 'Nepal Art Now', the largest modern and contemporary Nepal art exhibition organized outside Nepal to date, at the Worldmuseum in Vienna, Austria. Thus, the 2015 earthquakes still impact on the artists, both in their works and other activities, even though the community projects have ended. The earthquakes became a theme and a lens through which some artists continued to reflect on their role in society. In 'We Are in War without Enemies', Gurung shows a man with a bandaged face (to render him anonymous, vulnerable, and mute), holding a colour photograph of the house he has lost—the photo memory stands out in front of the main canvas which is painted in black–white–grey. The backdrop consists of dozens of small photographs taken by the artist and his friends, some downloaded from the internet, showing the earthquake landscape in 2015: 'The work is a critical commentary on [the] Nepal government's hypocritical behaviour as well as those involved in the rebuilding and resettlement process', reads the artist's statement (Artree Nepal 2016: 54). Gurung responds to the fact that despite the USD 4.4 billion pledged to the Government of Nepal as relief and rebuilding funds, thousands of families were still living in temporary shelters even after 2016. The work is dedicated to the earthquake survivors who lost their homes and family members in the earthquake (Figure 13.17).[10]

---

[10] I cannot elaborate further here on other artists' important contributions to the post-earthquake situation, but want to mention at least Sunita Maharjan's Earthquake Series (2016) where she responds to the earthquakes' impact on residential structures in the media of acrylic and charcoal on canvas, of print and stitching on fabric, or photo montage. The work is a combination of personal experiences and a community art project in Gatlang, outside the Kathmandu Valley, both related to the earthquakes.

Figure 13.16a Installation of Sheelasha Rajbhandari's community-based project from Camp.Hub, at Moesgaard Museum, Aarhus, Denmark, September 2016.

Source: From ArTree Facebook page.

Figure 13.16b Sanjeev Maharjan's Stories from Thulo Byasi: wall reconstruction at the exhibition 'Parallel Realities' in Moesgaard Museum, Aarhus, Denmark, September 2016.

Source: From Facebook posting by Sanjeev Maharjan.

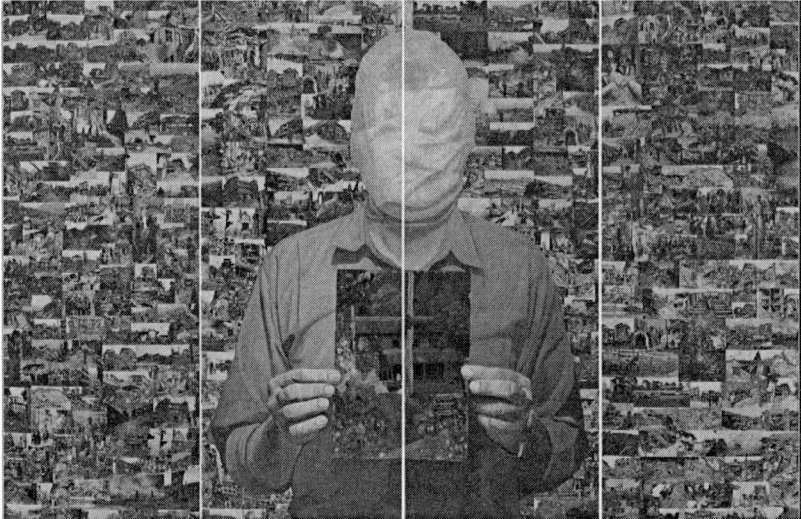

Figure 13.17 Hitman Gurung, 'We Are in War without enemies' (2016), from the series 'This Is My Home, My Land and My Country....' Stippling drawing on printed canvas, acrylic on canvas, 239 × 360 cm, 4 panels. Collection of Prem Prabhat Gurung.

Source: Courtesy of Artree Nepal.

Conclusion

A disaster such as an earthquake possesses a certain gravitation and non-linear temporality that is registered by artists in very diverse thematic ways, both political and personal.

In Maharjan's work, we can sense the enormous impact of the earthquake in the increased intensity and vulnerability of what it means to belong to a place, a neighbourhood, a civil society in the making, even if only in a person's imagination. We see it in the precariousness of life in a city with an uneven commitment to urban planning, and in the anxieties of fate and faith in a cityscape that has been radically transformed and made unhomely. Morever, there is an effort to trace what is at loss, excavate what could be overlooked in the turmoil of the aftermath, and hurried ventures of saving lives and giving relief. This ephemeral intangibility of everyday heritage is possibly one of the most revealing scales of artistic work in this case.

As I wrote in our 2017 volume (Brosius and Mahajan 2017),

> Maharjan's photographs, taken in the aftermath of the great earthquake of 2015, are withdrawn, cautious, humble, and sometimes even soothing messengers of what almost seems to be a 'normal world' in the midst of the catastrophe. Despite being an event that was heightened visually in, and digested through, global news media, Maharjan's work allows for—or even demands—other perspectives and positionings to challenge habitual ways of seeing, to reposition our scope so as to re-engage on a human scale. Maharjan's photographs return us to the street, to the everyday, to ordinary people and the lived reality of their lives. (Brosius 2017a: 109)

The urban archive that speaks through the series documents a fragmented society (with the neighbourhood and family as the gravitational centre), a city torn apart by different lifestyles and temporalities. In this scattered landscape, Maharjan sees cultural heritage as a social resource, for both continuity and innovation.

12 Baisakh and Camp.Hub's activities ask how a collective can contribute to alleviating the suffering and ruptures caused by an event such as an earthquake, how participation and co-production can be nourished, and how a local neighbourhood can find shelter and relief. Beyond the particular site, ArTree Nepal attempts to connect and contribute to society, to help shape a rooted and yet open society that keeps its Newar identity and prevents essentialized, ethno-chauvinist, and nationalist narratives from taking over. This enormous tension, crystallized by and through the earthquake's aftermath, surfaced centrally and yet retained an unsolvable asymmetry. The safe space created by the community art projects can thus be but a temporary moment in a larger field of becoming, sustaining, and aspiring. The firm belief, of ArTree and others, however, in the constructive force of sharing and debating, of challenging and working on social and political challenges—against all odds—is what the earthquake also triggered and further contained. The earthquake as art is certainly not *l'art pour l'art* and romanticizing beautification: it is a courageous inquiry into art's burden of representation and the artist's agentive role in the contemporary fabric of aesthetic formation in Nepal.

14

Gathering Absences and Presences

Memory Work, Photographs, and Affective Recovery in the Langtang Valley*

Austin Lord and *Jennifer Bradley*

Presences, Absences, Images

It was raining outside. We huddled under one umbrella and used a flashlight as we walked toward Pasang Dhindup's temporary post-earthquake 'home'. He opened the door, pulled out a water

* We are deeply grateful to the many people from the Langtangpa community who have participated in, contributed to, and supported the work of the Langtang Memory Project. We would especially like to thank Gyalpo Lama, Tsering Lama, Lhakpa Jangba, Norcho Lama, Temba Lama, Damjo Tamang, and Suppa Lama for their contributions and support. We also thank the many volunteers who have helped us, especially Nathaniel and Amanda Needham, Prasiit Sthapit, Jay Macmillan, Brigid McAuliffe and Patti Bonnet, Simon Ingall and Rhea Garen, Bob and Vera Bonnet, Sagar Chhetri, Johanna Fricke, Nima Pambar Tamang, and NayanTara Gurung Kakshapati. Thanks are also due to the many people around the world who have contributed photographs and other materials to the Langtang Memory Project archive. Our work with the Langtang Memory Project was financially supported by Engaged Cornell, the Falcon Fund, Friends of Nepal, the Firebird Foundation, We Help Nepal, the families of Sidney Schumacher and Bailey Meola, a digitization grant from the Cornell University Library, and a Lemelson Fellowship from the Society for Visual Anthropology. We are grateful for guidance, feedback, and comments from Kathryn March, Sienna Craig, Christopher Pinney, Caroline Heldman, Lucinda Ramberg, and the editors of this volume, as well as insights gained from other scholars who have worked in Langtang, such as Ayako Sadakane, Colleen McVeigh, and Francis Khek Gee Lim. We are also both thankful for the support of our families, who have loved and encouraged us throughout this process.

bottle of petrol, and we walked back to the newly-built community hall in Langtang Village. Inside were about twenty Langtangpas, almost all of them over forty years old, like most of the people living in Langtang these days. We filled the generator with petrol and the projector switched on, filling the white bed sheet we had attached to the wall with light.

The first image flickered to life: a photo of a young girl holding a wooden pail of water with a small black dog sitting at her feet. 'Di pomo su yin pa?' [Who is this young girl?] Everyone huddled together, pointing and discussing who she might be. Amongst their chatter in the local dialect of Tibetan, some questions in Nepali began to emerge, directed at me. 'When was this photo taken?' I explained that a Peace Corps Volunteer had taken the photo in the early 1960s. They shifted back to speaking in the Langtang language as I clicked through the images. 'How did you get all these photos...?' someone asked. I explained our project again.

We had been gathering photos from foreigners for about a year at that point, working with a handful of younger Langtangpa collaborators and keeping the broader community abreast of our progress. But this was the first time we had brought these images back to the Langtang Valley. We had been patient, waiting for the right time. Now it seemed that these projections had made this project more real to the older Langtangpas. We went through fifty images about three times that first evening. The Langtangpas were looking at the past with nostalgic eyes.

Before that night, I hadn't seen many people from the Langtangpa community wanting to look back into the past in this way. Their minds were focused on other things, especially rebuilding their homes. But now these photos seemed to help them see beyond the painful memories of the past two years since the earthquake. Everything about these photos recalled a more distant past: the Langtang of their parents and grandparents; a past that didn't hurt so much to look at.

The next morning, one of the older women stopped me on the village trail and said: 'Aja pheri dekhaunu, hai?' [Show us again tonight,

Figure 14.1 Photographs of Langtang village before and after the avalanche of 25 April 2015.

Source: Photographs by David Breashears.

okay?] Each night for the next several nights, following the evening meal, we reviewed the same photographs, again and again. (Field notes, Jennifer Bradley, Langtang, May 2017)

In the wake of the 25 April 2015 earthquake, the people of the Langtang Valley have had to navigate a damaged landscape full of absences and presences. When the earthquake struck, it triggered a massive co-seismic avalanche that buried Langtang, the ancestral village at the centre of the Langtang Valley (Figure 14.1). This disaster within a disaster was the deadliest and single most-destructive event caused by the earthquake: more than 300 people lost their lives, including 176 Langtangpas.[1] Every single

---

[1] The avalanche began 3,000 metres above the village on the southwest slopes of Langtang Lirung (7,234 metres) and it released a blast that carried more than half

one of the 485 surviving members of the Langtangpa community lost someone close to them. Now, almost five years after the disaster, the people of Langtang are still working to cope with the immensity of this tragedy and its uncertain legacies. They seek to recover a sense of normality within a present that can often seem unlivable, remembering and forgetting, while reckoning a variety of differently imagined pasts and possible futures.

In this chapter, we consider some of the social and cultural dynamics that shape processes of affective recovery within the Langtangpa community, focusing on the different kinds of memory work—understood as uneven processes of remembering and forgetting, of gathering and organizing absences and presences—that accompany other processes of resettlement, reconstruction, and recovery in Langtang. Because a village is not just a collection of buildings, post-disaster recovery in Langtang requires far more than physical reconstruction and material processes of repair. While doing this, we foreground two Langtangpa concepts—*sempa tserah* and *kipu sho*—which are affective sensibilities central to the ways in which Langtangpas think about recovery. The former is a way of talking about senses of loss and absence, and the latter is a way of inviting happiness and well-being back into their lives. Connecting these two concepts with anthropological scholarship that focuses on memory in the aftermath of disaster (Oliver-Smith 1986; Fortun 2001; Simpson 2013; Gordillo 2014; Barrios 2017), we show how memory work is an embodied process that shapes the very idea of post-disaster recovery.

Our analysis draws on more than three years of archival and ethnographic work with the Langtang Memory Project—a collaborative archival initiative we co-founded with a small group of Langtangpas in early 2016, which focuses on building a 'living archive' that can help honour, conserve, and sustain Langtangpa culture and heritage.[2] Working together

---

the force of the Hiroshima atomic bomb when it struck the valley floor (Kargel et al. 2016; Fujita et al. 2017). Though avalanches do occur regularly in the Langtang Valley (Lim 2008; Soden and Lord 2018), this particular avalanche was an event of a different magnitude—in fact, it was one of the deadliest avalanches in recorded history, globally.

[2] While the Langtang Memory Project is similar in some ways to other community-engaged archival projects initiated in the wake of disasters, such as Hurricane Katrina, the 2010 Haiti earthquake, or Japan's 3/11 disaster, our objectives and work processes are organized in ways that are highly specific to the tragedy that

Figure 14.2 The authors together with some of their Langtangpa collaborators and co-curators—*left to right*: Norcho Lama, Temba Lama, Ngawang Dorje Chusang, Austin Lord, Tsering Lama, Gyalpo Lama, and Jennifer Bradley—at the opening of a multimedia exhibition organized and collectively curated by the Langtang Memory Project (Kathmandu, October 2018).
Source: Photograph: The Langtang Memory Project.

with Langtangpa friends and collaborators over the past few years, we have collected tens of thousands of photographs of Langtang from around the world; digitized thousands of Langtangpa family photos; recorded a diverse array of interviews and oral histories with Langtangpas from different walks of life; organized visual storytelling workshops and trainings for Langtangpa colleagues; created two documentary films focused on post-earthquake rejuvenation; and curated multimedia exhibitions within and beyond Langtang (Figure 14.2).[3] Through working on this project, we are

occurred in the Langtang Valley and the particular qualities of its aftermath. Importantly, at all times, we work in ways that are appropriate for and respectful of the sociocultural contours of Langtangpa society, as well as the needs, desires, and sensitivities of the differently positioned Langtangpa community members and collaborators with whom we work.

3   At the time of writing, our team from the Langtang Memory Project is also working to design, build, and curate a Langtang Memory and Heritage Center, which we plan to begin constructing in Langtang village in the Spring of 2020.

constantly learning about the different ways that Langtangpas access, recall, respond to, and reconfigure memories, as well as how memory work can help people reorient themselves in relation to a shifting array of pasts, presents, and futures.

Like other Nepali communities that have struggled to rebuild and recover, the Langtangpa want to 'show that community and belonging, dignity and humanity, have not been buried under the rubble' (Brosius 2017a: 116). For this reason, the collective work of the Langtang Memory Project also focuses on creating new spaces and platforms where Langtangpas can tell their own stories—part of a broader effort to destabilize, complicate, and counter the simplistic narratives of disaster and aftermath that circulated in the wake of the 2015 earthquakes—often 'single stories' (Adichie 2009) that portray people like the Langtangpas as victims with limited agency. Because we seek to build an archive that exceeds and expands beyond the temporality of disaster, most of our work focuses on understanding broader patterns of continuity and change, rather than on the tragedies that occurred in April 2015, and on helping the Langtangpa community create a resource for future generations. Ultimately, the Langtang Memory Project is perhaps best understood as an open-ended intergenerational dialogue organized around a recurring question: What kinds of stories are Langtangpas interested in telling about their pasts, presents, and futures—and for whom?

Building upon our ongoing archival work, we examine the different ways in which photographs and other images are implicated in memory work within the Langtangpa community, as well as the ways in which these practices are shifting over time. To do this, we draw upon the work of scholars who have highlighted the materiality and social lives of images (for instance, Pinney 1997, 2004; C. Harris 2004; Azoulay 2008; Edwards 2012) or inquired into the ways that photographs and other visual media facilitate uneven acts of remembering and forgetting (for example, Edwards and Hart 2004; Kuhn and McAllister 2006; Sandbye 2014). Here, we show how Langtangpas have used photographs to reorient and relocate themselves in a variety of ways: to restore visual and symbolic order in newly rebuilt homes; to reaffirm certain values and identity claims; to recall and reconnect with the lives and deeds of those who have departed the living world; to reconfigure narratives about the disaster and its aftermath; to recreate their own visual histories that re-present Langtang to a variety of different audiences; and to evoke or re-enact social or cultural continuities that are critical within broader processes of affective recovery.

Focusing on Nepali artists' responses to the 2015 earthquakes in the Kathmandu Valley, Christiane Brosius has suggested that 'photography related to a catastrophe like an earthquake is work *on* the event itself' (Brosius 2017a: 114). In the Langtang Valley, where the material traces of disaster remain inescapably and overwhelmingly present and where the Langtangpas must reckon with absence and loss on an everyday basis, doing memory work with photographs is a means of working on an event that has not yet truly ended. In this chapter we consider the ways in which memory work with photographs articulates with other forms of memory work, including culturally specific approaches to processing grief and sorrow, as well as how hope, though uncertain, emerges for the Langtangpas in the wake of disaster.[4] By gathering—people and images, absences and presences, in many different ways—again and again in the wake of disaster, the Langtangpas are slowly reweaving the frayed threads of memories, histories, and personal narratives in ways that allow life to go on, so that something more hopeful remains.

Living with *sempa tserah* and *kipu sho*

The convoluted relationship between remembering and forgetting becomes increasingly complicated in the wake of a disaster, and central within conversations about recovery and aftermath.[5] While remembrance can serve as a means of re-enacting identities, cultural continuities, and a kind of hopefulness in the face of despair (Benjamin 1969; Oliver-Smith 1986; Lear 2006; Solnit 2016), remembering certain events, patterns, and people can also sometimes lead to suffering, grief, and hopelessness. Forgetting, either consciously or unconsciously, can also bring despair, anxiety, and anguish

---

4   Here we understand hope as a precarious and affective orientation that focuses on the possibilities of the 'not yet' or the 'yet to be' (Bloch 1986), and as a method for knowing uncertainties that can help to prevent the closure of imagined futures (Miyazaki 2004; Lear 2006; Solnit 2016).

5   Scholars of disaster have repeatedly highlighted the role that remembrance and memorialization play in the context of affective recovery, and the ways that invocations of different pasts shape patterns of post-disaster recovery (Oliver-Smith 1986; Hoffman 1999; Barrios 2017) as well as the politics and unevenness of memory (Fortun 2001; Hastrup 2011; Simpson 2013; Gordillo 2014).

(Solnit 2016), but in the wake of disaster or trauma, selective amnesia and forgetting can also emerge as a strategy for recovery, or as a source of hope (Fortun 2001; Connerton 2008; Simpson 2013). Patterns of remembering and forgetting shift over time, as aftermaths continue to unfold.

Over the course of our work with the Langtang Memory Project, the Langtangpas have repeatedly highlighted two significant concepts that speak to recurring tensions between remembering and forgetting, between longing for the past and moving forward: *sempa tserah* and *kipu sho*. In this section, we examine the ways that Langtangpas conceptualize these two often co-arising feelings, as they attempt to remember and forget. For the Langtangpas, affective recovery requires striking a balance: slowly coming to terms with *sempa tserah*, while inviting *kipu* back into their lives.

Sempa tserah

Sempa tserah is a phrase that people use to talk about feelings of unsettledness and helplessness, and, in this case, a sense of disorientation. From a linguistic perspective, *sempa tserah* is an articulation of one's *sem* or 'heart-mind' being in an unsettled or disturbed state, *tserah*. The Langtangpas experience visual and psychological confrontations of this feeling daily: while waking up and seeing the avalanche zone; while looking at photographs of deceased family members; while wanting to share experiences and talk with friends who have passed away. Tsering Lama, a young Langtangpa woman who is part of the Langtang Memory Project, described this feeling as a sense that 'something is missing'. She explains:

> The people of Langtang, after the earthquake, they use these words a lot.… It means that your heart and your state of mind—or you, yourself—are not in a good state. Now, in these days, the people we love are no longer with us. You want to meet them, but you cannot. They are still here in our hearts but they are not here in person. We lost a lot. When we think about it, it's *sempa tserah*. You miss them, you want to talk to them, you want to see them, but you cannot do that. It's *sempa tserah*. You can do nothing about it. You can do nothing.

While individuals and family groups may have experienced other states of unsettledness and uncertainty before, this feeling has never been so collectively experienced, so pervasive, or so enduring. These days the Langtangpas are faced with a constant sense of *sempa tserah*. Perhaps the ubiquity of *tserah* can be understood best through the words of Yangjen Tamang, a middle-aged Langtangpa woman who has resumed living in Langtang village:

> Before, our *gumba*s [temples] used to be really sacred. We even renovated Langtang Gumba because it was very old. But it was after not even one year that it was destroyed by the major earthquake. We never imagined in our dreams that this would happen. Now there is still no gumba in Langtang and when we look at the destroyed gumba, *tserah*. When we look at the new houses, *tserah*, because we don't see the traditional houses anymore. When we look at the people, they are so much fewer now, *tserah*. Now there is only *tserah* … there is nothing but *tserah*. There is not a time when we don't feel *tserah*. We lost so many things and when we remember this, it's *tserah*. But we cannot sit only with *tserah*; we have to move on.

Yangjen's words, and her rhythmic use of the word *tserah*, speak to the ways that this sense of being unsettled recurs in the everyday experiences of those Langtangpas who have resettled in the Langtang Valley since the 25 April earthquake. This account communicates the ways that mundane encounters with persons, places, and things that call innumerable absences to mind can generate feelings of *sempa tserah*.

However, while feelings of *sempa tserah* seem to be common within the Langtangpa community, people sense and experience this feeling unevenly and in different ways. Elders who have spent most of their lives in Langtang, for example, often experience the most acute sense of disorientation and absence. Langtang had already changed so much in recent years with the coming of tourism, and the earthquake made their birth villages almost unrecognizable. At the same time, many Langtangpa youths studying in Kathmandu also feel anxious about being too distant or removed from Langtang, about returning to a childhood home that is now gone or no longer as it once was—especially if one or both of their parents died during the earthquake. When they do return during school breaks, their sense of disorientation is very strong. Both older and younger Langtangpas are fearful that future generations will not know how things in Langtang once were.

Kipu sho

In the Langtang dialect of Tibetan, *kipu* is a term that means happiness, well-being, joy, or 'the good life' (Lim 2008), and *sho* is an invitation, a welcome in the imperative tense. In the aftermath of the earthquake, and especially after the conclusion of a three-year period of collective mourning (see later), many Langtangpas are now focused on inviting happiness back into their lives, and so they say *kipu sho*. This phrase functions as both a way of remembering 'the good life' and a call to rejuvenate the Langtang Valley; it demonstrates the ways that the Langtangpas conceptualize the possibility of affective recovery. Our colleague Tsering described this feeling as follows:

> In Langtang, there is a saying that if we cry after someone's death, then their spirit will feel bad. But when we are happy, they are also happy. We want *kipu* to come back to us. We want happiness once again to come back to us.... Maybe people will never be happy and satisfied like before but if they can make Langtang better now, it will benefit the young generations and coming generations.

Inviting *kipu* back is a particular kind of memory work: a practice of re-enactment that attempts to draw the best from the past, rebuilding community well-being, and maintaining Langtangpa traditions. However, as Lim (2008) has shown, Langtangpa concepts of *kipu* or 'the good life' have also changed in the past, and have been reimagined in response to social, economic, and cultural shifts. These days, intensive patterns of educational out-migration are also shifting Langtangpa lifepaths and aspirations, as they are in other parts of the Nepal Himalaya. Above all else, the Langtangpas are hoping for a better life for their children, away from and beyond the suffering caused by the earthquake. But while many Langtangpas are beginning to invite *kipu* into their lives, they are also not entirely sure what this new *kipu* will look like.

These days people locate *kipu* in houses being rebuilt and babies being born, in the reconstruction of the *gumba* or the re-establishment of yak herds, in wedding ceremonies conducted in the traditional style where people can gather to dance and sing again. The photographs of loved ones that people keep on their altars carry the possibility of *kipu* as does reprinting and hanging old photographs in the newly rebuilt community centre, because they remind people of the good times and help evoke a sense of cultural continuity. Whereas *kipu* was typically defined in opposition to material scarcity and hardship in the past (Lim 2008), in the wake of the disaster *kipu* is often conceptualized in opposition to the unsettled state of *sempa tserah*.

Welcoming *kipu* back is an active process of remembering which infuses a variety of individual and communal efforts to re-inhabit the landscape of Langtang. Some work to repair and rebuild community infrastructures, while others seek to restore frayed relations with local territorial deities. Elders commit themselves to their prayers, while urban Langtangpas create youth groups and YouTube channels dedicated to Langtangpa culture. As several Langtangpas have told us, in different ways: 'We can't just sit and cry or be sad all the time. We need to rebuild Langtang and remember our traditions.' While the ways in which Langtangpas conceptualize heritage are also in flux, many of these efforts seem to be imbued with a strong sense of a unique Langtangpa identity. Many people are looking to the past for guidance on what 'the good life' might be.

Living between sempa tserah *and* kipu sho

In the aftermath of the earthquake, the Langtangpas are constantly shifting back and forth between the grief and unrest of *sempa tserah* and the hopefulness of *kipu sho*—as is evident in this quote from our friend and collaborator Tsering Lama:

> Now you can see the progress after three years.... Even though people are having hard times, people are starting to sing, dance, they are starting to enjoy their life. They want to enjoy their life but they can't fully because they have grief in their heart. And they don't want this identity to get lost; they don't want their culture, traditions, their songs, their dance to get lost.... But we have to look at the present and move on with our life, do what we can do to preserve the humanity, preserve the compassion, preserve the culture, and preserve what we have left of us.

Several other Langtangpas have also described the affective intensities felt during community events. One described the anticipation and anxiety he felt before a major festival: 'I know that it will be great, and many people will be dancing. But this year will also be very hard, because we will look around and remember all the faces that we cannot see, those people who are missing.'

Many Langtangpas also describe feeling both *kipu* and *sempa tserah* when looking at the newly rebuilt guesthouses in Langtang—spaces that are both Langtangpa homes and the centre of local tourism-based economies (Lim 2008). There is *kipu* in the knowledge that each person now has shelter and a livelihood again, and some comfort comes from seeing most of their villages rebuilt after years of struggle. But *sempa tserah* also returns when the Langtangpas look at the design of these new guesthouses: the blue tin roofs, the plain concrete interiors, the lack of traditional wooden window carvings and places to keep animals. During the third anniversary of the 25 April earthquake, one of the Langtangpa leaders composed a poem called 'Sempa Tserah' that lamented the many changes brought by the earthquake, the avalanche, and the process of reconstruction. For the Langtangpas, living in a place filled by absences and presences also means living with, and sometimes in between, these two sensibilities.

Retaining and relinquishing: memory work in the wake of disaster

Memory work is a constant process of reconfiguration and reorientation that implies a layered conversation between multiple pasts and presents, as well as an array of differently intentional practices of remembering and forgetting. Scholarship focused on memory commonly highlights its manifold, uneven, and relational nature. Memory requires a variety of overlapping and imperfect processes of interpretation, inscription, consolidation, recall, contextualization, reinterpretation, and re-inscription that are socially, culturally, and spatially contoured (cf. Benjamin 1969; Casey 1987; Connerton 1989; Boyarin 1994; Ricouer 2000; Tortell, Turin, and Young 2018). As a way of locating oneself in social, spatial, and temporal contexts that are forever shifted or shifting, memory work is a significant part of the perpetual and multi-sensorial processes by which we re-organize meaning and identity.

In this section we outline and briefly describe a few of the ways in which the Langtangpas have used different kinds of memory work to reorient, recuperate, and sustain themselves in the face of intense dislocation and recurring disorientation. Memory work, undertaken individually and collectively, can also help with facing or avoiding trauma by moving certain memories to the foreground, shifting others into the background, and reworking narratives into more manageable forms (cf. Oliver-Smith 1986; Casey 1987; Connerton 2008; Simpson 2013). Struggling to move forward with their lives in a landscape marked by tragedy and overwhelming loss, the Langtangpas want to forget some things, but they are fearful of forgetting others.

In the immediate wake of the disaster, the Langtangpas had to perform a kind of memory work that was almost unthinkable: after being evacuated to Kathmandu, they had to conduct the funerary rites for 176 of their people. As per Tibetan Buddhist traditions, these funerary rites focused on generating virtue or *ghewa* that would help guide the souls of the deceased Langtangpas through an in-between realm of the afterlife called the *bardo* and toward fortunate rebirths (Childs 2004; Desjarlais 2016). These ceremonies, modified to account for the mass nature of the deaths in Langtang, required an intensely focused presence. Forty-nine days after the earthquake, the space of the Yellow Gomba, where the people of Langtang were living in a tent camp, was filled with dozens of chanting monks, rows of women seated on the ground in the heat, singing and sobbing, and hundreds of well-wishers (Lord 2015). This collective form of memory work was both a highly intentioned act of remembering and honouring the good deeds of the dead and an important part of the difficult process of letting them go (Figure 14.3).

Writing about death and dying in Nepal's Hyolmo communities, Robert Desjarlais has suggested that *ghewa* ceremonies and other funerary rites serve as a way of modulating grief, sorrow, and attachment by helping create 'a patterned scaffold of memories that moves people away from recalling the deceased in dangerously disruptive ways' (Desjarlai 2016: 226). Importantly, while this ceremonial process reflects Buddhist principles of impermanence and non-attachment, the goal is not to forget the dead entirely. Instead, the point is to remember *differently*: to reconfigure relations between the living and the dead in ways that help to resolve and dissolve the pain that comes with attachment. These deeply social rituals, which gather and refocus intention and energy, help people to 'retain, yet relinquish' (Desjarlais 2016: 227) in the wake of death.

In the aftermath of an unthinkable disaster, when the Langtangpas were both overcome with grief and struggling to make 'a good death' possible for their loved ones, these funerary rites, both traditional and unprecedented,

Figure 14.3 Langtangpas gathered in Kathmandu 49 days after the earthquake for a *ghewa* ceremony, marking the end of traditional funerary rites practised in Langtang.

Source: Photograph by Austin Lord.

were both the first stage in a long and uncertain process of affective recovery and a critical source of hope.

After the earthquake, the Langtangpas decided to collectively observe a three-year period of mourning that Langtangpas have often translated as a time of 'condolences'—an extension and intensification of traditional practices of mourning modified to account for the scale and intensity of mass death. This period of formalized remembrance was oriented around recognizing and honouring absence. During this time, the community did not engage in singing, dancing, or celebration of any kind. The Langtangpas also constructed a variety of commemorative structures in the Langtang landscape: most significantly a 'memorial stupa' in the upper valley near the recently reconstructed monastery at Kyangjin Gompa, and a 'memorial wall' built at the edge of the avalanche zone in Langtang village. Each year, according to the Tibetan calendar, the Langtangpas held a *puja* led by local *lamas*, lighting butter lamps, changing the prayer flags, and praying that the souls of their loved ones would find peace in their new lives.

In the summer of 2018 when the official period of mourning ended, the people of Langtang gathered for Dukpa Tse Shi, which many people hopefully referred to as 'a time for singing again'. Our team from the Langtang Memory Project worked to document these celebrations and to make a short film about this moment of transition—a gathering that embodied the rising sensibility of *kipu sho*, and an attempt to combat feelings of *sempa tserah* by rejuvenating this landscape. This was a deeply hopeful moment. But, at the same time, going back and remembering those who are gone was often extremely challenging. As the following field note, written as we travelled back to the Langtang Valley to make this film with a group of Langtangpa collaborators and friends, shows, embodied encounters with the absences that fill the Langtang Valley can bring forth unsettling waves of memories for everyone:

Coming back to Langtang is always hard, but walking up here again with Gyalpo and Tsering has been extremely emotional. This morning, Tsering was excited, telling us how happy she was about coming back up for Dukpa Tse Shi again, but she broke down crying when we walked through the ruins of the small settlement at Chyamki—the place where her parents died, where her home used to be. Gyalpo [who also lost both his parents during the earthquake], put his arm around her and spoke to her quietly as they walked, offering comfort and trying to help her keep moving. These small acts of kindness, solidarity, and strength in the face of overwhelming grief amaze me.

Just half an hour later we reached the main avalanche zone at Langtang village, and we walked once more across the field of debris that overwhelms the landscape—a massive and inescapable presence that speaks of so many absences. We crossed a stream flowing underneath a bridge made of rubble and compacted ice. Even three years later, the avalanche was still there, still melting....

Gyalpo told us that he tries not to think about anything when he walks through this place, that he resists the urge to locate himself or recall what this space once was. Though once before he had also pointed out a fragment of blue concrete amidst the rubble to Jennifer, saying: 'this is where my house used to be … my mother's body is maybe still lying under here somewhere'. When I cross the avalanche zone I can't help but remember his home, the way it was when I slept there the night before the earthquake. I can't imagine the way he might feel coming back here.

Reaching the edge of the debris field, where the grass begins again, we met the 'memorial wall' [a modified kind of *mani* wall inscribed with the names of all those who died in Langtang on 25 April 2015]. It was built for the one-year anniversary of the earthquake—a time when hundreds of Langtangpas, other survivors like me, family members of the many foreigners who died, and various supporters from around the world gathered together here for various acts of commemoration. I ran my hands across the prayer wheels embedded in the wall, remembering some of the words spoken during that ceremony.

Just behind the wall a group of workers were reconstructing a chorten that the lamas say was first built about five hundred years ago. Further afield, people were rebuilding their houses. Poles with new, long, white prayer flags raised just a few weeks before during the puja that marked the third anniversary of the earthquake flapped in the afternoon wind. On one end of the wall, the names of the dead were becoming faint and hard to read, after being exposed to more than two years of wind and rain. (Field notes, Austin Lord, Langtang, July 2018)

In the wake of disaster, in Langtang as elsewhere, memory work becomes a way of coping with rupture, restoring and reconfiguring the myriad connections that make social worlds, and helping us to respond to dislocation and disorientation. For the Langtangpas, funerary rites, the work of building memorials, restoring or renewing sites of cultural heritage, building archives, returning for festivals like Dukpa Tse Shi, or simply telling stories, emerges as a form of 'repair work' that 'fills in the moment of hope and fear in which bridges from old worlds to new worlds are built, and the continuity of order, value, and meaning gets woven, one tenuous thread at a time' (S. J. Jackson 2014: 223). As a critical complement to other reconstruction and recovery efforts, memory work (both remembering and forgetting) helps

Langtangpas to restore and re-animate fractured landscapes, rejuvenate social relations, and re-affirm their sense of sovereignty and place. Memory work becomes a way of reshaping the absences that fill their lives, while also reaffirming presences.

Haptic recoveries: emplacing photographs

In the wake of disaster, the work of recovering or collecting photographs and reorganizing them as archives frequently emerges as a practical and haptic mode of memory work that can support the processes of affective recovery (cf. Creighton 2015; Hastrup 2011; Liboiron 2015). In Langtang, photographs have also become an important medium for doing memory work, both before and after the 2015 disaster. Everyone hangs photographs of loved ones in their homes, and many people have salvaged photographs from the rubble and re-hung them in their newly rebuilt homes. Looking at people's photos on their phones, alone or clustered together in small groups, is also a favourite way to 'timepass'. In the wake of the earthquake, people also interact with photographs of the deceased on a regular basis: putting butter *tika* on the foreheads of people in photographs; placing scarves around framed family photographs; or just looking back at the photos near their puja altars while lighting butter lamps and pouring out cups of water for the gods during the morning prayer. Following an intense period of displacement and a struggle to return to Langtang, resituating photographs in the context of new homes and socialities is a significant act of *re-emplacement* for many Langtangpas.

Underlining the material and haptic qualities of photographs, the visual anthropologist Elizabeth Edwards has highlighted the embodied act of 'placing' images, suggesting that 'photographs are not merely surrogates for the absent, but powerful actants in social space intertwined with a larger process of maintaining different forms of sociality and personhood' (2012: 229). In Langtang, re-placing photographs is a way of re-establishing a symbolic visual and material order which carries significant cultural meaning, as it does in many other culturally Tibetan societies (C. Harris 2004).[6] In the

---

6   Tibetan Buddhist communities organize photographs, icons, and other images in ways that adhere to spatial hierarchies which place images of revered persons, places, or things at a greater height—a praxis-based system that indicates how

wake of disaster, reassembling images of deceased family members, children who are off studying elsewhere, religious leaders, pilgrimages to places like Bodhgaya, and other family photos is also an important form of memory work and a component of affective recovery. In a very material sense, this is a way of gathering and organizing presences and absences.

'Noree Didi, do you have any old photos from before the earthquake?' I asked in Nepali. Noree's automatic answer, like many other residents of Langtang Village, was no. All of the old photographs had been destroyed, along with her home, during the earthquake. I said that was okay. As we sat in her new guesthouse drinking tea, I talked to her about our archival project. Her young son whizzed past us, playing with a broken protractor and some ripped pages from a notebook.

While I was talking, Noree said something to the young girl who works in her guesthouse. The girl started rummaging around, looking through bags and inside of cabinets throughout the kitchen. Eventually she found something. Noree knelt down and pulled out a small plastic bag from a container on the floor. Inside the bag were nine photos. Noree smiled at me and asked if this was what I was asking for. We looked through the photos together. There was a photo of Noree's father from about twenty years earlier, photos of Noree with foreign guests, and a photo of Noree's son when he was still a small baby. We were both excited as we viewed the photos.

I finished the last of my tea and set the cup aside. 'Cha thung' (drink tea), Noree encouraged me again. It had become dark, so I thanked Noree for searching for the photos and explained to her that I would come back in the morning with our scanner to incorporate her photos in the community archive.

The next morning, I packed the scanner into my backpack and walked to Noree's guesthouse again. Walking in, I didn't see the plastic bag from the night before anywhere, and I was worried the photos may have been tucked away again. Noree asked me to follow her into the dining area where guests eat. Each of the photos that Noree had

---

'the materiality of photography is of the essence' within culturally Tibetan communities (C. Harris 2004: 143).

shown me the night before was displayed, tucked into the wooden framings of the walls. I smiled, pulled out the scanner, and began the work. (Field notes, Jennifer Bradley, Langtang, May 2017)

Over the past few years, we have scanned several thousand photographs from the personal and family collections that Langtangpas keep—as loose photos, stacks of prints, or in family albums. Several visual anthropologists have described the ways that domestic photographic collections can speak to broader processes of self-representation, identity formation, and cultural narratives (Edwards 2005; Pinney 1997; Sandbye 2014). Similarly, in our work with the Langtang Memory Project, we recognize the layers of meaning inherent within these collections and we take careful note of the ways in which Langtangpas have chosen to represent themselves and their families so that our archive, to the greatest extent possible, can help Langtangpas to be seen in the ways they want to be seen.

As the vignette above shows, our working process is organized around the kind of interactions that create new photographic events, understood as moments of entanglement that follow the 'photographed event' and facilitate processes of re-interpretation, continually reconfiguring relations between photographs, subjects, photographers, and viewers (Azoulay 2008). By reclaiming, reorganizing, recontextualizing, and recirculating photographs—be it a landscape photo taken by a tourist decades ago or a recent portrait taken by a Langtangpa youth—our work allows photographs to take on new meanings. Importantly, looking at photographs together is also an invitation to sit down and tell stories, which often makes another wave of photographic events possible.

Handling photographs is also very important in Langtang, to the extent that one of the most significant contributions of the Langtang Memory Project might just be simply locating old photographs and physically bringing them back. Several scholars of photography have highlighted the importance of touch and the sociocultural complexities of our haptic or embodied engagements with photographs (Pinney 2004; Pink 2006; Edwards 2012). The haptic experience of photographs is all the more important in a place where bringing anything up to villages located above 3,000 metres requires effort and signals intention. Of the countless tourists and foreigners who have visited and photographed Langtang over the years, only a small percentage have actually brought back copies of their photographs, despite frequent promises to do so. Further, in the wake of the earthquake, when so many

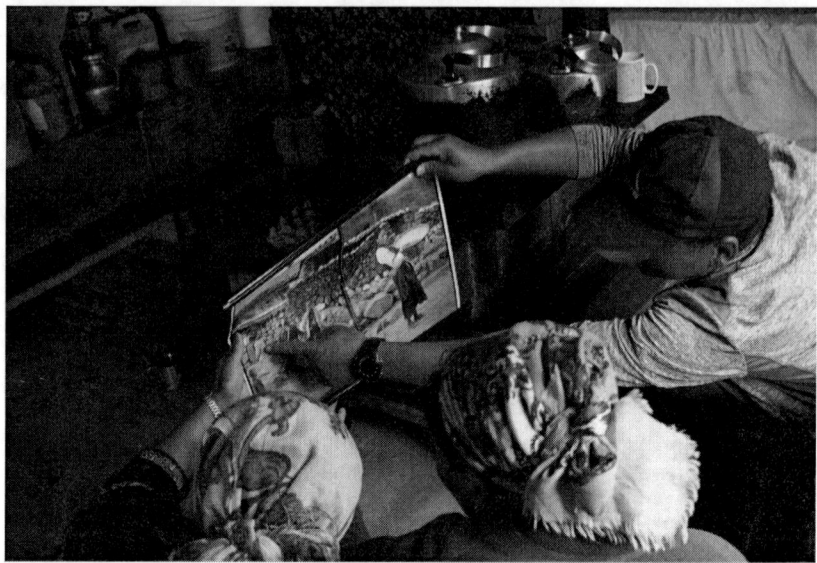

Figure 14.4 Friends in Langtang telling stories while handling a series of old photographs that we helped collect and return to the community.

Source: Photograph by Austin Lord.

Langtangpas' photographs were damaged and lost, many people in Langtang are grateful to have physical photographic objects to place in their homes (Figure 14.4). As Margaret Olin suggests in *Touching Photographs*, 'vision and touch are interchangeable in lived experience' and 'touching photographs can help us reach those who are distant or gone from our lives' (2012: 9).

Despite this, engaging with photographs is not always easy for the Langtangpas. Sometimes in the course of everyday life, while working with us or while flipping through photographs online, people encounter images that bring up a tumult of emotions, much like encountering traces of absence in the material landscape. Some are interested in looking at photographs of the past; others are not yet able to do so. Yangjen Tamang once told us:

> When we look at the old photos, we feel like these people are still with us. When we look at the old videos, when they are singing and dancing, it feels like they are still alive. But after the video is finished, we look around and we don't see these people and all the memories of these people come flooding into our minds....

Yangjen's reactions to these visual records of people who are absent reveal how *kipu* and *sempa tserah* often surface together. In this way, Yangjen is speaking to the sentiment that forgetting, or avoiding these visual representations at times, can also be helpful. Because we are deeply aware of these sensitivities, we always proceed slowly and cautiously with archival work in Langtang; indeed, shifting our methods and objectives in relation to people's different sensitivities is a critical part of our working process.[7] That said, these feelings are different for each Langtangpa, and not all images of the past stir negative emotions or painful attachment.

Over the past few years, we have also witnessed people's feelings change over time. Some days they want to see photographs and videos, and other days they do not. Many Langtangpas find comfort in photographs of a more distant past, long before the earthquake, images that evoke a sense of heritage and belonging. Recent images are often more fraught. While working with her own family photographs during one of the exhibitions we collectively curated through the Langtang Memory Project, Tsering described the complicated emotions she feels when she looks at photographs of her own parents, who passed away in the earthquake:

> Seeing these pictures, I feel happy and sad at the same time. I feel sad because they are no more with me. And I feel happy because they are still in the photographs. They are still with me in my heart....You think about them a lot when you look at the photos, when you look at the videos, when you talk to someone, when you go to a certain place. You keep reminiscing them, you remember them.... We can remember them, we will keep them in our heart. We will keep them safe, their memories safe.

The swirling emotions evident in Yangjen and Tsering's descriptions connect to inexorable questions about the temporalities of photography and photographs which can bring our pasts into the present, creating memento mori that 'testify to time's relentless melt' (Sontag 2001: 21). While looking at

---

7   Importantly, as the opening story mentions, we waited until almost two years after the disaster to truly begin the grounded phase of our archival work, though we had already been working within the Langtangpa community on several other issues related to disaster relief, camp management, recovery, and reconstruction of Langtang (see Lord and Murton 2017).

photographs of the deceased can sometimes 'wound' the viewer in different ways (Barthes 1981), this feeling is usually just one of many reactions—and the meanings that we attach to these scars are often a powerful affective force that can also rejuvenate and motivate us. For Langtangpas, photographs are both a reminder of the nature of impermanence and an invocation of alternative temporalities that exceed the disaster. They are a key technology for cultivating a sense of place and being in the world, while finding ways to 'retain, yet relinquish' (Desjarlais 2016: 227) in the aftermath of an unthinkable event.

For many Langtangpas, the material and affective labour of working with and re-placing photographs—identifying people and places, retelling stories, recontextualizing moments within multiple pasts—is also a way of reaffirming values and naming or organizing priorities for the present. By reconfiguring relations with and through photographs, the Langtangpas are both 'working on the event' (Brosius 2017a; this volume) that occurred in Langtang during the 2015 earthquake, and reworking connections between pasts and futures that are both constantly being reimagined.

Remembering differently: the politics of memory and representation

What is promised by remembering differently? The change mobilized by remembrance can be difficult to see. But it operates, reshaping what we think is possible, necessary, and good. A disaster can become a prism....

—Kim Fortun (2001: 354)

Remembering, which always operates on multiple registers, can also be a highly political act. In the wake of a crisis or disaster, powerful voices often propagate hegemonic narratives of these events that facilitate processes of selective remembering or structural amnesia (Boyarin 1994; Connerton 2008; Hastrup 2011; Simpson 2013; Gordillo 2014), bring about false closures (Oliver-Smith 1986; Das 1995), or reduce accounts of human tragedies to a series of statistics that silence other narratives (Liboiron 2015; Soden and Lord 2018). Similarly, popular media coverage of disasters often merely facilitates the short-term consumption of a disaster and its 'suffering subjects' in a frenzied attention economy (Sontag 2003;

Lord and Murton 2017). Alternative narratives of disaster and differently configured archives are needed to counter these trends, to fill the silences in official data and histories of disaster with diverse and systematically excluded voices.

In this sense, our work with the Langtang Memory Project is also a political commitment in that we actively seek to destabilize, complicate, and reconfigure dominant 'single stories' (Adichie 2009) that present the Langtangpas simply as 'earthquake victims' and to re-present the Langtangpas as a diverse group of people with agency. In the wake of the 2015 earthquakes, Langtangpa community members have been frustrated by solipsistic media coverage of the disaster, and repeatedly expressed a desire to 'let the world know that Langtang is not gone'. With the Langtang Memory Project, we are helping to create both an alternative archive that exceeds the disaster and new narrative platforms where Langtangpas can foreground their own stories of disaster, aftermath, recovery, and the future of the Langtang Valley. We seek to remember differently.

Practically, creating an archive focused explicitly on Langtang and its cultural heritage also requires us to gather photographs from around the world and bring them back to Langtang, where we ask our Langtangpa collaborators how they would like to repurpose, reinterpret, and re-present these images. We see this as an act of 'visual repatriation' that allows the Langtangpas to use 'photographs as foci for telling stories and claiming histories' (Edwards 2012: 229) on their own terms. This kind of re-presentation can also help de-centre visual histories shaped by chronic patterns of social exclusion and hierarchies of access (Onta 1998; Nepal Picture Library 2018) and counter the effects of a persistent orientalizing gaze that seeks to find and depict 'timeless Himalayan others' (Adams 1997; Lim 2008; C. Harris 2012).

Further, as part of a broader project effort to create discursive space for indigenous media (cf. Ginsburg 1994), the Langtang Memory Project archive actively seeks to foreground photographs and videos made by the Langtangpas themselves. To this end, we have gathered resources and tools for Langtangpas interested in photography and visual storytelling, and we have organized and collaboratively curated a variety of exhibitions that highlight the work of Langtangpa photographers, both in Nepal and

Figure 14.5 Tsering Lama (*centre*), our co-curator and co-filmmaker, sitting with two Langtangpa women during the Dukpa Tse Shi festival in July 2018.

Source: Photograph by Austin Lord.

elsewhere.[8] Like William Lempert (2018), we believe that such community-driven media projects can generate hope with communities affected by disasters to reclaim damaged pasts and presents, and help re-envision clouded futures. In no uncertain terms, we feel it is important that Langtangpas are now holding the camera rather than having it pointed at them, and we are committed to creating spaces where the Langtangpas can be seen in the ways they want to be seen (Figure 14.5).

Perhaps most importantly, the slow and careful work of the Langtang Memory Project is animated by a strong belief that creating a living archive will be of value to future generations of Langtangpas, and others around the world. As our close friend and collaborator Gyalpo Lama once said in the early stages of the Langtang Memory Project: 'We are now passing through

[8] We have featured the work of Langtangpa photographers in a variety of exhibitions—in Langtang Village, in the cafes of Boudhanath and the Taragaon Museum in Kathmandu, at the Hood Museum of Art at Dartmouth College, and at the Photo Kathmandu festival. More co-curated exhibitions are planned for the future.

this incident, so if we share what happened to us and what we did, by making photographs and writing stories, then I think people will learn something from us.'

Hopeful gatherings

Over the past five years, the Langtangpas have worked hard to reorient themselves and to revitalize the Langtang Valley—to bring presence to a landscape filled with absences. In the aftermath of the 2015 disaster, memory work has emerged as several different things: a technique of sense-making in response to intense disorientation; a way of metabolizing individual or collective grief; a technology of repair; a way of enacting cultural continuities; and a means of envisioning possible futures. Gatherings, of many kinds, have become an essential part of these collective healing processes. Gathering, even though some people will be absent. Gathering, even though the landscape has changed and the traditional houses are no longer here. Gathering, despite pervasive senses of *sempa tserah*. Gathering to preserve culture, to sing and dance, and to work collectively to invite *kipu* back in. Gathering presences and absences. Gathering, again and again.

In the end, the central goal of the Langtang Memory Project is also to facilitate a series of gatherings: of images and archival materials; of Langtangpas from the different generations; of ideas about the past and the future; of energy and attention. As researchers working across difference and as two people whose lives and heart-minds have become woven into Langtangpa social worlds, we too gather, slowly and carefully. Because memory work is a recursive and adaptive process of gathering, our working process must also be a recursive and adaptive form of gathering.

Memory work in the aftermath of a disaster can be a deeply uncertain, troubling process *and* it can be a hopeful process of reorientation. Often it is both. As Edward Simpson writes toward the end of his book about the 2001 Gujarat earthquake and its aftermath: 'Earthquakes are remembered, but in other ways they are forgotten; occasionally, forgetting and remembering touch one another' (2013: 263). Over the past several years, our friends and interlocutors from Langtang have repeatedly described the ways that feelings of loss and absence mix with their efforts to honour certain memories or welcome happiness back into their lives—the ways they live with co-arising feelings of *tserah* and *kipu*.

Patterns of remembering and forgetting, themselves a continuous gathering of presences and absences, continue to change as the aftermath continues to unfold. Our work with the Langtang Memory Project continues, changing as patterns and practices of memory work within the Langtangpa community shift over time. Life goes on within and through gatherings.

15

Bhukampa

Nepali Recitations of an Earthquake Aftermath*

Michael Hutt

Poetry comes nearer to vital truth than history.
—Ralph Waldo Emerson[1]

Introduction

This is a discussion of the local literary response to the 7.8 magnitude earthquake that struck the central hills of Nepal on Saturday, 25 April 2015 and the series of lesser earthquakes and aftershocks that followed—an aspect of this disaster that remains almost totally unstudied.[2]

After a disaster strikes, it is inevitable that disaster themes will dominate not only the news media content but also the literary production of the affected society for a period of time. As a contemporary reviewer of the great Lisbon earthquake of 1755 remarked:

---

* This chapter is based on research conducted as a part of the project 'After the Earth's Violent Sway: The Tangible and Intangible Legacies of a Natural Disaster' funded by the UK's Global Challenges Research Fund through the Arts and Humanities Research Council; grant number AH/P003648/1. My thanks go to Peshal Acharya, Govinda Raj Bhattarai, Biyogi Budhathoki, Claire Cox, Aidan Seale Feldman, Birkha Kranti, Mani Lohani, Francesca Orsini, Shyam Rimal, Shri Om Shrestha 'Rodan', Abhi Subedi, Gita Tripathi, and two anonymous reviewers of an earlier draft. All errors of emphasis, interpretation, and translation are of course my own.

[1] Orth (1966: 173*n*308) describes Emerson's famous aphorism as an 'amalgamation' of statements made by Aristotle and Plato.

[2] Gandhiraj Kaphle quotes from a small selection of Nepali earthquake poems in a chapter of his 2016 volume (Kaphle 2016: 72–89).

> Earthquakes are great plagues, as illuminated by the great quantity
> of bad writing that they produce in all parts from the ground and
> over which in recent years many a press has sighed. (Wilke 2017)

Of course, there will be major differences between the aftermaths of two disasters that were geographically and temporally so far apart. For instance, while Nepal's domestic news media were dominated by the earthquakes and their aftermath for many weeks, and the disaster was also reported on extensively in international news media, word of the Lisbon disaster took weeks even to reach other European capitals (Wilke 2017). But in certain other respects there are striking similarities. In Nepal, as in Portugal, a huge number of narrative accounts, opinion pieces, and more literary reflections on the earthquakes and their impact appeared during the early months of the aftermath. These texts, produced mostly in Nepali, but also in English and in other languages of Nepal, circulated nationally in print and globally online, via social media, and on platforms such as YouTube.

The local literature of a disaster aftermath not only sheds light on individual and personal responses to the disaster but also provides insights into the public mood of the aftermath and the terms of its political, cultural, and social discourse—the 'endogenous response', that is, which Albala-Bertrand (1993:23) argues has been overlooked or disregarded in most writings on disaster response. The content and tone of this literature raises a number of interesting questions. For instance: What is the relationship between a post-disaster literary outpouring and the broader 'endogenous response' to a disaster? How does this literature help us to distinguish the endogenous response from the 'exogenous' response that, according to Albala-Bertrand and others, dominates writing about disasters? Do the two discourses of response speak to one another, or are they conducted in isolation from one another? What might an analysis of the literary articulations of an endogenous response to a disaster tell us about the structure of public space within a disaster-affected society, laid bare as it may be by the chaos of the aftermath? Should we investigate not only what these voices say, but also to whom they belong, and where they are located?

To arrive at firm answers to such questions in the Nepali context, it would be necessary to survey and analyse the whole of Nepal's output of earthquake aftermath literature. Unfortunately, such a task would require a small, multilingual army of researchers. The quantity of textual production in the Nepali language is considerable: seven national daily newspapers, four weekly news magazines, dozens of literary journals, and approximately 600 books published each year.[3] And of the more than 100 languages recognized by Nepal's constitution, Newar, Tamang, Gurung, and several other minority languages are spoken by large populations in the most severely earthquake-affected districts. The Newar language has a developed formal literature of its own, while Tamang and Gurung are rich in oral literature, some of which has been committed to print.

Given the large quantity of close reading required, I decided to focus on a single genre (poetry) published in Nepal's dominant literary language (Nepali) for the purposes of this discussion. I chose poetry because verse was until quite recently the default genre for writing in Nepali, and because poetry has reflected patterns of social and political change and provided inspiration for political movements in Nepal since at least the early 20th century. Moreover, poems and lyrics are forms that can be produced more quickly and spontaneously than other literary genres. They are likely to appear in the public sphere, whether on paper or online, more immediately than essays or works of fiction, especially when they represent responses to a specific event.[4] The continued currency of a public belief in the power of poetry in Nepal was evident in the early aftermath of the 25 April 2015 earthquake, when Radio Nepal repeatedly broadcast Robin Sharma's recording of the song 'Kun Mandirma Janchau Yatri?' (Which Temple Will You Visit, Pilgrim?), based on the celebrated poem 'Yatri' (Pilgrim) by Nepal's greatest poet, Lakshmiprasad Devkota.[5] The message of this poem, beloved to generations of Nepalis, is that a temple is not merely a building, it is also a place in a person's heart. The choice of song was probably intended to console the many people, particularly members of the older generation, who had lost the temples and shrines at which they worshipped and attended rituals.

---

[3] Shri Om Shrestha 'Rodan', then editor of *Madhuparka*, personal communication, Kathmandu, 13 November 2017.

[4] For an interesting discussion of the political role of song and poetry in Nepal, see Subba (2073 v.s.).

[5] Aidan Seale Feldman, personal communication, Amsterdam, 22 March 2018. On YouTube, Robin Sharma's rendition of this song against the background of a photograph of the poet Devkota has been viewed over 3.5 million times. See https://www.youtube.com/watch?v=Gq4Ti4WQICA (accessed 29 January 2019).

Figure 15.1 The earthquake special
issue of *Madhuparka*
Source: Author's private collection.

Most of the poems that provide the basis for this discussion were
published in the *bhukampa visheshank* (special earthquake issues) of six
Kathmandu literary journals: *Madhupark* (Figure 15.1),[6] *Shabda Sanyojan*
(Figure 15.2),[7] *Shabdankur* (Figure 15.3),[8] *Dayitwa* (Figure 15.4),[9] *Kaushiki*
(Figure 15.5),[10] and *Kalashri*.[11] The sample also includes 15 poems published
in the first two post-earthquake issues of the Nepal Academy's quarterly

[6] *Madhuparka Mahabhukampa 2072 Visheshank, purnanka* 552, Jeth v.s. 2072
    (May–June 2015) (cited as *Madhuparka* hereafter).
[7] *Shabda Sanyojan Bhukampa Vishesh* 12(2), *purnanka* 133, Jeth v.s. 2072 (May–
    June 2015) (cited as *Shabda Sanyojan* hereafter).
[8] *Shabdankur Bhukampa Anubhuti Vishesh* 14(10), *purnanka* 166, Shravan v.s. 2072
    (July–August 2015) (cited as *Shabdankur* hereafter).
[9] *Dayitwa Mahabhukampa 2072 Visheshank, purnanka* 94, Jeth–Asar v.s. 2072
    (May/June–August/September 2015 (cited as *Dayitwa* hereafter).
[10] *Kaushiki* 25:1, *purnanka* 65, Baisakh–Jeth v.s. 2072 (April/May–May/June 2015)
    (cited as *Kaushiki* hereafter).
[11] *Kalashri Sahityik Varshik* 4(4), v.s. 2072 (2015/16). This annual publication contains
    a substantial section dedicated to earthquake poetry (cited as *Kalashri* hereafter).

Figure 15.2 The earthquake special issue of *Shabda Sanyojan*

Source: Author's private collection.

Figure 15.3 The earthquake special issue of *Shabdankur*

Source: Author's private collection.

Figure 15.4 The earthquake special issue of *Dayitwa*

Source: Author's private collection.

Figure 15.5 The earthquake special issue of *Kaushiki*

Source: Author's private collection.

Figure 15.6 The earthquake special issue of *Sahabhagita*

Source: Author's private collection.

Figure 15.7 The first post-earthquake issue of *Shivapuri Sandesh*

Source: Author's private collection.

poetry journal *Kavita*, three published in the special earthquake issue of *Sahabhagita*, the journal of NEPAN (Nepal Participatory Action Network) (Figure 15.6), four published in the first post-earthquake issue of the literary journal *Shivapuri Sandesh* (Figure 15.7), and thirteen published in the online journal *Setopati* during the first two months of the aftermath. Together this constitutes a corpus of 291 compositions by 256 poets.

Reciting the *bhukampa*

The main body of this chapter consists of a sample survey of this poetry, arranged thematically. However, before embarking upon this survey, I offer some tentative answers to the questions raised in my introduction.

Much of the poetry I will discuss below articulates anguish, grief, anger, guilt, and remorse, but also seeks to channel and turn these emotions into hope for the future and a determination to build Nepal anew. While this might seem at first glance to echo the externally generated discourse of 'building back better' which dominated the ensuing debates on reconstruction, it actually refers to much more than the concrete task of restoring the country's domestic housing stock.

It has already been noted in other contexts that a disaster may be constructed in quite different ways by those who suffer its impact directly and those who come to their aid from outside, and that the two perspectives may generate very different discourses. For instance, Bankoff and Borrinaga explain that the two designations of the major storm that struck the Philippines in late 2013 (the internationally designated 'Typhoon Haiyan' and the Filipino 'Typhoon Yolanda') came to represent 'two quite different discursive narratives about the typhoon and its aftermath':

Typhoon Haiyan is headline news that explains the storm in terms of climate change, freak storms (numerical calculation of risk), and poverty. Typhoon Yolanda, on the other hand, has a storyline to do with national politics, accusations of incompetence (national versus local), identity, and self worth. These very different narratives about blame and responsibility also lie at the heart of a fundamental difference in the way disasters are viewed from the standpoint of the developed and the developing worlds: to the former, the emphasis is now much more on resilience and people's capacity; to the latter, disasters are still very much about vulnerability and disentitlement. (Bankoff and Borrinaga 2016: 46)

As Anderson states in the introduction to his study of the literary mediation of Latin American disasters, 'each disaster engenders its own language, whose terms are often as symbolic as directly allusive' (2011: 7). While the international discourse on the Nepal disaster referred to it as the 'Gorkha Earthquake', after the district in which the epicentre of the first and biggest tremor was located, most of the Nepali-language discourse referred to it as the *bhukampa* or *maha* (great)-*bhukampa* of the year 2072 of the Bikram calendrical era.[12] Although 44 of Nepal's 75 districts were not deemed to have been directly affected by the earthquake, poets constructed it as a disaster on a national scale with very few references to specific localities. This mirrored the discourse of Nepal's political leaders who played up the national dimension of the disaster not only to maximize the quantity of incoming international aid but also to awaken the innate patriotism of Nepal's majority hill populations. Once mobilized, this provided them with a vehicle for the delivery of a long-awaited new constitution which largely denied the longstanding demands of the Madhesis of the plains (see Hutt 2020).

In many cases, this poetic mirroring of the national political discourse was intentional. In 2006, the Maoist-led 'People's War' had come to an end in a negotiated settlement, and in 2008 a Constituent Assembly had been tasked with agreeing to drafting a new national constitution, which it had signally failed to deliver. By the time the earthquake struck, the political forces that had dominated the early years of the constitutional debate, pursuing an agenda of social inclusion for marginalized minorities and of restructuring the state along lines of identity and ethnicity, were in retreat, and the earthquake provided further opportunity for their political opponents to represent their agenda as divisive.

Leo Lowenthal has argued that studies of the representation of society, state, or economy in the literature of a particular country or time contribute to our knowledge of 'the kind of perception which a specific social group—writers—has of specific social phenomena' and therefore

---

12 *Bhukampa* is a compound of *bhu*, 'the earth, land, ground' and *kampa*, 'trembling, tremor', which makes it very similar semiotically to the English word 'earthquake'.

to our knowledge of the 'history and sociology of shared consciousness' (1961: 143). In order to understand this intentional poetic mirroring of the post-disaster political discourse of national unity, it is necessary to locate and identify the voices, the 'specific social group', that gave it its poetic articulation. Of course, 'writers' constitute a tiny subset of any society, a subset which is not merely literate, but also literary—given to setting out its thoughts and reactions on paper or computer screens in the hope that they will be shared with others through publication and other forms of dissemination. As is almost always the case in Nepali-language literature, the voices of male authors from the politically and culturally hegemonic Khas-Arya segment of Nepal's population are most audible here: of the 256 poets whose work provides the basis for this discussion, only 38 appear from their names (and/or photos in the journals that include these) to be women, and there are only some 20 writers from indigenous minority (Adibasi Janajati) backgrounds. Support for a constitutional settlement that would maintain the dominance and hegemony of Nepal's higher castes, and of patriarchal social structures, will inevitably be found to be most prevalent among those who benefit from it. As Anderson observes in the Latin American context, 'the process of narrating the disaster mobilizes existing social and political power relations at the same time that it renegotiates them' (2011: 6–7).

It would also appear that the majority of these poems emanated from the capital valley of Kathmandu. The reason for this apparent underrepresentation of poets from the much more severely affected hill districts is not difficult to ascertain. In February 2018, I held roundtable discussions with writers and media workers in the towns of Charikot and Manthali, in the severely affected districts of Dolakha and Ramechhap. Literary organizations exist in most of Nepal's larger towns, and also spring up wherever Nepalis have settled in sufficient numbers in the diaspora, including in the West. The Charikot writers explained that their town had historically seen a high frequency of literary 'programmes' and that the earthquake of 25 April took place half way through a programme that many of them were attending. After the *bhukampa*, according to one,

> the literary programmes pretty much stopped.... This is not because writers were not mentally prepared to write. There was plenty of subject material, and there is an old saying (*ukti*) that writers write most when they are suffering. But the problem was that the writers

were also affected. They had to sort out their own internal affairs. Not just their own, but their children's, parents', wives', and husbands' etc. So they didn't have time to think.

Another writer explained that the house in which he was living had collapsed, burying and destroying his personal library. He then had to live for months in temporary accommodation, with five or six people sleeping in a single room. Several compared their experience of the earthquake with that of writers based in Kathmandu, where the level of damage to buildings and infrastructure and the loss of life were significantly lower:

> Their experience of the *bhukampa* was nothing more than a bit of shaking. But our experience was that we saw someone go inside a house to fetch a pot (*gagri*) and never come out again. It all happened in a single second. I was working on my laptop. If I hadn't run outside I'd have been lying there dead in a second.

Several of the Charikot and Manthali writers were contacted by Kathmandu-based editors, who invited them to contribute to the special journal issues they were assembling. But most felt unable to write in the circumstances and the journals were published without them.[13]

Many of these poetic echoes of the post-earthquake political discourse of national unity reflect a belief, prevalent among its largely high-caste, largely male authorship, that the drive to achieve a higher level of inclusivity for historically marginalized sections of the population represented a threat to their privileged position, which they cast as 'national unity'. However, others represented a political discourse that was quite radically opposed to this view. For these latter poets, the post-*bhukampa* 'new Nepal' of their dreams was one that would be built by 'the people', rejecting the erstwhile leaders who, in their perception, had not come to their aid in the aftermath. My sample includes a number of scathing political poems about the failure of the national political leadership, and visions of a society emerging from the disaster that would be more equal and more inclusive. There is of course no exact correlation between the caste, gender, and ethnicity of a poet and

---

[13] The roundtable discussions referred to here were held at Manthali on 3 February 2018 and at Charikot on 4 February 2018 and recorded with participants' permission.

the ideological thrust of his/her poem; nor does the content of every poem give clues to its author's political leanings. But these readings suggest that even if there existed a 'shared consciousness' of the aftermath of the 2015 earthquakes, this consciousness was variously nuanced. As a result, these texts had 'multiple, overlapping uses, from helping individuals to resolve traumatic experience to upholding explicit political platforms or challenging established political orders' (Anderson 2011: 191). For some, the disaster underlined a need for a national coming-together, at least of the affected hill populations, that would reaffirm the social and political order whose bases had come under sustained questioning since the end of Nepal's decade of lethal conflict. For others, national unity would serve the purpose of building a 'new Nepal' of greater equality and inclusion, in which a political leadership that was seen to have failed would have no role to play. For them, the earthquake was a social leveller, a 'socialist' (*samyavadi*) earthquake, in fact, affecting rich and poor alike. Now they would recognize their commonality and turn against those who had betrayed and misled them.

Some of this poetry speaks back to the exogenously generated response to the disaster. Nepal has a positive reputation worldwide as a place of spectacular natural beauty and cultural richness, and for periods of its history it has been the recipient of the world's highest per capita rates of development aid, not least because of its strategic location during the Cold War. Tourism, mountaineering, and (for the UK public at least) the Gurkha military tradition bestow upon Nepal an aura of deservingness, and this was reflected in a spectacularly generous international response, with international governments and donors pledging USD 4.4 billion to support the massive reconstruction effort. Some of the poetry considered here acknowledges this and expresses gratitude, but there are also some attacks on the mediatization and exploitation of the disaster, and implicitly on the notion that the Nepali people are 'resilient'. As Anderson writes:

> From the viewpoint of those who are affected, disaster cannot be addressed adequately from without, even when international aid and solidarity are involved in the disaster response. In this setting, academic narratives of disaster arising from broad, international scientific frameworks often have little weight in the political decision making surrounding disasters unless local narratives engage them to their own ends. Indeed, intellectual abstraction often becomes offensive for those who have suffered a disaster in the flesh. (2011: 192)

The analysis presented below is arranged thematically. Poetry does not lend itself easily to quantitative analysis, but I give some indication of the frequency with which a particular theme recurs within the sample. The discussion is illustrated with extracts from the poems under consideration, in my own English translation. Given the size of the corpus, it is possible to cite only a selection of poems as representative examples, and when choosing which poems to cite I allowed myself to be influenced by my own notions of literary quality. As far as possible, the discussion avoids what the Nepali poet Nasala Chitrakar (2017) might call 'The Obligatory Post-Earthquake Poems': those written by well-established poets who assumed that a poem was expected of them at such a time of crisis, and also knew that their poem would be published and widely read.

Theme one: poems of anguish and determination

A very large portion of the sample, probably more than half, consists of outpourings of anguish and sorrow at the destruction wrought by the *bhukampa*. These poems do not focus in any detail on particular instances of loss or destruction (though they will often list notable examples) but describe what happened to the country and population at large. Many (especially those composed in the traditional metrical forms) are straightforward narratives, almost mini-chronicles, which belie Cooley's (2014: 4) assertion that 'the poetry of disaster refuses chronology':

> In the year of two thousand and seventy two, on the twelfth day of Baisakh,
> There occurred a destructive *bhukampa* at about twelve o'clock,
> At the time of midday, on a Saturday,
> Everything fell down, just look, all in a single moment.[14]

Others make use of stock allegories and metaphors:

> A house was built with the earnings of a lifetime
> In just one moment the *bhukampa* made it a ruin.

---

[14] Devendra 'Amsu' Aryal, 'Aba Ke Ke Hola?' (What Things Will Happen Now?), *Dayitwa*, p. 120.

[It made] a labourer who worked day and night
Into a dependent who lived in the hope of others.

[It made] our fertile fields where grain would grow
Useless barren ground filled with holes.

The parting of one person's hair is empty, one person's lap is void
The *bhukampa* scattered families far and wide.[15]

Almost all of these narrative poems conclude with an exhortation to their readers to unite and rebuild, with a call to the nation to 'rise again', or with a statement of faith in the future. Nepalis should learn from Japan;[16] they should turn the challenge of the *bhukampa* into an opportunity;[17] they should stand shoulder to shoulder.[18] Nepalis are rich in spirit: they will cease fighting one another and engage in reconciliation, awaking to build a beautiful and peaceful country. Their political leaders will cease their infighting and unite to produce a constitution that will fill the land with peace.[19] The loss of loved ones, homes, and heritage buildings is greatly to be mourned, but all will be restored.[20]

Desire is expressed for the emotional unification of the nation:

And now
we have to see in the destroyed structure
a new dream,
and
we have to imagine
a new future,
and

---

[15]   *Sindur* (vermillion powder) is sprinkled into the parting of a Hindu woman's hair at her wedding; the absence of this powder signifies widowhood. Mohanmani Pokhrel, 'Gajal', *Dayitwa*, p. 108.

[16]   Kalpana Acharya, 'Ayo Bhukampa' (An Earthquake Has Come), *Dayitwa*, p. 107.

[17]   Ramkaji Kone, 'Muktak', *Madhuparka*, p. 34.

[18]   Thakur Sharma Bhandari, 'Mahabhukampa' (The Great Earthquake), *Dayitwa*, pp. 35–38.

[19]   Gokul Adhikari, 'Bhukampa' (Earthquake), *Dayitwa*, p. 123.

[20]   Jivnath Dhamala, 'Shraddhanjali' (Condolences), *Kaushiki*, pp. 8–9.

we have to draw the outline of a new Nepal[21]

and lines such as the following recur time and again throughout the sample:

samuhama bal huncha samuhama shakti
hami ek bhae milcha vipadbata mukti

In the collectivity there is strength, in the collectivity there is power,
If we unite we will be delivered from calamity.[22]

Normal daily life will resume, but an important lesson has been learned:

Now at last we have discovered
There will be nothing if we do not rely [on one another]
There will be no history, no geography
No politics, no literature
There will be only
The people....[23]

Ultimately, these poems take on the characteristics of a modernization or developmentalist narrative, envisioning a future of successful reconstruction by 'the people' for the nation.

Theme two: poems of witness

Particular instances of death, destruction, and personal and familial loss provide poets with subject matter. The recovery is described of a woman from the ruins of her home.[24] A set of lyrics purports to be the song inside

---

[21] L. B. Chetri, 'Akranta Nagariko Pida' (The Pain of an Assaulted City), *Kalashri*, pp. 346–48.

[22] Bhagavat Acharya, 'Git' (Song), *Shabda Sanyojan*, p. 55.

[23] Bimal Koirala, '… Tara Hamilai Desh Dukhiraheko Cha' ('… But the Country Is Hurting for Us'), *Kalashri*, pp. 336–37

[24] Nirajan Maudgalya, 'Bhagnavasheshbata Jhikieki Maiyadevi' (Maiyadevi, Pulled from the Ruins), *Dayitwa*, p. 109.

the hearts of 'ordinary Nepalis rendered homeless by the *bhukampa*'.[25] The ground trembles, houses collapse, people run, no one comes to assist, and the poet's eyes are so full of tears they are never empty no matter how long she weeps.[26] A man watches as his house collapses.[27] A lost house is described lovingly: built by a father with his bones, flesh, and blood, it had a roof of honour, windows of the mind, and stones of ideals, where swallows and sparrows built their nests. The country stands like a tree whose leaves have all fallen, but in the poet's mind there is a mountain of courage. Hands and arms are busy rebuilding every day, whether it be homes for people, gods, or animals.[28] God himself is seen 'weeping in a tent', and the *bhukampa* is roundly cursed and described as 'deceitful' (*jaali*) and 'dishonourable' (*beimaan*).[29]

Two of these poems were reprinted several times. In the first, a woman is described sitting in the ruins of her house 'stroking the fallen rocks and bricks single-mindedly', perhaps in search of her 'pregnant daughter/And her tiny grandsons and granddaughters'. Who was the most cruel, she wonders: was it

> ... the undiscerning Parameshvara, who did not hear
> The weeping and lamenting, and cries of distress
> Of the *lakhs*[30] of poor suffering villagers

or was it

> ... the selfish leaders
> Who did not even turn to look back

---

[25] Gyanendrabikram Basnet, 'Git' (Song), *Shabdankur*, pp. 58–59.

[26] Minakshi Dahal, 'Abiral Amsu Bagirahyo' ([My] Tears Flowed without Ceasing), *Sahabhagita Vinashkari Bhukampa 2072 Visheshanka* 50, Bhadau 2073 (August–September 2016), p. 33

[27] Rupesh Shrestha, 'Chora, Ghar ta Gayo' (Son, the House Is Gone), *Setopati*, 23 May 2015 (9 Jeth 2072), available at: http://archive.setopati.com/sahityapati/28537/ (accessed 18 July 2017).

[28] Rupak Alankar, 'Ghar' (House), *Kavita* 101, Baisakh–Saun 2072 (April/May–July/ August 2015), p. 58.

[29] Kamala 'Jyoti' Risal, 'Dui Muktak' (Two *Muktaks*), *Shabdankur*, p. 19.

[30] One *lakh* = 100,000.

After they had secured their votes?

'A famished boy' is encountered on the path, eating dry noodles and *chiura* from a spread-out newspaper, described in lines strongly redolent of Bhupi Sherchan's famous 'Ek Kavita' (A Poem) (see Hutt 2010: 123–24):

> In that newspaper, published five days after the *bhukampa*,
> A press statement from some big leader was published,
> 'To those who lost their lives in the *bhukampa*,
> Heartfelt homage and condolences,
> Best wishes for the speedy recovery of those injured.'[31]

The second is an articulation of communal grief which includes a mixture of sentiments about those who have come to assist in the relief effort. The aid-givers stand to take photographs on the ground where 'our rice husker, grinding stone and anvil' have been buried. They stand to write their news on the ground where 'our children's [hair]clips, ribbons and pencils' have been buried. Gratitude is expressed for the 'red tents, noodles, *chiura* and cameras' the visitors have brought ('We bend our heads and thank you— You remembered us and came so far') but any idea that they are able to empathize with the suffering of *bhukampa* victims is denied:

> Lest our tears wet the lens of your camera,
> We are crying carefully carefully,
> Lest blood stain the page in which you write your poems
> We are carefully carefully extracting our mother's dead body.

A spirit of hope is invoked:

> Now we will dig out the dust of the grave and gather the pieces of light,
> We will pick up the letters that fell from the pages of books
> And again create beautiful sentences of life....

but it is made very plain that outsiders will be marginal to this renewal:

---

[31] Kaliprasad Rijal, 'Tyo Aimai' (That Woman), *Madhuparka*, pp. 5–6

Our children are buried in this dust, please walk carefully along the
edge....

Our mothers are buried in this dust.
Do not think otherwise—please walk carefully from the land.[32]

It has not been possible to establish which of these poems narrate events
that their composers experienced at first hand, and which are based on the
experience of others, real or imagined. The words of one poem purport to
come from a youth named 'Jitendra Tamang', but it is clear from the poet's
Brahmin name that he does not belong to the indigenous Tamang ethnic
group himself. In another context (one thinks of the politically charged
aftermath of Hurricane Katrina in the United States, for example)[33] such an
act of ventriloquism, in which a member of the dominant social group puts
words into the mouth of a member of the marginalized community that was
the most severely affected by the disaster, would be politically contentious, to
say the least. As Cooley states, 'The poetry of disaster asks ethical questions
about voice.... Who is speaking and who can speak for whom? How close
to a disaster does a poet need to be to write about it? Can one write about a
disaster without first hand experience?' (Cooley 2014: 5).

In this instance, the poet has clearly reflected on these questions,
because the speaker in his poem criticizes the very act of writing poetry in
such circumstances:

I have watched my mother's corpse rotting before my eyes,
Ask me what suffering is like.
I am running away, insecure in my own courtyard,
Ask me what fear is like.
Enough, poet!
Do not write poems abusing the *bhukampa*,

---

[32] Biplav Dhakal, 'Bhukamp Dayari—Ek' (Earthquake diary—one), *Shabda
Sanyojan*, pp. 39–40, also published in *Kalashri*, pp. 337–38.
[33] Hurricane Katrina, which struck the US city of New Orleans in 2005, inspired
several collections of poetry by African American poets, including Brad Bechler
(*When Will the Sky Fall?*), Patricia Smith (*Blood Dazzler*), Nicole Cooley (*Breach*),
and Raymond McDaniel (*Saltwater Empire*). My thanks to Claire Cox for
introducing me to this material.

Instead, if you can, send a mouthful of grain,

And a wide-spreading (*pharakilo*) belief that we can rise from this condition.[34]

Curious to know the origins of this poem, I sought out Mani Lohani, its author. He kindly explained that he was working as a journalist for a Nepali TV channel at the time of the earthquake. He travelled with a small team to a Tamang village in Sindhupalchok with relief supplies and a film crew. He saw a young boy sitting there who had lost his family. The boy did not speak any of the words of the poem, but

> he sat there as we were distributing the relief, regarding us, and I grounded my poem on that. From the way he looked at us you could see real pain (*ekdam pidaa*) inside him. Because whatever balm (*malam*) we could give him was not enough. This really touched me. He was probably 8 or 10 years old, certainly less than 11. Very quiet and still, as if he was telling us that what we were doing would not put things right.

After Lohani returned to Kathmandu, he was invited to a poetry-reading programme, at which people were asked to recite poems they had written about the earthquake:

> And I thought of that boy again and asked myself, what would he gain from that? How would he feel if he heard that we were writing and reading out poems about this? He would tell us off ('give us *gaali*' [abuse]) he would be angry.[35]

Theme three: the *bhukampa* as a punisher

Blame for the calamity is cast repeatedly upon Nepali society itself in these poems. It is asserted that the *bhukampa* was a consequence of human venality, conceit, and ambition:

---

[34] Mani Lohani, 'Sukkha Pahiromuni' (Under a Dry Landslide), *Kalashri*, pp. 341–42.

[35] Mani Lohani, recorded interview, Patan, 28 February 2019.

Many we had become, who wished to be masters
Many we had become, who wished to be statues
Many we had become, who wished to be gods....[36]

If cowardly men had not tried to be emperors,
It seems to me,
Perhaps Nature would not have made itself despotic (*nirankush*).[37]

Those who suffered the effects of the *bhukampa* had forgotten 'the meaning of birth and the face of death' and had engaged merely in self-seeking competition with one another. They have now been awoken by their injuries and must face reality. But, although 'the underground ghost' may have demolished their homes, it has not brought down their desires and dreams.[38]

Human conceit and ambition are often seen as manifesting themselves in the building boom that has taken place in central urban areas of the Kathmandu Valley since the 1990s, and particularly in the construction of tall buildings. Regret is expressed that 'we did not learn from the 1990 [1934 CE] *bhukampa*' and allowed unrestricted construction, leaving few open spaces in Kathmandu. As a consequence, 'those tall houses of conceit and pride' collapsed. Humankind is responsible for the *bhukampa* because of its more generalized despoiling of the natural environment: 'It is we who spoiled the earth.'[39]

Nature, which is addressed as a female deity (usually Prithivi, sometimes Dharati or Dharati Mata) is implored to forgive the people their sins[40] but also accused of cruelty. In tones of hurt, the goddess (*devi*) is asked why she is angry, and assured that all the poet wishes to do is love and beautify her.[41]

---

[36] Dubasu Kshetri, 'Bhukampa 2072' (The 2072 Earthquake), *Dayitwa*, pp. 48–49.

[37] Mohan Duval, 'Ko Atankavadi Prakriti ki Manche?' (Who Is the Terrorist, Nature or Humankind?), *Shabda Sanyojan*, p. 22.

[38] Sojho Gaunle, 'Jakhampachi Jageko Man' (The Mind That Awakes after Injury), *Shabdankur*, pp. 37–38.

[39] Anantaraj Nyaupane, 'Hamile Nai Bigareko....' (It Is We Who Have Spoiled....), *Madhuparka*, p. 48.

[40] Ambika Rauna, 'Dhartimata' (Mother Earth), *Kaushiki*, p. 5.

[41] Ramsundar Deuja, 'Kina Risayo Timi' (Why Are You Angry?), *Shabda Sanyojan*, p. 83.

She is admonished and asked not to shake her motherly lap so violently.[42] She is asked which lifetime the anger she has unleashed comes from, that she no longer allows people to die of old age or to wither and fall like forest flowers.[43] She is accused of cruelty and wanton vandalism: she has destroyed built structures and natural environments that took her thousands of years to build, and caused untold human suffering. But her wrath (*prakop*) is being countered by the offspring (*santati*) of Mother Nepal (Nepal Ama), who will work together, shoulder to shoulder, to reconstruct what she has destroyed.[44] And she is called upon to desist:

> Our journey
> Is just a moment between birth and death,
> What harm would it do if you allowed us to play just that long?[45]

Mother Earth remains silent in these poems: she has nothing to say in response, it seems. But while the Mother does not speak, the Monster does (see Hoffman 2002), in a tone that is decidedly male. Sometimes the *bhukampa* declares itself to be powerful, uncompromising, remorseless, and blind to the suffering it causes[46] and sometimes it engages in dialogue. Often it is not to be trifled with, responding to a complaint about the injustice of its actions and those of its forefathers (Nepal's 1934 and 1988 earthquakes) as follows:

> You fall into a pit you have dug yourself,
> You are merely insulting me
> When you say that the *bhukampa* killed people.
> Was it me who built the five-storeyed house?
> Was it me who built the nine-storeyed palace?
> My grandfather taught you a lesson,

---

42 Jyoti Jangal, 'E prithvi' (Oh Earth), *Shabda Sanyojan*, p. 52.
43 Tekbahadur Jirel, 'Euta Prashna Dhartisita' (A Question for the Earth), *Madhuparka*, p. 51.
44 Napit Pasa, 'Prakop Prakriti' (Angry Nature), *Shabda Sanyojan*, p. 48.
45 Gobindaraj Bhattarai, 'Pheri Arko Ek Kodalo Hana' (Strike One More Time), *Kalashri*, pp. 342–45.
46 Dil Sahani, 'Mahabhukampko Bakpatra' (The Earthquake's Statement), *Dayitwa*, pp. 60–63.

My father showed you a miracle (*karamat*).
If your wisdom still has not sprouted forth
I will come again.
This time I came in daylight,
Next time I will come and destroy even more.[47]

Occasionally, the *bhukampa* expresses remorse and regret over the consequences of its actions. It explains that its motives were political, and that its destructive energies were aimed at a range of common enemies, including

those who called themselves the centre and scorned the 'remote' (*sudur*),
the skyscrapers that insulted the huts and humbler homes,
the capital that thinks it's the king,
the superstitious who don't believe in science,
those who ignore advice,
the many-tongued rich;
the wolves and tigers who eat the hearts and livers of the honest and simple,
those who play with the people's dreams but only fulfil their own,
those who build their own houses and spoil other people's,
doctors who treat their own parents and kill others' wives,
cities, bazaars, tall palaces,
people who wear the mask of nationalism but do their country down.[48]

In this poem, the *bhukampa* declares that its intention was to 'move those in heaven towards hell and those in hell toward heaven', but it admits that it has failed to achieve this, and instead it has destroyed 'Barpak, Laprak, beautiful Langtang, and the Durbar Squares'.[49] The poem ends by

---

[47] Prem Oli, 'Bhukampasanga Varta' (Talks with the Earthquake), *Shabdankur*, pp. 54–55.

[48] Punyaprasad Kharel, 'Bhukampako Atmapida' (The Earthquake's Remorse), *Shabda Sanyojan*, pp. 32–33.

[49] Barpak and Laprak are villages in the central Gorkha district close to the epicentre of the 25 April 2015 earthquake. Langtang is a high valley to the north of Kathmandu that was devastated by a massive avalanche set off by the tremor (see

quoting a well-known Nepali proverb about unintended consequences, 'the axe aims for the knee'.

There is little evidence in these poems of any echo of the intense debates on theodicy ('the justification of God's good government of the world in the face of evil and pain' [Wood 2010]) that followed the Lisbon Earthquake of 1755, drawing in philosophers such as Voltaire, Kant, and Rousseau (see Deneen 2010). This is perhaps less of a concern in a society where most people do not conceive of a monotheistic God, and in a cosmology whose deities may often struggle with and conspire against one another.

Theme four: the *bhukampa* as unifier and leveller

The levelling and unifying impact of the disaster is a theme that recurs frequently throughout the sample. One poem recites a long string of examples: two brothers who had divided their shared property with a wall after a quarrel over their inheritance are now sitting in the same tent and eating from the same cooking pot; the newly rich who were building their house taller and taller behind a high gate have to escape to nearby open ground where they are welcomed by neighbours they barely know; some Madhesis (lowlanders) living in rented rooms rescue their landlord's son from falling bricks; a soldier smiles as he finds someone alive under the rubble, even though he knows that some of his own relatives are dead; Nepalis living abroad spend their nights on social media trying to find ways of helping, and tourists raise donations.[50] Another relates that thousands have come out to live on the street under the open sky, including the millionaire who now shares a tent with his less prosperous neighbours. The rich, the poor, even foreign guests, have applied themselves to the task of relieving others. There is no longer any discrimination on grounds of ethnicity (the shapes of people's eyes or noses), language, or religion:

Lord and Bradley, this volume).. The Durbar Squares are the temple-filled squares adjacent to the medieval palaces of each of the three cities of the Kathmandu Valley.

[50] Ranjit Acharya, 'Mahabhukample Dekhaeko Adrishya Drishya' (An Unseen Sight Revealed by the Great Earthquake), *Setopati*, 9 May 2015 (26 Baisakh 2072), http://archive.setopati.com/sahityapati/27967/ (accessed 18 July 2017).

At last the leaders have understood unity, goodwill, and reconciliation
It passed in one vote, a proposal for a relief resolution
Let us turn our grief into strength, there will be no curses ahead
Let us consider the *bhukampa* an opportunity and build a new
prosperous Nepal.[51]

The *bhukampa* has made it possible for a boy from a humble household to
meet and play with the children of the big house next door:

When the *bhukampa* came, my son said:
The friends who latch the gate of the big house,
Before they played up there,
Now we get to play with them;
Now we get to sleep
With the landlord who would not let us enjoy the sunshine on the
roof.[52]

The food and drink of the humbler citizen suddenly becomes everyone's
staple:

The *chiura* and water we always eat and drink:
See how its importance has increased![53]

In fact, it was social inequality that brought the *bhukampa*, which has
now corrected the imbalance—'so why shouldn't there be a *bhukampa*?'[54]
By pulling people 'out of both hovels and palaces' and 'delivering them
straight to tents in public clearings', the *bhukampa* has at last introduced
true socialism to Nepal, mocking the political parties. One blow from the
bhukampa 'shook off the dust that lay on hearts, thought, wisdom, and
discernment', and in its 'socialist camps'

---

[51] Keshavraj Panta, 'Bhukampa' (Earthquake), *Dayitwa*, p. 85.
[52] Gita Sapkota, 'Bhuinchalo' (Earthquake), *Shabda Sanyojan*, p. 104.
[53] Gita Sapkota, 'Bhuinchalo' (Earthquake), *Shabda Sanyojan*, p. 104.
[54] Gita Sapkota, 'Bhuinchalo' (Earthquake), *Shabda Sanyojan*, p. 104.

It made a father and daughter who had not shared water for years speak on the telephone,
It made brothers who had fought for years over an irrigation channel greet one another with prostrations,
It made the wives of brothers-in-law who had divided their courtyard with a wall embrace one another,
It made co-wives share a bed who had always had separate cooking fires and veils before,
The ditch of electoral enmity was made level by a packet of relief noodles.
Breaking the red flag ban,
Beneath one tent
Hymns were sung to the gods,
Incense was lit for the ancestors.
And communal rites were performed for the dead.[55]

The *bhukampa* is a skilled (*daksha*) guru that comes and goes like lightning and terrifies the world. It comes carrying 'socialist dreams in a basket' to teach the Nepali people to live together, to share what they have to drink. Now there is a 'golden opportunity' to build village, town, city, and country:

The *bhukampa* of '72 has inflamed the brain,
The loss of lives and property has caused compassion to spring up,
Made us conscious of one another,
So let us unite, taking up an ideological tethering cord
For reconstruction and new construction,
Turning our grief into strength.[56]

In the end, people's dreams are all the same: all they needed in the immediate aftermath was food, shelter, and clothing. But for some poets, the *bhukampa*'s levelling effects were temporary. The *bhukampa* came 'in the way that

---

[55] Birkha Kranti, 'Bhuincalo ra Banmara' (The Earthquake and the Banmara Weed), *Madhuparka*, p. 26.
[56] Narmadeshvari Satyal, 'Jutaum Vaicarik Damlo Liera' (Let Us Unite with an Ideological Tether), *Shabda Sanyojan*, p. 23.

threats sometimes come' and left 'in the way that reassurances vanish'.[57] It is unfortunate that the people and the leaders so quickly forgot the lessons it taught them:

> It would have been best if people had not forgotten
> Those moments spent sleeping unafraid under a tent,
> The moments spent unsleeping in the fear of death in a mansion,
> The lessons taught continuously by the *bhukampa*,
> If they had torn apart for ever
> All of the delusions of discrimination.[58]

Theme five: the distribution of loss

Albala-Bertrand writes that the effects of a disaster 'are neither geographically homogenous nor socially indiscriminatory' (1993: 105). Some of this poetry disagrees: the *bhukampa*'s levelling effects, it says, were due precisely to the fact that it affected both rich and poor:

> Those who do not know the language of the earth say
> The *bhukampa* killed people,
> The flood and the landslide took lives,
> Caused damage to life and property;
> Those who know the language of the earth say
> *Bhukampa*, flood, landslide, tsunami, and volcano
> Never take people's lives,
> They never discriminate between those who offer their lives,
> Calling one their own, and another another's.[59]

Another poet considers that it is the rich who fear a disaster most, presumably because they have the most to lose:

---

[57] Peshal Acharya, 'Agaman' (Arrival), *Shivapuri Sandesh* 68, Baisakh–Asar 2072 (April/May–June/July 2015), p. 12 .

[58] Narayandev Panta, 'Bhukampa, Manche ra Jigisha' (Earthquake, Humankind and Survival), *Dayitwa*, p. 77.

[59] Gopalkumar Mainali, 'Bhukampa' (Earthquake), *Kaushiki*, p. 4.

Those who imprison the water sources
And rape the rivers and streams high up,
Those who pluck the beauty of flowers
And display their glory by putting on garlands to show how
important they are,
Those who see all things as money
And consider themselves great in their pride of money,
Why are they most afraid when a *bhukampa* happens?[60]

The sample also includes poems that draw attention to the way in which the disaster exposed the inequalities in Nepali society. When the earth 'begins to dance' a poor person and a rich person both run to open ground, crying and screaming, and then 'embrace one another for the first time'. As they run, the sandal on the poorer person's left foot snaps and he runs on without it; however, the other person is, as always, wearing *amerikané* boots. The richer person's seven-storeyed house collapses, reducing the poorer person's hut to dust in the process, and that night they sleep together under the open sky. The next day, one 'swims in a pond of beer' while the other stands in line for relief rations, and that night they share the tent he brings. For the richer person this is a picnic around a campfire, while the poorer person feels remorse at having to hold his hands out for help. In the end, the richer receives compensation and rebuilds his house, while the poorer cannot reconstruct his hut,

And it seems to me,
Why did I not fall among those thousands
Who became sun and moon in this great calamity?[61]

In another poem we meet 'Jaisi Budha', who does not qualify for aid or assistance and lives in a remote corner of the countryside, without phone reception or neighbours who can hear his cries for a sip of water: he dies as a consequence. This poem is one of a very few examples of an ironical or satirical treatment of the theme. If 'Jaisi Budha' had been a party worker, he

---

[60] Mohan Duval, 'Bhukampale Sandesh Die Jasto' (As if the Earthquake Delivered a Message), *Shabdankur*, p. 56.

[61] Nakima, 'Bhukampama Timi ra Ma' (In the Earthquake You and I), *Kalashri*, pp. 356–57.

might have been made a 'living martyr'; if he had been a member of a caste or ethnic grouping, he might have found shelter under the 'ethnic (*jatiya*) umbrella'; if he had been a woman, he might at least have had a reserved seat in an auto-rickshaw; if he had been a member of a religious organization, he might at least have had some influential mourners; if he had been a senior citizen, he might have secured some funds for his funeral. An 'all-party comrade' sits in the sunshine on his third-floor rooftop the next day and writes a 'secret poem' about '*bhukampa* equality', which goes viral in seconds, and is taken up by professors of social science and analysts of the constitution.[62]

Theme six: poems of political anger and distrust

The sample contains some caustic commentaries on the Nepal government's initial response to the disaster:

> The first thing to fall down
> As soon as the *bhukampa* came—
> That was my government.
>
> The first to hide under its bed
> As soon as the ground shook indistinctly—
> That was my government.[63]

Once relief aid began to arrive, the party-based competition for power and resources that is a characteristic feature of Nepali political culture resumed as normal:

> I watched the scrabbling and grabbing (*luchachundi*),
> I saw them favouring their own voters,
> I saw the tempting and pulling to themselves.

---

[62] Birkha Kranti, 'Bhukampiya Samanta ra Jaisi Budha' (The Earthquake Feudal Lord and Jaisi Budha), *Sahabhagita Vinashkari Bhukampa 2072 Visheshanka*, 50, Bhadau 2073 (August–September 2016), p. 14.

[63] Suresh Kiran, 'Tyo Mero Sarkar Thiyo' (That Was My Government), *Shabda Sanyojan*, p. 30.

Alas! Seeing that pitiable condition
For how long will this wrong politics persist?[64]

It is frequently asserted that the ultimate beneficiaries of the disaster will be the political elites. The *bhukampa* is characterized as 'a duty for the virtuous youths who understood dedication to the country' (a reference to the huge volunteer movement that emerged in the immediate aftermath, mainly of urban youth), but as 'commission and feasting for liars (*phataha*), exploiters, and takers of bribes'.[65] Wonder is expressed at the selflessness and energy of the young volunteers.[66] But the relief aid is not reaching those most in need of it[67] and the *bhukampa* is warned about the corruption of the people who occupy Singha Durbar, the main government secretariat:

Before you came they ate seeds and manure here,
After you came they ate the rice that came as relief.[68]

In Nepal there are many who can eat and digest, and are able to protect themselves from the government body that investigates cases of corruption. The *bhukampa* is warned that it will be consumed by them too, 'mixed with bribes and commission payments'.[69] The 'commission demon' (*kamishan danav*) is identified as the greatest threat.[70]

Nepal's Constituent Assembly had been promising but failing to deliver a new national constitution for seven years on the day the earthquake struck. The ready acceptance by several of its more prominent members of tents and other items of relief aid for themselves and their families provoked a media

---

[64] Birendrakumar Balami, 'Mahsus Gari Herem' (I Felt and Watched), *Shabdankur*, pp. 42–43.

[65] Sitaram Gurung, 'Bhukampa' (Earthquake), *Kaushiki*, p. 5.

[66] Bijayashri, 'Bhukampapachiko Urja' (Energy after the Earthquake), *Shabda Sanyojan*, p. 102.

[67] Marubhumi Narayan, 'Vyangya Gajal' (Satire *Gajal*), *Shabdankur*, p. 31.

[68] Punyaprasad 'Bachita' Acharya, 'Bhukamplai Dhamki' (Warning to the Earthquake), *Dayitwa*, p. 81.

[69] Punyaprasad 'Bachita' Acharya, 'Bhukamplai Dhamki' (Warning to the Earthquake), *Dayitwa*, p. 81.

[70] Vishvadip Adhikari, 'Bhukampka Panch Muktak' (Five Earthquake *Muktaks*), *Dayitwa*, p. 102.

furore, forcing them to return what they had received. One poet offers a tongue-in-cheek defence of their actions: the *bhukampa* had destroyed the coops and pens in which the leaders kept their chickens, the ministers kept their goats, the secretaries kept their dogs, and the personal assistants (PAs) kept their pigs: and were not these all living creatures too?

> They work day and night for the country,
> They give their very lives for the people,
> Our leaders, ministers, secretaries, and PAs....
> ...
> Where else do they have such lovers of development?
> They even build bridges where there is no river.

> Like saints, *sadhus*, and *jogis*
> The poor things are satisfied,
> They are happy to receive a tent,
> Those who have donated eight divine years to the constitution....[71]

Various allegories are offered to predict the ways in which the self-seeking political elite will quickly regain control and turn the situation to its own ends. In one poem, the *bhukampa* has shaken the rhododendrons, creepers, and grasses and made them bud and flower. However, a clump of the aggressively invasive 'forest killer' (*banmara*)[72] has sprung up from a *tulsi-math*[73] and is flourishing now:

> Eating up the relief supplies (*rasin-pani*) of the buried houses,
> It wraps itself in the tents from the helicopters....[74]

---

[71] Shiva Prakash, 'Bichara! Mantri-netale Ke Birae?' (Poor Things! What Wrong Did the Ministers and Leaders Do?), *Setopati*, 20 June 2015 (5 Ashadh 2072), http://archive.setopati.com/sahityapati/29786/ (accessed 18 July 2017).

[72] *Banmara*, literally 'forest killer', is Ageratina adenophora, an allelopathic exotic invasive originally from Central America, also known as crofton weed or sticky snakeroot. My thanks to Mark Liechty for this information.

[73] The sacred basil, planted outside the home of every high-caste Nepali family.

[74] Birkha Kranti, 'Bhuincalo ra Banmara' (The Earthquake and the Forest Killer), *Madhuparka*, p. 26.

In another, the people who come to deliver relief aid are characterized as a throng of predators:

Suddenly a throng entered that ruined house,
Of jackals, wolves, and vultures,
It is mocking and throwing mud
Into eyes lifted in the hope of sympathy,
Ripping away the blood and flesh
Of souls agitated by cries of pain.[75]

Once the emergency phase is over and the *bhukampa*'s levelling and unifying effects have waned,

Another messiah of the proletariat will be born,
Sitting on a pyramid of assurances
And giving out the magic words of dreams.

But this 'messiah' will simply turn into yet another cruel ruler who will 'live in a grand palace' and 'rape the dreams of the poor':

Displaying the knot of his tie
On the TV screens,
He will spit at the proposals of the UN, ADB, and EU
To his heart's content from *paan*-scented gums....[76]

A handful of poems express the fear that the disaster will spell the end of the constitution-drafting process:

The reciters and deputy reciters
of the Puranas of the constitution have disappeared,
And now in my country,
Spewing meetings and circulars,
There is a government of fear.

---

[75] Arjun Kumar Karki, 'U' [He/she], *Kavita* 102, Bhadau–Mangsir 2072 (August/September–November/December 2015), p. 15.

[76] Peshal Acharya, 'Agaman' (Arrival), *Shivapuri Sandesh*, 68, Baisakh–Asar 2072 (April/May–June/July 2015), p. 12.

For myself, all I need
is a tent.[77]

There is a danger that if the Nepali people do not receive their new national constitution soon, 'the land of true heroes' will break into pieces.[78] There are some optimistic voices, however. Despite the political deadlock that was ongoing on the day the *bhukampa* struck, the disaster will be of benefit to those who had failed to reach agreement on the constitution hitherto:

> The country's shaking was of benefit to some,
> Their flags were over the country,
> And they were standing on ground higher than the country,
> The orchestrators (*matiyar*) of shutdowns (*banda*) and strikes fomented disputes over the constitution,
> Chanting their rosaries of agreement, they had never been able to reach an agreement,
> In this present, this was the harsh reality we endured.[79]

Suffering imparts greater lessons than happiness, and now this 'sudden suffering' of the *bhukampa* has identified who is who. Now the very force of Nature, which 'identifies the demon of property and the human being of disaster', will give the country its constitution:

> and I understood—
> Nature is now going to give this country a constitution
> That identifies the demon of property and the human being of calamity.[80]

Other voices are less optimistic, and see the possibility of explosive change in the aftermath of the *bhukampa*:

---

[77] Peshal Acharya, 'Bhukampa-trasad' (Earthquake-tragedy), *Shabda Sanyojan*, p. 66.

[78] Vishveshvari Adhikari, 'Bhukampa ra daivajña' (The earthquake and the prophesier'), *Dayitwa*, p. 75.

[79] Chaviraman Silwal, 'Samay Trasadi' (Time Tragedy), *Shabdankur*, p. 22.

[80] Adarsh Pradhan, 'Jindagima Sarvocca Satya Dukha' (The Ultimate Truth of Life Is Suffering), *Kalashri,* pp. 357–58.

The economy seems sunk in mourning,
Politics is like a person who has lost his wits,
Maybe deep within, a fire of straw is being lit
In the feeble, obstructed, unsatisfied structure,
And an explosion is about to occur of another time of radical change.[81]

There is a need for a real tremor....
... We have to bring a political quake
Against the old political model of regime,
To establish a new political order.[82]

Nepal has been attacked by the gods and by Nature; it is suffering from injustice and discrimination. It is not a laboratory, a circus clown, or a madman at whom stones can be thrown. It is the country that has spread peace in the world, has written songs of courage, has lifted the world up to the highest peak. Where should its people go to seek justice, whom should they beg?

I will come, bringing parents who have lost their children,
I will come, bringing orphans,
I will come, bringing bricks made by 50 degrees of sunshine,
I will come, carrying the land that has split apart,
I will come, bringing the remnants of my monuments,
I will come with those who have lost their mental balance,
I will sit and fast unto death with my dear ones.

Send me an SMS
Telling me where I should go
With these cracked, demolished, dead, and wounded realities,
Because my country has been done an injustice,
My country needs justice.[83]

---

[81] Purna Inphada, 'Santrasta Hahakar' (Fearful Lamentation), *Kalashri*, pp. 354–55
[82] Omkumar Subedi, 'Kampa' (Tremor), *Kaushiki*, p. 6.
[83] Niru Tripathi, 'Mero Deshmathi Anyaya Bhaeko Cha' (My Country Has Been Done an Injustice), *Setopati*, 16 May 2015 (2 Jeth 2072), http://archive.setopati.com/sahityapati/28259/ (accessed 18 July 2017).

Figure 15.8 The earthquake special
issue of *Samakalin Sahitya*
Source: Author's private collection.

But the likelihood is that nothing will change and that Nepalis will have to continue to enjoy international paeons of praise for their 'resilience':

> For how many centuries will we helpless Nepalis
> Have to endure new editions of new *raksi* in an old bottle?
> Waiting for an answer,
> Sitting under a tent,
> I am scratching the design of a new Nepal,
> I am weeping, moved by the scream of the soil.[84]

Conclusion

The corpus of poetry considered here forms one segment of a spontaneous 'endogenous response' written for an imagined community of readers that extends beyond the urban elite and the inhabitants of the non-governmental organization (NGO) or international non-governmental organization

---

[84] Peshal Acharya, 'Agaman' (Arrival), *Shivapuri Sandesh* 68, Baisakh–Asar 2072 (April/May–June/July 2015), p. 12.

(INGO) and development spheres of Nepali society. For the latter, the great national *bhukampa* envisioned by both politicians and poets as a unifier, a leveller, a punishment, and an opportunity was merely the Gorkha Earthquake, to which the world would respond by helping Nepal to 'build back better' in physical terms.

The readership of this poetry will not have been extensive. The journals in which it appeared have circulations of a few thousand at most, mostly within the capital valley, and very little of this material is available online. The politically contentious content of some of this poetry is not found in the scores of earthquake-related Nepali music videos that were posted on YouTube in the early months of the aftermath, several of which have recorded hundreds of thousands of views by Nepalis all over the world (see Asambare 2016; Hutt forthcoming). As I will explain in a future paper, almost without exception these latter followed the 'anguish and determination' theme I have identified here. It is possible that the authors of the poetry I have discussed here felt freer to articulate political anger and dissent than they would have been if they knew their work was going to be more widely read.

A great deal of further research would be required to produce an account of the literary response to the 2015 Nepal earthquakes in its entirety. This would explore, *inter alia*, other Nepali literary genres; earthquake aftermath literature in other languages, especially the minority languages of the most-affected districts; folksong and oral literature; online music videos; and so on. A fuller appraisal of the endogenous response would help to bring divergent understandings of this disaster into a closer relationship with one another. In a wider context, taking proper account of the endogenous responses to disasters that are articulated in local literatures will help us to refine the models we employ to understand disaster aftermaths worldwide. For this we must attend not just to the English-language literature generated by the disasters that strike the societies of the Global North, but to that of all disaster-stricken societies.

REFERENCES

Achar, D. and S. K. Panikkar, eds. 2012. *Articulating Resistance. Art and Activism*. Delhi: Tulika Press.

Acharya, K. P. 2002. 'Twenty-four Years of Community Forestry in Nepal'. *International Forestry Review* 4(2): 149–56.

Adams, V. 1997. 'Dreams of a Final Sherpa'. *American Anthropologist* 99(1): 85–98. https://doi.org/10.1525/aa.1997.99.1.85.

Adhikari, D. 2018. 'Nepal's KP Sharma Oli Is Becoming Increasingly Authoritarian— And There's Little to Stop Him'. *Scroll.in*, 27 August. Available at: https://scroll. in/article/891656/nepals-kp-sharma-oli-is-becoming-increasingly-authoritarian- and-theres-little-to-stop-him (accessed 11 June 2020).

Adhikari, J. 2008. *Land Reform in Nepal: Problems and Prospects*. Action Aid. Available at: https://nepal.actionaid.org/sites/nepal/files/land_reform_complete_-_done. pdf (accessed 11 June 2020).

Adhikari, P. 2015. 'Quake Victims Stage Protest against Relief Distribution Delay'. *The Kathmandu Post*, 13 October. Available at: http://kathmandupost.ekantipur.com/ news/2015-10-13/quake-victims-stage-protest-against-relief-distribution-delay. html (accessed 11 June 2020).

Adichie, C. N. 2009. 'The Danger of a Single Story'. TED Talk. Available at: https:// www.ted.com/talks/chimamanda_adichie_the_danger_of_a_single_story (accessed 20 November 2020).

AFP. 2017. 'Lowest Bidders Threaten Nepal's Quake-hit Heritage'. *Daily Mail*, 24 March. Available at: http://www.dailymail.co.uk/wires/afp/article-4344866/ Lowest-bidders-threaten-Nepals-quake-hit-heritage.html (accessed 11 June 2020).

Agrawal, A. and E. Ostrom. 2001. 'Collective Action, Property Rights, and Devolution of Forest and Protected Area Management'. In *Collective Action, Property Rights and Devolution of Natural Resource Management: Exchange of Knowledge and Implications for Policy*, ed. R. S. Meinzen-Dick, A. Knox and M. Di Gregorio, pp. 73–109. Feldafing, Germany: Food and Agriculture Development Centre.

Agrawal, P. M. 1969. 'Structural Response Results during the June 27, 1966 Earthquake in Nepal–India Border Region'. *Bulletin of the Seismological Society of America* 59(2): 771–75.

Ahmed, F. 1988. 'Earthquake: Tremors Leave a Trail of Death and Damage in Bihar and Nepal'. *India Today*, 15 September.

Aijazi, O. 2016. 'Who Is Chandni Bibi? Survival as Embodiment in Disaster Disrupted Northern Pakistan'. *Women's Studies Quarterly* 44(1/2): 95–110. https://doi. org/10.1353/wsq.2016.0015.

Albala-Bertrand, J. M. 1993. *Political Economy of Large Natural Disasters: With Special Reference to Developing Countries.* Oxford: Clarendon Press.

Aldashev, G. and T. Verdier. 2010. 'Goodwill Bazaar: NGO Competition and Giving to Development'. *Journal of Development Economics* 91(1): 48–63. https://doi. org/10.1016/j.jdeveco.2008.11.010.

Aldrich, D. P. 2011. 'The Externalities of Strong Social Capital: Post-tsunami Recovery in Southeast India'. *Journal of Civil Society* 7(1): 81–99. https://doi.org/10.1080/17 448689.2011.553441.

Alfred, C. 2015. 'Nepal Desperately Needs Aid, but the Wrong Kind Could Make Things Worse'. *Huffington Post*, 30 April. Available at: https://www.huffingtonpost. com/2015/04/30/nepal-aid-needs_n_7173750.html (accessed 11 June 2020).

Allinger, E. and G. Melzer. 2010. 'A Pañcaraksa Manuscript from Year 39 of the Reign of Ramapala'. *Artibus Asiae* 70(2): 387–414.

Amatya, S. 2019. 'Role of Skilled Female Construction Worker (Mason)'. In *Post-earthquake Reconstruction and Their Socio-economic Changes: A Case of Gorkha Earthquake, Nepal.* Unpublished Masters Thesis, Brac University. Available at: http://dspace.bracu.ac.bd/xmlui/bitstream/handle/10361/12744/17262016_ MPSM.pdf?sequence=1&isAllowed=y (accessed 11 June 2020).

Amaya, V., S. Amir, A. Manna, and I. Matton. 2016. *Revitalizing Bungamati: An Action Plan. Design Investigations for a Post Earthquake Reconstruction Process in Bungamati, Kathmandu Valley, Nepal.* Studio Kathmandu Volume 1. Landscape Urbanism, K. U. Leuven. UN Habitat, Shelter Program. Available at: https://issuu.com/valentina_ amaya/docs/ktm_vol1_bgm_action_plan (accessed 20 November 2020).

Amnesty International. 2017. *Building Inequality: The Failure of the Nepali Government to Protect the Marginalised in Post-earthquake Reconstruction.* Amnesty International, ASA 31/6071/2017. Available at: https://www.amnesty. org/en/documents/asa31/6071/2017/en/ (accessed 11 June 2020).

Anderson, M. D. 2011. *Disaster Writing: The Cultural Politics of Catastrophe in Latin America.* Charlottesville and London: University of Virginia Press.

Andersson, R. 2014. *Illegality, Inc.: Clandestine Migration and the Business of Bordering Europe.* Oakland: University of California Press.

Appel, H., N. Anand, and A. Gupta. 2015. 'The Infrastructure Toolbox: Theorizing the Contemporary'. *Cultural Anthropology/Fieldsights*, 24 September. Available at: https://culanth.org/fieldsights/series/the-infrastructure-toolbox (accessed 20 November 2020).

Arnstein, S. R. 1969. 'A Ladder of Citizen Participation'. *Journal of the American Institute of Planners* 35(4): 216–24. https://doi.org/10.1080/01944366908977225.

ArTree Nepal. 2016. *12 Baisakh Post Earthquake Community Art Project*. Unpublished report.

———. 2018. *ArTree Nepal. Report 2016/2017.* Unpublished report.

Aryal, M. R. and S. S. Shrestha. 2016. *A Report on the Salvaging, Screening and Inventorying of Carved Wooden Elements of Hanuman Dhoka Complex*. Kathmandu: Department of Archaeology with support from UNESCO and in collaboration with ICOMOS. Available at: https://unesdoc.unesco.org/ark:/48223/pf0000246816 (accessed 20 November 2020).

Asambare, B. 2016. 'Myujik Bhidiyoma Bhukampako Prakop' (The Destructive Power of the Earthquake in Music Videos). *Lalitkala Patrika* 2(9) (January): 34–35.

Azoulay, A. 2008. *The Civil Contract of Photography*. Cambridge, MA, and London: MIT Press.

Bae, Y., Y. M. Joo, and S. Y. Won. 2016. 'Decentralization and Collaborative Disaster Governance: Evidence from South Korea'. *Habitat International* 52: 50–56. https://doi.10.1016/j.habitatint.2015.08.027.

Bajracharya, S., D. Manandhear, R. Meierhofer, S. Lama, O. Schwank, and D. Zurcher. 1995. *Development Trends in Dolakha and Sindhupalchok Nepal (1975–1995)*. Zurich/Kathmandu: INFRAS/SDC.

Bakkour, D., G. Enjolras, J. C. Thouret, R. Kast, E. T. W. Mei, and B. Prihatminingtyas. 2015. 'The Adaptive Governance of Natural Disaster Systems: Insights from the 2010 Mount Merapi Eruption in Indonesia'. *International Journal of Disaster Risk Reduction* 13: 167–88. https://doi.org/10.1016/j.ijdrr.2015.05.006.

Baltutis, M. C. 2018. 'Innovating the Ancient, Instantiating the Urban: The South Asian Indra Festival'. In *Ritual Innovation: Strategic Intervention in South Asian Religion*, ed. B. K. Pennington and A. L. Allocco, pp. 53–70. New York: Suny Press.

Bangdel, D. 2017. 'Post-earthquake Art Initiatives'. In *Breaking Views: Engaging Art in Post-earthquake Nepal*, ed. C. Brosius and S. Maharjan, pp. 59–70. Kathmandu: Social Science Baha/Himal Books.

Baniya, J., 2014. 'Civil Society, Social Movements and Democratization: A Case Study of Nepal'. Ph.D. thesis, University of Oslo, Norway.

———. 2018. 'Rebuilding "Homes" or "Houses"?'. SWAY project blogpost, 27 February. Available at: https://sway.soscbaha.org/blogs/rebuilding-homes-houses-jeevan-baniya/ (accessed 3 July 2020).

Bankoff, G. 2003. *Cultures of Disaster: Society and Natural Hazard in the Philippines*. London: Routledge Curzon.

Bankoff, G. and G. E. Borrinaga. 2016. 'Whethering the Storm: The Twin Natures of Typhoons Haiyan and Yolanda'. In *Contextualizing Disaster*, ed. G. V. Button and M. Schuller, pp. 44–65. New York and Oxford: Berghahn Books.

Barnett, M. N. 2011. *Empire of Humanity: A History of Humanitarianism*. Ithaca: Cornell University Press.

———. 2013. 'Humanitarian Governance'. *Annual Review of Political Science* 16(1): 379–98. https://doi.org/10.1146/annurev-polisci-012512-083711.

Barrios, R. E. 2016. 'Expert Knowledge and the Ethnography of Disaster Reconstruction'. In *Contextualizing Disaster*, ed. G. V. Button and M. Schuller, pp. 134–52. New York and Oxford: Berghahn Books.

———. 2017. *Governing Affect: Neoliberalism and Disaster Reconstruction*. London: University of Nebraska Press. https://doi: 10.2307/j.ctt1mtz7p9.

Barthes, R. 1981. *Camera Lucida: Reflections on Photography*. New York: Macmillan.

BBC News. 2015. 'Nepal Quake: What Is the World Doing to Help?' 27 April. Available at: https://www.bbc.com/news/world-asia-32477180 (accessed 19 March 2019).

Bell, T. 2016. 'A Second Disaster Awaits Nepal's Heritage'. *Al Jazeera*. Available at: http://www.aljazeera.com/indepth/opinion/2016/04/disaster-awaits-nepal-heritage-160417081759057.html (accessed 11 June 2020).

Benjamin, W. 1969. *Illuminations*. New York: Schocken Books.

Bennike, R. B. 2017. 'Aftershock: Reflections on the Politics of Reconstruction in Northern Gorkha'. *Himalaya: The Journal of the Association for Nepal and Himalayan Studies* 37(2): 55–64. Available at: http://digitalcommons.macalester.edu/himalaya/vol37/iss2/9 (accessed 20 November 2020).

Benson, C., J. Twigg, and M. Myers. 2002. 'NGO Initiatives in Risk Reduction: An Overview'. *Disasters* 25(3): 199–215. https://doi.org/10.1111/1467-7717.00172.

Bhattarai, A. 2018. 'Storeyed Past: The Movement to Rebuild an Iconic Monument in Earthquake-hit Nepal'. *Caravan Magazine*. Available at: https://caravanmagazine.in/reportage/storeyed-past (accessed 11 June 2020).

———. 2019. 'Seeing Like a Farmer: Socioecological Complexity of Constructing and Maintaining Ecologically Integrated Smallholder Family Farms'. Ph.D. thesis, University of Toronto.

Bhattarai, H., K. Acharya, and A. Land. 2018. 'Humanitarian Assistance: Is It Politically Instrumentalized?' *Health Prospect: Journal of Public Health* 17(1): 1–4.

Bhattarai, S. 2018a. 'Clash of Cultures in Bhaktapur'. *The Nepali Times*, 1 June. Available at: https://www.nepalitimes.com/banner/clash-of-cultures-in-bhaktapur/ (accessed 11 June 2020).

———. 2018b. 'Mapping the Earthquake with Art'. *The Nepali Times*, 6 July. Available at: https://www.nepalitimes.com/banner/mapping-the-earthquake-with-art/ (accessed 11 June 2020).

Bisri, M. B. F. and S. Beniya. 2016. 'Analyzing the National Disaster Response Framework and Inter-Organizational Network of the 2015 Nepal/Gorkha Earthquake'. *Provedia Engineering*, special issue 'Humanitarian Technology: Science, Systems and Global Impact' 159: 19–26. https://doi.org/10.1016/j.proeng.2016.08.059.

Bist, K. 2012. 'History's House'. *ESC Nepal* 126 (April). Available at: http://ecs.com.np/features/historys-house (accessed 11 June 2020).

Bista, D. B. 2000. *People of Nepal*, 7th ed. Kathmandu: Ratna Pustak Bhandar.

Bjønness, I. M. 1986. 'Mountain Hazard Perception and Risk-avoiding Strategies among the Sherpas of Khumbu Himal, Nepal'. *Mountain Research and Development* 6(4): 277–92.

Bloch, E. 1986. *The Principle of Hope*. Cambridge, MA: MIT Press.

Bodhi, B. 2010. 'Giving Dignity to Life: Access to Insight—Readings in Theravada Buddhism'. Available at: https://www.accesstoinsight.org/lib/authors/bodhi/bps-essay_38.html (accessed 20 November 2020).

Boersma, F. K., J. E. Ferguson, F. Mulder, and J. J. Wolbers. 2016. 'Humanitarian Response Coordination and Cooperation in Nepal: Coping with Challenges and Dilemmas'. White paper, VU Amsterdam.

Boin, A., A. McConnell, and P. Hart. 2008. 'Governing after Crisis'. In *Governing after Crisis: The Politics of Investigation, Accountability and Learning*, ed. A. Boin, A. McConnell, and P. Hart, pp. 3–32. Cambridge; New York: Cambridge University Press.

Boyarin, J. 1994. 'Space, Time, and the Politics of Memory'. In *Remapping Memory: The Politics of Timespace*, ed. C. Tilly, pp. 1–37. Minneapolis: University of Minnesota Press.

Brancati, D. 2007. 'Political Aftershocks: The Impact of Earthquakes on Intrastate Conflict'. *Journal of Conflict Resolution* 51(5): 715–43.

Brichta, T. 2014. 'The Late Completion of Prague and Cologne Cathedral: Design of Cathedrals, Gothic Revival Movement, Completion as Conservation'. M.Sc. thesis, University of Edinburgh.

Brosius, C. 2017a. 'Art in the Aftermath of a Catastrophe: Gazing, Walking, Participating in the City'. In *Breaking Views: Engaging Art in Post-earthquake Nepal*, ed. C. Brosius, and S. Maharjan, pp.107–35. Kathmandu: Social Science Baha/Himal Books.

———. 2017b. 'Heritage Dynamics in Times of Crisis'. *Material Religion* 13(3): 377–8. https://doi: 10.1080/17432200.2017.1335057.

Brosius, C. and S. Maharjan, eds. 2017. *Breaking Views: Engaging Art in Post-earthquake Nepal*. Kathmandu: Social Science Baha/Himal Books.

Buba, I. A. 2018. 'Aid, Intervention, and Neocolonial "Development" in Africa'. *Journal of Intervention and Statebuilding* 13(1): 131–38. https://doi.org/10.1080/17502977.2018.1470136.

Bukenya, B. 2016. 'From Social Accountability to a New Social Contract? The Role of NGOs in Protecting and Empowering PLHIV in Uganda'. *The Journal of Development Studies* 52(8): 1162–76. https://doi.org/10.1080/00220388.2015.1134775.

Burghart, R 1996. *The Conditions of Listening: Essays on Religion, History and Politics in South Asia*. Delhi: Oxford University Press.

Burke, J. and I. Rauniyar. 2015. 'Nepal Government Criticised for Blocking Earthquake Aid to Remote Areas'. *The Guardian*, 5 May. Available at: https://www.theguardian.com/world/2015/may/02/nepal-government-criticised-blocking-earthquake-aid-remote-areas (accessed 11 June 2020).

Butler, C. and M. Rest. 2017. 'Calculating Risk, Denying Uncertainty: Seismicity and Hydropower Development in Nepal'. *Himalaya: The Journal of the Association for Nepal and Himalayan Studies* 37(2): 15–25.

Button, G. V. and M. Schuller, eds. 2016. *Contextualizing Disaster*. New York and Oxford: Berghahn Books.

Campbell, A. 1833. 'Account of the Earthquake at Kathmandu'. *Journal of the Asiatic Society of Bengal* 2 (January–December): 564–67, 536–39. Available at: https://www.scribd.com/document/38135477/Nepal-Earthquake-of-26-August-1833 (accessed 11 June 2020).

Campbell, B. 2010. 'Rhetorical Routes for Development: A Road Project in Nepal'. *Contemporary South Asia* 18(3): 267–79. https://doi.org/10.1080/09584935.2010.5 01099.

———. 2017. 'Encountering Climate Change: Dialogues of Human and Non-human Relationships within Tamang Moral Ecology and Climate Policy Discourses'. *European Bulletin of Himalayan Research* 49: 59–87.

———. 2018. 'Communities in the Aftermath of Nepal's Earthquake'. In *Evolving Narratives of Hazard and Risk: The Gorkha Earthquake, Nepal 2015*, ed. L. Bracken, H. A. Ruszczyk, and T. Robinson, pp. 109–23. New York: Palgrave Macmillan.

Carrasco, S. and D. O'Brien. 2018. 'The Role of Humanitarian Agencies in Reconstruction and Development of Disaster Affected Communities in Japan and the Philippines'. *Procedia Engineering* 212: 606–13. https://doi.org/10.1016/j.proeng.2018.01.078.

Casey, E. S. 1987. *Remembering: A Phenomenological Study*. Bloomington: Indiana University Press.

Castel-Branco, C. N. 2008. 'Aid Dependency and Development: A Question of Ownership? A Critical View'. Instituto de Estudos Sociaise Económicos, Maputo, Working Paper 01/2008. Available at: www.iese.ac.mz/lib/saber/ead_34.pdf (accessed 11 June 2020).

Chakraborty, R. N. 2001. 'Stability and Outcomes of Common Property Institutions in Forestry: Evidence from the Terai Region of Nepal'. *Ecological Economics* 36(2): 341–53. https://doi.org/10.1016/S0921-8009(00)00237-8.

Chapagain, N. K. and S. R. Tiwari. 2018. 'Challenges to the Notion of Authenticity in the Context of Temples in Kathmandu Valley, Nepal'. In *Revisiting Authenticity in the Asian Context*, ed. G. Wijesuriya and J. Sweet, pp.133–40. Rome: International Centre for the Study of the Preservation and Restoration of Cultural Property.

Chase, L. E., K. Marahatta, K. Sidgel, S. Shrestha, K. Gautam, N. P. Luitel, B. R. Dotel, and R. Samuel. 2018. 'Building Back Better? Taking Stock of the Post-earthquake Mental Health and Psychosocial Response in Nepal'. *International Journal of Mental Health Systems* 12(44): 2–12. doi: 10.1186/s13033-018-0221-3.

Chan, Emily Ying Yan and Polly Po Yi Lee. 2016. 'III: Earthquakes in Nepal: the 2011 Sikkim Earthquake'. Collaborating Centre for Oxford University and CUHK for Disaster and Medical Humanitarian Response. Available at: http://ccouc.org/_asset/file/3nepal.pdf (accessed 1 May 2020),

Childs, G. 2004. *Tibetan Diary: From Birth to Death and Beyond in a Himalayan Valley of Nepal*. Berkeley: University of California Press.

Chitrakar, N. 2017. *Wandering Feet*. Word Warriors Chapbook 7. Lalitpur: Safu.

Cho, A. 2014. 'Post-tsunami Recovery and Reconstruction: Governance Issues and Implications of the Great East Japan Earthquake'. *Disasters* 38(S2): 157–78. https://doi.org/10.1111/disa.12068.

Choguill, M. B. G. 1996. 'A Ladder of Community Participation for Underdeveloped Countries'. *Habitat International* 20(3): 431–44. https://doi.org/10.1016/0197-3975(96)00020-3.

Choi, V. Y. 2015. 'Anticipatory States: Tsunami, War and Insecurity in Sri Lanka'. *Cultural Anthropology* 30(2): 286–309. https://doi.org/10.14506/ca30.2.09.

CHS Alliance, Group URD, and Sphere Project. 2014. *Core Humanitarian Standard on Quality and Accountability*. Available at: https://corehumanitarianstandard.org/files/files/Core%20Humanitarian%20Standard%20-%20English.pdf (accessed 8 November 2018).

Claire, A. 2015. 'Nepal's Earthquake and International Aid'. *The Diplomat*, 5 May. Available at: https://thediplomat.com/2015/05/nepals-earthquake-and-international-aid/ (accessed 11 June 2020).

Clancey, G. 2006. *Earthquake Nation: The Cultural Politics of Japanese Seismicity, 1868–1930*. Berkeley: University of California Press.

Coleman, J. 1990. *Foundations of Social Theory*. Cambridge, MA: Harvard University Press.

Comaroff, J. L. 2001. 'Colonialism, Culture, and the Law: A Foreword'. *Law & Social Inquiry* 26(2): 305–14.

Coningham, R. A. E., K. P. Acharya, C. E. Davis, R. B. Kunwar, I. A. Simpson, A. Schmidt, and J. C. Tremblay. 2016. 'Preliminary Results of Post-disaster Archaeological Investigations at the Kasthamandap and within Hanuman Dhoka, Kathmandu Valley UNESCO World Heritage Property (Nepal)'. *Ancient Nepal* 191–92: 28–51.

Connerton, P. 1989. *How Societies Remember*. Cambridge: Cambridge University Press.

———. 2008. 'Seven Types of Forgetting'. *Memory Studies* 1(1): 59–71.

Cooke, B. and U. Kothari. 2001. 'The Case for Participation as Tyranny'. In *Participation: The New Tyranny?* ed. B. Cooke and U. Kothari, pp. 1–15. London: Zed Books.

Cooley, A. and J. Ron. 2002. 'The NGO Scramble: Organizational Insecurity and the Political Economy of Transnational Action'. *International Security* 27(1): 5–39. https://doi.org/10.1162/016228802320231217.

Cooley, N. 2014. 'Poetry of Disaster'. Academy of American Poets. Available at: https://www.poets.org/poetsorg/text/poetry-disaster (accessed 20 November 2020).

Corbridge, S., G. Williams, M. Srivastava, and R. Véron. 2005. *Seeing the State: Governance and Governmentality in India*. Cambridge, NY: Cambridge University Press.

Cornish, F., C. Campbell, A. Shukla, and R. Banerji. 2012. 'From Brothel to Boardroom: Prospects for Community Leadership of HIV Interventions in the

Context of Global Funding Practices'. *Health & Place* 18(3): 468–74. https://doi.org/10.1016/j.healthplace.2011.08.018.

Cornwall, A. 2002. 'Making Spaces, Changing Places: Situating Participation in Development'. IDS Working Paper 170, pp. 1–35. Available at: https://www.ids.ac.uk/publications/making-spaces-changing-places-situating-participation-in-development/ (accessed 11 June 2020).

Cornwall, A. and K. Brock. 2005. 'What Do Buzzwords Do for Development Policy? A Critical Look at "Participation", "Empowerment" and "Poverty Reduction"'. *Third World Quarterly* 26(7): 1043–60. https://doi.org/10.1080/01436590500235603.

Creighton, M. 2015. '"Wasuren!—We Won't Forget!" The Work of Remembering and Commemorating Japan's and Tohoku's (3.11) Triple Disasters in Local Cities and Communities'. *Journal of Global Initiatives: Policy, Pedagogy, Perspective* 9(1): 97–120. Available at: http://digitalcommons.kennesaw.edu/jgi/vol9/iss1/8 (accessed 20 November 2020).

Cretney, R. M. 2018. 'Beyond Public Meetings: Diverse Forms of Community Led Recovery following Disaster'. *International Journal of Disaster Risk Reduction* 28: 122–30. https://doi.org/10.1016/j.ijdrr.2018.02.035.

Crooke, E. 2010. 'The Politics of Community Heritage: Motivations, Authority and Control'. *International Journal of Heritage Studies* 16(1–2): 16–29. https://doi.org/10.1080/13527250903441705.

Cuny, F. C. 1983. *Disasters and Development*. New York: Oxford University Press.

Curato, N. 2018. 'From Authoritarian Enclave to Deliberative Space: Governance Logics in Post-disaster Reconstruction'. *Disasters* 42(4): 635–54. https://doi.org/10.1111/disa.12280.

D'Ayala, D. and S. S. R. Bajracharya. 2003. *Housing Report Traditional Nawari House in Kathmandu Valley*. World Housing Encyclopedia. Earthquake Engineering Research Institute (EERI) and International Association for Earthquake Engineering (IAEE). Available at: http://www.world-housing.net/WHEReports/wh100103.pdf (accessed 24 June 2020).

Dahal, D. R. 2001. *Civil Society in Nepal: Opening the Ground for Questions*. Kathmandu: Centre for Development and Governance.

Daly, P. and B. Chan. 2016. 'Putting Broken Pieces Back Together: Reconciliation, Justice, and Heritage in Post-conflict Situations'. In *A Companion to Heritage Studies*, ed. W. Logan, M. Craith, and U. Kockel, pp. 491–506. London: John Wiley & Sons.

Daly, P. and T. Winter, eds. 2012. *Routledge Handbook of Heritage in Asia*. New York: Routledge.

Daly, P. and Y. Rahmayati. 2012. 'Cultural Heritage and Community Recovery in Post-tsunami Aceh'. In *From the Ground Up: Perspectives on Post-tsunami and Post-conflict Aceh*, ed. P. Daly, R.M. Feener, and A. Red, pp. 57–78. Singapore: Institute of Southeast Asian Studies.

Daly, P., S. Ninglekhu, P. Hollenbach, J. Duyne Barenstein, and D. Nguyen. 2017. 'Situating Local Stakeholders within National Disaster Governance

Structures: Rebuilding Urban Neighbourhoods following the 2015 Nepal Earthquake'. *Environment and Urbanization* 29(2): 403–24. https://doi. org/10.1177/0956247817721403.

Dangol, N. 2010. 'Sana Guthi and the Newars: Impacts of Modernization on Traditional Social Organizations'. MA. thesis, University of Tromsø.

Das, V. 1995. *Critical Events: An Anthropological Perspective on Contemporary India.* Oxford: Oxford University Press.

———. 2006. *Life and Words: Violence and the Descent into the Ordinary.* Berkeley and London: University of California Press.

Davidson, C. H., C. Johnson, G. Lizarralde, N. Dikmen, and A. Sliwinski. 2007. 'Truths and Myths about Community Participation in Post-disaster Housing Projects'. *Habitat International* 31(1): 100–15. http://dx.doi.org/10.1016/j. habitatint.2006.08.003.

Deen, T. 2015. 'Donors Pledge over 4.4 Billion Dollars to Nepal—But with a Caveat'. *IPS News*, 26 June. Available at: http://www.ipsnews.net/2015/06/donors-pledge-over-4-4-billion-dollars-to-nepal-but-with-a-caveat/ (accessed 11 June 2020).

Deneen, P. 2010. 'God of Earthquakes and Uncertainty'. Berkley Center for Religion, Peace and World Affairs (blog), 8 March. Available at: https://berkleycenter. georgetown.edu/posts/god-of-earthquakes-and-uncertainty-dbe4a666-c752-49d5-8d75-01f09f3d7441 (accessed 11 June 2020).

Desjarlais, R. 2016. *Subject to Death: Life and Loss in a Buddhist World.* Chicago: University of Chicago Press.

DfID-Nepal. 2017. 'Emergency Support to Vulnerable Households: Post-earthquake Housing Reconstruction in Nepal. Business Case Summary Sheet'. Available at: http://iati.dfid.gov.uk/iati_documents/15698505.odt (accessed 14 November 2020).

Dhungana, N. 2019. 'The Politics of Citizen-centric Governance in Post-earthquake Nepal'. Ph.D. thesis, London School of Economics and Political Science. Available at: http://etheses.lse.ac.uk/3923/ (accessed 12 April 2020).

DiCarlo, J., K. Epstein, R. Marsh, and I. Måren. 2018. 'Post-disaster Agricultural Transitions in Nepal'. *Ambio* 47: 794–805. https://doi.org/10.1007/s13280-018-1021-3.

Diwasa, T., C. M. Bandu, and B. Nepal. 2007. 'The Intangible Cultural Heritage of Nepal: Future Directions'. UNESCO Kathmandu Series of Monographs and Working Papers, 14, UNESCO Office Kathmandu.

Dixit, K. M. 2003. 'A New Abode for the Gods'. In *Patan Museum*, ed. G. Hagmüller, pp. 99–101. London: Serindia Publications.

Dombroski, K., G. Diprose, and I. Boles. 2019. 'Can the Commons Be Temporary? The Role of Transitional Commoning in Post-quake Christchurch'. *Local Environment* 24(4): 313–28. https://doi.org/10.1080/13549830902764688.

Dominguez, J. I. 2009. 'Don't Stay Home: The Utility of Area Studies for Political Science Scholarship'. In *The Future of Political Science: 100 Perspectives*, ed. G. King, K. L. Schlozman, and N. H. Nie, pp.180–82. New York: Routledge.

Drechsler, W. 2004. 'Governance, Good Governance, and Government: The Case for Estonian Administrative Capacity'. *Trames: A Journal of Humanities and Social Sciences* 4(8): 388–96.

———. 2009. 'Towards the Law & Economics of Development: Ragnar Nurkse (1907–1959)'. *European Journal of Law and Economics* 28(1): 19–37. https://doi.org/10.1007/s10657-009-9097-7.

———. 2019. 'The Reality and Diversity of Buddhist Economics (with Case Studies of Thailand, Bhutan and Yogyakarta)'. *American Journal of Economics and Sociology* 78(2): 524–60. https://doi.org/10.1111/ajes.12271.

Drury, A.C. and R. S. Olson. 1998. 'Disasters and Political Unrest: An Empirical Investigation'. *Journal of Contingencies and Crisis Management* 6(3): 153–61. https://doi.org/10.1111/1468-5973.00084. Calcutta: Geological Survey of India.

Dunn, J. A., J. B. Auden, and A. M. N. Ghosh. 1934. *Preliminary Report on the North Bihar Earthquake of the 15th January 1934*. Patna: Superintendent, Government Printing.

Dunn, J. A., J. B. Auden, A. M. N. Ghosh, and Wadia, D. N., 1939. 'The Bihar–Nepal Earthquake of 1934'. *Memoirs of the Geological Survey of India* 73. Calcutta: Geological Survey of India.

Dussaillant, F. and E. Guzmán. 2014. 'Trust via Disasters: The Case of Chile's 2010 Earthquake'. *Disasters* 38(4): 808–32. https://doi.org/10.1111/disa.12077.

Duyne Barenstein, J. 2006. 'Challenges and Risks in Post-tsunami Housing Reconstruction in Tamil Nadu'. *Humanitarian Exchange Magazine* 33: 38–39. Available at: https://odihpn.org/magazine/challenges-and-risks-in-post-tsunami-housing-reconstruction-in-tamil-nadu/ (accessed 11 June 2020).

Duyne Barenstein, J. and S. Iyengar. 2009. 'Towards Owner-driven Housing Reconstruction in India'. Paper presented at 'Development from Disaster: Scaling Up Owner-driven Reconstruction', IFRC, Practical Action, and London South Bank University, 19–20 March.

Dynes, R. R. 1999. 'The Dialogue between Voltaire and Rousseau on the Lisbon Earthquake: The Emergence of a Social Science View'. Preliminary papers; 293. Available at: http://udspace.udel.edu/handle/19716/435 (accessed 11 June 2020).

Easterly, W. 2002. 'The Cartel of Good Intentions: The Problem of Bureaucracy in Foreign Aid'. *The Journal of Policy Reform* 5(4): 223–50. https://doi.org/10.1080/1384128032000096823.

———. 2007. 'Was Development Assistance a Mistake?' *The American Economic Review* 97(2): 328–32.

Edwards, E. 2005. 'Photographs and the Sound of History'. *Visual Anthropology Review* 21(1–2): 27–46. https://doi.org/10.1525/var.2005.21.1-2.27.

———. 2012. 'Objects of Affect: Photography beyond the Image'. *Annual Review of Anthropology* 41: 221–34. https://doi.org/10.1146/annurev-anthro-092611-145708.

Edwards, E. and J. Hart, eds. 2004. *Photographs Objects Histories: On the Materiality of Images*. London and New York: Routledge.

EERI (Earthquake Engineering Research Institute). 2016. 'EERI Earthquake Reconnaissance Team Report: M7.8 Gorkha, Nepal Earthquake on April 25, 2015 and Its Aftershocks'. EERI. Oakland, CA. Available at: https://reliefweb.int/sites/reliefweb.int/files/resources/Nepal-Gorkha-Earthquake-Report-Reduced.pdf (accessed 18 December 2018).

Enns, C., B. Bersaglio, and T. Kepe. 2014. 'Indigenous Voices and the Making of the Post-2015 Development Agenda: The Recurring Tyranny of Participation'. *Third World Quarterly* 35(3): 358–75. https://doi.org/10.1080/01436597.2014.893482.

Epstein, K., J. DiCarlo, R. Marsh, B. Adhikari, D. Paudel, I. Ray, and I. Måren. 2018. 'Recovery and Adaptation after the 2015 Nepal Earthquakes: A Smallholder Household Perspective'. *Ecology and Society* 23(1): 29. https://doi.org/10.5751/ES-09909-230129.

Fortun, K. 2001. *Advocacy after Bhopal: Environmentalism, Disaster, New Global Orders*. Chicago and London: University of Chicago Press.

Foster, H. 1995. 'The Artist as Ethnographer?' In *The Traffic in Culture: Refiguring Art and Anthropology*, ed. G. Marcus and F. Myers, pp. 302–09. Berkeley and London: University of California Press.

Francis, A. 2015. 'Nepal Earthquake: Anger as Corruption, Red Tape Holds Up Aid Delivery in Remote Areas'. *ABC News*, 19 May. Available at: https://www.abc.net.au/news/2015-05-19/corruption,-red-tape-holds-up-nepal-earthquake-aid-delivery/6479052 (accessed 11 June 2020).

Frewer, T. 2013. 'Doing NGO Work: The Politics of Being "Civil Society" and Promoting "Good Governance" in Cambodia'. *Australian Geographer* 44(1): 97–114. https://doi.org/10.1080/00049182.2013.765350.

Froude, M. J. and D. N. Petley. 2018. 'Global Fatal Landslide Occurrence from 2004 to 2016'. *Natural Hazards and Earth System Sciences* 18(8): 2161–81. https://doi.org/10.5194/nhess-18-2161-2018.

Fujita, K., H. Inoue, T. Izumi, S. Yamaguchi, A. Sadakane, S. Sunako, K. Nishimura, W. W. Immerzeel, J. M. Shea, R. B. Kayastha, T. Sawagaki, D.F. Breashears, H. Yagi, and A. Sakai. 2017. 'Anomalous Winter-snow-amplified Earthquake-induced Disaster of the 2015 Langtang Avalanche in Nepal'. *Natural Hazards and Earth System Sciences* 17(5): 749–64. https://doi.org/10.5194/nhess-17-749-2017.

Fujiwara, T, T. Sato, T. Kubo, and H. O. Murakami. 1989. *Reconnaissance Report on the 21 August 1988 Earthquake in the Nepal–India Border Region*. Research report on natural disasters, supported by the Japanese Ministry of Education, Science and Culture, Grant No. 63115047. Available at: https://core.ac.uk/download/pdf/35430907.pdf (accessed 20 November 2020).

Gaire, S., R. Castro Delgado, and P. Arcos González. 2015. 'Disaster Risk Profile and Existing Legal Framework of Nepal: Floods and Landslides'. *Risk Management and Healthcare Policy* 8: 139–49. https://doi.org/10.2147/RMHP.S90238.

Gamburd, M. R. 2013. *The Golden Wave: Culture and Politics after Sri Lanka's Tsunami Disaster*. Bloomington and Indianapolis: Indiana University Press.

Gautam, R. 2046 v.s. (1989/90). *Nepalko Prajatantrik Andolanma Nepal Praja-Parishadko Bhumika* (The Role of Nepal Praja Parishad in Nepal's Democratic Movement). Kathmandu: Self-published.

Gaventa, J. 2006. 'Finding the Spaces for Change: A Power Analysis'. *IDS Bulletin* 37(6): 23–33. https://doi.org/10.1111/j.1759-5436.2006.tb00320.x.

Gellner, D. N. 1992. *Monk, Householder, and Tantric Priest: Newar Buddhism and Its Hierarchy of Ritual*. Cambridge: Cambridge University Press.

———. 2019. 'The Guthi System Should Be Regarded as Important Intangible Cultural Heritage'. *South Asia Time*, 21 June. Available at: https://www.southasiatime. com/2019/06/21/the-guthi-system-should-be-regarded-as-important-intangible-cultural-heritage-prof-david-gellner/ (accessed 11 June 2020).

Gellner, D. N. and D. Quigley, eds. 1995. *Contested Hierarchies: A Collaborative Ethnography of Caste among the Newars of the Kathmandu Valley, Nepal*. Oxford: Clarendon Press.

Toffin, G. 1995. 'The Social Organization of Rajopadhyaya Brahmans'. In *Contested Hierarchies: A Collaborative Ethnography of Caste among the Newars of the Kathmandu Valley, Nepal*, ed. D.N. Gellner and D. Quigley, pp. 186–209. Oxford: Clarendon Press.

Geographical. 2004. 'Dr John Auden (1903–91): An Outstanding Geologist and Surveyor Who Worked Primarily in India, John Auden Also Inspired the Writings of His Famous Brother, the Poet WH Auden'. *Geographical* 76(3) (March). Available at: https://www.questia.com/magazine/1G1-114239286/dr-john-auden-1903-91-an-outstanding-geologist (accessed 11June 2020).

Ghale, S. 2019. 'The Anti-reservation Brigade'. *The Record*, 4 July. Available at: https://www.recordnepal.com/featured/the-anti-reservation-brigade/?fbclid=IwAR2T0bCFrSlXP0t2K63_k_2VssaUpS6x2v2FqCALv2HgIcm5AMrZgE5AJnU (accessed 11 June 2020).

Gharti Magar, J. and D. B. Majhi. 2068 v.s. *Majhi Jatiko Chinari* (Introduction to the Majhi Ethnic Group). Lalitpur: National Foundation for Development of Indigenous Nationalities.

Ghimire, B. 2020. 'Why the MCC Compact Courted Controversy in Nepal'. *The Kathmandu Post*, 9 January. Available at: https://kathmandupost.com/national/2020/01/09/why-the-mcc-compact-courted-controversy-in-nepal (accessed 11 June 2020).

Ghimire, J. 2008. *Antarmanko Yatra* (Journey to Inner Heart). Kathmandu: Modern Books.

Ginsburg, F. 1994. 'Embedded Aesthetics: Creating a Discursive Space for Indigenous Media'. *Cultural Anthropology* 9(3): 365–82. https://doi.org/10.1525/can.1994.9.3.02a00080.

Giri, A. 2018. 'Integrity Policy Gathers Dust at PM's Office'. *The Kathmandu Post*, 29 December. Available at: https://kathmandupost.com/national/2018/12/29/integrity-policy-gathers-dust-at-pms-office (accessed 11 June 2020).

Giri, S. 2018. 'Restored Gaddi Baithak Sparks Controversy: Conservationists Point Out Design Alterations'. *The Kathmandu Post*, 26 June. Available at: https://kathmandupost.ekantipur.com/news/2018-06-26/restored-gaddi-baithak-sparks-controversy.html (accessed 11 June 2020).

Gong, T. B. 2014. 'The Fab Four: Youth Were Angered When Rana Regime Started Distributing Earthquake Relief in the Form of Loans'. *My Republica*, 1 February.

Gordillo, G. R. 2014. *Rubble: The Afterlife of Destruction*. Durham NC: Duke University Press.

Government of Nepal (GON), Ministry of Culture, Tourism and Civil Aviation, Department of Archaeology. 2018. *Updated Report: Kathmandu Valley World Heritage Property*. Available at: https://whc.unesco.org/document/165534 (accessed 20 November 2020).

Government of Nepal (GON), Ministry of Home Affairs. 2013. *Nepal Disaster Report 2013. Focus on Participation and Inclusion*. Kathmandu: GON MOHA, and Disaster Preparedness Network-Nepal. Available at: http://drrportal.gov.np/uploads/document/163.pdf (accessed 20 November 2020).

Government of Nepal (GON), Ministry of Law, Justice and Parliamentary Affairs. 2015. *Act Relating to Reconstruction of the Earthquake Affected Structures, 2015 (2072 v.s.)*. Available at: http://nra.gov.np/en/content/acts/0 (accessed 21 October 2018).

Government of Nepal (GON), Ministry of Urban Development. 2072 v.s. *Basti Bikas, Shahari Yojana Tatha Bhavan Nirman Sambandhi Adharbhut Nirman Mapdanda, 2072* (Basic Construction Standards for Settlement Development, Urban Planning and Building Construction, 2072 v.s.). Kathmandu: Ministry of Urban Development, Government of Nepal. Available at: moud.gov.np/images/category/Basti-Bikash-Mapdanda-2072-Final1.pdf (accessed 20 November 2020).

Government of Nepal (GON), Nepal Law Commission. 2008. *Good Governance (Management and Operation) Act, 2064 (2008)*. Available at: http://extwprlegs1.fao.org/docs/pdf/nep137755.pdf (accessed 2 October 2017).

Gupta, A. 2012. *Red Tape: Bureaucracy, Structural Violence, and Poverty in India*. Durham, NC: Duke University Press.

Gurung, B. 2010. 'One Decade of Upper Tamakoshi Hydroelectric Project'. *Energy Nepal* 2(3): 10–19.

Gutschow, N. 2011. *Architecture of the Newars: A History of Building Typologies and Details in Nepal—Documentation Drawings by Bijay Basukala*, 3 vols. Chicago: Serindia Publications.

———. 2017. 'Architectural Heritage Conservation in South and East Asia and in Europe: Contemporary Practices'. In *Authenticity in Architectural Heritage Conservation: Discourses, Opinions, Experiences in Europe, South and East Asia*, ed. K. Weiler and N. Gutschow, pp. 1–68. Cham: Springer.

———. 2019. *Preserving Hariśaṅkara: Lessons in Rebuilding on Patan's Royal Square in Nepal. 2015 to 2019*. Kathmandu: Kathmandu Valley Preservation Trust.

Gutschow, N. and R. Roka, eds. 2017. *Nepal. Patan Palace. The Restoration of Sundari Cok, 2006–2016*. Kathmandu: Kathmandu Valley Preservation Trust.

Hachhethu, K. 2009. 'The Communist Party of Nepal (Maoist): Transformation from an Insurgency Group to a Competitive Political Party'. *European Bulletin of Himalayan Research* 33/34: 39–71.

Hagmüller, G., ed. 2003. *Patan Museum*. London: Serindia Publications.

Hall, M. L., A. C. K. Lee, C. Cartwright, S. Maharatta, J. Karki, and P. Simkhada. 2017. 'The 2015 Nepal Earthquake Disaster: Lessons Learned One Year On'. *Public Health* 145: 39–44. https://doi.org/10.1016/j.puhe.2016.12.031.

Hall, S. 2007. 'Whose Heritage? Unsettling "The Heritage", Re-imagining the Post-nation'. In *Cultural Heritage*, ed. L. Smith, pp. 87–100. London: Routledge.

Hamad, R. 2015. 'Nepal Earthquake: How Religious Groups Prey on the Victims of Natural Disasters'. *Dailylife*, 30 April. Available at: http://www.dailylife.com.au/news-and-views/news-features/nepal-earthquake-how-religious-groups-prey-on-the-victims-of-natural-disasters-20150429-1mw0fu.html (accessed 11 June 2020).

Hammersley, M. 1992. *What's Wrong with Ethnography? Methodological Explorations*. London; New York: Routledge.

Hammersley, M. and P. Atkinson. 2007. *Ethnography: Principles in Practice*, 3rd ed. New York: Routledge.

Haraway, D. 1988. 'Situated Knowledges: The Science Question in Feminism and the Privilege of Partial Perspective'. *Feminist Studies* 14(3): 575–99.

Harles, M. and S. Rajbhandari . 2017. 'Contemporary Artists' Response to Heritage in Times of Crisis: 12 Baisakh and Photo Kathmandu'. *Material Religion: The Journal of Objects, Art and Belief* 13(3): 387–90. https://doi.org/10.1080/1743220 0.2017.1335058.

Harris, C., 2004. 'The Photograph Reincarnate: The Dynamics of Tibetan Relationships with Photography'. In *Photographs Objects Histories: On the Materiality of Images*, ed. E. Edwards and J. Hart, pp. 139–55. London and New York: Routledge.

———. 2012. *The Museum on the Roof of the World: Art, Politics, and the Representation of Tibet*. Chicago: University of Chicago Press.

Harris, G. 2015. 'Nepal's Bureaucracy is Blamed as Earthquake Relief Supplies Pile Up'. *The New York Times*, 3 May. Available at: https://www.nytimes.com/2015/05/04/world/asia/nepals-bureaucracy-is-blamed-as-quake-relief-supplies-pile-up.html (accessed 12 June 2020).

Harris, R., A. Jacquemin, S. Ponthagunta, J. Sah, and D. Shrestha. 2003. 'Rural Development with ICTs in Nepal: Integrating National Policy with Grassroots Resourcefulness'. *Electronic Journal of Information Systems in Developing Countries* 12(4): 1–12. http://doi: 10.1002/j.1681-4835.2003.tb00079.x.

Harvey, P., C. Jensen, and A. Morita. 2017. *Infrastructures and Social Complexity*. Oxford: Routledge.

Hassenforder, E., A. Smajgl, and J. Ward. 2015. 'Towards Understanding Participatory Processes: Framework, Application and Results'. *Journal of Environmental Management* 157: 84–95. https://doi.org/10.1016/j.jenvman.2015.04.012.

Hastrup, F. 2011. *Weathering the World: Recovery in the Wake of the Tsunami in a Tamil Fishing Village*. New York: Berghahn Books.

Haxby, A. 2019. 'A House Divided: Land, Kinship, and Bureaucracy in Post-earthquake Kathmandu'. Ph.D. thesis, University of Michigan.

Hayward, B. 2014. 'Reimagining and Rebuilding Local Democracy'. In *Once in a Lifetime: City-building after Disaster in Christchurch*, ed. B. Bennett, J. Dann, E. Johnson, and R. Reynolds, pp. 179–85. Christchurch: Freerange Press.

Heaton-Shrestha, C. and R. Adhikari. 2011. 'NGOization and De-NGOization of Public Action in Nepal: The Role of Organizational Culture in Civil Society Politicality'. *Journal of Civil Society* 7(1): 41–61. https://doi.org/10.1080/1744868 9.2011.553420.

Heydon, S. 2019. 'Death of the King: The Introduction of Vaccination into Nepal in 1816'. *Medical History* 63(2): 22–43. https://doi.org/10.1017/mdh.2018.61.

Hilhorst, D. 2004. 'Complexity and Diversity: Unlocking Social Domains of Disaster Response'. In *Mapping Vulnerability: Disasters, Development, and People*, ed. G. Bankoff, G. Frerks, and D. Hilhorst, pp. 52–66. New York: Earthscan.

Himalayan Risk Research Institute. n.d. 'Lo Mustang Earthquake, 1505'. Available at: https://hri.org.np/lo_mustang_earthquake_1505/ (accessed 20 November 2020).

Hirslund, D. V. 2019. 'Brokering Labour: The Politics of Markets in the Kathmandu Construction Industry'. *Ethnography*: 1–20. https://doi. org/10.1177/1466138119886601.

Hoffman, S. M. 1999. 'After Atlas Shrugs: Cultural Change or Persistence after a Disaster'. In *The Angry Earth: Disaster in Anthropological Perspective*, ed. A. Oliver-Smith and S. M. Hoffman, pp. 302–26. Hove: Psychology Press.

——. 2002. 'The Monster and the Mother: The Symbolism of Disaster'. In *Catastrophe and Culture: The Anthropology of Disaster*, ed. S. M. Hoffman and A. Oliver-Smith, pp. 113–42. Santa Fe and Oxford: School of American Research Press.

Hoftun, M., W. Raeper, and J. Whelpton. 1997. *People, Politics and Ideology: Democracy and Social Change in Nepal*. Kathmandu: Mandala Bookpoint.

Holmberg, D. H. and K. S. March. 2015. 'Tamsaling and the Toll of the Gorkha Earthquake'. *Fieldsights*, Hot Spots, 14 October. Available at: https://culanth. org/fieldsights/tamsaling-and-the-toll-of-the-gorkha-earthquake (accessed 20 November 2020).

Holston, J. 1995. 'Spaces of Insurgent Citizenship'. *Planning Theory* 13: 35–51.

Hörhager, E. 2015. 'Political Implications of Natural Disasters: Regime Consolidation and Political Contestation'. *WIT Transactions on the Built Environment*, 150: 271–281.

Housing Recovery and Reconstruction Platform (HRRP). 2018. *Women in Reconstruction Research Report*. Available at: https://digital.soas.ac.uk/SWAY002096/ (accessed 20 November 2020).

Hurlbert, M. and J. Gupta. 2015. 'The Split Ladder of Participation: A Diagnostic, Strategic, and Evaluation Tool to Assess When Participation is Necessary'. *Environmental Science & Policy* 50: 100–113. https://doi:10.1016/j.envsci.2015.01.011.

Hutt, M. J. 2010. *The Life of Bhupi Sherchan: Poetry and Politics in Post-Rana Nepal*. New Delhi: Oxford University Press.

———. 2019a. 'Area Studies and the Importance of "Somewheres"'. *South East Asia Research* 27(1): 21–25.

———. 2019b. 'Revealing What Is Dear: The Post-earthquake Iconisation of the Dharahara, Kathmandu'. *Journal of Asian Studies* 78(3): 549–76.

———. 2020. 'Before the Dust Settled: Is Nepal's 2015 Settlement a Seismic Constitution?' *Conflict Security and Development* 20(3): 379–400. https://doi.org/10.1080/14678802.2020.1771848.

———. Forthcoming. 'Earthquake Aftersongs: Music Videos and the Imagining of an Online Nepali Public'. *Popular Communication Journal*.

Hutt, M. J. and K. Shreesh. 2019. 'A Visit to the Epicentre'. SWAY project blog post, 28 March. Available at: https://sway.soscbaha.org/blogs/a-visit-to-the-epicentre/ (accessed 3 July 2020).

ICOMOS. 1965. International Charter for the Conservation and Restoration of Monuments and Sites (The Venice Charter). Approved by the Second International Congress of Architects and Technicians of Historic Monuments in Venice from 25 to 31 May 1964, adopted by ICOMOS in 1965. Available at: https://www.icomos.org/charters/venice_e.pdf (accessed 20 November 2020).

ILO (International Labour Organization). 2015. 'Nepal Post-earthquake: Rebuilding Lives!!!' *Decent Work: Biannual Newsletter of the ILO Country Office* (July). Available at: https://www.ilo.org/wcmsp5/groups/public/---asia/---ro-bangkok/---ilo-kathmandu/documents/publication/wcms_389359.pdf (accessed 20 November 2020).

ITUC–NAC (International Trade Union Confederation–Nepal Affiliated Council). 2015. 'Trade Union Road-map for Reconstruction and Development of Nepal: Statement from "Reconstruction by Creating Decent Jobs: International Solidarity Meeting on Nepal"'. Kathmandu, 3–4 September 2015. Available at: http://ntuc.org.np/uploads/docs/SnmvC9gL2F161224052059.pdf (accessed 11 November 2020).

Jackson, D. 2002. 'The Great Western-Himalayan Earthquake of 1505: A Rupture of the Central Himalayan Gap?' In *Tibet, Past and Present*, ed. H. Blezer, Brill's Tibetan Studies Library I, pp. 147–59. Leiden: Brill.

Jackson, S. J. 2014. 'Rethinking Repair'. In *Media Technologies: Essays on Communication, Materiality, and Society*, ed. T. Gillespie, P. J. Boczkowski, and K. A. Foot, pp. 221–39. Cambridge, MA, and London: MIT Press.

Janssen, P. 2016. 'Christianity's Rise Tests Nepal's New Secularism'. *Nikkei Asia*, 15 December. Available at: https://asia.nikkei.com/magazine/OVERWORKED/Life-Arts/Christianity-s-rise-tests-Nepal-s-new-secularism (accessed 11 November 2018).

Johnson, K., E. Olson, and S. Manandhar. 1982. 'Environmental Knowledge and Response to Natural Hazards in Mountainous Nepal'. *Mountain Research and Development* 2(2): 175–88. doi: 10.2307/3672962.

Jones, S., K. J. Oven, B. Manyena, and K. Aryal. 2014. 'Governance Struggles and Policy Processes in Disaster Risk Reduction: A Case Study from Nepal'. *Geoforum* 57: 78–90. doi.org/10.1016/j.geoforum.2014.07.011.

Joshi, S. 2072 v.s. (2015). '90 Salle Nepallai Usinachamal, Jastapata ra Siment Diyo' (1934 Gave Nepal Parboiled Rice, Corrugated Steel and Cement). *Himal KhabarPatrika* 20–26 (Baisakh), p. 45.

Kafle, L. 2019. 'Lalitpur Metropolis Bracing for VNY 2020'. *The Rising Nepal*, 17 September 2019. Available at: https://risingnepaldaily.com/detour/lalitpur-metropolis-bracing-for-vny-2020 (accessed 25 November 2020).

Kandel, R. C., B. H. Pandey, and A. M. Dixit. 2004. 'Investing in Future Generation: The School Earthquake Safety Program in Nepal'. Paper presented to 13th World Conference on Earthquake Engineering, Vancouver, 1–6 August.

Kaphle, G. 2016. *Shabdako Ainama Mahabhukampa* (The Great Earthquake in a Mirror of Words). Kathmandu: Oriental Publications.

Kargel, J. S., G. J. Leonard, D. H. Shugar, U. K. Haritashya, A. Bevington, and E. J. Fielding. 2016. 'Geomorphic and Geologic Controls of Geohazards Induced by Nepal's 2015 Gorkha Earthquake'. *Science* 351(6299). https://doi:10.1126/science.aac8353.

Karki, D. 2015. 'Sense of an Ending'. *The Kathmandu Post*, 28 April. Available at: https://kathmandupost.com/opinion/2015/04/28/sense-of-an-ending (accessed 2 July 2020).

Karki, L. M. S. 2015. 'Road to Recovery: Juddha Shamsher Tried to Utilize Domestic Resources As Much As Possible to Normalize Lives of People after the 1934 Earthquake'. *My Republica*, 23 May. Available at: http://archive.myrepublica.com/2015-16/opinion/story/21361/road-to-recovery.html (accessed 25 November 2020).

Kantipur Daily. 2071a v.s. 'Tamakoshi Bibaad Suljhiyo' ([Upper] Tamakoshi Disputes Resolved), *Kantipur Dainik*, 17 Chaitra.

———. 2071b v.s. 'Tamakoshi Tesro Din Pani Thappa' ([Upper] Tamakoshi [Construction Work] Halted Third Day Too), *Kantipur Dainik*, 2 Chaitra.

Kathmandu Valley Preservation Trust (KVPT). 2016. *Nepal. Patan Darbar Earthquake Response Campaign. Documentation of Work to Date. September 2016.* Kathmandu: KVPT.

Kawan, S. S. 2015. 'Heritage in All, Heritage for All: Integrity Overrides Authenticity'. In UNESCO, *Revisiting Kathmandu: Safeguarding Living Urban Heritage*, pp. 73–82. Kathmandu: UNESCO.

KC, C. 2016. 'Preserving the Intangible'. *The Nepali Times*, 30 September–6 October (828). Available at: http://nepalitimes.com/article/Nepali-Times-Buzz/saving-the-intangible,3303 (accessed 2 July 2020).

KC, C., S. Karuppannan, and A. Sivam. 2019. 'Importance of Cultural Heritage in a Post-disaster Setting: Perspectives from the Kathmandu Valley'. *Journal of Social and Political Sciences* 2(2): 429–42. doi: 10.31014/aior.1991.02.02.82.

KC, D. 2071a v.s. 'Sheyar Bibadle Tamakoshi Nirman Pheri Thappa' (Construction of [Upper] Tamakoshi Stopped Again due to Share Dispute). *Karobar Dainik*, 1 Chaitra.

———. 2071b v.s. 'Tamakoshima Pheri Sahamati' (Reconciliation at [Upper] Tamakoshi Again). *Karobar Dainik*, 17 Chaitra.

Khadka, P. 2017. 'Nepal: New Law Criminalizes Religious Conversion'. *Eurasia Review*, 6 September. Available at: https://www.eurasiareview.com/06092017-nepal-new-law-criminalizes-religious-conversion/ (accessed 20 November 2020).

Khaniya, G. 2005. *Traditional Water Management Practices: A Case Study of Bhaktapur City*. Internal report, Jalsrot Vikas Sanstha. Available at: https://jvs-nwp.org.np/wp-content/uploads/2018/07/Number-28.pdf (accessed 20 November 2020).

Khazai, B., J. Anhorn, S. Brink, T. Girard, G. K. Jimee, B. Parajuli, S. Wagle, O. Khanal, S. Shrestha, and R. Manandhar. 2015. *Emergent Issues and Vulnerability Factors in Temporary and Intermediate Shelters Following the 2015 Nepal Earthquake*. Centre for Disaster Management and Risk Reduction Technology, Karlsruhe Institute of Technology, South Asia Institute Heidelberg University, National Society for Earthquake Technology. Report No. 4, Shelter Report Following Field Mission. Available at: https://reliefweb.int/sites/reliefweb.int/files/resources/CEDIM_NepalEarthquake_Report4_ShelterFM.pdf (accessed 20 November 2020).

Kirshenblatt-Gimblett, B. 1998. *Destination Culture: Tourism, Museums, and Heritage*. Berkeley; Los Angeles; London: University of California Press.

Klein, N. 2007. *The Shock Doctrine: The Rise of Disaster Capitalism*. New York: Metropolitan Books.

Klinenberg, E. 2003. *Heat Wave: A Social Autopsy of Disaster in Chicago*. Chicago: University of Chicago Press.

Koirala, S. 1968. 'Koshi Pradeshka Majhi Jaati' (The Majhi Community of Koshi Region). *Ancient Nepal* 3 (April): 18–21.

Korn, W. 1976. *The Traditional Architecture of the Kathmandu Valley*. Kathmandu: Ratna Pustak Bhandar.

Krause, M. 2010. 'Accounting for State Intervention: The Social Histories of "Beneficiaries"'. *Qualitative Sociology* 33(4): 533–47.

Kuhn, A. and K. E. McAllister, eds. 2006. *Locating Memory: Photographic Acts*. Oxford: Berghahn Books.

Kunwar, N. 2015a. 'How a Local Artist Collective Is Responding to Nepal Earthquake'. *Huffington Post*. Available at: https://www.huffpost.com/entry/how-a-local-artist-collec_b_7528660 (accessed 20 November 2020).

———. 2015b. 'Nepali Artists Engage with Quake-hit Communities'. *Huffington Post*. Available at: https://www.huffingtonpost.com/niranjan-kunwar/nepali-artists-engage-wit_b_8202264.html (accessed 20 November 2020).

Labadi, S. and W. Logan, eds. 2016. *Urban Heritage, Development and Sustainability*. London: Routledge.

Lal, A. 2019. 'A Ghost Settlement in Gorkha'. *Record Nepal*, 18 June. Available at: https://www.recordnepal.com/wire/features/a-ghost-settlement-in-gorkha/ (accessed 20 November 2020).

Lama, S. C. 2019. '4 Years after Quake, Sankhu Rises from the Dust'. *The Nepali Times*. Available at: https://www.nepalitimes.com/here-now/4-years-after-quake-sankhu-rises-from-the-dust/ (accessed 20 November 2020).

Larkin, B. 2013. 'The Politics and Poetics of Infrastructure'. *Annual Review of Anthropology* 42: 327–43. https://doi.org/10.1146/annurev-anthro-092412-155522.

Lassa, J. 2018. 'Roles of Non-government Organizations in Disaster Risk Reduction'. In *Oxford Research Encyclopedia of Natural Hazard Science*, pp. 1–23. Oxford: Oxford University Press. https://doi.org/10.1093/acrefore/9780199389407.013.45.

Latif, S. A., N. Muniyati, N. Din, and Z. Mustapha. 2018. 'Good Waqf Governance and Its Contribution in Sustainable Development'. *Journal of ASIAN Behavioural Studies* 4(12): 37–47. https://doi.org/10.21834/jabs.v4i12.328.

Lauta, K. C. 2018. 'Disasters and Responsibility: Normative Issues for Law following Disasters'. In *Disasters: Core Concepts and Ethical Theories*, ed. D. P. O'Mathúna, V. Dranseika, and G. Gordijn, pp 43–54. Cham: Springer Open Series. https://doi.org/10.1007/978-3-319-92722-0.

Lave, J., D. Yule, S. Sapkota, K. Bassant, C. Madden, M. Attal, and R. Pandey. 2005. 'Evidence for a Great Medieval Earthquake (–1100 A.D.) in the Central Himalayas, Nepal'. *Science*, New Series, 307(5713): 1302–05.

Lawoti, M. 2003. 'Centralizing Politics and the Growth of the Maoist Insurgency in Nepal'. *Himalaya* 23(1): 47–58. Available at: http://digitalcommons.macalester.edu/himalaya/vol23/iss1/10 (accessed 20 November 2020).

Lear, J. 2006. *Radical Hope: Ethics in the Face of Cultural Devastation*. Cambridge, MA and London: Harvard University Press.

Le Billon, P., M. Suji, J. Baniya, B. Limbu, D. Paudel, K. Rankin, N. Rawal, and S. Shneiderman. 2020. 'Disaster Financialization: Earthquakes, Cashflows, and Shifting Household Economies in Nepal'. *Development and Change* 51(4): 939–69. https://doi.org/10.1111/dech.12603.

LeCompte, M. D. and J. J. Schensul. 2013. *Analysis and Interpretation of Ethnographic Data: A Mixed Methods Approach*, 2nd ed. Lanham, New York, Toronto and Plymouth: Altamira Rowman Littlefield.

Lefebvre, H. 1991. *The Production of Space*, trans. D. Nicholson-Smith. Oxford and Malden, MA: Blackwell Publishing.

———. 2003. *The Urban Revolution*. Minneapolis: University of Minnesota Press.

Lekakis, S., S. Shakya, and V. Kostakis. 2018. 'Bringing the Community Back: A Case Study of the Post-earthquake Heritage Restoration in Kathmandu Valley'. *Sustainability* 10(8): 2798. https://doi.org/10.3390/su10082798.

Lempert, W. 2018. 'Generative Hope in the Post-apocalyptic Present'. *Cultural Anthropology* 33(2): 202–12. https://doi.org/10.14506/ca33.2.04.

Levy, R. I. 1992. *Mesocosm: Hinduism and the Organization of a Traditional Newar City in Nepal*. Berkeley: University of California Press.

Lewis, D. 2014. *Non-Governmental Organizations, Management and Development*, 3rd ed. London and New York: Routledge.

Lewis, D. and D. Mosse. 2006. 'Theoretical Approaches to Brokerage and Translation in Development'. In *Development Brokers and Translators: The Ethnography of Aid and Agencies*, ed. D. Lewis and D. Mosse, pp. 1–26. Bloomfield, CT: Kumarian Press.

Lewsley, H. 2015. 'The Town as a Museum Piece'. *The Nepali Times*, 20–26 November (783). Available at: https://archive.nepalitimes.com/page/Patan-town-as-a-museum-piece (accessed 24 June 2020).

Liboiron, M. 2015. 'Disaster Data, Data Activism: Grassroots Responses to Representing Superstorm Sandy'. In *Extreme Weather and Global Media*, ed. J. Leyda and D. Negra, pp. 152–70. London and New York: Routledge.

Liechty, M. 1997. 'Selective Exclusion: Foreigners, Foreign Goods, and Foreignness in Modern Nepali History'. *Studies in Nepali History and Society* 2(1): 5–68.

———. 2003. *Suitably Modern: Making Middle-class Culture in a New Consumer Society*. Princeton: Princeton University Press.

———. 2020. 'Disasters and "Conditions of Possibility": Rethinking Causation Through an Analysis of Nepal Earthquakes'. *Disasters*, online publication 8 August. https://doi.org/10.1111/disa.12459.

Lim, F. K. G. 2008. *Imagining the Good Life: Negotiating Culture and Development in Nepal Himalaya*. Leiden: Boston: Brill.

Limbu, B., N. Rawal, M. Suji, P. C. Subedi, and J. Baniya. 2019. 'Reconstructing Nepal: Post-earthquake Experiences from Bhaktapur, Dhading and Sindhupalchowk'. Reconstructing Nepal Working Paper Series, Social Science Baha, Kathmandu. Available at: https://soscbaha.org/publication/reconstructing-nepal-post-earth quake-experiences-from-bhaktapur-dhading-and-sindhupalchowk (accessed 3 July 2020).

Lin, J. Y. 2012. *New Structural Economics: A Framework for Rethinking Development and Policy*. Washington DC: World Bank. Available at: http://hdl.handle. net/10986/2232 (accessed 20 November 2020).

Lindell, M. K. 2011. 'Disaster Studies'. *Current Sociology* 61(5–6): 797–825. https://doi. org/10.1177/0011392113484456.

Lizarralde, G., C. Johnson, and C. Davidson. 2009. *Rebuilding after Disasters: from Emergency to Sustainability*. London: Routledge. https://doi.org/10.4324/ 9780203892572.

Lizarralde, G., M. Fayazi, F. Kikano, and I. Thomas. 2016. 'Meta-patterns in Post-disaster Housing Reconstruction and Recovery'. In *Coming Home after Disaster: Multiple Dimensions of Housing Recovery*, ed. A. Sapat and A. M. Esnard, pp. 229–243. New York: Routledge. https://doi.org/10.4324/9781315404264.

'Lord, A. 2015. 'Langtang'. *Cultural Anthropology*, 14 October. Available at: https:// culanth.org/fieldsights/langtang (accessed 11 June 2020).

————. 2016. 'Citizens of a Hydropower Nation: Territory and Agency at the Frontiers of Hydropower Development in Nepal'. *Economic Anthropology* 3(1): 145–60. https://doi.org/10.1002/sea2.12051.

Lord, A. and G. Murton. 2017. 'Becoming Rasuwa Relief: Practices of Multiple Engagement in Post-earthquake Nepal'. *Himalaya: The Journal of the Association for Nepal and Himalayan Studies* 37(2): 87–102.

Lotter, S. 2019. 'From Ritual (Dis)continuity to Hurt National Pride: Limiting Outsider's Cultural Insensitivities in Heritage Conservation'. Unpublished paper.

Lowenthal, L. 1961. *Literature, Popular Culture, and Society*. Palo Alto: Pacific Books.

Lu, Y. and J. Xu. 2014. 'NGO Collaboration in Community Post-disaster Reconstruction: Field Research following the 2008 Wenchuan Earthquake in China'. *Disasters* 39(2): 258–78. https://doi.org/10.1111/disa.12098.

Magar, S. G. 2015. 'The Tamang Epicentre'. *The Nepali Times*, 10–16 July (766). Available at: http://archive.nepalitimes.com/article/nation/April-25-earthquake-Tamang-epicentre,2407 (accessed 3 July 2020).

Maharjan, M. 2013. 'Conflict in World Heritage Sites of Kathmandu Valley: A Case Study on the Conservation of Private Houses in Three Durbar Squares'. *Nepal Tourism and Development Review* 2(1): 87–104. https://doi:10.3126/ntdr.v2i1.7381.

Maharjan, M. and F. T. Barata. 2017. 'Living with Heritage: Including Tangible and Intangible Heritage in the Changing Time and Space'. *Journal of the Institute of Engineering* 13(1): 178–89. https://doi:10.3126/jie.v13i1.20365.

Mahatara, B. 2017. 'Earthquake Disaster: Reconstruction and Recovery'. *The Himalayan Times*, 12 December. Available at: https://thehimalayantimes.com/opinion/earthquake-disaster-reconstruction-recovery/ (accessed 3 July 2020).

Majhi, D. B. 2006. *Majhi Jatiko Sanskar ra Sanskriti* (The Customs and Culture of the Majhi Ethnic Group). Kathmandu: Majhi Bikash tatha Anusandhan Parishad, Nepal.

Malagodi, M. 2013. *Constitutional Nationalism and Legal Exclusion: Equality, Identity, Politics, and Democracy in Nepal (1990–2007)*. Oxford: Oxford University Press.

Manandhar, R. 2071 v.s. 'Tamakoshimaa Hadtaal: Gambhir Sankatko Ghoshana' (The Strike at [Upper] Tamakoshi: A Declaration of Serious Crisis). *Kantipur Dainik*, 1 Chaitra, p. 18.

Manandhar, S. 2018. 'Communist Government Moves to Curtail Civil Liberties'. *Record Nepal*, 15 June. Available at: https://www.recordnepal.com/wire/communist-government-moves-to-curtail-civil-liberties/ (accessed 3 July 2020).

Manandhar, T. 2014. 'Digu Puja: Lineage God Worship. A Cultural Study of the Kathmandu City'. Ph.D. thesis, Tribhuvan University, Nepal.

Mansuri, G. and V. Rao. 2012. *Localizing Development: Does Participation Work?* Washington D.C: The World Bank.

Marchezini, V. 2015. 'The Biopolitics of Disaster: Power, Discourses, and Practices'. *Human Organization* 74(4): 362–71. https://doi.org/10.17730/0018-7259-74.4.362.

Mateo, B. V. 2014. 'Community Based Development and Urban Conservation in Kathmandu Valley of Nepal: Learning from Conservation and Development'. MA thesis, Technische Universität Berlin.

Mathema, P. 2017. 'Contractors Threaten Nepal's Heritage'. *The Gulf Times*, 24 March. Available at: http://www.gulf-times.com/story/539799/Contractors-threaten-Nepal-s-heritage (accessed 2 July 2020).

Matthew, R. and B. R. Upreti. 2018. 'Disaster Capitalism in Nepal'. *Peace Review: A Journal for Social Justice* 30(2): 176–83. doi.org/10.1080/10402659.2018.1458946.

Mawdsley, E. 2018. 'Development Geography II: Financialization'. *Progress in Human Geography* 42(2): 264–74. doi.org/10.1177/0309132516678747.

Messerschmidt, D. 1981. '"Nogar" and Other Traditional Forms of Cooperation in Nepal: Significance for Development'. *Human Organization* 40(1): 40–47. Available at: https://www.jstor.org/stable/44125585 (accessed 20 November 2020).

Meyer, B. ed. 2009. *Aesthetic Formations: Media, Religion and the Senses*. New York: Palgrave MacMillan.

Mishra, S. and D. Aryal. 2015. '1934 Earthquake Revisited: A View from the Archives'. Paper presented at the Annual Kathmandu Conference on Nepal and the Himalaya, Kathmandu, 22–24 July. Available at: https://www.youtube.com/watch?v=eCA0XaEuuCw (accessed 2 July 2020).

Miyamoto. n.d. 'U.S. Embassy to Restore Iconic Nepal UNESCO-site Structure: Gaddi Baithak'. Available at: http://miyamotointernational.com/gaddi-baithak-restoration-project-us-embassy/ (accessed 22 January 2018).

Miyazaki, H. 2004. *The Method of Hope: Anthropology, Philosophy, and Fijian Knowledge*. Stanford: Stanford University Press.

Morsy, S. W. and M. A. Halim. 2015. 'Reasons Why the Great Pyramids of Giza Remain the Only Surviving Wonder of the Ancient World: Drawing Ideas from the Structure of the Giza Pyramids to Nuclear Power Plants'. *Journal of Civil Engineering and Architecture* 9: 1191–201. https://doi:10.17265/1934-7359/2015.10.007.

Moss, T. J., G. Pettersson, and N. van de Walle. 2006. 'An Aid-institutions Paradox? A Review Essay on Aid Dependency and State Building in Sub-Saharan Africa'. Working Paper 74, Center for Global Development, Washington D.C.

Mosse, D. 2004. 'Is Good Policy Unimplementable? Reflections on the Ethnography of Aid Policy and Practice'. *Development and Change* 35(4): 639–71.

Mubyazi, G.M. and G. Hutton. 2012. 'Rhetoric and Reality of Community Participation in Health Planning, Resource Allocation and Service Delivery: A Review of Reviews, Primary Publications and Grey Literature'. *Rwanda Journal of Health Sciences* 1(1): 51–65.

Muni, S. D. 2015. 'Nepal's New Constitution: Towards Progress or Chaos?' *Economic & Political Weekly* 50(40): 15–19.

Murphy, B. L. 2007. 'Locating Social Capital in Resilient Community-level Emergency Management'. *Natural Hazards* 41: 297–315. doi.org/10.1007/s11069-006-9037-6.

Murton, G. 2013. 'Himalayan Highways: STS, the Spatial Fix, and Socio-cultural Shifts in the Land of Zomia'. *Perspectives on Global Development and Technology* 12(5–6): 609–21. https://doi.org/10.1163/15691497-12341278.

———. 2017. 'Making Mountain Places into State Spaces: Infrastructure, Consumption, and Territorial Practice in a Himalayan Borderland'. *Annals of the American Association of Geographers* 107(2): 536–45. https://doi.org/10.1080/24694452.201 6.1232616.

Murton, G., A. Lord, and R. Beazley. 2016. 'A Handshake across the Himalayas: Chinese Investment, Hydropower Development, and State Formation in Nepal'. *Eurasian Geography and Economics* 57(3): 403–32. https://doi:10.1163/15691497-12341278.

Music Nepal. 2014. 'Majhi Jaatiko Samajik Sanskaar ra Sanskriti, Majhi Documentary: Pitra Puja/Thulo Kam' ([Majhi Caste's Social Culture and Tradition: Worship of Deities). Available at: https://www.youtube.com/watch?v=BxVwOrlLEwM (accessed 3 July 2020).

Mustafa, D. 2003. 'Reinforcing Vulnerability?: Disaster, Relief, Recovery and Response to the 2001 Flood in Rawalpindi, Pakistan'. *Environmental Hazards* 5(3–4): 71–82. https://doi:10.1016/j.hazards.2004.05.001.

My Republica. 2017. 'US Supports Restoration of Cultural Heritage in Nepal'. 12 August. Available at: https://myrepublica.nagariknetwork.com/mycity/news/us-supports-restoration-of-cultural-heritage-in-nepal (accessed 18 November 2017).

———. 2018a. 'Guthi-run Schools Told to Furnish Property Details'. 30 August. Available at: http://archive.myrepublica.com/2015-16/society/story/27272/guthi-run-schools-told-to-furnish-property-details.html (accessed 26 February 2019).

———. 2018b. 'PM Vents Ire on Foreign Missions, I/NGOs for "Unwarranted Interest" in Integrity Policy'. 27 July. Available at: https://myrepublica.nagariknetwork.com/news/pm-vents-ire-on-foreignmissions-i-ngos-for-unwarranted-interest-in-integrity-policy/ (accessed 23 November 2018).

———. 2019. 'Walkathon Raises Rs 1.2m for Patan Heritages'. 24 September. Available at: https://myrepublica.nagariknetwork.com/news/walkathon-raises-rs-1-2m-for-patan-heritages/ (accessed 12 November 2019).

Nagoda, S. and A. Nightingale. 2017. 'Participation and Power in Climate Change Adaptation Policies: Vulnerability in Food Security Programs in Nepal'. *World Development* 100: 85–93. doi.org/10.1016/j.worlddev.2017.07.022.

Naidu-Silverman, E. 2015. *The Contribution of Art and Culture in Peace and Reconciliation Processes in Asia: A Literature Review and Case Studies from Pakistan, Nepal, Myanmar, Indonesia, Afghanistan, Sri Lanka and Bangladesh*. Denmark: Centre for Culture and Development.

Nelson, A. 2017. 'Prestigious Houses or Provisional Homes? The *Ghar* as a Symbol of Kathmandu Valley Peri-urbanism'. *Himalaya: The Journal of the Association for Nepal and Himalayan Studies* 37(1): 57–71. https://digitalcommons.macalester.edu/himalaya/vol37/iss1/11 (accessed 20 November 2020).

————. 2018. 'Dalal Middlemen and Peri-urbanisation in Nepal'. *Economic and Political Weekly* 53(12): 61–67.

Nepal Picture Library. 2018. 'The Feminist Memory Project'. *The Kathmandu Post,* Special Supplement, 18 February. Available at: https://kathmandupost.ekantipur. com/news/2019-02-18/test-20190218154037.html (accessed 3 July 2020).

Nepal, P. 2016 (Magh 2073 v.s.). *2072 ko Bhukampa ra Bhukampa Itihas* (The 2015 Earthquake and Earthquake History). Kathmandu: Ratnasagar Prakashan.

Nepal, R. S. 2006. *My Life Story.* Kathmandu: Anita Nepal.

Nepali Times. 2018. 'Model Mayors'. 7 September. Available at: https://www. nepalitimes.com/editorial/model-mayors/ (accessed 14 May 2020).

Nepali, G. S. 2015. *The Newars: An Ethno-sociological Study of a Himalayan Community,* 2nd ed. Kathmandu: Mandala Book Point.

Nightingale, A. 2003. 'A Feminist in the Forest: Situated Knowledges and Mixing Methods in Natural Resource Management'. *ACME: An International E-Journal for Critical Geographies* 2(1): 77–90. Available at: http://hdl.handle.net/1842/1405 (accessed 25 November 2020).

Nightingale, A. J., A. Bhattarai, H. R. Ojha, T. S. Sigdel, and K. N. Rankin. 2018. 'Fragmented Public Authority and State Un/making in the "New" Republic of Nepal'. *Modern Asian Studies* 52(3): 849–82. https://doi.org/10.1017/ S0026749X16000500.

Ninglekhu, S. and K. Rankin. 2008. 'Neighborhood Associations as Civic Space in Kathmandu: Progressive and Regressive Possibilities'. In *The Politics of Civic Space in Asia: Building Urban Communities,* ed. A. Daniere and M. Douglass, pp. 151–74. New York: Routledge.

Northeast Now. 2018. 'Nepal Govt Seeks Suggestions for Amending Draft National Integrity Policy'. 7 May. Available at: https://nenow.in/neighbour/nepal-draft-national-integrity-policy.html (accessed 23 October 2018).

NPC (National Planning Commission Nepal). 2013. *National Priority Projects' Short Introduction and Progress.* Kathmandu: National Planning Commission.

————. 2015a. *Nepal Earthquake 2015: Post Disaster Needs Assessment, Vol. A: Key Findings.* Kathmandu: National Planning Commission. Available at: https:// reliefweb.int/report/nepal/nepal-earthquake-2015-post-disaster-needs-assessment-vol-key-findings (accessed 8 November 2020).

————. 2015b. *Nepal Earthquake 2015: Post Disaster Needs Assessment, Vol. B: Sector Reports.* Kathmandu: National Planning Commission. Available at: https:// ec.europa.eu/fpi/sites/fpi/files/pdna/pdna_nepal_2015_-_report_vol_b_0.pdf (accessed 11 July 2019).

NRA (National Reconstruction Authority). 2015a. *Grievances Management Related to Reconstruction and Rehabilitation Guidelines 2016 [2073 v.s.].* Kathmandu: National Reconstruction Authority, Government of Nepal. Available at: http://www.nra.gov. np/resources/details/bYI1dNmmAfcggmU2atIc8fiZ02PODtOvbCwlSq4k8WY (accessed 20 November 2020).

———. 2015b. *Grant Disbursement Procedures for Private Houses Destroyed by the Earthquakes 2015 [2072 v.s.].* Kathmandu: National Reconstruction Authority, Government of Nepal. Available at: http://nra.gov.np/resources/details/lDeFX wDc2J1HIsAWlIYsyUMVkjWdH9Z0UXk7ZSKmP_c (accessed 20 November 2020).

———. 2015c. *National Reconstruction and Resettlement Policy 2072 v.s.* Kathmandu: National Reconstruction Authority, Government of Nepal. Available at: http:// www.nra.gov.np/resources/details/a3o6SVhGxbfcvbeKBCRXnrRqiZQmraLbyF-4ujpnKls (accessed 20 November 2020).

———. 2015d. *Procedure for Private Housing Reconstruction Subsidized Loan for Earthquake Affected Households 2015 [2072 v.s.].* Kathmandu: National Reconstruction Authority, Government of Nepal. Available at: http://nra.gov.np/ resources/details/lDeFXwDc2J1HIsAWlIYsyUMVkjWdH9Z0UXk7ZSKmP_c (accessed 20 November 2020).

———. 2016a. Beneficiaries Selection Criteria for Cash Grant Distribution for the Reconstruction or Retrofitting of Private Houses Damaged by the Earthquakes 2016 (2073 v.s.). Kathmandu: National Reconstruction Authority, Government of Nepal. Available at: http://www.nra.gov.np/resources/details/ ebUVxZtX4uarwnIddiIrr4Ia7SwaObKpVmXg2wpApCs (accessed 20 November 2020).

———. 2016b. *Nepal Earthquake 2015: Post-disaster Recovery Framework, 2016–2020.* Kathmandu: National Reconstruction Authority, Government of Nepal. Available at: https://reliefweb.int/report/nepal/nepal-earthquake-2015-post-disaster-recovery-framework-2016-2020 (accessed 20 November 2020).

———. 2019. *Rebuilding Nepal* (November–December): 2. Available at: http://www.nra.gov.np/en/content/bulletins/.

———. 2072a v.s. *Punarnirman ra Punarsthapanako Lagi Gairsarkari Sanstha Parichalan Sambandhi Karyavidhi* (The Standard Operating Procedure for Guiding the Operation of the Non-Governmental Organizations for Reconstruction and Relocation). Kathmandu: National Reconstruction Authority, Government of Nepal. Available at: nra.gov.np/uploads/docs/1pSJn4nRAd170805073452.pdf (accessed 21 November 2020).

———. 2072b v.s. *Baseline Directory/Guideline for the Protection and Reconstruction of the Cultural Heritages Affected by the Earthquake 2072* (in Nepali). Kathmandu: National Reconstruction Authority, Government of Nepal.

———. 2074 v.s. *Jokhim Vargama Parne Bhukampabata Prabhavit Labhagrahi Pahichan Sambandhi Karyavidhi* (Operating Procedure for Identifying Affected Beneficiaries Belonging to the Vulnerable Sections of Society). Kathmandu: National Reconstruction Authority, Government of Nepal. Available at: http://nra.gov.np/ uploads/docs/wmcAaT6y7F180319082604.pdf (accessed 20 November 2020).

Nurkse, R. 1958. 'Trade Fluctuations and Buffer Policies of Low-income Countries'. *Kyklos* 11(2): 141–54. https://doi.org/10.1111/j.1467-6435.1958.tb02361.x.

O'Brien, K., S. Eriksen, L. P. Nygaard, and A. Schjolden. 2007. 'Why Different Interpretations of Vulnerability Matter in Climate Change Discourses'. *Climate Policy* 7(1): 73–88. https://doi.org/10.1080/14693062.2007.9685639.

O'Reilly, K. 2010. 'The Promise of Patronage: Adopting and Adapting Neo-Liberal Development'. *Antipode* 41(1): 179–200. https://doi.org/10.1111/j.1467-8330.2009.00736.x.

Ojha, A. 2017. 'KMC Threatens to Scrap Contractor's Deal over Rani Pokhari Project Delay'. *The Kathmandu Post*, 12 November. Available at: http://kathmandupost. ekantipur.com/news/2017-11-12/kmc-threatens-to-scrap-contractors-deal-over-rani-pokhari-project-delay.html (accessed 8 December 2017).

———. 2019a. 'In Biggest Protest since the 2006 People's Movement, Thousands of Protesters Gather to Oppose the Guthi Bill'. *The Kathmandu Post*, 19 June. Available at: https://kathmandupost.com/valley/2019/06/19/thousands-protest-against-the-guthi-bill-in-kathmandu (accessed 17 May 2020).

———. 2019b. 'Reconstruction Work of Rani Pokhari Resumes'. *The Kathmandu Post*, 6 March. Available at: http://kathmandupost.ekantipur.com/news/2019-03-06/reconstruction-work-of-rani-pokhari-resumes.html (accessed 12 June 2020).

Ojha, H. R., J. Cameron, and C. Kumar. 2009. 'Deliberation or Symbolic Violence? The Governance of Community Forestry in Nepal'. *Forest Policy and Economics* 11(5–6): 365–74. https://doi.org/10.1016/j.forpol.2008.11.003.

Olin, M. 2012. *Touching Photographs*. Berkeley: University of Chicago Press.

Oliver-Smith, A. 1986. *The Martyred City: Death and Rebirth in the Andes*. Albuquerque: University of New Mexico Press.

———. 1991. 'Successes and Failures in Post-disaster Resettlement'. *Disasters* 15(1): 12–19. https://doi.org/10.1111/j.1467-7717.1991.tb00423.x.

———. 1996. 'Anthropological Research on Hazards and Disasters'. *Annual Review of Anthropology* 25: 303–28. Available at: https://www.jstor.org/stable/2155829 (accessed 25 November 2020).

Oliver-Smith, A. and S. Hoffman., eds. 1999. *The Angry Earth: Disaster in an Anthropological Perspective*. London: Routledge.

———. 2001. 'Why Anthropologists Should Study Disasters'. In *Catastrophe and Culture: The Anthropology of Disaster*, ed. S. M. Hoffman and A. Oliver-Smith, pp. 3–22. Santa Fe and Oxford: School of American Research Press.

Olson, R. S. 2000. 'Toward a Politics of Disaster: Losses, Values, Agendas, and Blame'. *International Journal of Mass Emergencies and Disasters* 18(2): 265–87.

Onta, P. 1998. 'A Suggestive History of the First Century of Photographic Consumption in Kathmandu'. *Studies in Nepali History and Society* 3(1): 181–212.

Orth, R. H., ed. 1966. *The Journals and Miscellaneous Notebooks of Ralph Waldo Emerson, VI, 1824–1838*. Cambridge, MA: The Belknap Press of Harvard University Press.

Osnepal. 2019. 'Locals to Reconstruct Agamche Temple'. 26 February. Available at: https://www.osnepal.com/744469 (accessed 2 July 2020).

Oven, K. J. 2010. 'Landscape, Livelihoods and Risk: Community Vulnerability to Landslides in Nepal'. Ph.D. thesis, Durham University, UK.

Oven, K. J. and J. D. Rigg. 2015. 'The Best of Intentions? Managing Disasters and Constructions of Risk and Vulnerability in Asia'. *Asian Journal of Social Science* 43: 685–712.

Oven, K. J., J. D. Rigg, S. Rana, A. Gautum, and T. Singh. 2019. '#leavenoonebehind: Women, Gender Planning and Disaster Risk Reduction in Nepal'. In *Climate Hazards, Disasters and Gendered Ramifications*, ed. C. Kinnvall and H. Rydstrom, pp. 138–64. London: Routledge. http://doi:10.4324/9780429424861-8.

Palacios, C. M. 2010. 'Volunteer Tourism, Development and Education in a Postcolonial World: Conceiving Global Connections Beyond Aid'. *Journal of Sustainable Tourism* 18(7): 861–78. https://doi.org/10.1080/09669581003782739.

Pallister-Wilkins, P. 2018. 'Hotspots and the Geographies of Humanitarianism'. *Environment and Planning D: Society and Space.* 38(6): 991–1008. https://doi:10.1177/0263775818754884.

Palmer, J. 2012. *The Death of Mao: The Tangshan Earthquake and the Birth of the New China.* London: Faber & Faber.

Panday, D. R., ed. 1983. *Foreign Aid and Development in Nepal: Proceedings of a Seminar* (4–5 October 1983). Kathmandu: Integrated Development Systems.

———. 1999. *Nepal's Failed Development: Reflections on the Mission and the Maladies.* Kathmandu: Mandala Book Point.

———. 2011. *Looking at Development and Donors: Essays from Nepal.* Kathmandu: Martin Chautari.

Pande, S. 2016. 'Art and the Earthquake'. *The Kathmandu Post*, 23 April. Available at: https://kathmandupost.com/miscellaneous/2016/04/23/art-and-the-earthquake (accessed 12 June 2020).

Pandey, B., S. Brzev, R. Culbert, and G. Schoenfeld. 2016. *Illustrated Guidelines for Construction of Stone Masonry Houses in Seismic Regions of Nepal.* Kathmandu: NRA, BWB-Canada, BCIT, RJC and UNDP-Nepal.

Pandeya, G. P. 2015. 'Does Citizen Participation in Local Government Decision-making Contribute to Strengthening Local Planning and Accountability Systems? An Empirical Assessment of Stakeholders' Perceptions in Nepal'. *International Public Management Review* 16(1): 67–98.

Pant, M. R. 2002. 'A Step towards a Historical Seismicity of Nepal'. *Adarsa: A Supplement to Purnima* 2: 29–60. Available at: http://himalaya.socanth.cam.ac.uk/collections/journals/adarsha/pdf/Adarsha_02.pdf (accessed 14 June 2017).

Partridge, W. L. 1989. 'Involuntary Resettlement in Development Projects'. *Journal of Refugee Studies* 2(3): 373–84. https://doi.org/10.1093/jrs/2.3.373.

Paudel, D. 2017. 'Politics of Post-earthquake Reconstruction and the Early Forms of Disaster Capitalism in Nepal'. Public talk. Available at: https://www.colorado.edu/geography/2017/03/24/politics-post-earthquake-reconstruction-and-early-forms-disaster-capitalism-nepal (accessed 30 January 2020).

Paudel, D. and P. Le Billon. 2018. 'Geo-logics of Power: Disaster Capitalism, Himalayan Materialities, and the Geopolitical Economy of Reconstruction in Post-earthquake Nepal'. *Geopolitics* 96(2): 137–60. https://doi:10.1080/14650045. 2018.1533818.

Paudel, D., K. Rankin, and P. Le Billon. 2020. 'Lucrative Disaster: Financialization, Accumulation and Post-earthquake Reconstruction in Nepal'. *Economic Geography*. https://doi.org/10.1080/00130095.2020.1722635.

Paudel, U. 2017. *Data Analysis of the Household Survey Data*. Report submitted to Durable Solutions Project. Kathmandu, Nepal. Available at: https://www. hrrpnepal.org/uploads/media/HH-Survey-Report-Final-DurableSoluti ons-170731_20190813201248.pdf (accessed 12 June 2020).

Paudyal, M. and K. R. Koirala. 2018. 'Oli Government Is Moving from Populism Toward Authoritarianism'. *My Republica*, 8 July. Available at: https://myrepublica. nagariknetwork.com/news/oli-government-is-moving-from-populism-toward-authoritarianism/ (accessed 11 November 2018).

Pelling, M. 1998. 'Participation, Social Capital and Vulnerability to Urban Flooding in Guyana'. *Journal of International Development: The Journal of the Development Studies Association* 10(4): 469–86. https://doi.org/10.1002/(SICI)1099-1328(199806)10:4<469::AID-JID539>3.0.CO;2-4.

Pelling, M. and K. Dill. 2010. 'Disaster Politics: Tipping Points for Change in the Adaptation of Socio-political Regimes'. *Progress in Human Geography* 34(1): 21–37. https://doi.org/10.1177/0309132509105004.

Petal, M., S. Baral, S. Giri, S. Rajbanshi, S. Gajurel, R. Paci, P. Green, B. Pandey, and K. Shoaf. 2017. *Causes of Deaths and Injuries in the 2015 Gorkha (Nepal) Earthquake*. Kathmandu: Save the Children. Available at: https://resourcecentre. savethechildren.net/node/14168/pdf/causes_of_deaths_and_injuries_nepal_ earthquake_report_eng_2017.pdf (accessed 20 November 2020).

Petech, L. 1984. *Mediaeval History of Nepal*, 2nd ed. Roma: Istituto Italiano per il Medio ed Estremo Oriente.

Petley, D. N., G. J. Hearn, A. Hart, N. J. Rosser, S. A. Dunning, K. J. Oven, and W. A. Mitchell. 2007. 'Trends in Landslide Occurrence in Nepal'. *Natural Hazards* 43: 23–44. https://doi.org/10.1007/s11069-006-9100-3.

Phuyal, S. 2018. 'The Women of Bhajya Pukhu'. *The Kathmandu Post*, 30 June. Available at: http://kathmandupost.ekantipur.com/news/2018-06-30/the-women-of-bhajya-pukhu.html (accessed 12 June 2020).

Pink, S. 2006. *The Future of Visual Anthropology: Engaging the Senses*. London: Routledge.

Pinney, C. 1997. *Camera Indica: The Social Life of Indian Photographs*. Chicago: University of Chicago Press, Reaction Books.

———. 2004. *Photos of the Gods*. Chicago: University of Chicago Press, Reaction Books.

Poudel, R. 2015. 'Worst-hit S'palchok Villages Still without Relief Materials'. *The Kathmandu Post*, 7 May. Available at: http://kathmandupost.ekantipur.com/

news/2015-05-07/worst-hit-spalchok-villages-still-without-relief-materials.html (accessed 16 October 2018).

Powell, C. 2016. 'Art and Catastrophe: A Manifesto'. *Medium*, 16 November. Available at: https://medium.com/@cepowell08/art-and-catastrophe-a-manifesto-7bd48a2 78f27 (accessed 12 June 2020).

Pradhan, K. L. 2001. *Brian Hodgson at the Kathmandu Residency*. Delhi: Spectrum Publications.

———. 2012. *Thapa Politics in Nepal: With Special Reference to Bhim Sen Thapa, 1806– 1839*. New Delhi: Concept Publishing Company.

Pradhananga, N., K. K. Shrestha, and J. Dee. 2010. 'Sustaining Indigenous Heritage: Learning from the Guthi System in Nepal'. New Zealand Geographical Society Conference, Christchurch, New Zealand, 5–8 July.

Pradhananga, S. B. 2017. 'The Tussle for Kasthamandap'. *The Kathmandu Post*, 1 July. Available at: https://kathmandupost.com/miscellaneous/2017/07/01/the-tussle-for-kasthamandap (accessed 11. November 2020).

Prajapati, S. 2018. 'Bhaktapur Shows the Way by Rebuilding Itself'. *The Nepali Times*, 1 March. Available at: https://www.nepalitimes.com/here-now/bhaktapur-shows-the-way-by-rebuilding-itself/ (accessed 27 April 2018).

Prasad, I. 1975. *Biography of Juddha Shamsher J. B. Rana*. New Delhi: Ashish Publications.

PTI (Press Trust of India). 2015. 'Chaos Reigns at Nepal's Only International Airport in Kathmandu'. *NDTV*, 27 April. Available at: https://www.ndtv.com/world-news/chaos-reigns-at-nepals-only-international-airport-in-kathmandu-758498 (accessed 2 July 2020).

Pun, S. 2018. 'Nepal's Heritage Reconstruction after the Earthquake: Kathmandu's Temple Troubles'. *Spotlight Magazine* 12(10), 21 December (6 Poush 2075). doi: 584/074-75.

Putnam, R. 1995. 'Bowling Alone: America's Declining Social Capital'. *Journal of Democracy* 6(1): 65–78. Available at: http://www.socialcapitalgateway.org/content/paper/putnam-r-d-1995-bowling-alone-americas-declining-social-capital-journal-democracy-6-1- (accessed 25 November 2020).

Quigley, D. 1985. 'The Guthi Organizations of Dhulikhel Shresthas'. *Kailash* 12(1): 5–61.

Rai, J. and S. Shneiderman. 2019. 'Identity, Society, and State: Citizenship and Inclusion in Nepal'. In *The Politics of Change: Reflections on Contemporary Nepal*, ed. D. Thapa, pp. 83–108. Kathmandu: Social Science Baha.

Rai, L. 2071 v.s. 'Khulyo tamakoshi' ([Upper] Tamakoshi Work Resumed). *Kantipur Dainik*, 12 Chaitra.

Rai, O. A. 2018. 'A Monumental Rivalry'. *The Nepali Times*, 1 March. Available at: https://www.nepalitimes.com/here-now/a-monumental-rivalry/ (accessed 12 June 2020).

Rai, R. 2008. 'Threats to the Spirit of the Place: Urban Space and Squares, Historic City Core, Kathmandu'. In 16th ICOMOS General Assembly and International

Symposium: 'Finding the Spirit of Place: Between the Tangible and the Intangible',
29 September–4 October, Quebec, Canada. Available at: https://openarchive.
icomos.org/227/ (accessed 21 November 2020).

Raj, Y. and B. Gautam. 2015. *Courage in Chaos: Early Rescue and Relief after the April
Earthquake*. Kathmandu: Martin Chautari.

Raju, E. and K. da Costa. 2018. 'Governance in the Sendai: A Way Ahead?' *Disaster
Prevention and Management: An International Journal* 27(3): 278–91. https://doi.
org/10.1108/DPM-08-2017-0190.

Rana, B. S. J. B. 2013. *The Great Earthquake in Nepal (1934 A.D.)*, trans. Kesar Lall.
Kathmandu: Ratna Pustak Bhandar.

Rana, P. S. J. B. 2062 v.s. (2005). *Shri Teenharuko Tathya Vrittanta* (Factual Account of
the Rana Maharajas), vol. II. Kathmandu: Vidyarthi Pustak Bhandar.

Rana, S. S. J. B. 2017. *Singha Durbar: Rise and Fall of the Rana Regime of Nepal*. New
Delhi: Rupa Publications.

Rankin, K. N. 2001. 'Planning and the Politics of Social Needs: Lessons from Financial
Market Regulation in Nepal'. *International Planning Studies* 6(1): 89–102. https://
doi.org/10.1080/13563470120026550.

Rankin, K. N, A. J. Nightingale, P. Hamal, and T. S. Sigdel. 2018. 'Roads of Change:
Political Transition and State Formation in Nepal's Agrarian Districts'. *The
Journal of Peasant Studies* 45(2): 280–99. https://doi.org/10.1080/03066150.2016.
1216985.

Rankin, K. N., T. Sigdel, L. Rai, S. Kunwar, and P. Hamal. 2017. 'Political Economies
and Political Rationalities of Road Building in Nepal'. *Studies in Nepali Society
and History* 22(1): 43–84.

Rao, V. and P. Sanyal. 2010. 'Dignity through Discourse: Poverty and the
Culture of Deliberation in Indian Village Democracies'. *The ANNALS of the
American Academy of Political and Social Science* 629(1): 146–72. https://doi.
org/10.1177/0002716209357402.

Rastriya Samachar Samiti. 2016. 'Kerauja VDC at High Risk of Landslides'. *The
Himalayan Times*, 2 July. Available at: https://thehimalayantimes.com/nepal/
kerauja-vdc-high-risk-landslides/ (accessed 11 July 2020).

Razani, R. 1984. 'Earthquake Disaster Area Reconstruction Experience in Iran'. In
Earthquake Relief in Less Industrialized Areas, ed. S. Schuppisser and J. Studer,
pp. 79–86. Rotterdam and Boston: AA Balkema.

Regmi, D. R. 1950. *A Century of Family Autocracy in Nepal*. Benaras: Nepali National
Congress. Available at: https://archive.org/details/in.ernet.dli.2015.15650
(accessed 29 May 2017).

Regmi, K. D. 2016. 'The Political Economy of 2015 Nepal Earthquake: Some Critical
Reflections'. *Asian Geographer* 33(2): 77–96. https://doi.org/10.1080/10225706.20
16.1235053.

Regmi, M. C. 1965. *Land Tenure and Taxation in Nepal*. Berkeley: University of
California Press.

———. ed. 1976. Regmi Research Series 8(1).

———. 1977. *Landownership in Nepal*, 3rd ed. Delhi: Adroit Publishers.

Reid-Henry, S. 2013. 'Review Essay: On the Politics of Our Humanitarian Present'. *Environment and Planning D: Society and Space* 31: 753–60. https://doi.org/10.1068/d3104rev.

———. 2014. 'Humanitarianism as Liberal Diagnostic: Humanitarian Reason and the Political Rationalities of the Liberal Will-to-care'. *Transactions of the Institute of British Geographers* 39(3): 418–31. http//:doi: 10.1111/tran.12029.

Remes, J. A. C. 2016. *Disaster Citizenship: Survivors, Solidarity, and Power in the Progressive Era*. Urbana: University of Illinois Press.

Riaz, A. and S. Basu. 2010. *Paradise Lost? State Failure in Nepal*. Delhi: Adarsh Books.

Ricoeur, P. 2000. *Memory, History, Forgetting*. Chicago: University of Chicago Press.

Rigg, J. D., A. Salamanca, and M. Parnwell. 2012. 'Joining the Dots of Agrarian Change in Asia: A 25 Year View from Thailand'. *World Development* 40(7): 1469–81. http://doi: 10.1016/j.worlddev.2012.03.001.

Roback, K., M. K. Clark, A. J. West, D. Zekkos, G. Li, S. F. Gallen, D. Chamlagaine, and J. W. Godt. 2018. 'The Size, Distribution, and Mobility of Landslides Caused by the 2015 Mw 7.8 Gorkha Earthquake, Nepal'. *Geomorphology* 301: 121–38. http://doi: 10.1016/j.geomorph.2017.01.030.

Robinson, A. 2016. *Earth-shattering Events: Earthquakes, Nations and Civilization*. London: Thames & Hudson.

Rose, L. 1970. *Nepal: Strategy for Survival*. Berkeley: University of California Press.

Rosser, N. J., Z. M. Swirad, M. Kincey, T. Robinson, R. Shrestha, D. Pujari, K. Oven, J. Williams, and A. L. Densmore. 2019. 'Validating Modelled Post-earthquake Landslide Runout Using Timeseries Landslide Inventories: Nepal 2015'. NH33E-0970, American Geoscience Union Fall Meeting, San Francisco, December.

Sandbye, M. 2014. 'Looking at the Family Photo Album: A Resumed Theoretical Discussion of Why and How'. *Journal of Aesthetics & Culture* 6(1): 1–17. https://doi.org/10.3402/jac.v6.25419.

Sangroula, P. 2020. 'Secrecy over the New Guthi Bill Adds to Old Suspicion'. *The Annapurna Express*, 14 February. Available at: https://theannapurnaexpress.com/news/secrecy-over-the-new-guthi-bill-adds-to-old-suspicion-2236 (accessed 20 February 2020).

Sangroula, S. 2017. 'Failure to Train Masons On Time Slows Reconstruction'. *My Republica*, 20 January. Available at: www.myrepublica.com/news/13982 (accessed 15 January 2020).

Sansom, A. 2019. 'It's Official: French Tycoons Finalise €300m Donations for Fire-ravaged Notre Dame'. *The Art Newspaper*, 17 April. Available at: https://www.theartnewspaper.com/news/french-tycoons-donations-notre-dame-restoration (accessed 12 June 2020).

Sapkota, R. 2018. 'Singati Locals Rebuilding Houses on Landslide Prone Area Ignoring Warning'. *The Himalayan Times*, 4 December. Available at: https:// thehimalayantimes.com/nepal/singati-locals-rebuilding-houses-on-landslide-prone-area-ignoring-warning/ (accessed 12 June 2020).

Sapkota, S. N., L. Bollinger, Y. Klinger, P. Tapponnier, Y. Gaudemer, and D. Tiwari. 2013. 'Primary Surface Ruptures of the Great Himalayan Earthquakes in 1934 and 1255'. *Nature Geoscience* 6: 71–76. https://doi.org/10.1038/ngeo1669.

Satyal, U. 2018. '85pc Heritage Monuments Yet to Be Rebuilt'. *The Himalayan Times*, 25 April. Available at: https://thehimalayantimes.com/kathmandu/85-per-cent-heritage-monuments-yet-to-be-rebuilt/ (accessed 27 April 2018).

———. 2019a. 'Thousands of Newars Gather against Guthi Bill in Show of Strength Protest'. *The Himalayan Times*, 20 June. Available at: https://thehimalayantimes. com/kathmandu/thousands-of-newars-gather-against-guthi-bill-in-show-of-strength-protest/ (accessed 7 July 2019).

———. 2019b. 'UNESCO Pulls Out of Reconstruction Project'. *The Himalayan Times*, 10 July. Available at: https://thehimalayantimes.com/kathmandu/united-nations-educational-scientific-and-cultural-organisation-pulls-out-of-reconstruction-project/ (accessed 14 April 2020).

Schaffner, U. 1987. 'Road Construction in the Nepal Himalaya: The Experience from the Lamosangu–Jiri Road Project'. Occasional paper no. 8, ICIMOD, Kathmandu. Available at: http://himaldoc.icimod.org/record/7750.

Schild, P. 2012. 'Struggling for Reconstruction: Houses, Homes and "the State" after the Earthquake in Muzaffarabad, Azad Kashmir'. *Scrutiny* 5/6: 33–51.

Schuller, M. 2012. *Killing with Kindness: Haiti, International Aid, and NGOs*. New Brunswick, NJ: Rutgers University Press.

Seale-Feldman, A. 2020. 'The Work of Disaster: Building Back Otherwise in Post-earthquake Nepal'. *Cultural Anthropology* 35(2): 237–63. doi: 10.14506/ca35.2.07. https://journal.culanth.org/index.php/ca/article/view/4167/540 (accessed 21 November 2020).

Sen, P. K. 2015. 'Will Nepal Once Again Become a Hindu State?' *East Asia Forum*, 12 September. Available at: from http://www.eastasiaforum.org/2015/09/12/will-nepal-once-again-become-a-hindu-state/ (accessed 11 November 2018).

Sengupta, K. 2015. 'Nepal Earthquake: The Task to Conserve What Survived at the UNESCO World Heritage Site in Kathmandu'. *The Independent*, 3 May. Available at: http://www.independent.co.uk/news/world/asia/nepal-earthquake-the-task-to-conserve-what-survived-at-the-unesco-world-heritage-site-in-kathmandu-10221688.html (accessed 18 November 2017).

Setopati. 2018. 'Bhaktapur Municipality Unveils Annual Budget of Rs 1.73 Billion'. 17 July. Available at: https://setopati.net/social/125540 (accessed 11 April 2019).

Sever, A. 1993. *Nepal under the Ranas*. New Delhi: Oxford and IBH Publishing.

Shah, S. 2008. 'Civil Society in Uncivil Places: Soft State and Regime Change in Nepal'. Policy Studies No. 48. East–West Centre, Washington. Available at: https://www. jstor.org/stable/resrep06500 (25 November 2020).

Shaha, R. 1990. *Modern Nepal: A Political History 1769–1955*. New Delhi: Manohar.

Shakya, M. 2015. 'The Question of Locality in Rupture'. *Cultural Anthropology*, 14 October. Available at: https://culanth.org/fieldsights/the-question-of-locality-in-rupture (accessed 11 June 2020).

———. 2018. *Death of an Industry: The Cultural Politics of Garment Manufacturing, Development and Revolution in Nepal*. Cambridge: Cambridge University Press.

Shakya, S. and W. Drechsler. 2019. 'The Guthis: Buddhist Societal Organization for the 21st Century'. In *Buddhism around the World*, ed. T. N. Tu, pp. 501–27. Hanoi: Religion Publisher.

Sharma, A. 2017. 'Architectural Considerations in Restoration of Heritage Buildings Damaged by Earthquake'. *Disaster Advances* 10(7): 27–36.

Sharma, B. 2072 v.s. (2015). 'Purkhako Tyo Tatvabodh' (The Ancestors' Material Understanding). *Himal KhabarPatrika*, 27 Baisakh–2 Jeth, p. 29.

Sharma, M. 2072 v.s. (2015). 'Kaha Paune Juddhashamsher Jasta Pradhan Mantri?' (Where to Find a Prime Minister like Juddhashamsher?). *Annapurna Post*, 17 Baisakh (30 April), p. 7.

Sharma, P. R. 2015. *Land, Lineage and State: A Study of Newar Society in Mediaeval Nepal*. Kathmandu: Himal Books.

Sharma, R. 2013. 'Kun Mandirma Janchau Yatri'. Available at: https://www.youtube.com/watch?v=Gq4Ti4WQICA (accessed 29 January 2019).

Sherry, J., A. Curtis, E. Mendham, and E. Toman. 2018. 'Cultural Landscapes at Risk: Exploring the Meaning of Place in a Sacred Valley of Nepal'. *Global Environmental Change* 52: 190–200. https://doi.org/10.1016/j.gloenvcha.2018.07.007.

Shneiderman, S. 2015a. 'Regionalism, Mobility, and "the Village" as a Set of Social Relations: Himalayan Reflections on a South Asian Theme'. *Critique of Anthropology* 35(3): 318–37. https://doi.org/10.1177/0308275X15588962.

———. 2015b. *Rituals of Ethnicity: Thangmi Identities between Nepal and India*. Philadelphia: University of Pennsylvania Press.

Shrestha, A. 2017. 'Patan Museum Sees Influx of Visitors'. *My Republica*, 18 December. Available at: https://myrepublica.nagariknetwork.com/news/patan-museum-sees-influx-of-visitors/ (accessed 11 June 2020).

Shrestha, B. G. 1999. *The Newars: The Indigenous Population of the Kathmandu Valley in the Modern State of Nepal*. Kirtipur: Center for Nepal and Asian Studies.

———. 2012. *The Sacred Town of Sankhu: The Anthropology of Newar Ritual, Religion and Society in Nepal*. Newcastle upon Tyne: Cambridge Scholars Publishing.

Shrestha, B. K. and G. C. Mamta. 2010. 'Managing Cultural Heritage of Ancient Settlement of Kisipidi through Urban Design'. *Administration and Management Review* 22(1): 88–102.

Shrestha, H. K. 2018. 'Small-scale Community Water Supply System as an Alternate to Privatized Water Supply: An Experience from Kathmandu'. In *Globalization of Water Governance in South Asia*, ed. V. Narain, C. G. Goodrich, J. Chourey, and A. Prakash, pp. 137–58. Delhi: Routledge India.

Shrestha, K. K. and P. McManus. 2008. 'The Politics of Community Participation in Natural Resource Management: Lessons from Community Forestry in Nepal'. *Australian Forestry* 71(2): 135–46. http//doi:10.1080/00049158.2008.10676280.

Shrestha, P. M., 2019. 'Non-government Organisations Concerned over a New Law to Regulate Them'. *The Kathmandu Post*, 12 April. Available at: https://kathmandupost.com/national/2019/11/03/non-government-organisations-concerned-over-a-new-law-to-regulate-them (accessed 11 June 2020).

Shrestha, S., B. Shrestha, M. Shakya, and P. N. Maskey. 2017. 'Damage Assessment of Cultural Heritage Structures after the 2015 Gorkha, Nepal, Earthquake: A Case Study of Jagannath Temple'. *Earthquake Spectra* 33(S1): 363–76. https://doi.org/10.1193/121616eqs241m.

Shrestha, S. K. 2014. 'Average Bid Method: An Alternative to Low Bid Method in Public Sector Construction Procurement in Nepal'. *Journal of the Institute of Engineering* 10(1): 125–29.

Shroder, J. F. and T. Davies, T., eds. 2015. *Landslide Hazards, Risks and Disasters*. Amsterdam: Elsevier.

Silva, K. and N. Chapagain, eds. 2013. *Asian Heritage Management: Concepts, Concerns and Prospects*. London: Taylor and Francis.

Simpson, E. 2013. *The Political Biography of an Earthquake: Aftermath and Amnesia in Gujarat, India*. Oxford: Oxford University Press.

Sinha, A. K. 2001. *The Gujarat Earthquake 2001*. Kobe: Asian Disaster Reduction Center. Available at: https://www.recoveryplatform.org/assets/publication/ADRC_Gujarat.pdf (accessed 12 June 2020).

Smadja, J., ed. 2009. *Reading Himalayan Landscapes over Time: Environmental Perception, Knowledge and Practice in Nepal and Ladakh*, translated from French by B. Sellers. Collection Sciences Sociales 14. Pondichéry: Institut Français de Pondichéry.

Smillie, I. 1995. *Alms Bazaar: Altruism under Fire: Non-profit Organizations and International Development*. Canada: International Development Research Centre.

Smolders, B. 2015. *Nepal Urban Recovery and Development Support Initiative*. Kathmandu Valley Master Planning Assessment, Bungamati Recovery and Development Support. United Habitat, Shelter Program.

Social Welfare Council Nepal. n.d. 'NGOs Affiliated with Social Welfare Council (2034–2076 Asadh)'. Available at: http://www.swc.org.np/sites/default/files/downloads/NGOs-affiliated-to-SWC-compressed.pdf (accessed 30 November 2020).

Soden, R. and A. Lord. 2018. 'Mapping Silences, Reconfiguring Loss: Practices of Damage Assessment & Repair in Post-earthquake Nepal'. Proceedings of the ACM on Human-Computer Interaction (CSCW), November, Article 161. https://doi.org/10.1145/3274430.

Solnit, R. 2016. *Hope in the Dark: Untold Histories, Wild Possibilities*. Edinburgh: Canongate Books.

Sonda, D., K. Miyamoto, S. Kast, and A. Khanal. 2019. 'The Restoration and Seismic Strengthening of the Earthquake-damaged UNESCO Heritage Palace in Kathmandu'. *International Journal of Architectural Heritage* 13(1): 153–71. https://doi.org/10.1080/15583058.2018.1497229.

Sontag, S. 2001 [1973]. *On Photography*. London: Macmillan.

———. 2003. *Regarding the Pain of Others*. New York: Macmillan.

Spotlight. 2017. 'Nepal's President Signs Law Criminalizing Evangelism, Christian Solidarity Worldwide Warns'. 22 October. Available at: https://www.spotlightnepal.com/2017/10/22/nepals-president-signs-law-criminalizing-evangelism-christian-solidarity-worldwide-warns/ (accessed 25 October 2018).

———. 2020. 'Temple Reconstruction: Lalitpur Takes Lead'. 12 February. Available at: https://www.spotlightnepal.com/2020/02/12/temple-reconstruction-lalitpur-takes-lead/ (accessed 15 April 2020).

Stiller, Ludwig F. 1975. *An Introduction to Hanuman Dhoka: Based on the Nepali Text of Gautam Vajra Vajracharya*. Kirtipur: Institute of Nepal and Asian Studies.

Subba, B. 2073 v.s. 'Adhikansh Nepali Kaviharuko Rachanama Matoko Suvas Painna' (The Scent of the Soil Cannot Be Found in the Works of Most Nepali Poets). *Kavita* 106 (Pus–Chait): 145–52.

Suhag, S. A. 2015. 'Bread Not Bibles for Nepal'. *Huffington Post*, last updated 1 May 2016. Available at: https://www.huffpost.com/entry/bread-not-bibles-for-nepal-_b_7192146 (accessed 12 June 2020).

Suji, M., B. Limbu, N. Rawal, P. C. Subedi, and J. Baniya. 2020. *Reconstructing Nepal: Bhaktapur—Heritage and Reconstruction*. Kathmandu: Social Science Baha.

Suleiman, L. 2013. 'The NGOs and the Grand Illusions of Development and Democracy'. *Voluntas* 24(1): 241–61. Available at: https://www.jstor.org/stable/42629801 (accessed 21 November 2020).

Szeliga, W., S. Hough, S. Martin, and R. Bilham. 2010. 'Intensity, Magnitude, Location, and Attenuation in India for Felt Earthquakes since 1762'. *Bulletin of the Seismological Society of America* 100: 570–84.

Tamang, M. S. 2017. 'Nepal'. In *Routledge Handbook of Civil Society in Asia*, ed. A. Ogawa, pp. 278–92. London: Routledge.

Tamang, S. 2005. 'The Politics of "Developing Nepali Women"'. In *State of Nepal*, ed. K. M. Dixit and R. Shastri, pp. 161–75. Lalitpur: Himal Books.

———. 2015. 'Bureaucratising Relief'. *The Kathmandu Post*, 5 May. Available at: https://kathmandupost.com/opinion/2015/05/05/bureaucratising-relief (accessed 12 June 2020).

———. 2018a. 'Democratic Deceits: Embedding the Constitution and Elections in Arrested Political and Social Change in Post-earthquake Nepal'. Keynote Lecture, 16th British-Nepal Academic Council Study Days, Durham University, UK, 16–17 April.

———. 2018b. '"Paint-on-the Road" Nationalism'. *The Kathmandu Post*, 14 April. Available at: https://kathmandupost.com/opinion/2018/04/04/paint-on-the-road-nationalism (accessed 14 May 2020).

———. 2019. 'The Limits of Expertise: Public Anthropology after the Nepal Earthquake'. Paper presented at the Fourth Northern European Conference of Emergencies and Disaster Studies, Uppsala, 10–12 June 2019.

Tandon, Y. 2008. *Ending Aid Dependence*. Cape Town, Dakar, Nairobi and Oxford: Fahamu, Network for Social Justice.

Telford, J. and J. Cosgrave. 2007. 'The International Humanitarian System and the 2004 Indian Ocean Earthquake and Tsunamis'. *Disasters* 31(1): 1–28. https://doi. org/10.1111/j.1467-7717.2007.00337.x.

Teplitz, A. B. 2018. 'Yes, Ask Those Tough Questions about Foreign Assistance! U.S. Embassy in Nepal'. Available at: https://np.usembassy.gov/yes-ask-those-tough-questions-about-foreign-assistance/ (accessed 12 June 2020).

Thapa, K. B. 2010. 'Religion and Law in Nepal'. *BYU Law Review* 3: 921–30. https:// digitalcommons.law.byu.edu/lawreview/vol2010/iss3/12 (accessed 25 November 2020).

Thapa, N. 2045 v.s. (1988/89). *Bhadau Panchko Bhukampa 2045* (Earthquake of 21 August 1988). Kathmandu: Self-published.

The Asia Foundation. 2017. *Independent Impacts and Recovery Monitoring Phase 4: April 2017. Synthesis Report*. San Francisco: The Asia Foundation. https:// asiafoundation.org/wp-content/uploads/2017/10/Aid-and-Recovery-in-Post-Earthquake-Nepal-Synthesis-Report-Phase-4-1.pdf (accessed 20 November 2020).

The Sphere Project. 2011. *Humanitarian Charter and Minimum Standards in Disaster Response*. Available at: https://www.ifrc.org/PageFiles/95530/The-Sphere-Project-Handbook-20111.pdf (accessed 9 October 2018).

The Himalayan Times. 2015. 'Protesters Demanding Hindu State Clash with Police in Kathmandu'. 5 August. Available at: https://thehimalayantimes.com/kathmandu/ protesters-clash-with-police-in-nepal-demanding-hindu-state/ (accessed 25 October 2018).

———. 2016. 'Reconstruction of Earthquake-damaged Heritages in Bhaktapur Begins'. 9 April. Available at: https://thehimalayantimes.com/kathmandu/reconstruction-earthquake-damaged-heritages-bhaktapur-begins/ (accessed 2 November 2018).

———. 2017a. 'Govt Bars NGOs, Individuals from Collecting Funds'. 15 August. Available at: https://thehimalayantimes.com/kathmandu/govt-bars-ngos-individuals-collecting-funds/ (accessed 15 September 2018).

———. 2017b. 'Only 6.6 pc of Quake-damaged Houses Rebuilt till Date'. 2 October. Available at: https://thehimalayantimes.com/business/6-6-per-cent-quake-damaged-houses-rebuilt-till-date/ (accessed 2 July 2020).

———. 2018a. 'KfW Pulls Out from Heritages Reconstruction Task Commitment'. 26 April. Available at: https://thehimalayantimes.com/kathmandu/kfw-pulls-out-from-heritages-reconstruction-task-commitment/ (accessed 27 April 2018).

———. 2018b. 'OPMCM Drafts National Integrity Policy'. 25 April. Available at: https://thehimalayantimes.com/nepal/opmcm-drafts-national-integrity-policy/ (accessed 10 September 2018).

———. 2018c. 'Plan to Allow JICA to Rebuild Temple Decried'. 5 September. Available at: https://thehimalayantimes.com/kathmandu/plan-to-allow-jica-to-rebuild-temple-decried/ (accessed 21 November 2020).

———. 2018d. 'Right to Roam'. 28 September. Available at: https://thehimalayantimes.com/opinion/editorial-right-to-roam/ (accessed 21 November 2018).

———. 2019a. 'Kasthamandap Reconstruction in Full Swing'. 23 October. Available at: https://thehimalayantimes.com/kathmandu/kasthamandap-reconstruction-in-full-swing/ (accessed 24 November 2019).

———. 2019b. 'Rs 10ml Donated for Reconstruction of Quake-damaged Bhimsen Temple'. 11 July. Available at: https://thehimalayantimes.com/kathmandu/rs-10ml-donated-for-reconstruction-of-quake-damaged-bhimsen-temple/ (accessed 12 December 2019).

The Kathmandu Post. 2015a. 'Distribute Edible Relief Items after Lab Tests: PMO'. 17 June. Available at: https://kathmandupost.com/money/2015/06/17/distribute-edible-relief-items-after-lab-tests-pmo (accessed 16 October 2018).

———. 2015b. 'WFP Takes Back Rotten Rice in Gorkha'. 2 July. Available at: https://kathmandupost.com/miscellaneous/2015/07/02/wfp-takes-back-rotten-rice-in-gorkha (accessed 16 October 2018).

———. 2016a. 'Bhaktapur Monument Reconstruction Begins'. 10 April. Available at: http://kathmandupost.ekantipur.com/news/2016-04-10/bhaktapur-monument-reconstruction-begins.html (accessed 27 April 2018).

———. 2016b. 'NRA to Distribute First Installment of Grant', 6 March.

———. 2016c. 'NRA Unveils Four-phase Reconstruction Plan'. 13 January.

———. 2017. 'New Agreement to Reconstruct Kasthamandap in 2 Yrs'. 12 May. Available at: http://kathmandupost.ekantipur.com/news/2017-05-12/new-agreement-to-reconstruct-kasthamandap-in-2-yrs.html (accessed 27 April 2018).

———. 2018a. 'Centre Mulls Review of Proposed National Integrity Policy after Flak'. 10 August. http://kathmandupost.ekantipur.com/news/2018-08-10/centre-mulls-review-after-flak.html (accessed 10 September 2018).

———. 2018b. 'Integrity Policy Draft Draws NGOs' Flak'. 15 April. Available at: http://kathmandupost.ekantipur.com/news/2018-04-15/integrity-policy-draft-draws-ngos-flak.html (accessed 10 September 2018).

The Times of India. 2015. 'A 102-year-old Recalls the Monster Earthquake of 1934'. Available at: https://www.youtube.com/watch?v=6Uk-18VvloE (accessed 30 May 2017).

The Week. 2019. 'Nepal Party Demands Govt to Declare Country as Hindu State'. 15 March. Available at: https://www.theweek.in/news/world/2019/03/15/nepal-party-demands-govt-to-declare-country-as-hindu-state.html (accessed 25 October 2019).

Theophile, E. 2019. 'New Wisdom from Nepal: Earthquakes, Local Practice, and World Heritage'. The 2019 Paul Mellon Lecture, 5 March 2019, hosted by the World Monuments Fund in New York. Available at: https://www.youtube.com/watch?v=YHDkypj1qX4 (accessed 12 June 2020).

Theophile, E. and E. Newman. 2016. 'The Slow Job of Restoring Nepal's Earthquake-damaged Heritage'. *Apollo Magazine*, 26 April. Available at: https://www.apollo-magazine.com/one-year-on-an-update-from-nepals-earthquake-damaged-heritage-sites/ (accessed 18 November 2017).

Tierney, K. 2012. 'Disaster Governance: Social, Political, and Economic Dimensions'. *Annual Review of Environment and Resources* 37(1): 341–63. https://doi.org/10.1146/annurev-environ-020911-095618.

Tiwari, S. 2007. 'Transforming Patan's Cultural Heritage into Sustainable Future'. In *Urban Crisis: Culture and the Sustainability of Cities*, ed. M. Nadarajah. and A. T. Yamamoto, pp. 62–106. Hong Kong: United Nations University Press.

———. 2015. 'Reclaiming Newar Urbanism from the Debris of 2072 Earthquake'. Presentation given at Martin Chautari, Kathmandu, Nepal, 9 August.

———. 2016. 'Reclaiming and Restoring Newar Urbanism from the Disaster of 2015 Gorkha Earthquake'. Keynote paper, International Conference on Earthquake Engineering and Post Disaster Reconstruction Planning, Khopa Engineering College, Bhaktapur.

Toffin, G. 1992. 'The Indra Jatra of Kathmandu as a Royal Festival'. *Contributions to Nepalese Studies* 19(1): 73–92.

———. 1995. 'The Social Organization of Rajopadhyaya Brahmans'. In *Contested Hierarchies: A Collaborative Ethnography of Caste among the Newars of the Kathmandu Valley, Nepal*, ed. D.N. Gellner and D. Quigley, pp. 186–209. Oxford: Clarendon Press.

———. 2005. 'From Kin to Caste: The Role of Guthis in Newar Society and Culture'. The Mahesh Chandra Regmi Lecture, Social Science Baha. Available at: https://soscbaha.org/wp-content/uploads/2019/11/mcrl2005.pdf (accessed 12 June 2020).

———. 2008. *Newar Society: City, Village and Periphery*, 2nd ed. Kathmandu: Social Science Baha.

———. 2019. 'Why Newars Are Raging'. *My Republica*, 27 July. Available at: https://myrepublica.nagariknetwork.com/news/why-newars-are-raging/ (accessed 12 July 2020).

Tortell, P., M. Turin, and M. Young. 2018. *Memory*. Vancouver: University of British Columbia Press.

Tripathi, N. 2015. 'Mero Deshmathi Anyaya Bhaeko Cha' (My Country Has Been Done an Injustice). *Setopati*, 16 May (2 Jeth 2072 v.s.). Available at: http://archive.setopati.com/sahityapati/28259/ (accessed 18 July 2017).

Tuladhar, A. 2018. 'The Movement to Rebuild Kasthamandap'. *The Nepali Times*, 3–9 November (822). Available at: http://archive.nepalitimes.com/article/Nepali-Times-Buzz/rebuilding-kasthamandap-nepal,4012 (accessed 27 April 2018).

UN (United Nations). 2015. *Transforming Our World: The 2030 Agenda for Sustainable Development*. A/RES/70/1. United Nations Department of Economic and Social Affairs. https://doi:.org/10.1080/02513625.2015.1038080.

———. 2016. *The Sustainable Development Goals Report 2016*. New York: United Nations. Available at: https://unstats.un.org/sdgs/report/2016/ (accessed 20 November 2020).

UN Office for the Coordination of Human Affairs. 2015. *Nepal Earthquake Humanitarian Response: April to September 2015*. OCHA 20 November. Available at: https://reliefweb.int/report/nepal/nepal-earthquake-humanitarian-response-april-september-2015 (accessed 12 June 2020).

UNDP (United Nations Development Programme). 2014. *Nepal Human Development Report 2014: Beyond Geography: Unlocking Human Potential*. Kathmandu: Government of Nepal, National Planning Commission and UNDP. Available at: http://www.hdr.undp.org/sites/default/files/nepal_nhdr_2014-final.pdf (accessed 14 May 2020).

———. 2018. Human Development Indices and Indicators. 2018 Statistical Update. Available at: http://hdr.undp.org/en/2018-update (accessed 20 November 2020).

UNESCO (United Nations Educational, Scientific and Cultural Organization). 1982. 'World Conference on Cultural Policies'. UNESCO, Paris. Available at: https://unesdoc.unesco.org/ark:/48223/pf0000052505 (accessed 20 November 2020).

———. 1983. 'Convention Concerning the Protection of the World Cultural and Natural Heritage'. World Heritage Committee, Sixth Session, Paris, 13–17 December. Report of the Rapporteur. Available at: http://whc.unesco.org/archive/1982/clt-82-conf015-8e.pdf (21 November 2020).

———. 2015. *Revisiting Kathmandu: Safeguarding Living Urban Heritage—A Contribution to the Discourse on Better Understanding Living Urban Heritage through the Four Themes of Authenticity, Heritage Management, Community Involvement and Disaster Risk Reduction and their Inter-linkages. The Proceedings of an International Symposium that Took Place in the Kathmandu Valley from 25 to 29 November 2013*, ed. K. Weise. Paris, France: UNESCO; Kathmandu: UNESCO Office in Kathmandu.

———. 2019. 'UNESCO Regrets to Withdraw from the Restoration of Jagannath and Shree Krishna Mahavishnu (Gopinath) Temples Damaged by the 2015 Earthquake at Hanumandhoka Durbar Square World Heritage Site'. Press release. Available at: https://en.unesco.org/news/unesco-withdraws-restoration-jagannath-and-gopinath-temples-hanumandhoka-durbar-square-world-0 (accessed 12 June 2020).

———. n.d. 'Kathmandu Valley: UNESCO World Heritage Centre'. Available at: https://whc.unesco.org/en/list/121 (accessed 2 July 2018).

UNESCO and World Bank 2018. 'Culture in City Reconstruction and Recovery'. Position paper. Available at: https://unesdoc.unesco.org/ark:/48223/pf0000265981 (accessed 12 June 2020).

UNISDR (United Nations Office for Disaster Risk Reduction). 2005. 'Hyogo Framework for Action 2005–2015: International Strategy for Disaster Reduction'.

Available at: https://www.unisdr.org/2005/wcdr/intergover/official-doc/L-docs/ Hyogo-framework-for-action-english.pdf (accessed 3 July 2020).

——. 2015. 'Sendai Framework for Disaster Risk Reduction 2015–2030: United Nations International Strategy for Disaster Reduction'. Available at: https://www. undrr.org/publication/sendai-framework-disaster-risk-reduction-2015-2030 (accessed 12 June 2020).

United States Department of State, Bureau of Democracy, Human Rights and Labor. 2016. *Nepal 2016 International Religious Freedom Report*. Available at: https://np.usembassy.gov/wp-content/uploads/sites/79/2017/08/Nepal-2016-International-Religious-Freedom-Report.pdf (accessed 11 November 2018).

Upreti, B. C. 2006. 'The Maoist Insurgency in Nepal'. *South Asian Survey* 13(1): 35–50. doi.org/10.1177/097152310501300103.

Uprety, P. R. 1984. *Nepal: A Small Nation in the Vortex of International Conflicts*. Kathmandu: Pugo Mi.

Vajracharya, D. 1973. *Lichavikalka Abhilekh* (Inscriptions from the Licchhavi Era). Kathmandu: Tribhuvan University Press.

Vajracharya, G. V. 1975. *An Introduction to the Hanuman Dhoka*. Kirtipur: Institute of Nepal and Asian Studies.

van der Geest, K. 2018. 'Landslide Loss and Damage in Sindhupalchok District, Nepal: Comparing Income Groups with Implications for Compensation and Relief'. *International Journal of Disaster Risk Science* 9(2): 157–66. https://doi.org/10.1007/s13753-018-0178-5.

Varughese, G. and E. Ostrom. 2001. 'The Contested Role of Heterogeneity in Collective Action: Some Evidence from Community Forestry in Nepal'. *World Development* 29(5): 747–65. https://doi.org/10.1016/S0305-750X(01)00012-2.

Venugopal, R. and S. Yasir. 2017. 'The Politics of Natural Disasters in Protracted Conflict: The 2014 Flood in Kashmir'. *Oxford Development Studies* 45(4): 424–42. http//:doi: 10.1080/13600818.2016.1276160.

von Rospatt, A. 2011. 'The Past Renovations of the Svayambhu Caitya'. In *Light of the Valley: Renewing the Sacred Art and Traditions of Svayambhu*, ed. T.P. Gellek and P.D. Maitland, pp. 157–206. Cazadero, CA: Dharma Publishing.

Ward, M. 2011. 'Disaster Risk Reduction: U.S. Responses to the 2005 Earthquake and 2010 Floods in Pakistan'. *Georgetown Journal of International Affairs* 12(2): 56–63.

Watanabe, C. 2015. 'Commitments of Debt: Temporality and the Meanings of Aid Work in a Japanese NGO in Myanmar'. *American Anthropologist* 117(3): 468–79. https://doi.org/10.1111/aman.12287.

Waterton, E. and L. Smith. 2010. 'The Recognition and Misrecognition of Community Heritage'. *International Journal of Heritage Studies* 16(1–2): 4–15. https://doi.org/10.1080/13527250903441671.

Weiler, K. 2017a. 'Authenticity and the Re-evaluation of Cultural Heritage: The Revival of Patan Darbar Square's Sacred Sites'. *Material Religion* 13(3): 382–84. https://doi:10.1080/17432200.2017.1335086.

———. 2017b. 'Introduction'. In *Authenticity in Architectural Heritage Conservation: Discourses, Opinions, Experiences in Europe, South and East Asia*, ed. K. Weiler and N. Gutschow, pp. xvii–xxiv. Cham: Springer.

Weise, K. 2016. 'Cultural Continuity in Post-Gorkha Earthquake Rehabilitation'. *Nepal Engineers' Association* XLIII-EC 30(1): 99–102.

Weise, K., G. Gautam, and G. Rodrigues. 2018. 'Response and Rehabilitation of Historic Monuments after the Gorkha Earthquake'. In *Impacts and Insights of the Gorkha Earthquake*, ed. D. Gautam and G. Rodrigues, pp. 65–94. Amsterdam: Elsevier.

Weisenfeld, G. 2012. *Imaging Disaster: Tokyo and the Visual Culture of Japan's Great Earthquake of 1923*. Berkeley: University of California Press.

Weizman, E. 2012. *The Least of All Possible Evils: Humanitarian Violence from Arendt to Gaza*. London: Verso Books.

Werbner, P., M. Webb, and K. Spellman-Poots. eds. 2014. *Political Aesthetics of Global Protest: The Arab Spring and Beyond*. Edinburgh: Edinburgh University Press.

Whelpton, J. 1991. *Kings, Soldiers and Priests: Nepalese Politics and the Rise of Jang Bahadur Rana, 1830–1857*. New Delhi: Manohar.

———. 2005. *A History of Nepal*. Cambridge: Cambridge University Press.

———. 2018. 'Bhimsen Thapa Award Lecture'. Delivered at the Nepal Academy, Kathmandu, 25 July. Available at: https://linguae.weebly.com/bhimsen-thapa-award-lecture.html (accessed 12 June 2020).

———. 2019. 'Between Two Big Ones: Earthquakes in the Nepali Consciousness 1934–2015'. Paper presented at the Annual Conference on Nepal and the Himalaya, Kathmandu, 24–26 July.

White, S. C. 1996. 'Depoliticising Development: The Uses and Abuses of Participation'. *Development in Practice* 6(1): 6–15. https://doi.org/10.1080/0961452961000157564.

Whitmarsh B. 2018. 'Narayanhiti Palace Museum: Memory, Power, National Identity'. PhD thesis, SOAS University of London.

———. 2017. 'Staging Memories at the Narayanhiti Palace Museum, Kathmandu'. *Himalaya: The Journal of the Association for Nepal and Himalayan Studies* 37(1): 84–97. https://digitalcommons.macalester.edu/himalaya/vol37/iss1/13.

Wilke, J. 2017. 'The Lisbon Earthquake (1755)'. European History Online (EGO). Mainz: Leibniz Institute of European History. Available at: http://ieg-ego.eu/en/threads/european-media/european-media-events/juergen-wilke-the-lisbon-earthquake-1755/view#Theextentofreporting (accessed 30 November 2018).

Wilson, G. 2012. 'Community Resilience, Globalization, and Transitional Pathways of Decision-making'. *Geoforum* 43(6): 1218–31. http://dx.doi.org/10.1016/j.geoforum.2012.03.008.

Wolff, A. 1999. *The Cologne Cathedral*. Cologne: Verlag Kölner Dom.

Wood, J. 2010. 'Between God and a Hard Place'. *The New York Times*, 24 January. Available at: https://www.nytimes.com/2010/01/24/opinion/24wood.html (accessed 25 June 2020).

World Bank. 1989. *Nepal: Municipal Development and Earthquake Emergency Housing Reconstruction Project*. Washington, DC: World Bank. Report No 7413. 27 January. Available at: http://documents.worldbank.org/curated/en/593391468289864709/Nepal-Municipal-Development-and-Earthquake-Emergency-Housing-Reconstruction-Project (accessed 23 December 2018).

———. 1997a. *World Development Report 1997: The State in a Changing World*. Oxford: Oxford University Press. Available at: https://openknowledge.worldbank.org/handle/10986/5980 License: CC BY 3.0 IGO (accessed 21 November 2020).

———. 1997b. *Implementation Completion Report. Nepal. Municipal Development and Earthquake Emergency Housing Reconstruction Project* (Credit1988-NEP). Available at: http://documents1.worldbank.org/curated/en/785251468061735231/pdf/multi-page.pdf (accessed 30 May 2019).

———. 2011. *Large-scale Migration and Remittance in Nepal: Issues, Challenges, and Opportunities*. Report No. 44390-NP. Poverty Reduction and Economic Management Sector Unit, South Asia Region.

World Politics Review. 2017. 'Peaceful Municipal Elections Show That Nepal Is Not as Divided at the Local Level'. 25 October. Available at: https://www.worldpoliticsreview.com/trend-lines/23457/peaceful-municipal-elections-show-that-nepal-is-not-as-divided-at-the-local-level (accessed 20 November 2020).

World Watch Monitor. 2018. 'Nepali Law Criminalising "Hurting of Religious Feelings" Comes into Force'. 17 August. Available at: https://www.worldwatchmonitor.org/2018/08/nepali-law-criminalising-hurting-of-religious-feelings-comes-into-force/ (accessed 11 November 2018).

Wright, D. 1966 [1877]. *History of Nepal*. Calcutta: Ranjan Gupta.

Yu, Z. 2017. 'China Will Restore Nepali Heritage Site'. *China Daily*, 5 May. Available at: http://usa.chinadaily.com.cn/epaper/2017-05/05/content_29219527.htm (accessed 18 November 2017).

Zhang, Q. and E. P. Wang. 2010. 'Local Political Trust: The Antecedents and Effects on Earthquake Victims' Choice for Allocation of Resources'. *Social Behavior and Personality: An International Journal* 38(7): 929–39. https://doi.org/10.2224/sbp.2010.38.7.929.

Zhao, Y. 2013. 'Social Networks and Reduction of Risk in Disasters: An Example of the Wenchuan Earthquake'. In *Economic Stress, Human Capital, and Families in Asia*, ed. W. J. J. Yeung and M. T. Yap, pp. 171–82. Dordrecht: Springer. http://doi:10.1007/978-94-007-7386-8_10.

Zyck, S. A. and H. B. Krebs. 2015. 'Localising Humanitarianism: Improving Effectiveness through Inclusive Action'. London: Overseas Development Institute. Available at: https://www.odi.org/sites/odi.org.uk/files/odi-assets/publications-opinion-files/9720.pdf (accessed 10 June 2020).

ABOUT THE CONTRIBUTORS

Jeevan Baniya is Assistant Director at Social Science Baha, Kathmandu, Nepal. He is a researcher for the project 'After the Earth's Violent Sway: The Tangible and Intangible Legacies of a Natural Disaster' and research coordinator of the project 'Expertise, Labour and Mobility in Nepal's Post-conflict, Post-disaster Reconstruction'.

Gopi K. Basyal is a doctoral student in the Department of Geography and the Institute of Hazard, Risk and Resilience at Durham University, UK, and a geographer at the National Society for Earthquake Technology (NSET-Nepal), Lalitpur, Nepal.

Jennifer Bradley is the co-facilitator of the Langtang Memory Project, the country representative for NYINGTHOP, and an independent researcher focused on issues of gender and exclusion in Nepal.

Christiane Brosius is Professor of Visual and Media Anthropology at the Heidelberg Centre for Transcultural Studies, Germany. She heads the Nepal Heritage Documentation Project (NHDP) jointly with Axel Michaels, Academy of Sciences at Heidelberg.

Patrick Daly is a Senior Research Fellow at the Earth Observatory of Singapore, Nanyang Technological University, Singapore.

Nimesh Dhungana is an LSE Fellow in the Departments of Methodology and International Development at the London School of Economics and Political Science, UK.

Amrita Gurung worked as a Senior Research Associate at Social Science Baha, Kathmandu, Nepal. She is currently a doctoral student at Concordia University, Canada.

Dan V. Hirslund is an Associate Professor in the Department of Cross Cultural and Regional Studies at the University of Copenhagen, Denmark.

Pia Hollenbach is a Senior Researcher at the Department of Geography, University of Zurich, Switzerland.

Michael Hutt is Emeritus Professor of Nepali and Himalayan Studies at SOAS, University of London, UK, and Principal Investigator for the project 'After the Earth's Violent Sway: The Tangible and Intangible Legacies of a Natural Disaster'.

Mark Kincey is a Post-Doctoral Research Associate in the Department of Geography and the Institute of Hazard, Risk and Resilience at Durham University, UK. He was lead researcher on the SHEAR-funded project on earthquake-triggered landslides in Nepal.

Shyam Kunwar is currently working as a research associate in the project 'Infrastructures of Democracy: State Building as Everyday Practice in Nepal's Agrarian Districts', a collaboration between the Universities of Toronto and British Columba, Canada, and Martin Chautari in Kathmandu. He has completed an MPhil in the Central Department of Anthropology at Tribhuvan University in Kathmandu, Nepal.

Philippe Le Billon is Professor at the Department of Geography and the School of Public Policy Global Affairs at the University of British Columbia, Vancouver, Canada.

Elsie Lewison is a graduate student in the Department of Geography at the University of Toronto, Canada.

Mark Liechty is Professor of Anthropology and History at the University of Illinois at Chicago, USA, and International Co-Investigator for the project 'After the Earth's Violent Sway: The Tangible and Intangible Legacies of a Natural Disaster'.

Bina Limbu is an independent researcher, and was previously a Research Associate at Social Science Baha in Kathmandu, Nepal.

Austin Lord is a PhD candidate in the Department of Anthropology at Cornell University, Ithaca, USA, and the co-facilitator of the Langtang Memory Project in Nepal.

Stefanie Lotter is a Research Fellow and Senior Teaching Fellow at SOAS University of London, UK, and Co-Investigator for the project 'After the Earth's Violent Sway: The Tangible and Intangible Legacies of a Natural Disaster'.

Sabin Ninglekhu is a Postdoctoral Research Fellow at Nanyang Technological University, Singapore

Katie Oven is a Vice Chancellor's Senior Research Fellow in the Department of Geography and Environmental Sciences, Northumbria University, UK. She is a Co-Investigator on the SHEAR-funded project on earthquake-triggered landslides in Nepal.

Bishnu Pandey is an Instructor in Civil Engineering in the School of Construction and the Environment at the British Columbia Institute of Technology, Vancouver, Canada.

Shubheksha Rana is Head of the Monitoring, Evaluation, Research and Learning Department at Plan International, Lalitpur, Nepal. She was previously an independent social scientist and researcher on the SHEAR-funded project on earthquake-triggered landslides in Nepal.

Katharine Rankin is Professor in the Department of Geography and Planning at the University of Toronto, Canada.

Nabin Rawal teaches at the Central Department of Anthropology at Tribhuvan University, Kathmandu, and is also a Senior Researcher at Social Science Baha, Kathmandu, Nepal.

Nick Rosser is a Professor in the Department of Geography and the Institute of Hazard, Risk and Resilience at Durham University, UK. He is Principal Investigator on the SHEAR-funded project on earthquake-triggered landslides in Nepal.

Shobhit Shakya is a doctoral student in Ragnar Nurkse Department of Innovation and Governance at Tallinn University of Technology, Estonia.

Sara Shneiderman is Associate Professor in the Department of Anthropology and the School of Public Policy and Global Affairs at the University of British Columbia, Vancouver, Canada, and Principal Investigator of the project 'Expertise, Labor and Mobility in Nepal's Post-Conflict, Post-Disaster Reconstruction'.

Prakash Chandra Subedi is currently pursuing a Master's in Social Work at Western Sydney University, Australia. He was previously a Research Associate at Social Science Baha, Kathmandu, Nepal.

Manoj Suji is a consultant at The Asia Foundation, Nepal. He previously worked as a Senior Research Associate at Social Science Baha, Kathmandu, Nepal.

Deepak Thapa is Director of Social Science Baha, Kathmandu, Nepal. He is also a political analyst and columnist with *The Kathmandu Post*.

Cameron Warner is Associate Professor of Anthropology at Aarhus University, Denmark.

Katharina Weiler is an art historian and the Provenance Researcher at the Museum Angewandte Kunst in Frankfurt am Main, Germany.

John Whelpton is an independent researcher. He was formerly an Honorary Research Associate of the Chinese University of Hong Kong and a researcher for the project 'After the Earth's Violent Sway: The Tangible and Intangible Legacies of a Natural Disaster'.

INDEX